American Baseball

AMERICAN BASEBALL

Volume I

From Gentleman's Sport
to the
Commissioner System

DAVID QUENTIN VOIGT

Foreword by
Allan Nevins

The Pennsylvania State University Press
University Park and London

Library of Congress Cataloging in Publication Data

Voigt, David Quentin.
　American baseball.

　　Vol. 1 foreword by Allan Nevins; v. 2 foreword by Ronald A. Smith; v. 3 foreword
by Clifford Kachline.
　　Vol. 1–2 are reprints. Originally published: Norman : University of Oklahoma
Press, 1966–1970.
　　Includes bibliographies and indexes.
　　Contents: v. 1. From gentleman's sport to the commissioner system—v. 2. From the
commissioners to continental expansion—v. 3. From postwar expansion to the
electronic age.

　　1. Baseball—United States—History—Collected
works.　I. Title.
GV863.A1V65　1983　　　796.357′64′0973　　　83-2300
ISBN　0-271-00331-6　(v. 1)
ISBN　0-271-00334-0　(pbk. : V. 1)
ISBN　0-271-00330-8　(v. 2)
ISBN　0-271-00333-2　(pbk. : V. 2)
ISBN　0-271-00329-4　(v. 3)
ISBN　0-271-00332-4　(pbk. : V. 3)

Printed in the United States of America

With the publication of Volume 3 of Voigt's *American Baseball*, Penn State Press
reissues Volumes 1 and 2 in order to complete the series.

Third printing, 1992

To Virginia, whose sacrifices helped bring this book "home."

Foreword

M R. VOIGT'S BOOK has two exceptional merits. It is a work of true historical thoroughness. Better than any other writer since Albert G. Spalding broke ground with *America's National Game* in 1911, he has investigated all aspects of the subject; the origins and evolution of the game, the professionalism that grew out of it, and the big business that was reared upon it. He has done this in a rapid, well proportioned, and critically objective narrative. At the same time, though with less emphasis, he has brought out the sociological and psychological significance of baseball, relating this to national change and development. We can no longer speak of it with the oldtime certainty as our national sport. Basketball and football vie with it in popularity as mass-spectator attractions. But that both participants and watchers feel it a true expression of the American spirit few will deny. Its strenuosity, excitement, speed, and drama endear it to our hearts. It is American, too, in the way in which it combines the zest of the amateur, the expertness of the professional, and the business appeal of the big gate. Mr. Voigt sees all the color of its history, sometimes bright, sometimes dark and seamy. He sees also how strikingly the game mirrors the American character; and he combines the two elements in a most satisfying way.

Of the annals of baseball, from the days when it appealed to gentlemen players as a form of conspicuous leisure, and to nostalgic town-dwelling spectators for the memories it evoked of village greens and district-school intermissions, we can never tire. Mr. Voigt casts aside the nationalistic pretense that baseball was a pure

American invention. He equally discards the foreign view that it was "rounders made scientific." As he states, it was an evolution, and he reveals just what were its evolutionary elements. By the 1840's at least, and probably earlier, it was something quite new under the sun. He shows how in 1859 the "New York game" and the attempt by the Knickerbocker Club to gain a dominant place led to a revolt by younger organizations that resulted in the National Association of Base Ball Players; how the Civil War lent an unexpected stimulus; how Lincoln himself showed a mild interest in impromptu matches; and how an East-West rivalry appeared. By the late 1860's clubs were not merely trying to win for the glory of the town; they were becoming professional in character and commercial in their instincts.

What a great day it was when, before 1870, the Cincinnati Red Stockings emerged as the first all-salaried team, placing every player on contract for the season at a negotiated wage!—a great day, that is, for those who saw the dollar-future of baseball. Well-paid clubs came in with a rush, five of them before 1870 closed. They played better ball for paying onlookers. The great names began to appear; first of all the English-born Henry Chadwick, of whom Mr. Voigt justly makes much; then Spalding; then Harry Wright, hero and idol of Cincinnati until the Bostonians lured him East. The gamblers, the players willing to "throw" games, the shifty managers, and the organizers of pools came like scum to the top of the stream. They foreshadowed the scandals of Black Sox days. But the healthy features that were to shape future baseball also began to exert their power. They included a strategy of play, in which managers learned which men to use in pinches, which substitutes to throw in, which signals to have made by the catchers; a strategy of running, with coaches at two bases; a science of hitting, and a greater science of pitching.

Thus it was that baseball came into the glorious days for which Chadwick had laid a foundation, and Harry Wright, Spalding, and Anson had fixed the standards. These were the days when Christy Matthewson would pitch three World Series shutouts for the Giants; when Ty Cobb of the Detroit Tigers would steal 96 bases in one season, a record bettered only as Maury Wills stole 104 for the Los Angeles Dodgers; when "Tinker to Evers to Chance" became a temporary national chant; when Babe Ruth for the Yankees hit sixty homers in a summer; and when Lou Gehrig, Joe DiMaggio, and Jackie Robinson—not to mention Honus Wagner—were heroes that every schoolboy knew. Mr. Voigt relates his story with sparkle and accuracy. He does not skip unpleasant pages, and he analyzes the disadvantages as well as advantages of the control by commissioners that the Black Sox trouble made unavoidable. The new scale of the baseball industry, the commercialism that has rendered six-figure salaries for popular heroes commonplace, and the heavy betting—approaching six billion dollars, estimates Max Lerner—on games, must be viewed with distaste. But it is clear that they do not greatly trouble the American public.

The author has given us a careful book on an important subject; a book that will interest multitudes, and deserves a wide reading by those who wish to understand the American scene.

ALLAN NEVINS

Introduction

THE CENTURY-LONG DEVELOPMENT of major league baseball as a leading entertainment institution is but a facet of a much broader movement, which might be termed America's leisure revolution. Without being dramatic, one may speak of the leisure revolution of the past hundred years, a change so momentous now as to occupy at last the attention of social scientists. Like many other changes that are revolutionary because they affect all of us, this one escaped notice until recently because Americans were preoccupied with "more important things." Even now serious students of leisure carry welts from a "backlash" of snobbery, laid on by the "more serious scholars," who look upon leisure studies as frivolous.

That some social scientists study leisure anyway may be due less to courage than to the current romantic notion that leisure has become a social problem. Today we hear of the "emerging leisure problem," a frightening apparition to those persons who envision devils popping out of the Pandora's box of shortened working hours. In their view the urgent need is for restraints in order that fewer people may succumb to temptations to use their leisure time unwisely.

The first problem in discussing the leisure revolution is to know what we are talking about. At present, social scientists offer a bewildering variety of definitions, many focusing on leisure "time" rather than on leisure "behavior." At least their definition of leisure time as free time, or time not needed for earning one's living, provides some consensus. Defined in this broad context, leisure time is hardly new. After all, the aristocratic Athenians who contributed so much to our intellectual granaries were men with leisure time, freed by fortune from having to earn a living, and men in similar circumstances have turned up in nearly every epoch of Western civilization. What is revolutionary in our era is that most people have large blocks of free time. In short, what was once the opportunity of a privileged few is now everybody's expectation. Herein is the essence of the leisure-time revolution.[1]

This quantitative approach raises several conceptual problems. Although it is tempting to depict American society in general terms, it is more realistic to regard our 200,000,000 population as perplexingly varied. People behave differently in America; they think, talk, work, worship, and play differently. The fact that they are active at different times during a day makes for leisure behavior differences. Thus, leisure behavior in America is a function of time, and one takes one's leisure when he is free to do so. Some persons get summer vacations, some winter vacations, some none at all, and many work to provide fun for vacationers. Under the rational organization of our urban-industrial society, division of labor is a powerful differentiator in all institutional areas, leisure included. But the common denominator is that urban-industrialism has made possible a majority's enjoyment of an abundance of time for something other than gainful employment.

The use of this free time depends upon personal values. Values move men to act; some, under the stimulus of the old Protestant value of "work for the night is coming," feel that they should use their free time for more work. "Moonlighting" is an example, and its widespread practice suggests that for a significant number of individuals, additional work is the answer to free time. Many of these apparently still heed the old saying that the devil finds work for idle hands. The new leisure ethic, however, is substituting "leisure" for "idleness" and telling us to value fun rather than condemn it;[2] but for many the shift from an implanted "work

[1] Bennett Berger, "The Sociology of Leisure: Some Suggestions," *Work and Leisure* (ed. by E. O. Smigel), 21–29.

[2] Russell Baker, "Poor Richard's Almanac," *Times* (New York), March 7, 1965.

ethic" to the new "fun morality" is a wrenching adjustment. Moreover, people of different sex, age, and education have different values. To meet their varied needs, our society offers a variety of leisure outlets, one of which is major league baseball.

This *smörgasbord* of outlets reminds us that one man's leisure may be another's boredom. To one man an annual vacation trip to a shore resort represents a concession to family peace; he himself might well prefer to go bowling or to stay on the job and enjoy the company of his cronies at work. The point here is that values, by constraining the choice of leisure outlets, really provide neither free time nor free choice in the matter, since ideological commitments dominate. Of course, American society is characterized by polytypical value systems, which broaden the number of leisure outlets to meet the many tastes. Such a God's plenty apparently offers free choice, but in reality an individual's choice is limited by the boundaries of his personal value system. One man's leisure is another man's sin, as major league baseball's long fight for Sunday games neatly illustrates.

Pondering the leisure revolution also raises the question of whether we are dealing with a new social institution, or whether leisure is merely bound up with familiar institutions like families, schools, and churches. In its present form leisure looks like a segmented institution, and many individuals argue that "fun" is a basic need of man. If this is true, man historically has found fun through other institutional behavior, such as working, raising a family, or worshiping. Only recently has he deliberately set out to look for fun, which means that only lately has he thought of his leisure needs as a separate dimension of his existence.

With many of us now looking for fun, many new enterprises profit from helping us to find it. Hence, for a fee one can go bowling, to a ball game, or to any of a host of commercialized outlets that sell fun either as participation or as spectacle. But the fact that so many of us now sally forth with the intention of finding fun suggests the existence of a separate institution of leisure, with a structure as clear-cut as that of the more obvious institutions.

Among the many studies delving into the nature of the leisure institution, one catches interesting glimpses of the complexity of human behavior, including play and fun. In the relatively brief time that man has scientifically studied himself, he has defined himself as a single species of animal life, with certain basic needs common to all members. In baring these needs, man has scrutinized himself from many different angles. Whether seen as learner, lover, worker, conformer, tool-maker, or worshiper, man emerges as a special kind of animal whose behavior is culturally conditioned through social institutions. In trying to account for differential human behavior, scientists have given weight to certain institutions; hence, students like Alfred Kroeber, Karl Marx, and Sigmund Freud have each nominated his favorite institution as the salient approach to understanding man's ways.

Man's current preoccupation with his leisure pursuits may be taken as another institutional approach to understanding human behavior. For now this former "dark side" of our nature has been examined and described by a perceptive Dutch historian, the late Johan Huizinga, in his book *Homo ludens* ("Man the Player"). To Huizinga, fun is a basic need of man. Marshaling a variety of historical data, Huizinga advanced the proposition that human behavior is a function of man's play needs.[3] Today, this hypothesis is widely accepted, and the leisure revolution has inspired certain scholars to work on the problem of fulfilling this human need for play.

As a statement of principle, the notion that man needs leisure is deceptively simple. Yet, as Alfred North Whitehead reminded us, the genius of science is its willingness to analyze the obvious. Having ventured a clear explanation of man's need for play, Huizinga stressed the importance of an element of our humanity too long ignored as "trivial." Yet at no time did scholarly contempt stop man from exercising his need. To the confusion and anger of some Christian churchmen of the past, this human penchant for play turned up as mimicry of the sacred, such as love-making in cathedrals, or in the consumption of forbidden Christmas puddings in Cromwell's England. To the outraged clerics, such

[3] Johan Huizinga, *Homo Ludens: A Study of the Play Element In Culture*, xii.

behavior was taken as evidence of the old deluder Satan's work.[4]

Spurred by pioneers like Huizinga, social scientists now seek to build a general theory of leisure which will explain this natural aspect of humanity. Although this goal is far from being achieved, limited theoretical insights already gained have sharpened our perception of leisure components. Among other elements a good theory requires a set of useful definitions, which adequately describe the data observed.

In the study of leisure, useful terms include Huizinga's definition of play as a creative and unrestricted leisure expression, and as such, man's oldest and most pervasive form of fun. One example would be "kolf" as first played by Dutch peasants without rules or formalities; another would be the many informal ball games which preceded the game of baseball. The point is that play is fun for fun's sake, a product of individual taste and inventiveness. The creative aspect of play is seen in man's endless invention of new forms. So unpredictable and unpremeditated are these that not even the most totalitarian society has been able to channel or restrict this human talent. Today, new play forms continually emerge in modern industrial settings, and sociologists have observed play forms cropping up in religious rites, weddings, and funerals—indeed, in almost any kind of human activity, however serious.

Sport differs from play. Unlike play, sport suggests formal organization, characterized by rules and the presence of officials. The rise of organized sports reflects man's rational approach to fun, and, indeed, most sports have developed in civilized societies where the rational-scientific world view is strong. However, if a society is too rational in its leisure, such behavior ceases to be free. Certainly, the rise of modern sports has brought many restrictions and rules. Because of these, major league baseball "players" are really "workers." Recognizing this aspect of sport, Huizinga proposed treating sports as a kind of antiplay, because sports tend to drive the "play element" into other avenues of human behavior, at times threatening the social system by injecting frivolity into

[4] J. A. R. Pimlott, "Christmas Under the Puritans," *History Today*, Vol. X, No. 11 (December, 1960), 832–39.

serious situations.[5] But if sports and play conflict, they also complement each other. In modern baseball the interplay between the two sometimes finds players engaging in horseplay during the course of a game. A candid observer of this play-within-a-play aspect of the game was pitcher Jim Brosnan, who told recently how his Cincinnati mates found fun during a game by engaging in an impromptu contest of long-range tobacco-juice spitting.[6] This example shows professional players working at a sport (baseball), yet demonstrating their need for fun (play) while on the job.

The interaction of play and sport is further clarified by Gregory Stone, a sociologist who uses the words "Play" and "Dis-play" to distinguish between them. While accepting Huizinga's definition of play and the proposition that play is older and more important than sport, Stone, nevertheless, argues that our urban-industrial way of life has made sports far more important. The great revolution in population and production has created a need for more and varied leisure outlets, which organized sports have helped to meet. Since many people choose to watch baseball games, baseball has passed from a game to be played to a sport to be watched by adult urbanites. From modest beginnings as a participation sport for gentlemen with leisure time to fill, the game became professionalized and commercialized—in short it is now a "dis-play." In this new form players are ruled by administrative bosses or, as Stone states, "With the massification of sport spectators begin to outnumber participants in overwhelming proportions, and the spectator, as the name implies, encourages the spectacular—the display."[7]

It is my thesis that baseball is a pioneer sports form which came to be widely imitated. In time other American team sports like football, hockey, and basketball imitated baseball's structural pattern in order to compete as commercialized spectacles. This competitive growth of sports spectacles was a function of the ideology of industrial-urbanism, which encouraged people to contract for

[5] Huizinga, *op. cit.*, xii.

[6] Jim Brosnan, *The Long Season*, 134, 168.

[7] Gregory Stone, "American Sports: Play and Dis-Play," *Mass Leisure* (ed. by Eric Larrabee and Rolf Meyersohn), 253–63.

their needs-satisfactions. Hence, with people willing and able to pay for fun, our society now offers a cafeteria line of catchpenny leisure outlets which fall roughly into two categories—play participation and spectator sport. The American cornucopia of fun forms is a result of our pluralistic culture, which tolerates a variety of tastes and choices. This ever flowing variety of fun-offerings constantly provides new ones, and the shifting of attention from one form to another, from old to new, is stimulated by the emotional impact of fads and crazes. If sports indeed explain the nation, such instability suggests a people groping for value patterns to fit a fast-changing way of life.

America's shift to commercialized spectacles forces the social scientist to consider the moral impact of this trend. Seemingly, the rise of professionalized sports was accompanied by the social ethic of "sportsmanship." As interpreted recently by James W. Keating, this code is derived from upper-class European values and implies playing games for the immediate pleasure which one derives from the activity itself. Thus, "sportsmanship" stresses indulgence for fun, and although competition may be present, the virtues of "generosity, exaltation, and joy" predominate. With the commercialization of sports, however, one could not logically expect a paid athlete to abide by this ethic. After all, professional players earn their living by working at a game. Their wages hinge on their sustaining a high level of performance in a competitive milieu. If a man should slip, another would replace him; hence, one would hardly expect the professional athlete to be overly generous or "sportsmanlike" to his rivals. And, yet, because society at large values the ethic of sportsmanship, professional athletes are forced to accept a watered-down brand of sportsmanship: a code calling for gracious acceptance of the rules of the game together with a posture of "modesty in victory and a quiet composure in defeat"—in short, demonstrate trained self-control.[8]

In other ways sports lend support to society's values. Since American values are diverse, some persons see play and leisure as

[8] James W. Keating, "Sportsmanship as a Moral Category," *Ethics*, Vol. LXXV, No. 1 (October, 1964), 25–35.

a threat, whereas others regard them as a step to a fuller life. Obviously, the leisure revolution in itself is neither bad nor good, even though many popular definitions impart a moral judgment. Today, those who approve of sports argue that sports give relief from tensions in our culture. As a force for maintaining culture, both play and sports help to adapt children and adults to society's ways. As a tension-reliever, sports are seen to rescue one from drudgery by temporarily freeing him from disagreeable aspects of social life.[9] Indeed, one might speculate about how many marriages are sustained (or broken) because one or both partners are able to withdraw into the world of sports, either directly or vicariously as in the pages of the sporting journals.

Leisureways also function to support society's work expectations. Since work in an automated society is often humdrum, leisure outlets offer "re-creation," the renewal of energy for further work performance.

Various forms of play and sport aid in the attainment of social goals and statuses. As one may join a church partly to meet the right people, so one joins sporting clubs, plays certain games, or attends certain scarce and expensive spectacles, such as the World Series, in order to validate his "social worth" in a society which demands never ending validation of one's status claims.

Sports and play may also assist in the social integration of individuals. For example, if one supports the National League in a World Series, he may gain social acceptance in the company of like-minded people.[10] The convivial ritual whereby such congenial characters identify themselves suggests a surrogate form of kinship, which has its counterpart among the Australian aborigines, whose kinship systems can be widened to admit any outsider. Certainly our sports function as social icebreakers and as launching pads for further social interaction.

Changes in the leisureways of a society may reflect broader currents of change. Once again the truth of the proposition that sports

---

[9] Stone, *op. cit.*, 253–63.

[10] Edward Gross, "A Functional Approach to Leisure Analysis," *Social Problems*, Vol. IX, No. 1 (Summer, 1961), 2–8.

explain the nation is apparent when one embarks on a brief excursion into the history of leisure. In the American time dimension such a trip not only places baseball in a broader cultural setting, but casts further light on the leisure revolution. The trip begins in Europe, because America is an integral part of Western civilization and our attitudes toward leisure are rooted deeply in European traditions.

To probe the preindustrial backgrounds of our modern world is to get a different perspective on the leisure revolution of today. Hence, we find that to define the leisure revolution solely in terms of more time free from work is to have no "revolution" at all. While it is true of preindustrial Europe that leisure time was the hallmark of elite groups, it is also true that lowly agricultural pursuits like herding offered plenty of free time, which was used partly to produce a wealth of folklore, folk dances, and folk songs. Similar large blocks of free time were part of the lot of soldiers and sailors in the past, and preindustrial urbanites had much time off from work; Rome had its plethora of Roman holidays, and Europe of the Middle Ages had an average of 115 holidays a year. Even serfs enjoyed time off to play or to attend such spectacles as fairs and religious rites. Yet nowhere did a society grapple with leisure as if it were a basic need of man, nor did anyone study leisure behavior. Such studies awaited the acceptance of the world view of a rational science.

The notion that leisure behavior in the past existed for the elite suffers when one learns how the elite regarded leisure. For the ancient Athenians leisure was defined by Aristotle as the pursuit of understanding, and free time was best thought of as the time for intellectual questing for wisdom. While marching to different drummers, the same ideal dominated the leisure attitudes of the clerics of Europe in the Middle Ages and the scholarly mandarins of China. Today remnants of the Greek and Christian tradition are with us yet, as is evidenced by our word "school," which was derived from the Greek word *schole*, meaning leisure.[11]

[11] Ida Craver, "Leisure," *The Encyclopedia of the Social Sciences*, Vol. V, 402–405; L. H. Weir, *Europe at Play: A Study of Recreation and Leisure Time Activities*, 1–19.

Since our forebears gave little thought to leisure as a basic need of man, one finds few prescriptions for guiding ordinary people in their use of leisure. To be sure, the elite generally agreed on what course was right for themselves, and many set the tone of Western civilization through their leisure pursuits in art, sculpture, philosophy, and, eventually, science. But because later historians so admired the elitist view of the "proper use" of leisure, we find this "humanistic fallacy" getting in the way of an objective consideration of leisure. In its present form this fallacy emerges as a highbrow attitude toward leisure behavior, a posture which cavalierly condemns a wide variety of leisure outlets as beneath the dignity of intellectuals. Today this view condemns much of our movies, popular literature, television, and mass sports, and in the academic vineyards the professor who engages in any of the despised forms soon becomes prudent about disclosing his interests to his colleagues.

Along with the humanistic fallacy goes another survival of past elitist thinking, which also exerts a ghostly effect on our ideas of proper leisure. This is the "gentlemanly fallacy," a class-bound notion that some leisure outlets properly belong to gentlemen and ought not to be used by the masses. Thus, if the humanistic fallacy holds that the best leisure behavior promotes powerful brains, the gentlemanly fallacy holds that the best leisure behavior validates one's claim to high status. From this aristocratic notion stems the distinction between amateur and professional sportsmen. As defined in 1897 by the Earl of Suffolk and Berkshire, an amateur must be a "gentleman of means," who may bet on sports, but who must never betray his "gentle birth" by teaching or practicing an athletic exercise in order to earn a living.[12]

The tenacity of this class-bound attitude throughout history may be seen in the way commitments to dogs and horses continue to evoke memories of knightly status. But it is this tradition which has been forcibly redefined under the impact of professionalized sports. Although American history shows neither clear-cut tradi-

[12] The Earl of Suffolk and Berkshire Hedley Peek and F. G. Aflalo (eds.), *The Encyclopedia of Sport*, 1–3.

tion of an aristocracy nor even a clear understanding of the word "gentleman,"[13] it still records the efforts of many would-be aristocrats to press their pedigree claims through their leisure behavior. In its earliest phase, organized baseball was dominated by would-be gentlemen, who tried to monopolize the sport as their form of conspicuous leisure. However, industrial democracy, with its dynamic ability to mass produce cheap copies of scarce commodities, soon destroyed this effort.

An early phase of industrial capitalism was closely identified with a set of quasi-religious values, now known as the Protestant ethic. Basic to this value complex is a notion that heavenly and earthly fortune comes to him who works hard and continuously, avoiding the pitfalls of idleness and luxury. In northern Europe and North America such a belief was a constraining influence on leisure, and the only approved type of leisure behavior was that which provided "a renewal or preparation for the continuance of routine and necessary work."[14]

In early America this value set was strongest in the colonies where Calvinist Protestantism held sway, but in many other places religion teamed with economic scarcity to impose a pattern of leisure austerity. Rooted firmly in the traditions of colonial America, such attitudes made a profound and lasting impression upon our national character. If on the one hand this ethic made Americans feel guilty about fun, on the other it helped lay the foundations of urban-industrialism, which would soon revolutionize both our economy and our social structure. Imbued with the value of hard work, Americans of 1850 seemingly did not know how to play. As Henry T. Tuckerman observed, Americans entered into festivities as "if [they] were a serious business." To take leisure "leisurely" was alien to our "national temper" during much of our history, and today remnants of this attitude continue to clash with the fun ethic.[15]

Paradoxically, the harder Americans labored, the more free

13 E. H. Cady, *The Gentleman in America*, 2–32, 209–11.
14 Max Kaplan, *Leisure in America: A Social Inquiry*, 24.
15 Foster R. Dulles, *America Learns to Play*, 9; A. M. Schlesinger, *Paths to the Present*, 1–7.

hours came to be available to more people. This phenomenon occurred because the application of rational science to the needs of life unleashed power sources which led to more efficient machines, better methods of distribution, bigger cities, and a widening of the rational approach to include morality and personal behavior. Significant for the present time was the fact that after 1870 there came a steady decline in the average working day. After 1900 further decreases in work hours followed the development of more ingenious, labor-saving machinery.[16]

Of equal significance to the leisure revolution was the rise of industrial cities, a trend profoundly disturbing to the lives of many persons. In two brief generations after the founding of the nation, Americans could point out that one of every six persons in 1860 lived in cities of eight thousand or more; forty years later, it was one in three. One might say that the city forced Americans to invent new patterns of fun, including the spectacle sports; and through widened channels of communication, such as the newspapers, cityways of leisure radiated "to the very fingertips of the whole land."[17]

The march of urban-industrial democracy sorely tested the staying power of rural-based religious values. In general, Christianity had always treated fun suspiciously, and extreme brands of Calvinistic Puritanism actively tried to repress play and sports. In colonial New England religious zealots promoted laws banning leisure activities such as playing at dice and cards, dances, and theaters. Just what kind of behavior these extremists aimed for may be inferred from an entry in the journal of that seventeenth-century worthy, Judge Samuel Sewell. At the time frivolous Christmas celebrations were forbidden, but Sewell found smug satisfaction in his own grim celebration. "Twas an awful yet pleasing Treat," he wrote concerning his experience in passing the day in

[16] M. H. Keir, *The Epic of Industry*, 1–6; Joseph S. Zeisel, "The Workweek in American Industry, 1850–1956," *Mass Leisure* (ed. by Eric Larrabee and Rolf Meyersohn), 145–52.

[17] Schlesinger, *op. cit.*, 23, 210–33; Schlesinger, *The Rise of the City, 1878–1898*, chapters iii, iv, ix; Allan Nevins, *Emergence of Modern America, 1865–1878*, 75–100, 203–27.

the family mausoleum. On other occasions he derived somber joy from attending public hangings and whippings and by serving as pallbearer.

The antileisure laws, however, were easier to enact than to enforce. As Huizinga pointed out, man's need for play is basic and will find an outlet. Thus, John Winthrop worried that his people were too willing to drop work in order to attend midweek church services, and other watchdogs bristled at the sounds of revelry emanating from colonial taverns. But in a fundamental sense, religiously inspired laws against fun failed because of the very diversity of American religion. In the middle colonies more tolerant forms of Protestantism allowed the pursuit of fun, and in the South, where Puritanism was weak, a variety of leisureways developed. In that region one might get away with playing on Sunday, and the wealthy had no trouble forming fancy, class-bound leisure groups for gambling and fox hunting.[18] Over the years ever widening religious diversity demanded toleration of another's ways of worship and play as basic to an orderly society.

Notwithstanding recurring waves of religious excitation in the wake of nineteenth-century revivals, the steady growth of a rational-scientific world view helped to undermine religious opposition to fun. Back in the eighteenth century Benjamin Franklin and Benjamin Rush had defended adult play and sport as positively healthful. In 1820, Stuart Skinner told American farmers that sports and play were basic to life, although he stressed the recreative value of them.[19] And by 1870, Dr. A. K. Gardner defended the integrative function of sports and play when he said, "What is more conducive to real family happiness than the family whist-table?" Noticing that leisure also reinforced socially useful goals and statuses, he added, "A finished cardplayer is of necessity gentlemanly in deportment, considerate in his demeanor toward others, and under proper self control."[20]

Of course such advice was superfluous for those already en-

[18] Dulles, *op. cit.*, 3–22.
[19] Marshall Davidson, *Life in America*, Vol. II, 6–37; Jennie Holliman, *American Sports, 1785–1835*, 178–92.
[20] *Leslie's Illustrated Weekly*, January 8, 29, 1870.

rolled in fashionable clubs organized for play purposes. Although a clear title to highest prestige eluded them, men of business enterprise tried hard over the last century to validate their place in a plutocracy. As Dixon Wecter noted, every city, town, and village in the land has a record of social aspiration with its tragicomic blending of snobbery, wisdom, and folly. With free time and fat purses as basic requirements, memberships in exclusive sporting clubs were used as proof that the bearer was not to be counted among the mortals, and at certain times and places these clubs did work to sort local gentlemen of leisure from the riffraff. But mostly the expansion of urban industrialism added new pretenders, so that by 1865 such clubs were so numerous that it was hard to distinguish the great from the near-great.

As outlets for conspicuous leisure, these clubs often focused on a single sport. Aping British styles, many stuck to horse racing, hunting, hounds, and polo. Others chose less pretentious activities, but whenever a rising standard of living allowed "the rabble to invade the diversions of gentlemen," the elitists practiced snobbery by abandoning the bastardized activity and regrouping around a scarcer leisure form. Of course, the unintended effect of such behavior was a further broadening of the leisure base and a consequent hastening of the leisure revolution.[21]

However, a frantic concern over one's social status is only one aspect of American culture reflected in our sports. Certainly, the notion that sports explain the nation, first voiced by Plato, promises many more insights into American culture. If one can detach himself from the humanistic fallacy and force himself to survey the broad variety of our leisureways, he can gain significant insight into the culture.

Certainly the dominant theme of individualism is reflected in our leisureways. In colonial America it showed up in a variety of activities, such as horse racing, hunting, fishing, and certain tavern sports enjoyed with variations in all parts of the United States. Because most of these were British imports, they reveal the impact

[21] Dixon Wecter, *The Saga of American Society: A Record of Social Aspiration, 1607–1937*, 245–79, 428–51.

of Britain upon our culture. But the shaping influence of American lifeways transformed many imports, thereby reflecting the emergence of a new species of English-speaking civilization. In an early form this transformation was reflected in brutal spectacles like wrestling and gouging, with participation outlets like wolf drives, shooting contests, and tomahawk-throwing testifying to the rugged way of life that put a high value on individual toughness.

While many early leisure outlets reflected a predominantly rural way of life, the rising urban areas added diversity. In the colonial era wealthy city-dwellers formed associations strictly for the pursuit of pleasure, thereby risking the opprobrium of religious moralists. Nevertheless, such clubs flourished and in time inspired lower classes to imitate their elegant ways of life.

America's growing commitment to a rational-scientific world view is reflected in our leisureways. Indeed, the rising popularity of sports roughly parallels the lessening of religious influence over American minds. This growing rational approach to leisure shows itself in Jefferson's concern over the relative value of certain sports. While Jefferson never doubted that men needed fun, he questioned whether "games played with ball" were as useful in character-building as those involving horses and guns.[22] His countrymen set his mind at rest by going mostly for martial sports. Freedom to hunt, gun, or fish was seldom restricted at the time, and those laws that did restrict did so to conserve game animals for food. Moreover, religious zealots hardly dared attack such outlets, and many individuals rationalized their own interest by arguing that gunning and fishing allowed time for meditation. Such tolerance made it easy for aspiring gentlemen to form elite hunting and fishing clubs, revealing their strong desire to validate their pretensions to status by betting, hunting with elaborate equipment, and fishing with the finest tackle.

Yet if Jefferson downgraded ball playing, many Americans were ever ready to throw, chase, catch, kick, and bat balls. So popular were ball games by 1787 that Princeton College authorities tried to ban them because they interfered with studies. Also, by 1816,

[22] *Ibid.*, 428.

several towns had passed laws curbing ball playing, because such play threatened both person and property. Nevertheless, ball play persisted, especially those British imports of town ball, cricket, and football. Other favorites included paddle ball, trap ball (played with bats), primitive golf, and such familiars as hockey, hurling, and shuttlecock.

As a precursor of baseball, town ball demands attention. As played in the early years, it required a square field with a base at each corner. Each side of the square was sixty feet long, and the batter stood inside a four-foot square located between first and fourth base. The pitcher threw from the center of the square, and a batter was out if he flied out, or if his batted ball was caught on the first bounce, or if he was hit by a fielder's return throw while running bases. Teams of ten to twenty could play, and each side got only one out. This simple team sport attracted sizable crowds, making town ball a primitive example of a field sport spectacular.

The above form of town ball was known as the "Massachusetts Game" and was one of several varieties. Around 1835, Alexander Cartwright developed the "New York Game," which utilized the familiar diamond-shaped infield. For a time it seemed as if a variety of town ball would be institutionalized as a favorite American game which could offer both group participation and spectator identification.

Meanwhile, other leisure spectacles were developing in the cities. Despite clerical opposition in the 1840's, horse racing flourished along with cockfighting and animal-baiting. Boxing matches, though fought under the English Broughton code of 1743, remained as bloody, bare-knuckled spectacles so offensive to many persons that this spectacle was forced to operate clandestinely. Other spectacles like wrestling matches, walking races, and boat races flourished, the last a rising favorite among would-be plutocrats.[23]

By the 1850's, America's heightened interest in such sports caught the notice of *Harper's Weekly*. Noting that the increase

[23] Holliman, *op. cit.*, 13–39, 53–103, 107–63; Davidson, *op. cit.*, Vol. II 6–37.

followed the waning of the urban religious revivals of the period, *Harper's* listed a host of commercialized outlets available for New Yorkers. Besides theaters, amusement parks, dance halls, and beer gardens, P. T. Barnum reigned as king of indoor urban spectacles with his combined circus and freak show.

At this time urbanites seemed content to watch others play rather than participate themselves. In 1860, *Harper's* editors worried about the consequences to the health of urbanites. Recalling that in past times city-dwellers played more, the editor warned that passive onlooking would produce "pulmonary men and women . . . childless wives . . . dyspeptic men . . . puny forms, and . . . bloodless cheeks," and he urged more "muscular education in general."[24] Scoring those merchants for making "a business of pleasure" by capitalizing on the underdeveloped leisure tastes of the poor, a *Harper's* editor irately sketched a typical Sunday at "Jones Woods" with its garish atmosphere of motion pictures, shooting galleries, and billiard tents. Damning the beer sales, the editor blamed the "German spirit" along with Jewish and Irish profanation of the Sabbath, thereby revealing his own rural Protestant bias and his culture-bound notion of proper leisure behavior.[25]

Nevertheless, urban leisure outlets multiplied, and in 1859 a *Harper's* editor refereed a lively debate on whether baseball or "free for all football" deserved to be called the national game.[26] Such diversity was apparent in the late 1850's, but after the Civil War the flood tide of urban leisure, dammed up by five years of war, burst. It seemed as if Americans were ready and willing as never before to spend time and money watching and playing games. For those wanting participation sports, there was a croquet mania in 1866, followed three years later by a velocipede mania. In the late 1860's in New York, Central Park was opened, offering seasonal opportunities to skaters, sleighers, swimmers, and picnickers. At the same time Coney Island Beach became a proletarian watering spot as the elite moved to the Catskills.

[24] *Harper's Weekly*, January 28, September 22, 1860.
[25] *Ibid.*, November 5, 1859.
[26] *Ibid.*, October 15, November 5, 1859, August 31, 1861; John A. Kouvenhoven, *Adventures in America, 1857–1900*, 24–25.

The rapid development of commercialized field sports like baseball struck a new note in urban leisure. With frank disapproval *Harper's* reported throngs of spectators on hand for the 1867 Harvard-Yale baseball game. And *Leslie's* was amazed that the pedestrian races could attract five thousand viewers. Indeed, any new spectacle attracted passive gawkers, including the balloon ascensions, ladies' equestrian competitions, and yacht races.[27]

If many spectacles were fly-by-night gimmicks, this was not true of baseball in the postwar era. In vain a *Harper's* editor urged young men to choose the YMCA reading room over the betting which accompanied the "championship follies" of baseball.[28] Just why baseball should have become an urban mania is not easily explained. In Bruce Catton's opinion the game's popularity grew out of its ability to invoke rural nostalgia.[29] If true, people were acting on a myth which is hardly a new phenomenon. At the time many urbanites were rural migrants for whom baseball may have conjured up an image of tidy village greens in small Protestant farm villages, where once one sported with old dog Tray. No doubt such sites were the scenes of ball games, but the game that we know as baseball was primarily an urban invention. It was also a rational invention, "Rounders made scientific," according to a British observer.[30] Although the game continues to strike a rural response, it developed in the cities and came to be played by professionals who manifested far more the new urban values. This we shall see as we turn to the origins of organized baseball.

[27] *Harper's Weekly*, August 3, 1867; *Leslie's Illustrated*, September 16, 1871.

[28] *Harper's Weekly*, October 26, 1867; *Leslie's Illustrated*, November 4, 1871.

[29] Bruce Catton, "The Great American Game," *American Heritage*, Vol. X, No. 3 (April, 1959), 17–25, 86.

[30] R. G. Knowles, "Baseball," *The Encyclopedia of Sport* (ed. by Hedley Peek and F. G. Aflalo), 73.

Contents

Illustrations

 I. *The Gentleman's Era of Baseball*

1

The Amateur Era

BASEBALL'S SURGE to prominence as a spectator sport in the 1850's amazed even seasoned observers of the contemporary scene. Writing in *Harper's*, one observer tried to restrain the enthusiasm of those *aficionados* who were touting the game as America's national sport. Was it not after all only a concoction of the big city papers? After all, he declared, baseball of the 1850's really was a city-slicker's pastime, not a favorite of rural villages and towns. Emboldened by his own logic, the critic sought to dampen the ardor of urban baseball buffs, saying, "We see no evidence that either base-ball or any athletic game is so generally practiced by our people as to be fairly called a popular American game." Yet he had to concede that Americans had radically changed their attitudes toward sport; back in the 1830's, sports were scorned by schoolmasters and employers. But in 1859 leading families wanted boys to learn "base-ball" as much as their "prosody or conic sections." If they should continue this passion, the editor thought Americans would soon rival the English in their love of sports, and the ensuing muscular development "will surprise physiologists."[1]

Stung by such talk, the baseball buffs were quick to reply. Writing from Steuben County, New York, F. H. Guivits argued that baseball was popular in rural America. Having dwelt in rural Ohio, Indiana, and Michigan, Guivits found ruralites in all these areas using baseball as a social accompaniment to barn-raisings over the past twenty years. He admitted that the rural brand of ball was unorganized, but he insisted that "It is the game at our district schools during intermission hours, and often enjoyed by youths of both sexes."[2]

The above exchange says much about the game's status in the 1850's. Men like Guivits saw it as a play-participation activity, whereas members of formally organized city "clubs" saw it as a spectator sport. Of the two forms it is the latter that contributed most to the leisure revolution, for in only a decade the sport had grown from modest urban beginnings to profitable commercial proportions, and in this brief span people came to accept the paid player as the skilled performer whose efforts were worth paying to see. Furthermore, by 1869 the promotional myth that baseball was the "national game" had rooted itself into the culture.

That baseball should have undergone so swift a transformation from rudimentary child's-play origins to a stage of formal organization with the feature of gentlemen's baseball clubs, and even farther, to the point where it was becoming an organized spectator sport for mass consumption, is perhaps best explained in terms of the leisure revolution. It was as if Americans needed new rituals to unify and sustain themselves in the new world of city and factory. As a sports spectacular, baseball met both challenges by providing fans with a tension-relieving spectacle of two hours' duration, played by skilled new heroes. Beyond this the hope of becoming a player offered poor boys a bit of the American dream

---

[1] *Harper's Weekly*, October 15, 22, 1859.
[2] *Ibid.*, November 5, 1859.

of cash and glory. In short, baseball mirrored the "exuberant energies" of Americans and was "suited to a people who feel that careers are open for skill and resourcefulness."[3]

However, the theory of the rapid evolution of baseball from primitive child's play to commercialized spectacular clashes with an old legend, which describes the game's immaculate conception. The "Doubleday legend" tells of the game's invention at Cooperstown, New York, in 1839 by an inspired youth, Abner Doubleday, who later became a Civil War hero. This tale gained wide acceptance sixty years ago, when major league owners ordered a committee of the game's elder statesmen to inquire into the origins of the game. Meeting in 1907, the committee of inquiry was headed by the millionaire sporting-goods baron Albert G. Spalding, and it supposedly met several times. Later, however, it was sadly reported that the committee's wealth of data had been destroyed by fire and that Spalding's final report rested mostly on the testimony of an aged mining engineer, Abner Graves, who advanced the Doubleday myth.[4] Since Spalding favored this version, the committee, except for one member who since had died, dutifully concurred, signing the final report on December 30, 1907.[5] In turn this report was quickly accepted by the major league brass and certified as official. Seldom in the history of ideas was a myth easier to track down; yet in 1939 the professional baseball world with solemn ritual proclaimed a season-long celebration of the centenary of the game's "birth."

Nurtured in the critical method of inquiry, historians naturally find fault with the Doubleday origin; indeed, Spalding must have doubted it himself since his own ghost-written history of the sport records accounts of games played prior to 1839 which would support the evolutionary hypothesis. But in seeking a motive for Spalding's deliberate myth making, one finds him unscrupulous in his chauvinistic determination to "prove" the American origin of the game. In his history he repeatedly argues that baseball is

[3] Max Lerner, *America As A Civilization*, 812–19.

[4] Arthur Bartlett, *Baseball and Mr. Spalding: The History and Romance of Baseball*, 1–11.

[5] Albert G. Spalding, *America's National Game*, 18–26.

5

wholly American. The game, "as no other form of sport . . . is the exponent of American Courage, Confidence, Combativeness; American Dash, Discipline, Determination; American Energy, Eagerness, Enthusiasm."[6]

Better-qualified historians than Spalding had already written histories which reported baseball games played prior to 1839. Three such writers, Francis C. Richter, Jacob C. Morse, and Henry Chadwick, refused to accept Spalding's version.

Easily the most productive and authoritative of the early baseball writers was Henry Chadwick. His career as a sportswriter spanned fifty years and earned him the title of "Father of the Game." With Harry Wright, Chadwick believed that British standards of sportsmanship should dominate organized baseball. Although born in England in 1824, Chadwick lived most his life in Brooklyn. When he was a boy, his journalist father groomed him for a career as a music teacher, but he practiced this calling only briefly. In 1848, at twenty-four years of age, he turned to journalism and soon specialized in sportswriting.[7]

Chadwick's columns soon appeared in every sports-minded paper in New York, and his tireless efficiency also won him the editorship of most of the early baseball guides. As his output increased, so, too, did his reputation as the leading authority and critic on baseball matters. By 1870, his pontifications could be read in guides like *Chadwick's Base Ball Manual, Beadle's Dime Base Ball Player, De Witt's Base Ball Guide,* and in the weekly variety journal, the New York *Clipper.*[8] As an authority he could draw upon his own background as a cricketer and baseball player, but mostly he was sustained by his close personal contacts with baseball men and by his unflagging zeal as an observer and student of the game. By the time he was fifty years old, his reputation was secured, and he proudly wore the title of "Father of the Game."

Although he was no blazing Anglophile, Chadwick insisted that baseball was an outgrowth of "rounders," a favorite game of

[6] *Ibid.*, 4.

[7] *Spalding's Official Base Ball Guide*, 1900, p. 206; *ibid.*, 1877.

[8] Harry Wright to William A. Hulbert, May 6, 1875. Wright, Correspondence, Vol. VI.

English children. He was supported in this contention by the studious Francis C. Richter, who edited the breezy *Sporting Life*, a Philadelphia journal devoted to baseball and other sports. Jacob Morse, long-time sports editor of the Boston *Herald*, also agreed that the game was an outgrowth of informal bat and ball games that children had played for generations. In general, this trio believed the "old cat" games to be the likeliest ancestor of baseball in America.[9]

But Spalding, brushing aside such dissent as almost treasonous, argued that baseball, like America, must be "free from the trammels of English traditions, customs, conventionalities."[10] And in his day such patriotic pap could and did clinch an argument.

In fact, baseball owes a debt to cricket. Comparing the two in 1859, *Harper's* suggested that baseball was at last crowding out cricket. But if cricket was shunted into a few fashionable enclaves of American society, it left its mark on baseball. The umpire is common to both, and the language of early baseball writers drew heavily from cricket, with such expressions as "excellent field," "batsman," "punish loose bowling," and "playing for the side." Further, it was the cricket experience of pioneer baseball men like Chadwick and Wright which inspired many of the innovations which they introduced into baseball.[11]

While some sportswriters still cling to the Doubleday legend, most historians, convinced by the scholarly work of Robert W. Henderson, accept the evolutionary thesis. Henderson's documented studies of eighteenth-century English and American children's picture books, which show pictures of children playing bat and ball games, offer hard evidence in support of the multilinear evolution of baseball.[12]

If not by the 1820's,[13] certainly by the 1840's, baseball evolved

[9] Jacob C. Morse, *Sphere and Ash: History of Baseball*, 5–15; Francis C. Richter, *A Brief History of Baseball*, 1–13.

[10] Spalding, *op. cit.*, 9.

[11] *Harper's Weekly*, October 18, 1858, October 22, 1859.

[12] Robert W. Henderson, *Baseball: Notes and Materials on its Origin*.

[13] Samuel Hopkins Adams, "Baseball in Mumford's Pasture Lot," *Grandfather Stories*, 121–31.

to a point where a twentieth-century observer, watching a team like the aristocratic New York Knickerbockers, would have recognized the game. The diamond, with bases set forty-five feet apart, was the work of an 1845 committee of Knickerbockers, headed by Alexander Cartwright. This committee later organized the Knickerbocker Club with a special set of playing rules and a code of conduct aimed at instilling gentlemanly decorum. In time this "New York Game" won nation-wide acceptance, overshadowing the "Massachusetts Game" and catapulting the Knickerbockers into a dominant position in baseball councils. As baseball's fashion-makers, the Knickerbockers took a condescending view of other clubs which sought to ape their style, and it soon became apparent that they were out to establish themselves as the social arbiters of baseball, after the manner of the Marylebone Cricket Club, then presiding over English cricket.

Unhappily for Knickerbocker hopes, they, like so many other Americans, really did not know what gentlemanly behavior meant. By any standards, some of the men in the Knickerbocker ranks were would-be gentlemen; of fifty names on the rosters of 1845–60, seventeen were listed as merchants, twelve as clerks, five as brokers, and two as insurance men. There was also a "segar dealer," a hatter, a cooperage owner, a stationer, and a U.S. marshal. Later on, as competition grew tougher, the members invited Harry Wright, a jeweler's apprentice and bowler with the St. George Cricket Club, to join their club; and then we see the paradox of gentlemanly American amateurism: Americans, although they seem to like the idea of being gentlemanly sportsmen in the British sense, really want to win.[14]

In failing to convince other clubs of their superior pedigrees and their diamond invincibility, the Knickerbockers found themselves bluntly rejected as baseball's fashion dictators. In 1858, some twenty-five rivals, all organized after the Knickerbocker pattern, lured their overlord into a convention ostensibly called in order

[14] Dr. Daniel Adams' account in *The Sporting News*, February 29, 1896; Spalding, *op. cit.*, 51–70; Morse, *op. cit.*, 5–15; Harold Seymour, *Baseball, The Early Years*, 16–18.

to consolidate the rules. Meeting in 1859, the newer clubs voted suddenly to organize themselves into the "National Association of Base Ball Players." This new organization effectively cut the Knickerbockers out of executive councils and also added a modified set of playing rules. Having thus slain the New York father, the Association extended its own loose control over organized baseball.

By 1860, some sixty clubs had joined the Association with most coming from the East, although St. Louis and Chicago were important western bastions.[15] Because the cotton curtain then divided North and South, the East-West pattern of major league competition became established and continued as the "proper" pattern until far into the twentieth century.

In its brief and impotent heyday, the new Association clung to the notion that organized baseball ought to be a gentleman's game. For this reason amateurism was applauded, and participants were expected to be persons of means and local social standing. Years later, E. H. Tobias, a member of the St. Louis Empire Club of the 1860's, recalled that a member was expected to invest much time and money in his hobby. Uniforms, dues, assessments for grounds maintenance, and fines for profanity and for missing meetings were all part of the expenses. And until a member paid for a quarrel with an umpire, he was subjected to "personal disgrace if not financial bankruptcy."

A typical Association team customarily ranked each member according to his prowess as a player. The Empire Club had the equivalent of three teams, with the most skilled occupying first-string berths.

Tobias also revealed some of the measures taken to keep the Empires exclusive. He noted that the club scheduled games only with teams of similar organization; in doing this, the Empires competed only with social equals.[16]

The 1860 Washington team tried to validate its gentlemanly claims in the same manner. A. H. Ragan proudly recalled that

[15] Spalding, *op. cit.*, 51–70.
[16] *The Sporting News*, November 2, 1895.

Washington players jealously guarded their amateur status by refusing all payments, including travel expenses.[17]

When two such gentlemanly clubs played, they potlatched with each other in an effort to show which was the more aristocratic. In line with the British ethic of sportsmanship, essential postures were magnanimity in victory and friendliness in defeat. Thus, even when the Washington Nationals slaughtered the Cincinnati Buckeyes, eighty-eight to twelve, the Buckeye hosts remained gracious to the end. Indeed, they afterwards "spread an excellent lunch before the Nationals which they disposed of 'on the fly.' "[18]

But more dominant American values, such as fierce competition and creeping commercialism, disrupted the climate of sportsmanship. As early as 1858, clubs were charging admission prices, although the gallant Washington clubs gave free tickets to ladies and sportswriters.[19] Another crass element was the intense interest of the gentlemen in getting newspaper publicity. Also, many clubs seeking to enhance their prestige padded their membership rolls with the names of prominent Americans: an example was the Empire Club, which listed as members General William T. Sherman and General Fred Benteen.[20]

None of the ingenious attempts to keep the game exclusive prevented the working classes from participating. To be sure, the long working day posed a problem for many men, but one team was so dedicated to the game that its members turned out for practice at five in the morning.[21] The rise of such teams posed a "vulgarizing" threat to the gentlemen, but the post–Civil War era stimulated their increase.

The Civil War was hard on the gentlemen clubs, although most managed to hold on and even flourished during those years. Some border-state clubs tried hard to keep the partisan passions out of their games. In the Pastime Club of Baltimore, William Griffith

[17] *The Evening Star* (Washington, D.C.), July 12, 1914.
[18] *Ibid.*, July 19, 1867.
[19] John C. Proctor, *ibid.*, March 26, 1944.
[20] *The Sporting News*, December 14, 1895.
[21] Dulles, *op. cit.*, 182–91.

recalled that they were able to hold both Northern and Southern sympathizers in line by banning all talk about the war.

When peace came, the Pastime Club built expensive grounds, with seats, fences, and clubhouse. However, the cost of the venture forced the club to seek new subscribers, to expand membership rolls, and, finally, to charge admissions. A fifteen-cent fee was imposed, and additional revenue came from renting the grounds to neighboring clubs.[22]

During the Civil War, baseball was played among Union troops, thereby threatening the gentlemanly monopoly. A. G. Mills, later a National League president, remembered packing his bat and ball with his field equipment, because he found as much use for them as for his side arms.[23] And the war also converted another future National League president, Norman E. Young, from an earlier commitment to cricket. When mustered out, Young helped found the Olympic Club of Washington.[24]

In relieving the monotony of camp life, the game early demonstrated an ability to attract hordes of spectators. Perhaps the largest crowd of the nineteenth century was the throng of forty thousand Union soldiers who watched a Christmas Day game in 1862 between two picked nines of their comrades. And in southern prison camps, northern prisoners found the game useful as a tension-reliever; sometimes teams of inmates played teams of guards.[25] Evidence of one such match is a lithograph showing two teams of Union prisoners playing at Salisbury, North Carolina.[26]

President Lincoln apparently had a mild interest in the game. Years after the Civil War, Winfield Scott Larner of Washington remembered attending a game played on an old Washington circus lot in 1862. The game was already under way when Larner saw a modest black carriage drawn by two black horses pull up. Out

---

[22] William R. Griffith, *The Early History of Amateur Base Ball in the State of Maryland, 1858–1871*, 10–11.

[23] Cincinnati Public Library, "Newspaper Clippings on Cincinnati," Vol. XXIX, 79.

[24] *Spalding's Official Base Ball Guide*, 1895, p. 137.

[25] Spalding, *op. cit.*, 95–97.

[26] Davidson, *op cit.*, II, 58–59.

stepped Lincoln, followed by his son Tad. Taking Tad's hand, the President "modestly and unobtrusively . . . made his way up to where he could see the game and sat down in sawdust left over from the late circus." Choosing a spot along the first-base line, he held Tad between his knees and watched the rest of the game, sometimes cheering like "the most enthusiastic fan of the day." On departing, Lincoln and Tad accepted three loud cheers from the crowd.[27]

More evidence of baseball's growing popularity is seen in some of Currier and Ives' political cartoons, which borrowed the baseball theme. Shortly after the war, these lithographers published a color print of "The American National Game of Base Ball," showing two teams competing for the championship at the Elysian Fields of Hoboken, New Jersey.[28]

It is not surprising then that the stimulating influence of the Civil War triggered a veritable baseball "mania" in eastern cities during the late 1860's. Such fierce interest forced clubs to put more effort into winning for the glory of the town.[29] Catering to public desire for winning baseball games, clubs changed some of their class-bound policies and invited husky yeomen into the ranks. For a time a few resisted this trend, but competition for the services of skilled players soon produced a paid class of players, whose skill and opportunism fostered professionalization.

A pattern of commercial baseball was set in the 1860's as clubs began charging admission and dividing some of the receipts among their best players. Nor did this hurt attendance, for fans showed increasing willingness to pay to see outstanding players perform. And because the game lends itself admirably to betting, other interests helped swell the growing ranks of the spectators.[30]

Because of keen public interest, the style of play changed rapidly. Standardization of rules came as a result of suggestions from the professional players, whose voices dominated Association

[27] *The Evening Star*, (Washington, D.C.), July 12, 1914.
[28] *Ibid.*, April 13, 1954.
[29] Davidson, *op. cit.*, II, 61.
[30] Carl Wittke, "Baseball in Its Adolescence," *The Ohio State Archeological and Historical Quarterly*, Vol. LX (April, 1952), 118-21.

councils. As early as 1857, the Association chose a nine-inning game, with five innings constituting a legal contest. No balls were called on a batter, who had only to swing at a pitch he liked. Six years later, in 1863, the Association revised the rules. Now iron plates marked the pitcher's box and home plate. Catching a foul ball on a bounce still put a man out, but fair flies had to be caught before touching ground. Pitchers threw underhanded from a box located forty-five feet from home plate, and the umpire was instructed to call balls or strikes against pitchers or batters who delayed the game or showed poor "form."

Until the 1880's batters had the advantage of being able to request a pitcher to throw either high or low strikes. Yet pitchers soon developed counter weapons. In 1865, young Arthur Cummings noticed that clam shells tossed underhanded would curve to the right. Impressed, Cummings experimented with a baseball at boarding sehool and, despite ridicule, learned to throw "a raise and a drop ball." The curve came from snapping his wrist and the second finger of his right hand, although once the effort dislocated a wrist bone, forcing him to wear a support. A few years later his underhand curve-ball pitching helped subdue Harvard College for his Brooklyn Excelsior team.[31]

With teams like the Excelsiors touring the Eastern seaboard in 1860, with clubs ready to pay skilled men like James Creighton, and with clubs building commodious grounds, the commercialization of baseball as a sports spectacle was a trend of the 1860's.[32] By the end of the decade it appeared that many baseball men would willingly trade the elusive claim of gentleman for the certainty of hard cash.

[31] *The Sporting News*, January 26, 1897.
[32] Spalding, *op. cit.*, 79.

2

Creeping Commercialism

BASEBALL'S MYTHMAKERS seemingly have an unholy penchant for immaculate conceptions; no doubt they believe that if Venus could emerge full grown from a seashell, why not the game of baseball? While such logic saves its user the burden of thought, its repeated use in baseball leads one to suspect that the user has something against natural procreation and growth processes. Be that as it may, another official baseball saga holds that professional baseball appeared, fully matured, in the year 1869. As the story goes, the Cincinnati Red Stocking Club simply decided to field the nation's top team by offering enticing salaries to the best players of the day. Once whipped into shape, this team won more than eighty consecutive games before bowing for the first time in 1870. Today, the staying power of this myth is evidenced in the

14

work of modern sportswriters who use it as a historical explanation of commercial baseball's origins.

Actually, the origins of commercialized baseball were less dramatic and more complicated. The play-for-pay movement began at least a decade before 1869, with various rewards going covertly to players. According to Chadwick, one of the best paid was star pitcher Jim Creighton, who received *sub rosa* rewards from the Brooklyn Excelsiors.[1] A fast-ball pitcher with a baffling twist delivery, Creighton led his team to a string of victories in 1860. Afterwards, the Excelsiors continued to dominate organized baseball until Creighton became one of the game's first casualties in 1862. While batting in a game, Creighton sustained "an internal injury occasioned by strain," and died a few days later in great pain. Shocked by his passing, his mates proceeded to canonize him as a baseball saint by erecting a garish monument in Brooklyn's Greenwood Cemetery. Carved on the granite monument were oak leaves, crossed bats, a baseball cap, base, and scorebook. With the top shaped like a giant baseball, "it would never be mistaken for anything else than the grave of a ball player."[2]

With high-priced stars raising the costs of competition among "amateur" clubs, many were obliged to seek new ways of meeting costs of travel, maintenance, and equipment. Now the ethic of victory first touched off a talent hunt among clubs, which soon relegated the gentlemen members to the side lines and to the vicarious enjoyment that goes with being a spectator. Also, it was evident that gentlemen members were no longer depended upon for financial support; in 1863, Porter's *Spirit of the Times* reported that many clubs were charging admission rates of as much as twenty-five cents.[3] At their Union Grounds in 1864, the New York Mutuals charged ten cents a head and regularly divided receipts among players. The same policy was followed by the Brooklyn Atlantics at their Capitoline Grounds.[4]

[1] *Spalding's Official Base Ball Guide,* 1898.
[2] Spalding, *op. cit.,* 79–88.
[3] Wittke, "Baseball in Its Adolescence," *The Ohio State Archeological and Historical Quarterly,* Vol. LX (April, 1952), 118–21.
[4] *Spalding's Official Base Ball Guide,* 1898.

The new approach not only attracted spectators who liked to watch skilled play, but also pulled in those who took fierce partisan delight in the local team's ability to beat the outlanders, and inevitably some came to bet on the action. "So common has betting become at baseball matches," complained a *Harper's* editor, "that the most respectable clubs in the country indulge in it to a highly culpable degree, and so common . . . the tricks by which games have been 'sold' for the benefit of gamblers that the most respectable of participants have been suspected of this baseness."[5]

For partisan-minded fans the 1860's provided invaders aplenty. In 1861, the Atlantics of Brooklyn dominated amateur circles, and over the next two seasons the Brooklyn Eckfords seized the national title; indeed, the Eckfords were undefeated in 1863. But the Atlantics came back in 1864 and 1865 with two consecutive undefeated seasons to regain the title.[6]

Admittedly, championships of the 1860's differed considerably from the tightly structured schedules of today. In those days competing clubs scheduled one another by the gentlemanly device of written invitation. Since certain clubs were ruled by aristocratic codes, they often refused to contest with some rivals on the grounds that they were ungentlemanly. Indeed, at this time the Brooklyn Excelsiors refused to have any dealings with the Atlantics, because in 1860 the Excelsiors were offended by the vulgar crowd and the loud-mouthed gamblers who harassed them in a game at the Atlantic's grounds. Hence, from 1860 to the disbandment of both clubs in 1871, playing relations were never resumed.[7] The incident underscores the limited meaning of the national championship title of that day; moreover, it suggests the democratization of baseball crowds and the growing importance of the game as a leisure outlet for ordinary people.

The fierce rivalry between eastern and western clubs in this era further explains the persistence of the East-West pattern of baseball organization. Helping to kindle this sectional rivalry

[5] *Harper's Weekly*, October 26, 1867.
[6] Richter, *op. cit.*, 1–4; Morse, *op. cit.*, 15.
[7] Spalding, *op. cit.*, 85; *Harper's Weekly*, October 26, 1867.

16

was the success of the Washington Nationals of 1867. Touring the West and defeating the top clubs of that region, the Washington Nationals crushed western pride until a Cinderella team, the Forest City Club of Rockford, Illinois, defeated the Nationals, twenty-nine to twenty-three, at Chicago's Dexter Park. Exulted by victory, the Rockford *Register* boasted the victory of its "country club" and loudly touted the pitching prowess of young Albert Spalding, "undoubtedly the best pitcher in the West."[8] Out of pride-filled hearts, the Rockford citizenry honored its heroes with watches, gold pins, and other gifts. Nor did local pride end there, for the town celebrated for a week and calmed down only when the Nationals sent an open letter denying that the Nationals were the "national champions."[9]

In an attempt to clarify the question of national champions, editor Frank Queen of the *Clipper* in 1868 offered a gold ball to the championship team and individual medals to the outstanding player at each position. That year the Athletics of Philadelphia took five individual medals,[10] but no gold ball was awarded because the two favorites, the Athletics and Mutuals, failed to schedule a playoff game.[11]

With good players winning increased recognition, many clubs began bidding for their services. At first the talent struggle was a covert one, with *sub rosa* offers made in the form of shares of gate receipts, bribes from gamblers, offers of political sinecures, and offers of cash or gifts. Cash payments were the last resort, and such offers went only to exceptional players. Nor were players slow to take advantage of the bull market. One who succeeded in getting a straight salary was Al Reach, star infielder of the Athletics. Back in 1862, he had turned down an attractive offer from Baltimore because his connection with the Athletics allowed him to commute to Philadelphia from his Brooklyn home.[12]

Of course, Reach's success strained the meaning of amateurism,

---

8 *Register* (Rockford, Illinois), July 27, 1867.
9 *Ibid.*, August 17, 1867.
10 Adrian C. Anson, *A Ball Player's Career*, 21–28.
11 *New York Clipper*, January 30, 1869, p. 339.
12 Fred Lieb, *The Baltimore Orioles*, 6.

so much so that at the Association's 1863 meeting the amateurs declared that the professionals should be separated from amateurs,[13] although professionals were allowed to remain in the Association. The next year the Association defined a "professional player" as one who "plays base ball for money, place, or emolument."[14]

However, such discrimination failed to halt the tide of commercialism. In 1863, Harry Wright wrote that he was being "honored" by a benefit along with his brother Sam and others. To finance the affair, a 25-cent admission charge was asked, and all comers were also encouraged to part with an extra 25 cents for a souvenir ticket with "a picture of a Professional on each." While the latter gimmick has a very modern sound, Wright was more interested in his cash cut, which came to $29.65.[15]

Fearing the power of entrenched amateurism in Association councils, professionals prudently treaded lightly. Typical of the amateur contempt for the mercenaries was Tobias' scornful summary of the dodges used to pay professionals. Tobias said that the Mutual's technique was to hand them political jobs from New York City's patronage pool, a favorite spot being the coroner's office. Other clubs using the same device were the Atlantics, Athletics, and the Unions of Morrisania, New York. At Troy the Haymakers were able to give good players easy work and good-paying jobs in local industries in addition to political sinecure.

In 1869 two upstate New York clubs reportedly were paying outright salaries to a few stars, and similar reports came from Chicago, Pittsburgh, Cincinnati, Fort Wayne, and Columbus.[16]

Such revelations of early commercialism are verified by reports from the Washington *Evening Star*. One writer, Thomas Henry, said the U. S. Treasury Department was "the real birthplace of professional base ball in Washington." As a source of patronage for good players, this bureau was widely exploited after the Civil War.

---

13 Morse, *op. cit.*, 5–15.

14 *Sporting Life*, January 26, 1887. Chadwick's column.

15 Harry Wright, Note and Account Books, Vol. I.

16 *The Sporting News.* December 14, 1895.

In addition Washington players benefited from the collection plates passed at games. By this kind of enterprise Washington clubs were able to keep a cadre of good players and to offer excellent accommodations. In 1867 the National's park was located on a field four hundred feet square, surrounded by a ten foot fence, and shaded on the north side by roofed stands. To discourage gamblers, a sign which read "Betting Positively Prohibited" was posted.[17]

The close of the decade saw a definite trend toward paying straight salaries. In 1866, Harry Wright reported that the Athletics were paying three players salaries of twenty dollars a week.[18] At the same time, the Athletics, like the Atlantics, were getting as much as two hundred dollars a season through division of gate receipts.[19]

The lure of good pay soon made professional ball playing a coveted career. That working-class youths were snatching at such an opportunity for fame and fortune was apparent from a study of the backgrounds of certain Brooklyn players of 1869. Compiled by the New York *Tribune*, the study revealed a youthful team, averaging twenty-three years in age, of working-class backgrounds. The pitcher was a former stonemason; the catcher, a postal employee; the infielders worked as compositor, machinist, shipping clerk, and compositor. Among the outfielders, two were without previous job experience and the other worked as a compositor. The team substitute once worked as a glass blower.[20]

By 1868 not only did newspapers tell of whole teams that were being paid for playing, but few even expressed surprise. Late in January, 1868, Chadwick, reviewing the prospects of the Atlantics, commented that the club "will have their regular professional ten," along with two other squads, "their amateur first-nine, and their muffins."[21] Such a comment says much about changes taking

[17] *The Evening Star* (Washington, D.C.), August 14, 1927, October 1, 1933.

[18] Wright, Note and Account Books, Vol. I.

[19] U.S. Congress, House Subcommittee Study, *Organized Baseball* (82 Cong., 2 sess., *House Report Doc. No. 95*), Report No. 2002, p. 17.

[20] *Commercial*, (Cincinnati) August 9, 1869.

[21] Chadwick, Scrapbooks, I, 17.

place in baseball. The professionals were often from working-class backgrounds, as were some of the first-ranked amateurs, who were looked upon as promising future professionals. Most significant, however, is the fact that the high status gentlemen, once the backbone of the club, were now the lowly "muffins," a term roughly comparable to the modern epithet of "duffer" in golf. Moreover, by 1869, it was probably painfully obvious to the muffins that the professional team was the darling of both the spectators and club directors. Clearly, baseball was becoming a sports spectacular.

Of course, not all forms of player remuneration were equally honored. Clubs with gambling and unsavory political connections drew scorn from moralists. While covering the fourteenth annual convention of the Association in 1870, Chadwick reported a hot argument stemming from an accusation that the infamous William M. (Boss) Tweed had invested $7,500 in the Mutuals. One attacker vehemently stated "that Mr. Tweed probably got his money back again."[22] Similar charges of bribery and corruption in baseball were heard with increasing frequency by the end of the 1860's.

Such charges prompted cries for reform, but many writers doubted the Association's ability to lead a reform movement. Alleging that the Association's antiprofessional resolves were "mere dead letters," realists urged the professionals to take the lead in correcting the evils of betting, gambling, and "hippodroming." The last term implied fixing the outcome of games in advance, then staging them as if they were legitimate contests.

Calling on unorganized professionals to lead a reform program was asking a lot, but it was a realistic approach. Commercialized baseball, in the opinion of even its harshest critics, was a *fait accompli*, and New York City was identified as the chief player market. As the center of such sales, New York was also at the vortex of baseball problems. Hence, clubs in that city were urged to work toward the elimination of such abuses as contract jumping, or "revolving," as it was then called. The elimination of revolving was crucial to the recognition of professional baseball as a legiti-

[22] *Ibid.*, article dated May, 1870.

mate business. This was Chadwick's line of argument when he scathingly denounced a revolver as a villain who thought nothing of leaving his club "in the lurch" to grab at a better offer. Now Chadwick was urging clubs to eliminate the evil by refusing to sign revolvers. He also warned players of the Association's latest rule calling for a player to give sixty days' notice of intention to leave one club for another.[23] Years later, major league baseball solved this problem by insisting on a reserve clause in player contracts, but in these formative years the revolving evil remained as the crucial stumbling block to the orderly and profitable promotion of big-time baseball.

Perhaps the most interesting point of Chadwick's argument was his 1868 admission that "professional baseball" was "a business." Indeed, while urging reform, he readily conceded the fact that the game had become a commercialized spectacle. Furthermore, at the beginning of the 1869 season, he listed several commercialized teams that were ready for action, including the Haymakers, the Atlantics, the Athletics, the Mutuals, the Chicago White Stockings, the Unions of Lansingburgh, New York, the Buckeyes of Cincinnati, and the Marylands of Baltimore; also mentioned was the rather obscure Red Stocking Club of Cincinnati, which now styled itself as the first all-salaried team in the sense that every player was under contract for a season's service at a negotiated rate of pay.[24] Here, then, was the chief difference between Wright's Reds and other commercialized clubs.

Yet this Red Stocking team was to become a baseball legend as the first "professional team." Fortifying the legend was the team's future record of success on the field. That they were neither the first paid players nor the first team to put together an impressive string of consecutive victories does not detract from their positive influence on the rise of professional baseball. They proved to be a powerful stimulant for commercial-minded clubs to reorganize the game under a regime of frank commercialism. Also, the Reds

---

[23] *Ibid.*, I, 17–18; *New York Clipper*, February 13, 20, 1869.
[24] Chadwick, Scrapbooks, I, 26; *New York Clipper*, January 23, February 13, 1869.

promoted the game beyond the Middle West by invading the hitherto untapped Far West. In short, this club brought favorable publicity to the commercial cause and made it easier for organizers to follow up by creating the first commercial major league.

3

Mr. Champion's Champions

W HILE NOT THE FIRST "PROFESSIONAL TEAM" in organized baseball, the Cincinnati Reds of 1869 were unique, because they alone among the many professional teams girding for the diamond wars chose to be an all-salaried team, using this device to hold each man to his contract for a full season.

But in the spring of 1869 few baseball experts predicted an Olympian effort from the Cincinnatians. Since most experts wrote for eastern papers, they understandably focused on the prospects of such eastern powers as the Mutuals and Athletics. Yet one *Clipper* writer waxed prophetic when he said, "Contestants for the championship next season will have to keep one eye turned towards Porkopolis."[1]

Meanwhile in the hog-butchering capital of America, as the

[1] *New York Clipper*, January 9, 1869.

Queen City of Cincinnati was styled, the Red Stockings were wrapped in a power struggle with a local rival, the Buckeyes. As late as February, 1869, the older Buckeye club debated whether to go all out for professionalism in order to compete with the Reds.[2] But when the Reds lured away the star of the Buckeye nine and when the administration of the Buckeyes passed into conservative hands, the club decided to remain proudly amateur. Thus, by default, the Reds in 1869 found themselves the most powerful team in town.

To be sure the Red Stocking ascendancy was a sudden event, but so too was baseball in Cincinnati. Prior to 1867 the game was almost nonexistent, but in that year Aaron B. Champion, a young lawyer, became interested in baseball's ability to stimulate local business. Champion was the son of a prosperous merchant, and his talents included mercantile promotion, which he harnessed to his sports interest. Champion already was testing his theory through the Union Cricket Club, which he organized in 1865. Two years later he switched his interest to baseball and became president and organizer of the new amateur baseball team, the Red Stockings. Although overshadowed by the older Buckeye club, the Reds under Champion attracted supporters by their flashy uniforms and equally flashy players.[3]

Helping to dazzle local fans was Champion's all-out commercial expansion program. In 1868, he got the club directors to approve an $11,000 stock issue in order to refit the Union Grounds. This was big spending, indeed, for the early days of baseball, but it was only a beginning. In spite of an 1868 seasonal deficit, Champion followed with a bigger spending program for next year on the theory that one must spend greenbacks to make them. Accordingly, $15,000 of new stock was sold, half to members and the rest to new investors. With this money the doughty Champion engaged in hot competition for the services of the nation's top players.[4]

2 *Ibid.*, February 13, 1869.

3 Charles F. Goss, *Cincinnati the Queen City*, III, 370–74; *New York Clipper*, April 3, 1869.

4 *Sporting Life*, January 23, 1884; *Commercial* (Cincinnati), November 24, 1868; *New York Clipper*, March 13, 1869.

Uncertain himself how to go about it, Champion delegated the ivory hunt to a committee of two, George Ellard and Alfred Gosham. Ellard was to head the committee because he owned a sporting goods store, and it was assumed that a knowledge of the artifacts of baseball also included a knowledge of key players. It soon became apparent, however, that the committee's not too subtle policy was simply to try to buy the nine *Clipper* gold medal winners of 1868. Today this would be like trying to buy up the National League all-star team, but in those days the *Clipper* medals supposedly went to the best nine players in the land. It was possible to attract such stars because in the 1860's players were not bound by a reserve clause. Indeed, at one point the committee boasted to a reporter that it already had signed five of the nine medalists. However, this tip-off boomeranged by warning rivals to take countermeasures against the "more than ordinarily strong" Red Stockings.[5]

A few weeks later, to the horror of the committee, two of the five medalists, John Radcliffe and John Hatfield, jumped their Cincinnati contracts and returned to their old clubs. It seems as if this clever pair merely used the Cincinnati offer as a ceremonial bluff to cadge more money from their old bosses. Apparently it worked, but Champion was so outraged that he set himself up as head of an *ad hoc* prosecution committee. Charging the two with dishonesty, contract jumping, and the "ungentlemanly conduct"— then a terrible epithet to apply—he accused the directors of the Athletics and Mutuals of tampering with contracts. These allegations the defendants not only parried, but also produced evidence showing that Radcliffe was under contract when the Reds signed him. Forced to beat a retreat, Champion and his committee nursed badly burned fingers.[6]

At this point the steady hand of Manager Harry Wright was felt. The team's field manager, he was a veteran of ten years' experience as a top player. It was the consensus of sportswriters of

[5] Harry Ellard, *Baseball in Cincinnati: A History*, 138–209; *New York Clipper*, January 9, 1869.

[6] *New York Clipper*, March 13, 1869.

the day that he knew what he was doing, and some held him to be the ablest field manager in the game. "Wright is unapproachable in his good generalship and management," commented the *Clipper*. And Chadwick added his accolade, saying that Wright's men are "better trained and more practiced."[7]

Certainly few others could match his sports-oriented background. Born in England in 1835 to a professional cricketer who emigrated with his family to America, Wright was weaned on field sports. In this country his father was the professional at the St. George Cricket Club of Staten Island, and two other sons followed Harry in emulating their father making a career of sports. Of the three, Harry and George made the most important contributions to American baseball. Both became first-rate players, with George becoming a brilliant shortstop. Although not his brother's equal as a player, Harry made a more fundamental contribution to the organization of major league baseball. As player, manager, league organizer, and theorist on commercial baseball's profit potential, he devoted his life to building baseball as a spectacle. Before his death in 1895, he was nationally acclaimed as "the father of the professional game."

But in early 1869, as he readied his team for the playing season which was to find his Reds invading the eastern baseball strongholds, Wright's future was uncertain. Only two years had passed since he left a $1,200 job as bowler for the Union Cricket Club in order to try his hand with the new game of baseball. Indeed, he never discarded his cricket experience, for throughout his career in baseball he tried to apply its code of sportsmanship to baseball. Nor did he ever abandon the idea that baseball fans were like cricket devotees, that they were rational in their desire to see a well-played, well-trained team compete.[8]

Since baseball as a gentleman's pastime aped British traditions, Wright's British system worked for a time. But Wright also added gimmicks like flashy uniforms, designed by a "female tailor." He

---

[7] *Ibid.*, January 9, 1869; Chadwick, Scrapbooks, VI, 21.

[8] John Kiernan, "Henry Wright," *Dictionary of American Biography* (ed. by Dumas Malone), XX, 554; Nevins, *op. cit.*, 216–27.

also dazzled the fans with good players, and after the Reds scored an unexpected victory over the rival Buckeyes in 1868, Wright became "the hero and idol of the Cincinnati Base Ball Club."[9]

Having taken over the task of recruiting from the committee, Wright had his 1869 line-up set by the end of March. Actually only a little tinkering was needed, since the manager retained six holdovers from his 1868 squad. Besides himself, these included catcher Doug Allison, first-baseman Charles Gould, third-baseman Fred Waterman, fielder Cal McVey, and pitcher Asa Brainard. To round out the team, he added his brother George and Dave Birdsall from the Morrisania Unions, and snared Andy Leonard, Dick Hurley, and Cal Sweasy from the Buckeyes. In all the squad numbered ten men, with Hurley as utility man and Wright himself as relief pitcher. Thus Cincinnati's novel, salaried, "picked nine" was fashioned, and this was the team that Wright proposed to lead against all comers, east and west. Any club could play the Reds simply by promising to give Wright's team one-third of the gate receipts.

Costwise, salaries constituted the greatest expense. Years later a director's son said that each contract ran from March 15 to November 15, and that George Wright, the star shortstop, drew highest pay at $1,400. The same source said that Harry received $1,200, Brainard, $1,100, Waterman, $1,000, five others received $800 each, and substitute Hurley received $600. But George Wright later challenged this list, saying that Harry received $2,000, and he himself, $1,800.[10]

Depending upon big receipts to pay the salaries, Wright bore down hard on training. He worked the men hard, but he also taught them useful tactics that welded them into an efficient machine. Wright's zeal as field manager and trainer soon won him applause from that king of sportswriters, Chadwick, who slyly suggested that New York managers might start winning when they "adopt the same course."[11]

[9] Ellard, *op. cit.*, 42–45, 96.
[10] *Commercial* (Cincinnati) August 26, September 3, 1868, March 21, 1869; *ibid.*, 138–209.
[11] Chadwick, Scrapbooks, VI, 21.

Some of the glamour that still clings to the memory of this team can be laid to President Champion's activities, for he was not one to shun publicity. He managed to get the Cincinnati *Commercial* to appoint Henry Millar as full-time reporter, and Millar never failed to lick Champion's hand. From the start he lavished praise on the Reds, and much of his copy reflected a boyish admiration of Wright. Yet one of his most glowing accounts included this piece of prophecy: "The nine has had plenty of exercise and practice, and is so well regulated that it should avail itself of its capabilities of defeating every club with which it contests." At this point it is worth noting that this well-regulated club required a bed check by the zealous Champion on the eve of its departure for the East.

Heading east, the club carried an early season record of seven wins and no losses, thanks to tune-up victories over weak western opponents and picked nines of local all-stars. On the way to New York the team added another ten victories. By then it was mid-June, and Champion's promotion campaign was in high gear, stressing mostly the novelty of the Cinderella team that dared to take on peerless eastern clubs in their own lairs. But propaganda became legend on June 14 when a partisan New York crowd saw the Reds beat the powerful Mutuals, four to two, on the Union Grounds in Brooklyn. Back home, when the news came, the streets filled with people raising "cheer after cheer for their pet club." "Go on with the noble work," rang a telegram, "our expectations have been met."[12]

By rolling over other formidable opponents, the Reds caught the fancy of eastern fans, who turned out in large numbers at some games. In Washington, President Grant met with the club, "treated them cordially and complimented them on their play." And a Washington sportswriter, betraying his own status dreams, commented that the Reds "drew the most aristocratic assemblage at its games that ever put in an appearance at a base ball match."[13]

As the eastern tour ended with a pile of victories, more sophisticated journals took note. *Harper's* published a page of cuts de-

[12] Ellard, *op. cit.*, 138–209.
[13] *Ibid.*, 138–209.

picting the "picked nine," including a team picture which showed grim young faces protected by beards and sideburns.[14] Returning in late June, the Reds were feted by rabid hero-worshipers, whose behavior looked outlandish to eastern sophisticates. Even the partisan *Commercial* admitted that local fans "get so excited that they ... cheer and applaud before either player or spectator knows what decision the umpire has to give." Also some enthusiasts were not genuine *aficionados*; one old gent, when interviewed, said, "Well, I don't know anything about base ball, or town ball, now-a-days, but it does me good to see those fellows. They've done something to add to the glory of our city." A companion chimed in, "Glory, they've advertised the city—advertised us, sir, and helped our business, sir."

Fanning the high spirits was Champion, who put in a busy day of speechmaking and bow-taking. Speaking at the station, he accepted the gift of a twenty-seven-foot bat from the Cincinnati Lumber Company. On it were carved the players' names, along with that of a substitute named "Fowler." On the run all day and far into the evening when he was guest of honor at a ball, the much-toasted Champion finally relaxed under the "Welcome Red Stocking" banner and allowed that at that moment he would rather be president of the Reds than President Grant.[15]

During the long home stand that followed, the Reds continued their winning ways, although one tie game marred the record. However, official legend passes over this blotch on the escutcheon by blaming the visiting Troy "Haymakers" for an ungentlemanly sin. The official Cincinnati version states that with the score tied, seventeen to seventeen, after five innings, the Troy captain argued violently with the umpire. Joined by his club president, the two cursed the umpire and angrily ordered their team to leave the field. At this point the crowd turned ugly and threatened the Troys, but Umpire Brockway quieted the crowd by forfeiting the game to the Reds. Later the *Commercial* blamed the whole affair on New York gamblers, led by kingpin John Morrisey, who feared

[14] *Harper's Weekly*, July 3, 1869, July 2, 1870.
[15] *Commercial* (Cincinnati), May 25, 1868, July 1, 2, 1869.

losing $17,000 they had bet on a Troy victory. According to this tale, it was the gamblers who tempted the Troys to stage their phoney strike. However, the Association did not accept this explanation, and overruled the forfeit, declaring the outcome a tie.[16]

On the road again in September the Reds toured the Far West by train and took on opponents from Ohio to California. They closed the season with a total log of fifty-seven wins, one tie, and no losses. Thus the official account of the 1869 season reads, and one is left with the impression that the achievement was a logical outcome of virtuous practices like clean living, hard practice, and honest capitalism.

However, even the briefest study of source materials leads one to conclude that the Reds were quite human. Manager Wright's personal record shows that no one more than he knew the mixed joys and sorrows of managing this club. To be sure, there were days when they drew very well, like the time 15,000 persons saw them play in Philadelphia. In six games played in the New York City area, they drew 23,217, enough to make their one-third share of gate receipts come to $4,474.[17] But then, too, there were days when modest receipts made the Reds' share meager. In Mansfield, Ohio, the club collected $50, and in Cleveland $81. And when the team arrived for a scheduled match in Syracuse, Wright was horrified to find a live pigeon shoot going on at the park. Much of the fence was down, and in spots the outfield grass was a foot high. On inquiring, Wright learned that nobody remembered scheduling a ball game, and so the manager contented himself and his men with the therapeutic consolation of a salt bath at a nearby spa at a cost of 35 cents.

The very next day brought a new challenge, but this time Wright was equal to the problem. Arriving in Rochester, he found the park in good shape and a good crowd on hand, but with the first inning barely underway, a sudden downpour soaked the field. Determined to save the receipts, Wright and his men, working furiously, "got

16 *Ibid.*, August 27, 1869.
17 Chadwick, Scrapbooks, I, 26; *Sporting Life*, February 16, 1887.

some brooms, swept the water off, and put sawdust in the muddy places and commenced playing again."

Wright's record also helps to dispel the "Superman myth" that drapes a halo effect over the team's group picture. Although well trained and disciplined, Wright's young men gave their manager many hard times. At times they straggled, missed trains, and ducked out on practices. Pitcher Asa Brainard was a leading offender, but others, including brother George, cut practice sessions. Brainard's temperament led him into a maze of trouble-making channels, and he was difficult to manage. In those days physical exertion was more a part of "work" than now, and baseball pitchers were expected to work all of the games. Of course, with a forty-five-foot pitching distance and an underhanded delivery, this was less brutal than it sounds. Yet it was Wright's misfortune to be saddled with a hypochondriac pitcher, who often complained of imaginary ailments. On those days Wright sometimes had to pitch himself and hope that his "dewdrop" was baffling enough to keep the enemy at bay, assuming the Reds were also hitting their hardest.

Aside from his hypochondria, Brainard was a night owl. Once when the exhausted team detrained at Buffalo in the early morning hours, all were ready for sleep save Brainard and his pal Waterman, who wanted to roam the streets seeking action. Although Wright knew Brainard was a gifted pitcher, who fought extra-hard in close contests, at times he had to threaten to cut his pay to get him to work harder. In short, Brainard was a character; in George Wright's words, he got "odd notions." During a game in 1869 a wild rabbit scampered across the diamond directly in front of the pitcher. Forgetting batter and runners, the irrepressible Brainard threw at the bunny and missed. As the ball rolled among the crowd, two rival runners scored.[18]

At times every member of this "super team" needed bracing, and one general problem was keeping the spirited team away from whisky. Although Wright was a temperance man, he realized that

[18] Wright, Note and Account Books, Vol. I; Wright, Correspondence, Vol. V, 236–37; *Reach's Official Base Ball Guide, 1894,* 79–85.

total abstinence ran counter to the prevailing American belief that ability to hold liquor was a measure of manliness. Apparently Wright fought a losing battle, because in 1870 the *Commercial* sarcastically suggested that the 1870 club contracts should stipulate that no man be permitted to use alcohol "unless prescribed by a physician in good standing."[19]

No doubt the Red Stocking victories compensated for some of his worries, but then victory also brought problems. In 1869 after the New York victories, some Gotham papers, showing the hostile envy of the vanquished, downgraded the feat and sneered at Cincinnati's brand of commercialism. Using a scattergun approach, the *Day Book* questioned the whole idea of paying ball players, saying that a youth who accepted pay ought to be "disgraced." If he held a position of financial responsibility, it was declared, he should be fired because one could not play for pay and remain honest. The editor suggested that paid players were "at the beck and call of the sporting men, who bring them into the ring, game-cock fashion, and pit them against each other for money."

Others singled out the Cincinnati style of commercialism and accused the Reds of being an "eclectic nine." By this the *Sun* and the *World* meant that by importing stars from other towns, the Reds were not native to Cincinnati. One must remember that urban loyalties and rivalries ran much higher than today, so that this charge was regarded as serious. Chadwick defended Wright, pointing out that in 1869 all major clubs were "eclectic," especially the Mutuals.

Wright soon discovered that his greatest problem was his success in demonstrating a new approach to big-time baseball. With the 1870 season about to begin, he noticed that rivals were copying his example, but he hoped that he had at least a year of experience over his imitators. He was wrong, for other clubs quickly closed the gap.

After winning the first twenty-seven games of 1870, Wright ran into this reality. Playing at the Capitoline Grounds in Brooklyn, the Reds lost their first game since 1868 to the Brooklyn Atlantics,

[19] *Commercial* (Cincinnati), October 29, 1870.

eight to seven. With the score tied, seven to seven, after nine innings, Wright could have settled for a tie, but he and Champion chose to gamble on an extra-inning win. Brooklyn scored the winning run in the eleventh inning on a throwing error by Gould. Lacking none of the spirit of later-day Brooklyn crowds, this one went wild, and the beaten Reds ran a gauntlet of jeers and catcalls before escaping. The ordeal lasted all the way to the hotel, and when Champion gained the safety of his room, he broke down and cried. Later he sent a telegram to the *Commercial* saying, "Atlantics 8, Cincinnatis 7. The finest game ever played. Our boys did nobly, but fortune was against us. Though beaten, not disgraced."[20]

The *Clipper*'s story of the game furnishes an example of the rapid advances in sportswriting, already becoming a major force for fans to identify vicariously with teams and player-heroes. In wordy headlines the *Clipper* announced the outcome of "the finest game on record," and reported a crowd of twenty thousand on hand. Larded with classical allusions, lead paragraphs reminded the reader of the uncertainties of baseball games: "for the door is always left open for aspirants to baseball fame to enter the portals of the temple of the goddess and grasp the laurels in the face of the strongest opposition." But if such prose was tossed in for the benefit of the elite fans, the reporter's objective discussion of the contest was intelligible to most. Indeed, the game was being thrown open as a leisure outlet for all classes of fans, and when newspapers realized the profit potential in this larger market, sportswriters would continue to write on a more elementary plane.[21]

Although under way before the Wrights burst on the scene, the flames of popular interest in baseball were certainly fanned by Wright's Reds. But it was surprising how quickly Cincinnatians lost interest. After the Brooklyn victory attendance fell off, both at home and abroad, and local fair-weather fans were frosted out forever when the club lost a late-season game to Chicago. Because this defeat left the Reds in second place among the 1870 western teams, an aura of gloom pervaded the annual meeting of the Red

[20] *Ibid.*, April 7, June 15, 1870.
[21] Ellard, *op. cit.*, 190–95.

Stocking club directors. At the November meeting, Champion was ousted by a conservative regime that was angered by the treasurer's report that the club had only broken even over the two years. Perhaps the Wrights knew now which way the wind was blowing because they announced their intention to leave Cincinnati for Boston. This disclosure was seized upon by the new president, who now denounced the evils of salaried teams, blaming the system for jealousy between stockholders and players. This salvo was followed by the announcement that the Reds would return to amateurism for 1871.[22]

Elsewhere the story was different. Other cities with big-time baseball aspirations were impressed by the Reds and decided to imitate their pattern. At the end of 1870, a reporter counted five clubs that planned to use the all-salaried plan in 1871. One of these was a newly established Boston Club, whose directors lured the Wrights to the "Hub of the Universe." Except in Cincinnati, the Wrights' move was regarded as a proper advancement for successful professionals, and one New York paper soberly commented that the heightened popularity of baseball would prompt most "A No. 1 players" to set new prices on their "muscles, endurance and skill. . . . base ball has become a paying institution to players."[23] He might have added that for the moment it was a player's market; time and the reserve clause would soon limit a player's freedom to contract annually to the highest bidder.

As for the Cincinnati Reds, they quickly became a memory, for Wright took not only the best players with him, but even the team name. Back in Cincinnati not even his best friends forgave him for taking the name "Red Stockings" to Beantown. In Boston the name would take on a new measure of glory as Wright's Red Stockings dominated the first professional league.

[22] *Ibid.*, 210–13; *Sporting Life*, January 23, 1884; Hy Turkin and S. C. Thompson (eds.), *The Official Encyclopedia of Baseball*, 381.

[23] *Sporting Times and Theatrical News*, June 11, July 2, 1870.

4

Harry Wright's League

IN 1870 THE SMOLDERING CONFLICT that had marked relations between the Association's amateur and professional elements at last burst into flame. The fall meeting of the Association was a fiery affair marked by hot words between the two camps, and it ended with the amateurs staging a walkout. But the incident gave the commercialized clubs a long-sought opportunity to strike out on their own. With little time remaining for prolonged discussion, they decided to make a single meeting suffice for the task of organizing their own league. Hence, on March 17, 1871, ten representatives of professional baseball met at the Colliers Rooms in New York City to stage their coup.[1]

It was a foul night, weatherwise, for such work, but all realized the urgency of the situation since but a month remained before the

[1] Morse, *op. cit.*, 25.

season must begin.[2] Moreover, they were well aware that they shouldered the burden of a hundred players whose careers depended on prompt action.[3]

Moving quickly, the delegates elected temporary leaders and agreed to call the league "The National Association of Professional Base Ball Players." Except for the addition of the word "Professional" it was the same title as that of the old organization, a fact which shows their reluctance to depart too far from the old pattern.

With remarkable accord the delegates adopted a constitution which was flexible and assured free entry for almost any commercial club. To gain a franchise—a license which one day in the near future would cost thousands of dollars—all a club had to do was to petition the permanent committee before May 1, 1871, and submit a ten-dollar entry fee. Indeed, the delegates sheepishly defended the high fee as necessary for purchasing the annual pennant. And since the delegates assumed that all promoters were gentlemen, nobody proposed any other membership restrictions.

Although each club was free to arrange its own playing dates, it was agreed that each must meet every other club at least five times before the close of the season on November 1. The pennant was to go to the team posting the greatest number of wins, and in the event of a tie, a steering committee was empowered to decide on the basis of seasonal performance which one had the better claim.

Having made this decision, the convention fell into temporary disorder as delegates scurried to and fro seeking to arrange advantageous playing dates. Without doubt this was the new league's worst feature, one that would lead to endless arguments. It had been the custom of gentlemen sponsors to depend on written and verbal promises, and in sticking to this policy, the gentlemen professionals were keeping faith with the old order.

In other ways these conservative rebels clung to a cherished

[2] *New York Clipper*, March 25, 1871.

[3] *Proceedings of the National Association of Professional Base Ball Players Held in New York City, March 17, 1871,* 1–11; *Beadles Dime Base Ball Player,* 1872, pp. 41–44.

amateur past. For one, they managed to save time by simply adopting the constitution and playing rules of the old Association, "so far as they do not conflict with the interests of professional clubs." This decision committed the circuit to the old, clumsy system of volunteer umpires, whose only qualification was that they were gentlemen members of a club and "acknowledged as competent men for their position." In choosing an umpire, the home team picked a man from a list of five names submitted by the visitors. Since the gentlemen professionals regarded umpiring as an honorary task, the umpire was not to be paid. Should a man so honored fail to show up by game time, the contending captains must agree on a substitute.

In facing the problem of revolving players, the delegates failed again, trusting too much in the good faith of players and directors. A player's contract, they urged, must be "honorably canceled" before he could sign with another club. In the event of a dispute over a player's services, a board of arbitration, chosen from "neutral clubs," would examine "persons and papers" and settle the matter. And if a club failed to live up to a contract, a player could appeal to the championship committee for a judgment.

Still another weakness was the delegates' inability to agree on basic admission rates. Most favored a half-dollar rate, with proceeds to be divided into two-thirds for the home team and the remainder for the visitors. But once again the vague language proved crippling and annoying, and this point, too, remained a troublesome one for the future of major league baseball.[4]

In retrospect the results of the coup were hardly revolutionary; indeed, it was a conservative effort. Yet notwithstanding the unwieldy and cumbersome planning, it was a memorable evening's work. In a real sense a major professional league was born, which would have far-reaching effects upon diverse interest groups such as players, owners, stockholders, sportswriters, and spectators. If the delegates had managed in a night's work to fashion a permanently stable organization, with no guide except the shopworn

---

[4] *Proceedings of the National Association of Professional Base Ball Players Held in New York City, March 17, 1871*, 1–11; *New York Clipper*, March 25, 1871.

amateur constitution, it would have been miraculous. Although it was not a night of miracles, the result did provide urban leisure seekers with five years of first-rate baseball.

Happily for the rebels, nobody challenged their creation; the old Association never recovered from the blow and "died of inanition, after an innocuous existence." In 1872 there was an abortive attempt to organize an "Amateur National Association," but the ten clubs and seven colleges backing the move ceased to exist after 1874. Thus by default the professionals came to dominate organized baseball. From 1871 onward, they dictated the major changes in rules and style of play. In years to come, some interest groups, like the Amateur Athletic Union, the collegiate associations, and softball associations, secured some influence, but the main course of development continued to be set by organized professionals.[5]

With the opening of the first campaign, optimism reigned, but as the season wore on, overtones of discord and disaster plagued the contenders. Certainly the rivals prepared enthusiastically. In Chicago, a city whose population had risen 296,000 over the past thirty years, the White Stocking management was confident. A friendly reporter declared the team to be "better qualified to face the stirring 'music of the spheres' than previous Chicago clubs." A dumping ground along the lake front was converted into a ball park which could seat seven thousand shaded spectators, with segregated sections for ladies and city officials. Surrounding the entire enclosure was a six-foot fence kept free of posted bills. A fifteen-dollar season ticket entitled the holder to the same seat all year, and the club promised not to sell it when the owner was absent. By March the project was nearing completion, although more investment capital was urged.[6]

Meanwhile at the home of the Mutuals, enthusiasm over the new league was equally intense. If ladies were less accommodated than in Chicago, at least the gamblers were well taken care of.[7] An early-season game with Chicago attracted six thousand fans and

[5] Francis C. Richter, *Richter's History and Records of Baseball*, 39–40.

[6] *Tribune* (Chicago), January 18, 21, 22, 28, 29, March 8, 1871.

[7] *Ibid.*, January 20, 1871.

returned receipts of over $3,000. Inside, pool sellers did a thriving business, and outside, three thousand "fence-peepers" posed a problem; and at various telegraph centers throughout New York thousands more enjoyed the action vicariously.[8]

Of the five NAPBBP compaigns the 1871 battle was clearly the most interesting from a competitive standpoint. Nine clubs entered the lists at the start, four from the West; but midway the balance was destroyed when the "Kekiongas" of Fort Wayne, Indiana, quit after winning the distinction of scoring the first victory under the new league. Replacing the western entry were the Brooklyn Eckfords, which had refused to join earlier on the grounds that the entry fee was too high. As prodigal sons, all they could hope for was money, because the terms of their belated entry stated that their won-loss record would not count.[9]

With ranks reformed, the NAPBBP now proved to be a viable circuit, and crowds thronged to watch the tight, three-cornered race. Up to the final month the only other drawback was the inefficient schedule system. Even so the outlook was bright, until dimmed by new disasters.[10]

Disaster struck Chicago's fine team when the Great Fire destroyed the club's physical assets, crushed its hopes for a good home attendance in the last month, and forced the team to take to the road for its stretch drive. When the fire struck, twenty-six hundred acres of buildings were consumed, including the Lake Front ball park, which was in the heart of the burned-over area. So numbing was the effect of the fire that from October 11 to October 23 the *Tribune* ignored baseball completely. When again it took notice, it was to say that "the White Stockings would sever their connection with Chicago at the close of the present season."[11] From *Clipper* correspondents came more somber news: "Chicago will want all her means to supply the necessities of life, and in re-building homes for their suffering people for a year at least . . .

8 Chadwick, Scrapbooks, Vol. I, 69.

9 *New York Clipper*, May 13, 1871.

10 *North American and United States Gazette* (Philadelphia), August 8, 17, 1871.

11 *Ibid.*, October 7, 1871; *Tribune* (Chicago), October 23, 1871.

therefore . . . dealing in such a recreative luxury as a professional base ball club" was out of the question.

But the players were determined to see the season through. In a letter to the *Clipper*, Captain Wood accepted an offer of free train tickets, making possible their playing the rest of the season on the road. Virtually penniless and without uniforms, the team threw itself on the generosity of rivals. In response to a *Clipper* appeal, three eastern clubs scheduled benefit games for the homeless team.[12]

Even against these odds, Chicago stayed in the race until the last day. Then the team lost to the Athletics in a poorly attended contest, the players' motley appearance saddening the *Tribune*'s correspondent.[13]

Without records or accounts the club secretary delivered a final report to stockholders from memory, stating that even with insurance payments of only ten cents on the dollar, the club made $2,000. Of this sum the directors gave $500 to Captain Wood, along with their thanks; afterwards they terminated the club's membership in the Association.[14]

Meanwhile discord joined forces with disaster to mar the circuit's first season. Boston protested the decision to hand Philadelphia the championship, but when the protest was disallowed, the Athletics laid claim to the American baseball championship. As pictured, they were a formidable-looking crew. All wore blazers and sported mustaches, the single exception being pitcher Dick McBride, who made up for a naked upper lip with an impressive sideburn growth extending to his chin.[15] Financially this team did well; after paying all debts, it showed a modest profit of $150.[16]

Pleased with their success, Association leaders met and elected a player as president.[17] At this point, indeed, the professional play-

12 *New York Clipper*, October 14, 21, 1871.

13 *Tribune* (Chicago), November 3, 1871.

14 *Ibid.*, November 10, 13, 26, 1871; Federal Writers Project, *Baseball in Old Chicago*, 26. Chicago rejoined the NAPBBP in 1874.

15 *New York Clipper*, November 18, 1871; *DeWitt's Base Ball Guide*, 1872, pp. 69, 90–91, 1873, p. 68.

16 *North American and United States Gazette* (Philadelphia), November 14, 1871.

17 Richter, *op. cit.*, 44.

ers held firm control of the Association, but it was to be a short-lived worker's paradise. That player control over big-time baseball failed was due to the consistent inability of players to run a strong, responsible league. Instead, their leaders chose to muddle along until tough-minded investors, wearied of the gentlemen who sponsored clubs as a hobby, took command.

Ironically it was the gentlemanly Harry Wright who did most to advance the coming capitalist taking of control from the gentlemen dilettantes. This apparent paradox is explained when one remembers that while Wright upheld the British ethic of sportsmanship on the playing field, he also was a strong advocate of a profitable baseball establishment. Having lost the 1871 race by the narrowest of margins, his Boston team now stood poised to win the first of four consecutive pennants. Indeed, so thoroughly and efficiently would his teams dominate the Association that by discouraging rivals, he also contributed to the downfall of this rickety circuit and its concept of player control.

An astute judge of playing talent, Wright had the ability to develop little-known men into stars. If some of his men were less brilliant than those of other clubs, Wright's discipline of constant practice and rigid training narrowed the gap, for versatility was the key trait in Wright's system.

As a manager, he expected his men to behave like professionals, to live up to their contracts. No one was permitted to report late; "Delays," he said, "create a feeling of indifference among the players to fulfill whatever regulations we may make. . . . Professional ball playing is *business*, and as such, I trust you will regard it while the season lasts."[18]

To a young hopeful who wrote asking what he must do to become a professional player, Wright could be gentle and helpful. "In regard to diet," he told one, "eat hearty, Roast Beef rare will aid, live regularly, keep good hours, and abstain from intoxicating drinks and tobacco." As for the necessary skills, he continued, "learn to be a sure catch, a good thrower—strong and accurate—a reliable

[18] Wright to John Clapp, January 18, 1872; Wright to Fred Rogers, March 11, 1872. Wright, Correspondence, Vol. V, 467–70.

batter, and a good runner, all to be brought out—if in you—by steady and persevering practice."[19]

If newspapers of the 1870's tended to overpraise good men, Wright kept a balanced view. In a letter to Chadwick, he reviewed the good and bad points of his men. It bothered him to hear that his team was openly envied by other managers, who sneered that they could do as well with his stars. Did such covetousness include the logic that all a manager had to do was field a good team and wait for the pennant to fall? Wright thought not. Managing a team involved human relations, and that neighborly science demanded an ability to see a player as a bundle of skills and weaknesses. Getting the best, even from a star, required skilled psychology. To succeed at this required a manager to be a teacher as well as a strategist.[20]

Wright was one of the first to perceive the fatal effect of too rigid a policy of player discipline. If a player was branded by another manager as a troublemaker, Wright did not regard him as lost. Tom Bond, a pitcher, left the Hartford team in 1876 after a row with his hot-tempered manager, Bob Ferguson. Wright took him on because he thought he could give Bond the kind of handling that the tactless Ferguson could not. "With us I have no fear but he will prove a different person. It shall be our endeavor to develop all the good there is in him, and restrain the bad. In fact to make a man of him, if it is in him. . . . A pitcher we know he is."[21]

Although idealistic and overly rational in his vision of the future of major league baseball, Wright was tough-minded about practical realities. From the beginning, he wanted a basic admission price of fifty cents, arguing that if a team was well trained, serious, sober, and honest to the man, it was worth the price to spectators. The public, he argued, will pay "75cts to $1.50 to go to the theatre, and numbers prefer base ball to theatricals. We must make the games worth witnessing and there will be no fault found with the price. . . . A good game is worth 50cts, a poor one is dear at 25cts."[22]

[19] Wright to Charles Tubbs, December 2, 1874. *Ibid.*, Vol. VI, 83–84.
[20] Wright to Chadwick, January 2, 1875. *Ibid.*, Vol. VI.
[21] Wright to Chadwick, September 14, 1876. *Ibid.*, Vol. VI.
[22] Wright to Norman (Nick) Young, May 12, 1873. *Ibid.*, Vol. V.

This approximates Wright's confession of faith in the future of commercial baseball and in the rationality of those fans who chose it as a leisure outlet.

Among modern clubs matters such as finances, road expenses, salary payments, and other administrative details are the responsibility of front-office administrators, and such staffs outnumber players. However, in Boston in 1872, such details rested on Wright's shoulders, to be taken care of in addition to his duties as player, field manager, and trainer. Of all his chores he found scheduling the most frustrating. Since the Association had no regular schedule of games, Wright cultivated the friendships of secretaries everywhere. Although he enjoyed these contacts, the problem was complicated by the constant turnover of clubs. With free entry into the Association guaranteed, many towns, large and small, grabbed the opportunity, only to withdraw shortly because of defeats or financial losses. Appalled by the situation, Wright urged the adoption of restrictive measures, but when these were not forthcoming, he at last threw his support behind men seeking to build a new league which would do this job. Wright wanted a major league with a stable membership and a firm schedule of games. For a time he hoped by his own example to inspire rival clubs to follow his lead and thus make the Association a stable league.[23]

His own teams were models of disciplined efficiency, and they reflected his own philosophy of commercial baseball—that people were sportsmanlike and would pay to see clean, well-ordered baseball. However fallacious this view, Wright's successes helped to drive it into the traditions of major league baseball. Vestiges of his belief survive today as reminders to the present generation of promoters that the game once was in the hands of gentlemen sportsmen; as such, it remains a subtle barrier to crass commercialism.

Proof of the power of Wright's system was evidenced by the strength of his teams. Only once, in 1873 when the Philadelphia "Whites" almost won, did the opposition come close. The team which he fashioned was formidable, and he kept seeking ways of

[23] Wright to William Hulbert, February 5, 1875. *Ibid.*, Vol. VI. The same volume contains many letters that attempt to schedule championship games.

making it even better. Performance and conduct were the prime virtues he sought in a player, and by 1875 his qualitative selection process had produced a colossus.

A cadre of veteran players formed the core of his team, and they came to know Wright's system intimately. One of them was brother George, perhaps the most versatile player of the formative years. More brilliant than his brother as a player, George shared Wright's dedication to the game, although in future years his interests turned to the production of the implements or equipment used in sports.

Young Albert G. Spalding was Wright's pitching mainstay. Born in Rockford, Illinois, he overcame the protests of his status-minded mother to become a seventeen-year-old pitching prodigy with the local team. At nineteen he was captain of the great Rockford team of 1870 and was acclaimed the leading pitcher in the country. According to one writer, he had "a peculiar manner of delivering the ball to the batsman suddenly, calculating to bother or to deceive him. . . . His pitching is very accurate." He was over six feet tall and slim, and his personal ambitions matched his physical stature, for he was shrewd, calculating, and a born promoter. As a Rockford schoolboy, he conned his principal into excusing him from class so that he could pitch for the home team. His decision to come to Boston was motivated more by the business possibilities in that city than by his love of pitching.

Like other hard-driving business innovators of the day, he had a fierce hunger to succeed; it was so strong that he readily abandoned pitching when an opportunity to enter the infant sporting goods industry beckoned.[24] Thus, at the very height of his pitching career, he left Boston in 1875 to open a sporting goods firm in Chicago. Sustained by his favorite motto, "Everything is possible to him who dares," he led his brother into the venture with a joint investment of $800.[25] Two years later he was considered "estab-

[24] *Register* (Rockford, Ill.), March 25, 1871; *Beadle's Dime Base Ball Player*, 1872, 41–44.

[25] *Register* (Rockford, Ill.), September 10, 1915.

lished," and after another decade he was acknowledged as the millionaire head of a vast sporting goods trust, which was to absorb such rivals as Wright and Ditson and A. J. Reach. Through it all, he functioned as the strong man in the councils of major league baseball. His career contrasts sharply with that of his manager, for if Wright symbolized the best of the gentlemen's era, Spalding epitomized the values of rugged commercialism.

The fourth member of Wright's nucleus was Roscoe "Ross" Barnes. Thanks to the Association rule permitting "fair-foul hitting," this diminutive player was the perennial league batting champion. A hit had only to touch fair territory before rolling foul, and such hits were the secret of Barnes's success until the National League changed the rules.[26]

Because of the fierce rivalry that developed between the Bostons and the Athletics over the 1871 season, Wright sorely wanted the 1872 pennant. Because Wright had protested the Athletics' right to the pennant, Manager Hayhurst of the Athletics had written Wright a sarcastic letter asking where his team ought to hang the "streamer." Wright's reply was caustic: "If I had them," said he, "I should fly them both in all the games we play next season." And he included this reprimand: "I think the proper place is or would be the Athletic Club room or some place where *all* who wish could go and see them," instead of the saloon in which it was presently hung. He advised Hayhurst to remember his obligation to "elevate the National Game," and as the "first legal and recognized Champions of the United States," to remember that commercial baseball had a long way to go to become financially remunerative.[27]

A few months later Wright settled his Athletics account in grand style. With the two rivals in hot competition in midseason, "All Boston took a half holiday" when the hated Athletics came to town. Betting odds were even, but Boston belied this by crushing

---

[26] George Wright, *Record of the Boston Base Ball Club Since Its Organization,* 8–16.

[27] Wright to E. H. Hayhurst. Wright, Correspondence, Vol. V.

their rivals thirteen to four. A highlight was a great catch by Harry Wright, who responded to "cheer on cheer" by "very politely . . . lifting his hat."[28]

After that nothing stopped the Reds. They went on to post a final log of thirty-nine and eight. Since this far outdistanced most rivals, five discouraged entries dropped out before the season ended. In all the six second-division clubs recorded only sixteen victories out of ninety-four decisions.[29] While these defections played havoc with attendance, Wright won a resounding vote of confidence from the Boston directors, who also voted a new stock issue to cover the seasonal losses.[30]

With renewed hope, Wright launched a second pennant drive the following year, although George Wright's rheumatism accounted for a sluggish start. However, two brilliant rookies, Jim O'Rourke and "Deacon" Jim White, took up the slack by showing the promise that would make them two of the mightiest stars of the century. By August the team was whole again, but by then it stood ten games behind the front-running Philadelphia "Whites," a new entry from Quakertown. A month of desperate pressing closed the gap to two and one-half games, and although the Phillies hung on through September, they collapsed in October after dropping five games in a row. One of the losses came at the hands of Boston before a partisan crowd of five thousand Philadelphians.[31]

Boston's pennant-winning record in 1873 was forty-three games won to sixteen lost, and the tight pennant race probably explains why the Association set a record for endurance. That year only a single entry dropped out along the way.[32]

Over the winter much talk centered around a major change in

---

[28] Chadwick, Scrapbooks, I, 88.

[29] *DeWitt's Base Ball Guide*, 1873, pp. 54–57, 68–69; Wright to Alex Davidson, chairman of the championship committee, October 30, 1872. Wright, Correspondence, Vol. V, 464–66.

[30] Wright to James White, December 27, 1872. Wright, Correspondence, Vol. V, 462.

[31] George Wright, *op. cit.*, 8–16; *New York Clipper*, June 21, July 26, September 27, October 25, 1873; *Herald* (Boston), May 31, 1873.

[32] *New York Clipper*, November 22, 1873; *Beadle's Dime Base Ball Player*, 1874, pp. 49–50, 66.

playing rules, which threatened to revolutionize the style of play. This was Chadwick's idea for a ten-man game. As Chadwick explained, the game was "lopsided," making it easy for hitters to get hits in the big hole between first and second. Chadwick proposed to station a "right short" in the gap, which would allow the second baseman to cover his base more closely. Of course, the real purpose was to allow first and third basemen to range further into foul territory for elusive "fair-foul" hits. Although Chadwick's idea was an effort to remedy the imbalance of fair-foul hitting, one wonders why he did not choose the simpler remedy of disallowing such a hit. When such action was taken a few years later, basemen would play their positions as they do today. But in 1874 the ten-man game seemed to be the answer, for, as Chadwick said, "There is not a reasonable objection that can be brought against it."[33] Before the innovation had been tried one year, however, opposition developed that led to its abandonment.

While pondering the new rule, Wright also faced a challenge of his own making. Shortly after the 1873 season, he and Spalding hatched a plan to take two major league teams to England in hopes of planting the game in the motherland. Here we see another side to Wright's character. As a baseball advocate he wanted to spread the game, but unlike Moody and Sankey, who were then taking their gospel to the common people of England, Wright chose to sell his game through the exclusive British cricket clubs. After all, this was the gentlemanly way to act.

But selling the plan to the Boston directorate meant answering their protests about its effects on the Association pennant race. In the end a tight schedule was worked out permitting both the Reds and the Athletics to telescope most of their championship games into the beginning and at the end of the championship season. This freed both clubs to spend half the season abroad selling baseball to the British.

With Chadwick providing support and advice, Spalding left for England early in 1874 to lay the groundwork. Meanwhile, Wright

[33] *Beadle's Dime Base Ball Player*, 1874, pp. 45–48, 1875, pp. 45–46, 1876, pp. 70–71; Richter, *op. cit.*, 39–49.

completed the task of lining up the Athletics, promising that the clubs would be gone no more than six weeks and saying that at the very least they should make expenses and gain nation-wide publicity.

For his part the ebullient Spalding carried the plan right to the officials of the famous Marylebone Cricket Club, then the reigning monarch of all England's cricket clubs. Since their consent was necessary to the plan's success, Spalding poured all his persuasive powers into his speech to the membership, making much out of the possibility for a number of contests. After some debate the club members voted to welcome the American ball players, although the prospect of cricket matches was the deciding factor. Nevertheless, Spalding was grateful enough to accept this stipulation.

Meanwhile, back home Wright for some time remained in the dark on the cricket matter. He expected that his men would be asked to play some cricket, but when letters of invitation arrived in large numbers, he began to get the picture. He realized that Spalding was booking combined baseball-cricket contests all over the Isles.[34]

After a nervous voyage Wright faced the prospect of engaging the Marylebone Club's "All-English eleven" in cricket. Nearly desperate over his men's lack of experience (some had never even seen a game), he felt somewhat easier when the British captain graciously allowed him to play all eighteen of his men in the field.

Because most of the inexperienced players approached cricket play in the same way they did batting a baseball, the Americans managed to beat all British comers.[35] However, what they did was "not cricket," something Spalding never quite understood. But the form-conscious Wright brothers, along with pitcher McBride of the Athletics, knew what effect this performance would have on their reputation. Possibly this factor explains why the trip was a financial failure. When not parodying cricket, the Americans sand-

---

[34] Spalding, *op. cit.*, 175–86; *New York Clipper*, June 20, 1874; Wright to James Ferguson, January 5, 1874. Wright, Correspondence, Vol. V, 377–78.

[35] Spalding, *op. cit.*, 175–86; Anson, *op. cit.*, 78–85.

Lithograph of Currier & Ives portraying the Elysian Fields, Hoboken, New Jersey, and the first formal match game between men's teams, the Knickerbockers versus New Yorks, June 19, 1846.

*Scene of the first extra-inning baseball game on record, in which
the Knickerbockers defeated Washington in ten innings with
22–20 score on June 17, 1851.*

Presentation of the championship bat to the Red Stockings on their return to Cincinnati from their triumphal tour of 1869.

Match between the Red Stockings and the Atlantics in 1870.

Harper's Weekly

The home of the Chicago White Stockings in 1885.

New York Clipper

This painting, "Slide, Kelly, Slide," by Frank O. Small, shows the famous Mike Kelly stealing second base during the 1880's.

MacGreevy Collection, Boston Public Library

Although two hours remained before the game, Boston fans, even with tickets, could not gain admission to their National League park during the 1880's.

Sketches of Cincinnati Association team drawn by newsman A. Faris from photographs taken by C. A. LeBoutillier. These sketches appeared in the Illustrated Graphic News, June 19, 1886.

wiched in fourteen baseball games, the Reds winning eight, the Athletics six. Although the travelers were warmly received in cricket clubrooms in London, Liverpool, Manchester, Sheffield, and Dublin, the baseball games drew poorly.

From a publicity standpoint the trip won for baseball a sympathetic review by the editor of the influential London *Field* magazine. He described baseball as "a scientific game, more difficult than any . . . can possibly imagine. It is . . . the cricket of the American continent, considerably altered . . . by the experiences of each season." In the editor's opinion baseball was faster and more exciting than cricket, and in fielding especially it far outshone the British game.

In September the two contenders returned home to finish the 1874 championship season. Among their heartiest greeters was Chadwick, who toasted the Americans in his columns for showing John Bull "that we are not so neglectful of athletic sports as he thought." Indeed, by the baseball players' more manly physiques and "abstemious habits," Chadwick declared that Americans had taught the aristocratic "beer-drinking professional cricketers" some lessons.

Such talk was cheap, for the trip was a financial failure. To recoup losses of over $3,000, the participants were obliged to take pay cuts. Although Wright foresaw this possibility and allowed for it by making the men sign statements in advance agreeing to such cuts, it left a residue of ill will.[36] But if Wright had learned a lesson from this bitter experience, the chauvinistic Spalding had not. That player's strong sense of moral mission, which assumed that the world must come to be like America, never flagged. In time he would try again, with similar dismal results. In all, there would be four such expeditions by 1920, and except for Japan, the Old World remained quite content to leave baseball to Americans.

But in 1874 the failure of baseball's British mission was almost overshadowed by the Association's dismal campaign. Although only one team dropped out, only Boston fulfilled its schedule obli-

---

[36] *Beadle's Dime Base Ball Player*, 1875, pp. 56–59; Wright, Correspondence, Vols. I, IV, VI, *passim*; Richter, *op. cit.*, 42–46.

gations. The others, perhaps bored by Boston's easy victory, fell victim to disinterest, mismanagement, and financial distress. In addition to pandemics of such illness, Chadwick now hurled a charge of dishonesty. Noting the number of "rather questionable" games played that year, he hinted at collusion with gamblers and suggested this cause for the "falling off of patronage." To restore public confidence, he now demanded the ouster of suspected players.

New charges of dishonesty circulated as the 1875 campaign approached.[37] Nevertheless, the spirit of the contenders ran high; in addition to seven holdovers from 1874, six other clubs paid the token entry fee and girded for action. This gave the Association a peak enrollment of thirteen teams, and since three of the newcomers came from the West, the geographical balance looked better.[38] Yet far from portending good times ahead, this new interest merely helped to deepen existing weaknesses. Given the economic depression of the times and the obvious superiority of Boston, it was unrealistic for newcomers to hope for large crowds.

As for Wright's 1875 team, it was at its pinnacle of power, and the manager saw no reason for tinkering with the lineup. With such power waiting to be unleashed, Harry was understandably impatient for spring to arrive. The winter was a cold one that carried into March, yet it would have been better for the rivals if it had never ended. Except for Chicago and the Athletics, which fought well, the other ten teams were hopelessly outclassed. As the defeated ten watched dreams and gate receipts fade, some openly demanded the breakup of Wright's team. Such unrest was ominous, but a greater threat to the league was the conflict stirred up by the Force case.

A celebrated revolver, Dave Force, jumped a Chicago contract to play with the Athletics, and when Chicago's formal protest was disallowed, Wright entered the fight and accused the Athletics of using the circuit's arbitration committee to its own advantage.[39]

---

[37] *Beadle's Dime Base Ball Player*, 1875, pp. 55–56, 64–65; *New York Clipper*, April 24, 1875.

[38] *Beadle's Dime Base Ball Player*, 1876, pp. 63–64.

Soon tensions engendered by the dispute spilled over on the playing fields. On several occasions players and spectators engaged in bitter brawls. At Philadelphia crowds surged on the playing field and hampered Boston fielders; in Boston, spectator conduct was no better. It took forthright diplomacy on the part of the embattled gentlemen directors to restore order in the name of sportsmanship.[40] Finally, by midseason, tempers cooled and clubs returned to playing baseball, an enterprise in which Boston's superiority was obvious.

In driving his club to its fourth straight pennant, Wright crushed all opposition. In no other major league campaign did a team's superiority show as in 1875. Of the Association's twenty leading hitters, eight were Boston men, including the top four. That season Harry Wright was the only Boston regular to average less than one safe hit a game, and he was nearing the end of his active career. It is noteworthy also that in an age of bare-handed fielding, Boston fielding records approached modern standards. Along with Spalding's pitching, such prowess carried Boston to a record of seventy-one and eight, and the team finished fifteen games ahead of its nearest rival.

For the weaker half of the circuit it was a nightmarish season. Among the newcomers, only St. Louis stuck it out; the others quit, leaving behind frightful records of futility. Keokuk, Iowa, won one out of thirteen starts and quit, and after winning two of forty-four, the Atlantics understandably quit. Four other clubs, with the combined record of seventeen wins and eighty-eight losses, also chose to drop out.[41]

Clearly the Association's lack of balance was killing commercial baseball as a spectacle, and promoters knew it. Before the 1875 season ended, some were conspiring to end both the rickety Association and the Boston tyranny. In this venture Chicago took the lead by luring four of the Reds' ablest men to the Windy City. To avoid charges of revolving, the secret deal was negotiated in

[39] *New York Clipper*, March 26, 1875; Spalding, *op. cit.*, 200–14; Wright to Charles Gould, March 15, 1875. Wright, Correspondence, Vol. VI.

[40] *New York Clipper*, July 10, 1875.

[41] *Beadle's Dime Base Ball Player*, 1876, pp. 63–64.

June, but news leaked out after a few weeks. When Boston fans learned that its "big four," Spalding, Barnes, White, and McVey, planned to desert, the four were villified for the remainder of the season.[42]

At the close of the campaign, a group of promoters moved to end the Association. Those proposing reforms wanted to eliminate the abuses of the player-dominated circuit. A new league, they thought, must be stable in organization, balanced enough to appeal to fans, and, most important, profitable to investors. Clearly the Association had accomplished none of these goals. Only the ball players had derived any profits from the old order, and some of the promoters thought the men were getting too much. Some compared players to industrial workers and pointed out that in industry profits were for investors, not workers.[43] Although this philosophy soon overshadowed the gentlemanly approach to baseball promotion, it never won a total victory. While the new breed of promoters would take big profits from the game, they shied away from completely mercenary exploitation. Today, this odd mixture of baseball-promotion motives, which combines profit-seeking with the older gentlemanly values, still survives. For this reason it remains a debatable point how much of major league baseball is entertainment industry and how much is a public service "sport."

In the 1870's, Spalding typified the new mercenary approach. As a Boston player, he studied both the administrative and managerial policies of Wright and the weaknesses of the NAPBBP. In the Association's failure to retain its members, to discipline players and directors, or to make money, Spalding saw the chief weakness in this approach to commercial baseball.

To Spalding the chief weakness lay in "the irrepressible conflict between Capital and Labor." Briefly, Spalding saw the present era as one of player (or labor) control over baseball. Such control was a function of persisting gentlemanly traditions: the earliest clubs had been designed for gentlemen players, the amateur Association was a player organization, and so was the present Association, the

---

[42] Spalding, *op. cit.*, 200–207; *New York Clipper*, December 25, 1875.
[43] Spalding, *op. cit.*, 189–96.

NAPBBP. In each of the preceding stages, it was the players who made most of the decisions and pocketed what money had been made out of baseball.

To be sure, NAPBBP clubs were nominally stock companies, but few of the gentlemanly investors really expected profits; instead, they regarded their investment and club membership as a status symbol. But as long as such a philosophy prevailed, only the players would make money.

In challenging this traditional approach, Spalding attacked the system of player control and suggested that capital take over. Chicago director William Hulbert's agreement was one reason why Spalding decided to leave Boston for Chicago in 1875. Years later, in defending his decision to throw his lot in with the directors, he argued that to be a good player meant giving one's whole efforts to it. Thus players ought to delegate to businessmen the task of "conducting the details of managing men, administering discipline, arranging schedules and finding ways and means of financing a team."[44]

By 1875 there were many persons involved who agreed with Spalding and Hulbert. In analyzing the failure of the Mutuals, a *Clipper* reporter blamed naïve managerial policies, noting that instead of paying each man a salary based on ability, the club paid some men salaries and the rest a percentage of the gate receipts. Since poor performance lowered gate receipts, factionalism was rife, leading to poorer play and even lower gate receipts. The reporter's tough-minded remedy paralleled Spalding's philosophy: get rid of "halfway measures" and put the club on a sound business basis, for "until it is those who invest in the business of engaging the club players cannot expect to run the machine successfully."[45]

Like the Mutuals, other players were uncertain about their pay; hence some aligned themselves with gamblers who paid them to "fix" games. In addition to this blotch, the Association's escutcheon was marred by incidents of "drunkenness and riot" resulting from

[44] *Ibid.*, 189–96.
[45] *New York Clipper*, December 25, 1875.

sales of liquor at some of the games. Moreover, "almost every team had its 'lushers.' "[46] But with players holding key spots in the Association's councils, there was little disposition to act; and even if the players submitted proposals for reforms, the Association lacked the executive machinery to enforce them, for member clubs valued their independence and only by making them accept authority from the top could a reform program stand a chance.

However, the mere substitution of a new league with executive authority would not guarantee profits to all members. Good administrative policies were needed, and there were some precedents to be followed. Certainly Boston had set an example with a sound approach to club management.[47]

As measured by profits and pennants, no Association club was so ably managed and directed as was the Boston Red Stockings. Yet it was a new organization, having been founded on the eve of the Association's birth. Chartered as a stock company under President Ivers Adams, the investors, having studied the structure of other clubs of 1870, approached Wright and offered him the reins.[48] It was a brilliantly simple choice, because for $2,500 a season, they bought themselves a field manager whose administrative ability matched his reputation as a field strategist. Furthermore, the gentlemanly Harry fit their hazy image of gentlemanly behavior, a factor which won for Harry the confidence of the Boston directors.[49]

Probably the worst of Wright's administrative headaches was scheduling. In dickering for playing dates, he was a tough haggler who knew the value of summer holidays for attracting large crowds, and on such dates he tried to schedule first-rate opposition on the grounds that crowds of 8,000 to 10,000 were better "than the 3,000 to 5,000."[50]

His standard policy in bargaining for playing dates, was to consider the drawing power of the cities involved. It disturbed his

46 Spalding, *op. cit.*, 189–96.
47 Chadwick, Scrapbooks, I, 89; *Beadle's Dime Base Ball Player*, 1875, pp. 55–56.
48 George Wright, *op. cit.*, 8.
49 Wright, Note and Account Books, Vol. II.
50 Wright to Norman Gassette, March 23, 1874. Wright, Correspondence, Vol. V.

orderly, profit-oriented mind that baseball management should be at so low a standard in populous cities like New York and Philadelphia.[51] Elsewhere, opportunities were worse, but Wright was determined to make the best of the situation. Knowing the drawing power of Boston in rival towns, Wright usually demanded one-third of the gross receipts when playing in the larger towns. Insisting on this point, he argued that if he did not, some of the big city clubs might not choose to come to Boston. Indeed, because they could count on good attendance most of the time, big city clubs tended to ignore their obligation to visit smaller towns.[52] As for weaker clubs, in scheduling games with them, Wright demanded as much as 60 per cent of the gross receipts. Once again, reciprocity was the rule, and Wright's motive was to force clubs to live up to their scheduling obligations.

As an administrator, Wright also fought the battle of the 50-cent admission rate. Because some clubs, discouraged over poor attendance, would sometimes drop the basic rate to 25 cents, Wright told them either to charge 50 cents when Boston came to town or else give his team a $150 guarantee.

Less justifiable was Wright's notion that because his team was the champion, he was "entitled to have the first game of the series with each club played upon our grounds."[53] But if somewhat dictatorial, such methods showed other clubs the profit potential awaiting a more rational, businesslike approach to major league baseball.

In general Wright's system worked rather well, but there were times when visitors failed to appear for games. On such occasions Wright wielded a scathing pen, once berating a Phillies' official, whose team failed to show up on a day when snow flurries blew in Boston, for shaking "the confidence of the public in our management."[54] Perhaps a fear of Wright's wrath prodded rivals into

[51] Wright to Cammeyer, April 27, 1874. *Ibid.*, Vol. VI. *New York Clipper*, August 7, 1873.

[52] Wright to W. H. Ray, April 14, 1871; Wright to Young, April 25, 1871. Wright, Correspondence, Vol. V.

[53] Wright to W. Miller, April 14, 1871; Wright to Mason Graffen, February 25, 1875. *Ibid.*, Vol. V.

[54] Wright to David Reid, April 29, 1874. *Ibid.*, Vol. VI.

meeting their schedule obligations with Boston; at any rate, in 1875, he missed playing all required games only because the St. Louis Reds refused to come East for a return game. That same season only five of the thirteen Association clubs even bothered to turn in their seasonal records to the championship committee, and of those which did, Boston's log was by far the most complete.[55]

One marvels that Wright, with so much frustration arising from scheduling championship games, should also have scheduled so many exhibitions. His policy for exhibition games was that the Reds should receive either 60 per cent of the gross or else a guarantee of $150. Since the Reds were superior to nonleague clubs, Wright often suggested that a rival club take five outs to the Reds' three. Far from being insulting, such an offer aimed at attracting more spectators by offering hope of a closer game.

Nor was Wright so craven as to demand money always. If worthy charities were to be served through baseball, he often brought his team to a town for nothing more than the cost of lodging and train fare.[56]

Of course the Wright system was not foolproof. For one thing, he was slow to grasp the possibilities of playing games on the Fourth of July.[57] Then there was the fiasco of the baseball mission to England in 1874, an affair which put nostalgia over commercial realities; and in 1872 his miscalculation that the public might pay well to see a postseason playoff among the three top teams cost the club $3,000.[58] Yet it might have been a harbinger of profitable World Series games to come.

On the whole, Boston's financial successes overshadowed the blunders, and the club's performance suggests that the gentlemanly Association might have prospered if more clubs had adopted the Wright system. Certainly the most striking proof of Boston's financial success is in the salaries paid to its players. In 1871, the total payroll came to $14,400; in 1872, $16,700; in 1873, $14,900;

[55] Wright to championship committee, NAPBBP, November 15, 1875. *Ibid.*, Vol. II.

[56] Wright to James Moorhouse, May 15, 1873; Wright to F. Todd, April 18, 1875. *Ibid.*, Vol. V.

[57] *Herald* (Boston), July 9, 1872.

[58] *Ibid.*, October 4, 1872; Chadwick, Scrapbooks, I, 89; Wright, *op. cit.*, 29–40.

in 1874, $15,800;[59] and in 1875, $20,685.[60] Not until the 1880's would player salaries or club payrolls surpass this Boston mark of 1875.

Yet one must remember that players, rather than investors, were reaping the biggest rewards under the Association. If there had been no disastrous fire in 1871, Chicago's 1872 payroll would have set a record. Tentative salary schedules listed three $2,500 men, four $2,000 men, and a total projected payroll of $24,100.[61] And in 1875, even the weak New Haven club boasted that it paid its men $1,600 each.[62]

However, it is quite possible that high salaries frightened investment capital away from a player's league. Wright agreed that this might be so, and suggested that good playing talent could be had for much less. He thought high salaries spoiled players and held back the progress of big-time baseball. Also, "What do the majority of the players do with all this money? Spend it foolishly to the injury of themselves, and consequently to the club engaging them, or with which they are playing."[63]

In truth investors did pocket fewer profits than players. After losing $3,000 in 1872, Boston showed a net profit of $4,020.38 in 1873. But most of the latter gains were plowed back into the club, leaving a true 1873 profit of $767.93. In 1874, again, the club netted a modest sum, this time $833.13. Finally in 1875 when the club netted $3,261.07, the stockholders voted not to take dividends, but rather to return the money to the club. Such behavior typified the era of gentlemen professionalism and contrasts sharply with the mercenary philosophy of the next decade. In that later era, directors would hungrily devour profit melons of as much as $100,-000, with players being looked upon as laborers.[64]

In retrospect, the Association era pioneered in the development

---

[59] Wright, Note and Account Books, Vol. II.

[60] *Beadle's Dime Base Ball Player*, 1876, p. 67. A sample Boston contract is in Wright, Correspondence, Vol. I.

[61] *New York Clipper*, October 21, 1871.

[62] *Ibid.*, February 12, 1876.

[63] Wright to Hulbert, December 29, 1874. Wright, Correspondence, Vol. VI.

[64] Chadwick, Scrapbooks, I, 99; Wright, Note and Account Books, Vol. II; *Beadle's Dime Base Ball Player*, 1876, p. 67; Morse, *op. cit.*, 60.

of major league baseball as a later-day entertainment business. In grappling on a small scale with such modern administrative problems as advertising, plant operation, equipment procurement, travel scheduling, and salary negotiations, Boston had a total 1875 operating cost of $34,505.99, which seems modest enough. Yet it was larger than for any previous Association year, and certainly it showed the way for future larger operations.[65]

Club managers of the 1870's also stumbled upon a modern device for making money out of baseball—the sale of players. Although contracts lacked a reserve clause, which would facilitate player sales later on, the Philadelphia Centennials of 1875, because they planned to quit the league, managed to sell two of their best men to the Athletics for $1,500. In the best gentlemanly style a wealthy Athletics director, anxious to strengthen his team, personally paid for the release of the two Centennials. The deal helped the Athletics reach second place in 1875,[66] and the future possibilities of such a tactic captured the imagination of more mercenary promoters.

In other ways this era was a proving ground for later business-like operations. As Boston manager, Wright became an expert in administration by investigating the significance of road costs, uniform procurement, and plant management. On the road he allowed $1.00 a day for each man's room and board.[67] By modern standards this is unthinkable, yet for $1,161.03, a dozen Reds spent twenty days in western hotels and had their food and travel to boot. On this trip the Reds grossed $3,537.22 from gate receipts, which shows the profits to be made in 1875.[68] When playing at home, Wright arranged room and board for his bachelor players for $1.00 a day at "Mrs. Parker's."[69]

Wright also became a first-rate baseball quartermaster. In those years the Reds used cricket flannel, costing up to $3.50 a yard. The shirts were of American flannel and were contracted to George

[65] *Beadle's Dime Base Ball Player*, 1876, pp. 63–64, 67.
[66] Richter, *op. cit.*, 39–49.
[67] Wright to A. Childs, April 10, 1875. Wright, Correspondence, Vol. VI.
[68] Wright, Note and Account Books, Vol. II.
[69] Wright to John Ryan, March 4, 1872. Wright, Correspondence, Vol. V.

Wright's fledgling sporting goods outlet. Figuring that each man wore out three uniforms a year, Wright shrewdly ordered all uniforms in three basic sizes so that a man could find parts to fit a uniform when necessary.[70]

The Boston manager's wide knowledge and experience in baseball matters caused others to seek advice from him. Such requests were willingly answered and covered a wide range of problems of baseball management. Once Wright gave advice on how to lay out a diamond, including suggestions on seating construction, infield grading, drainage, and the best kind of grass to plant in the outfield.[71]

A successful manager in an age when it took unusual ability to run a successful franchise under the rickety Association, Wright nevertheless cast his lot with rebels seeking to build a better order. He entered the conspiracy because he believed the Association to be a disciplinary failure; in its present form he found it incapable of exploiting the vast profit potential of this leisure outlet. "Professional clubs," he wrote to archconspirator Hulbert, "to keep in existence, must have gate money, to receive gate money they must play games, and to enable them to play games, their opponents must have faith that such games will prove remunerative."

Grateful for Wright's backing, Hulbert pronounced Wright's ideas for reform to be so sound that they would one day earn Wright the title of "Father of the Game." But this honor Wright brushed aside with drollery, saying that it made him feel old and, more seriously, that Chadwick had the better claim. Also, having just watched his "seventh . . . base bawler" enter the world, he stated that it was enough "to be considered the father of this little game, but I wish it to go no farther. Seven is plenty, thank you."[72]

[70] Wright to Hulbert, March 20, 1875. *Ibid.*, Vol. VI.
[71] Wright's unaddressed letter. *Ibid.*, Vol. I.
[72] Wright to Hulbert, December 29, 1874. *Ibid.*, Vol. VI.

5

The National League Coup

Wiтн a мonotonous penchant for *deus ex machina* explanations, baseball mythmakers depicted the National League of 1876 as a reforming force for major league baseball. The legend tells how the white knights of the league quickly brought honesty and prosperity to baseball by overcoming the discredited Association. In truth it did neither. In its first four years its franchises were seldom profitable and its claim to honesty was tarnished by the Louisville affair. Further, the moralizing founders undermined the stability of the league by barring membership to New York and Philadelphia, two of the most lucrative cities. Even during the 1880's, when general prosperity won wide public support for organized baseball, the league seemed more interested in dominating the game, regardless of costs. This its members managed to do by the 1890's only to discover that anticipated profits did not follow.

Thus, it is more accurate to say that the National League founders made their contribution by their stubborn staying power rather than by any superior insight.

Yet in 1875 the Association's weaknesses were painfully evident to thoughtful baseball men. In the East, Chadwick exposed the pernicious influence of gamblers, the selling of games by players, the mismanagement of directors, and the generally hostile reaction of the public. In demanding reform, he called for a convention that would stop fraudulent play by punishing crooked officials and blacklisting corrupt players. After the rotten timbers had been torn out, his next recommendation called for elimination of profitless, small-town franchises.[1]

Meanwhile, in Chicago, President Hulbert completed the reorganization of the White Stockings. With Boston's "big four" under contract, the 1876 pennant lay within his grasp, but he worried over the threat of an eastern counterplot that could nullify his gains. If successful, the plot might put control of Association policies in Philadelphia, and possibly force him to relinquish his players. This the portly Chicagoan became determined to prevent.

The forty-four-year-old Hulbert knew how to fight such fires. A son of pioneer parents, he had lived in Chicago since the age of two. Graduating from Belard College, he picked up enough business wisdom to acquire a profitable coal dealership, and in time, sought-after social recognition came his way with his admission to Chicago business organizations and to membership in the White Stocking Base Ball Club.

His baseball background differed from that of the typical gentlemanly promoter. Having had no playing experience, he liked the game more for its profit potential and its ability to stimulate local business than for pleasure. When the White Stocking Club was formed in 1870, he became a stockholder, and in 1876 he gained the presidency.[2]

As president he decided to give Chicago a first-rate club, and young Spalding was captivated by his drive and his civic pride.

[1] *New York Clipper*, February 12, 1876.
[2] *Tribune* (Chicago), April 11, 1882.

61

Indeed, the latter quality in Hulbert bordered on chauvinism. Once he told Spalding, "I would rather be a lamp-post in Chicago than a millionaire in another city." It was the kind of leadership that the opportunistic Spalding was seeking, and together the pair made a good combination, Hulbert providing the business acumen and the zealous Spalding acting as apprentice. With hard-driving Hulbert as his mentor, Spalding did not wait long for action. The idea of a coup against the Association was announced to Spalding with blunt suddenness: "Spalding, I have a scheme. Let us anticipate the Eastern cusses and organize a new association before the March meeting, and then see who will do the expelling."[3]

It was no impulsive remark, for the two soon drafted by-laws for a new league. Later Wright was brought in, and from him Hulbert got more ideas for changing the structure of baseball. Other key men were consulted, including some who had no idea why their advice was sought. Among the unenlightened was Chadwick, who was quizzed on specific weaknesses in the areas of playing rules and club management. As the outline took shape, Hulbert took shrewd advantage of western resentment of eastern domination to win support for his plan. By catering to western interests at a secret meeting in Louisville, he won the support of St. Louis, Cincinnati, and Louisville.

Wright's support of the move must be studied in the light of the Force case. Embittered over what he perceived as a clumsy attempt by the Athletics to dominate the Association and fearful of further plots, he wanted to crush the Philadelphians. However, he also saw Hulbert's plan as one that would open the way to greater profits by eliminating weak, fly-by-night franchises. He noted with alarm that fifteen clubs were seeking to join the Association in 1876 and urged Hulbert to push his coup.[4]

At this stage the plotters chose to bypass Chadwick. Certainly the westerners resented Chadwick's charges of corruption; Hulbert himself felt that his consistent hammerings in this area were

[3] Spalding, *op. cit.*, 200–14.

[4] Wright to Hulbert, March 23, December 30, 1875. Wright, Correspondence, Vol. VI

hurting baseball's popularity. Also, westerners disliked his dictatorial control over the rules committee, an influence that led to the unpopular and widely ridiculed ten-man plan. In short, the West wanted a rules committee that would be freed from this czar. Consequently, Chadwick remained in the dark during the formative stages of the coup, although he was brought in from the cold once the league was established.[5]

In addition to his organizing ability, Hulbert had a flair for the dramatic, and his usually serious mien was brightened with flashes of conviviality. His occasional pranks, like spiking a long-winded speaker's drink with red pepper, added color, because they were unexpected. Once, when his dog contributed to a Chicago victory by frightening a rival outfielder, Hulbert's sly reply to the protest was that the rules did not exclude dogs from the playing fields.[6]

Although skeptical of the durability of his newly created constitution, he decided to present it at a general meeting in New York. Anticipating a bitter struggle, he told Spalding "that the wit of man cannot devise a plan" that would regulate major league baseball for more than five years.[7] Nevertheless, armed with the backing of the directors of western clubs, including Charles Fowle of St. Louis, he pressed on with the meeting, which was scheduled for noon, February 2, 1876, at the Grand Central Hotel in New York.

Five prominent eastern clubs met with Hulbert and Fowle, with the latter pair carrying the proxies of two other western entries. In confronting this array of baseball brass, Hulbert dramatically locked the door and dropped the key into his pocket. Taking full charge, he reminded delegates of the Association's weaknesses. Moving from general grievances to particular solutions, he produced his constitution and read the preamble. It promised to "encourage, foster and elevate" the game by creating a new order. The over-all aim was to make the game "respectable and Honorable" and to protect the interests of owners and players by establishing

[5] Wright to Hulbert, January 24, 1876. *Ibid.*, Vol. VI.

[6] Anson, *op. cit.*, 92–93; *Daily Globe* (Boston), March 4, 1891; *Tribune* (Chicago), June 12, 1881.

[7] Spalding, *op. cit.*, 200–14.

a new league. To do so meant subordinating the players, and the title of the new league, "The National League of Professional Base Ball Clubs," made it plain that Hulbert intended to make the game more profitable to club owners.

Moved by his words, the delegates first voted to accept the title. Next, they listened while Fowle read the thirteen-point constitution, and to Hulbert's surprise they were receptive. Except for a few amendments adopted during the course of brief debate, the delegates approved the document in its entirety.

Important changes in the structure and conduct of major league baseball were bound up in that baker's dozen of articles. Of greatest significance was the transfer of power from players to owners. Rigid measures were enacted binding players more tightly to clubs. Among them was one provision granting a club the right to expel players from the League. Another established a new contract form binding players to all rules laid down by a club. Although no reserve clause was added yet, a strong effort was made to curb revolving by forbidding players to negotiate with another club until the playing season was over.

A vital concern of the new league was that the game be made to pay. No longer must it be a hobby for status-seeking gentlemen. Measures were adopted to attract serious investors by insuring the admission of potentially profitable franchises. One such measure decreed that a member club must come from a town of at least seventy-five thousand people. Also petitioners for a franchise must be voted in by current franchise holders, with two blackballs sufficient to bar an applicant.

To foster profits, another rule protected the territory of each franchise, granting each club full control over a five-mile radius of territory extending from its city center. Within this domain a club might bar any interloper from playing except by permission. In plain language it was stated that only one club would represent a league city.

On the theory that it would draw more fans, the league affected a lofty, moral image. Sunday games were forbidden along with betting or pool selling on any club's grounds. Also, police protec-

tion was to be provided, players were to be barred from fraterniz-
ing with fans, and rowdy fans were to be ejected from the game
by the umpire.

By adopting a regular playing schedule beginning with its 1877
season, the league remedied this traditional problem. An enabling
act, threatening expulsion to any club failing to meet its schedule
obligations, was added, and the same grim sanction was to be used
against any club disbanding before the season's end or flaunting
any part of the constitution. Adding teeth to the threat was a rule
making reinstatement virtually impossible, since a unanimous vote
of all member clubs was required.

To regulate the behavior of member clubs, the league established
a central bureaucracy, paid for by an annual $100 assessment
from each member. Extraordinary costs of supervision would call
for special assessments. The act created the permanent post of
secretary-treasurer, who was to be paid $400 a year for record
keeping. Hence, it was ordered that after each championship game,
a club was to telegraph results to the central office within twenty-
four hours. Further supervision would come from the president and
a board of directors. The latter group was a final court for settling
interclub disputes. Membership on this board was limited to
owners, and no club was to have more than a single member.

The constitution followed the traditional East-West pattern of
organization and took account of the limitations of existing transportation. By creating an eight-club league, another trend was set.
The eight-club model dominated the major league structure far
into the twentieth century, abandoned only briefly in the 1890's
and restored with penance in 1900.

Except for a rule calling for uniform scoring and a "foul balk"
rule aimed at stopping a trend toward overhand pitching, playing
rules remained the same. But the planners adopted uniform admission prices and set a uniform policy of distributing receipts.
Still another stride toward uniformity was a decision to pay umpires five dollars a game. This last rule paved the way for a professional staff of umpires and represented a major break with Chadwick's beloved volunteer system.

Upon approval of the thirteen points, Hulbert asked each delegate to sign a statement, burying the old Association and blaming that body for insidious abuses "growing out of an imperfect and unsystematized code." And so by unanimous accord, the modern era of major league baseball began.

In choosing officers, Hulbert named Morgan Bulkeley, a well-known Connecticut politician, as president. It was thought that such a name would go far towards endowing the league with respectability. Afterwards the arbitration board was chosen, three members coming from the East and two from the West, and the paid post of secretary-treasurer went to another easterner, Nicholas (Nick) Young.[8]

Young's election began his long career of National League service. A former player and club director, he eventually became president-secretary of the league in 1888. Not a strong personality nor even a resolute one, he was proficient in the arts of tact and compromise. By judicious use of both he retained his office until the early 1900's amidst all the storms that buffeted the league. Notwithstanding his lack of leadership ability, he served the league well as an administrator; especially noteworthy was his work as scheduler, supervisor of umpires, and league record keeper.[9]

The ease with which players were herded under the new regime furnishes further proof of the successful power play. Lacking organized opposition, the new rulers merely dispatched new contracts to each player which required his submission. Under his new contract a player agreed to play whatever position his captain asked him to fill. Management assumed broad disciplinary powers, demanding that a player perform at his utmost skill, accept authority "cheerfully," refrain from excess dissipation, and "submit to a medical examination." Illness, injury, and insubordination were indiscriminately linked as causes for dismissal.[10]

---

[8] *New York Clipper*, February 12, 1876; *Constitution and Playing Rules of the National League of Professional Base Ball Clubs*, 5–44.

[9] *Spalding's Official Base Ball Guide*, 1889, p. 52, 1896, p. 198.

[10] *Constitution and Playing Rules of the National League of Professional Base Ball Clubs*, 5–44; Wright, Correspondence, Vol. I, for a copy of a League player contract.

Not only were players taken by surprise, but so was the Association. At its March meeting its defenders tried to regroup, but a call for support drew responses only from small Pennsylvania towns like Reading, Allentown, and New Castle. Convinced of the hopelessness of their cause, the leaders allowed the old circuit to die quietly.[11]

Although spared the threat of formal opposition, the coup did not escape bitter criticism. In the East, tempers rose high. Leading the protest was the *Clipper*, along with reporters from bypassed towns. The strongest defense came from the West, with the Chicago *Tribune*, in on the plot from the start, leading. A *Tribune* writer attended the New York meeting, and, given a scoop, his paper voiced its approval with its headline, "The Diamond Squared." Forecasting a new era of honest play, the *Tribune* approved both the subordination of players and the ousting of unproductive franchises. In praising the western origins of the coup, the paper took a generous share of the credit. The writer needled Chadwick, crowing at the way that "the Old Man of the Sea . . . a dead weight on the neck of the game," was bypassed. Proclaiming the new circuit as a true major league, the writer cavalierly advised outside clubs to fulfill their proper role of nourishing players for the National League, a prophetic proposal in the light of things to come.[12]

Counterattacking in the *Clipper* a few days after the coup, Chadwick demanded to know why it had been necessary to use cloak-and-dagger tactics to achieve a moral end. "Reform should not fear the light of day," he chided, protesting the summary dismissal of certain clubs. If they were not given fair hearings, he warned, the arbitrary action of the league framers would only add to public distrust. To Chadwick the coup was "a sad blunder . . . and a star-chamber method of attaining . . . objects." Better, thought he, would it have been to have issued open invitations to all professional teams; as it was, twenty professional players were now without jobs for 1876.

From another quarter, the St. Louis *Globe-Democrat* questioned

[11] *World* (New York), March 5, 1876.
[12] *Tribune* (Chicago), February 4, 7, 13, 1876.

the logic of the reformers' morality. If the Phillies were kicked out for gambling, why not the Mutuals, whose record for crooked play was notorious? Begging the question, he suggested that the reformers could not bear to cut themselves out of the lucrative New York area.

In New Haven the *Register* protested the local club's ouster and argued that it had been a profitable organization. It stressed the fact that the club was a solid joint-stock venture, far superior in structure to the Mutuals. Similar protests came from Philadelphia demanding to know why the Athletics were retained and not the Phillies.[13]

Back in Chicago, sheltered from the protesting victims of Hulbert's judgment day, Spalding stepped into his new managerial role. To a *Tribune* man he predicted that "championship matches will draw a better average attendance . . . the public will feel confident that strong men will meet." Although training the White Stockings kept him busy, he found time to open "a large emporium in Chicago where he will sell all kinds of base ball goods and turn his place into the headquarters for the Western Ball Clubs."[14] Still in his early twenties, Spalding now took on multiple roles of manager, team captain, pitcher, and merchant. From the start he showed an ability to combine them, for as he clothed his team in uniforms from his own shelves, he provided a different-colored hat for each position. The effect was to make the team look like a "Dutch bed of tulips."[15]

Such frivolity did not detract from his serious desire to capture the pennant. The success of Chicago's league leadership hinged on it; besides, Hulbert and he had invested heavily in playing talent. Also, 1876 being the centenary of our national proclamation of independence, extra glory would come from winning baseball's "Centennial season."

The stakes were high and the opposition worried Spalding, but as the season unfolded, his anxieties abated. Boston, weakened by

---

[13] *New York Clipper*, February 12, 19, 1876; *World* (New York), April 2, 1876.
[14] *Tribune* (Chicago), February 13, 1876.
[15] *Ibid.*, March 12, April 23, 1876.

the losses of key players and hurt by Wright's early-season illness, never threatened. Only Hartford challenged the White Stockings, and near the end they rallied, winning nine in a row. But Chicago's seasonal pace was too much; the team closed with a percentage of .867, based on fifty-two wins and fourteen losses. The *Tribune* lavished tributes on the White Stockings, praising their teamwork, which stood "in glaring contrast with some gangs of quarrelsome bummers," and crediting "Capt. Spalding" for doing the job. The writer promised more glory for 1877, adding that steamcars would replace horsecars on the transit run to the park, which should enable businessmen to do more work on days that they wanted to go to the ball game.

Only one discordant note marred Chicago's pride. In a post-season test of strength that was directly ancestral to the modern world series, St. Louis beat the Whites, three games to two, to win the Northwest Championship series.

Yet it was a great personal triumph for Spalding. Along with his new reputation as a manager, his sporting goods store was thriving. In 1876 the league dropped two plums in his lap, a monopoly to supply the league's official balls and the right to publish the official league organ. Thus boosted, his business did even better, so that the very next year he began his gradual retirement from active play.[16]

By now the chastened Chadwick was sharing in the league's success, and following the death of Lewis Meacham, Spalding named Chadwick editor of his *Spalding's Official Base Ball Guide*. This appointment signified Chadwick's restoration to favor, and the grateful writer praised the league in return. His only criticism was levied at the fad of curve-ball pitching.[17]

But the season of 1876 had its black moment. Just before the close the Athletics and Mutuals refused to go west for their final scheduled games; both pleaded that they had lost money and did not want to go any deeper into the hole. This was a direct challenge to the league's authority, and naturally all eyes focused on the leaders and how they would meet the challenge. At the league's

[16] *Ibid.*, October 1, 8, 1876; *Spalding's Official Base Ball Guide*, 1877, pp. 50–56.
[17] *DeWitt's Base Ball Guide*, 1877, pp. 53–58.

annual meeting in December, Hulbert, after gaining the presidency, moved immediately against the offenders. With A. G. Mills as prosecuting attorney, the league moved to expel both clubs. The Draconian action shocked everybody. Spalding described a pathetic scene in which a weeping Athletics president begged for another chance. It moved Wright to intervene and to plead that the Athletics had "repented and . . . 'put on clean linen.' " But Hulbert was pitiless; after presenting charges, he demanded and got a unanimous vote for dismissal. It was a bold stand in behalf of the new league's authority, but it cost the league its two largest cities. Disregarding the potential profit losses, the leaders named no replacements, but chose to make the league a six-club circuit in 1877.[18]

To prevent a repetition of such a violation, Hulbert and Wright together fashioned the first uniform playing schedule. It was mostly Wright's work, and while some protested the imposition of playing dates,[19] the move was a major step in regularizing the conduct of the spectacle. Now fans would know well in advance when a club was home or away.

Otherwise, the league's failure to make expected profits in 1876 led to further restrictions on the players. Beginning in 1877, each player was charged thirty dollars a season for uniforms, to be procured by the club and maintained at his own expense. Another economy measure levied a half-dollar charge for each day a player was on the road with the team. This action drew protests from players, who got nowhere with the owners, and drew sarcasm from reporters, like the Louisville writer who gibed about players' complaining over assessments when really they had never had it so good.[20]

Indeed, other incidents lead one to suspect that owners now were united in a general get-tough policy against players. In Chicago,

[18] *New York Clipper*, September 30, 1876; Spalding, *op. cit.*, 312–13; Wright to Hulbert, March 23, 1877. Wright, Correspondence, Vol. VI.

[19] Wright to Robert Ferguson, April 13, 1877. Wright, Correspondence, Vol. VI. *Courier-Journal* (Louisville), April 1, 1877.

[20] Spalding's Official Base Ball Guide, 1877, pp. 23–26, 36–38; *Beadle's Dime Base Ball Player*, 1877, p. 77; *Courier-Journal* (Louisville), January 4, 1877.

Hulbert publicly rebuked Paul Hines, a brilliant outfielder, for alleged indifference, poor attitude, and poor play. In an open letter published in a Chicago newspaper, Hines was told to "attend to your business in first class shape," or suffer loss of pay. Furthermore, Hulbert threatened to tell Hines's father about his son's poor play. The implication that players were children to Hulbert hit home, and the Chicago *Post* received letters of angry protest from players siding with Hines. Hulbert, said the *Post*, was fast becoming *persona non grata* to players and spectators.[21]

Rumblings of player unrest were heard in other league towns. In Louisville rumors were spread of a rift between the club owners and pitcher Jim Devlin. In this case the *Courier-Journal* sided with the owners and said that the player was at fault. Although the player got nowhere with his demands, the ensuing ill feeling did not die.

That year newsmen eyed the Louisville team as a likely winner. Along with the brilliant Devlin, the club now had hard-hitting George Hall, who came from the ousted Athletics along with his reputation for consorting with gamblers. Two other players included Captain William Craver, the second baseman, and outfielder Al Nichols, a most recent acquisition. This quartet soon formed a clique within the team, which, popularly known as the Grays, kept their manager John C. Chapman on edge with their fun-loving antics. Very much the overgrown boy, Devlin was given to nocturnal tomfoolery like feigning sleepwalking in hotel corridors.

As a pitcher, however, Devlin was a team in himself; by mid-August his pitching had built up such a lead that a reporter estimated that seven wins in the team's final fifteen games would land the pennant. The nearest challenger, Wright's Bostons, needed to win thirteen of their last fifteen in order to take it away,[22] and the only basis for the Bostons' hope lay in the fact that they finished at home while the Grays were on the road.

[21] Hulbert to Paul Hines, July 20, 1877. Article in Wright, Correspondence, Vol. I.

[22] *Courier-Journal* (Louisville), January 4, 21, February 18, March 4, 18, April 1, August 6, 15, 1877.

Nevertheless, Boston fans were too sophisticated to believe in miracles, and only when the Grays posted a string of losses did optimism emerge. After errors cost the Grays defeats in Boston and Hartford, the *Courier-Journal* expressed bewilderment in headlines like, "!!!—???—!!!," and "What's the Matter?" After another loss to Boston the paper commented on Devlin's ineffectiveness and the loss of the team's offensive power: "Men struck out in every inning, but the fifth and ninth and but one man reached third." And when Devlin or Craver got on base, they were caught napping.[23]

Near the end of September, Boston took first place, and on October 1 the pennant was theirs. Although some believed that they smelled a rat, the *Daily Globe* loyally chalked up the victory to the fighting prowess of the Reds, who under "Old Man Wright" played "as gentlemen," "worked hard," and gave no thought to "crooked playing."[24]

While sadly writing off the pennant, the *Courier-Journal* began to marshall facts pointing to the conclusion that the Grays had thrown the pennant. Devlin was singled out as a possible culprit, because after losing his vaunted "ground shoot" (sinker ball) during the stretch drive, he suddenly regained his winning ways with some brilliant postseason pitching victories. "The Celt has completely given himself away," commented the editor.[25]

Prompted by the *Courier-Journal*'s evidence, the league launched a full-scale investigation, which resulted in confessions from three players. Acting on these, the league directors expelled Devlin, Hall, Nichols, and Craver for insubordination, selling games, and general misconduct. When the directors finally released their account to the press, Nichols was branded as the archconspirator. It was revealed that he had connections with a New York pool seller named McCloud. These two had hatched a plot calling on the four to throw games to the opposition, enabling McCloud

23 *Ibid.*, August 24, 28, 29, September 1, 1877; *Daily Globe* (Boston), August 29, 1877.

24 *Daily Globe* (Boston), October 1, 1877.

25 *Courier-Journal* (Louisville), September 8, 14, 27, October 1, 9, 18, 1877.

to profit from his inside knowledge. As a payoff the quartet were to receive a portion of McCloud's winnings. At first the operation began modestly, and only exhibition games were thrown. But when Hall suggested that more could be made by throwing championship games, it was arranged that they would throw the league race. The above account was pieced together from grilling the accused, three of whom filled the air with accusations while protesting their own innocence. It was generally agreed that, all together, the men were paid about $300, half of which went to Devlin.

The four were expelled from major league baseball for life. Shocked by the disclosure, reporters predicted the decline of baseball as a leisure outlet, since people would regard it as a tool of gamblers. Almost alone Chadwick kept the faith, basing his optimism on the purifying effects of forthcoming antipooling laws. One such law was adopted in New York State in 1877.[26]

While propaganda raged, the league directors fought to save their creation. At the winter meeting these aroused crusaders, led by Hulbert, launched a holy war against sinful players and franchises. Now umpires were empowered to levy fines up to twenty dollars against players who used abusive or threatening language, and on the assumption that low profits also were immoral, Hartford was dropped from the league. And for the immoral act of nonpayment of dues, Cincinnati's 1877 record was disallowed.

But almost unnoticed amongst the torrent of punitive laws was an act destined to provide a pattern for National League control over organized baseball. This act established a "League Alliance" for all professional clubs, whose goals "are not inconsistent with the objects of this League." Under its terms payment of a ten-dollar membership fee would secure the protection of the league. Such protection included recognition of a member's territorial rights and its player contracts. Also, by accepting each other's black lists, the Alliance promised to enforce member clubs' punitive acts. Later replaced by the National Agreement, the Alliance was a long step

[26] *Ibid.*, October 31, November 1, 2, 4, 1877; *DeWitt's Base Ball Guide*, 1878, pp. 36–38; *Laws of the State of New York* (100th session, January 2–May 24, 1877), Chapter 178, "An act in relation to bets, wagers and pools."

73

toward National League control over commercial baseball and the careers of professional players.[27]

Meanwhile, the exploitation of the Louisville incident was enabling league men to tighten control over their own players. In the press, sentiment continued to brand the Louisville quartet as crooks who almost ruined baseball, while Hulbert emerged as the saint whose righteous wrath saved the game. Thus did another myth find its way into baseball history.

The myth explains that baseball was once corrupt because it lacked businesslike leadership, but with the arrival of the National League clubowners, the players' instincts for corruption were curbed by the marvelous disciplinary measures enacted in 1878. At any rate, one sees few of the convivial gentlemen-sponsors after this year; in their place there now emerged the impersonal, profit-seeking owner type. Their new ethic may be glimpsed in Secretary Young's attitude toward players. In 1878, Wright asked Young for permission to sign catcher Charles Snyder of the disbanded Louisvilles. In giving approval, Young advised Wright to reduce his $1,500 offer to $1,280 since no other club was seeking a catcher. Young's comment typified the new managerial ethic. His contempt for players showed in his characterization of Snyder as one "not loaded down with brains," whose kind "like to receive a large sum more for the name . . . than . . . the judicious use of it. It comes and goes, and at the end of the season they are hard up as usual, and have little or no idea what has become of it, unless, perchance, some one has induced him to invest in a large gold watch."[28]

However, since Wright was used to having players respond and confide in him, he could not bring himself to accept Young's view. Now even the Louisville culprits sought him out, begging him to reveal evidence in their behalf that would lessen the enormity of their crime and perhaps lighten their sentence. The evidence to which they pointed suggested that the Louisville directors had failed to meet regular salary payments. In the case of Devlin, who had a wife and child to support, failure to receive his salary could

---

[27] *Spalding's Official Base Ball Guide*, 1878, pp. 1–23.
[28] Young to Wright, December 20, 1877. Wright, Correspondence, Vol. I.

have driven him to commit the rash act. This side of the story the semiliterate pitcher presented to Wright in three eloquently pathetic letters. Although hardly exonerating Devlin, they suggest that not all the guilt belonged to the players. As Devlin wrote, "I am Satisfied Harry that I have Done wrong . . . our Club did not do right with me or I wold never Done what I Did I was compeled at the time I had no money   the club wold not Pay me and I had a wife and Child in want. . . . All of our men got away out of town in the Dead hour of the night So as not to Pay there Bills the Club wold not Pay them and they cold not Pay anyone."[29]

Spalding later described a scene in which the threadbare pitcher entered Hulbert's Chicago office to beg for reinstatement. Visibly moved, Hulbert gave him fifty dollars to return home, but would do no more. For the next five years Devlin haunted league meetings, hoping for reinstatement, but Hulbert was relentless. Through the League Alliance he kept the four from playing professionally, and once warned a San Francisco team that if it played against Devlin, he would ruin its members' "professional chances."[30] At last Devlin, a pathetic baseball villain or a victim of niggardly club directors, gave up and became, of all things, a Philadelphia policeman. He died in 1884, but his misdeed followed him to the grave as is evidenced by his Louisville obituary, which reminded young players of the "fruits of crookedness."[31]

At least Chadwick had the courage to speak out against excessive and unjust disciplinary action on the part of directors. While approving the action against the Louisville men, Chadwick warned of the dangers of unfair purges, and criticized some directors for abusing their powers by black-listing for such "crimes" as drinking and disobedience. Such behavior must not be confused with dishonesty, he warned.[32]

But the grim atmosphere of the times encouraged tyranny by owners everywhere. In Boston, after two financially poor seasons, Boston's new president, Arthur Soden, seized personal control and

[29] James Devlin to Wright, November 2, 1877. Wright, Correspondence, Vol. I.
[30] *Tribune* (Chicago), April 18, 1880; Spalding, *op. cit.*, 227–29.
[31] *Courier-Journal* (Louisville), October 15, 1884.
[32] *DeWitt's Base Ball Guide*, 1879, pp. 44–46, 53–54.

imposed rigid economies. As Soden's secretary, Wright was now obliged to haggle with hotel managers over something like an alleged $1.67 overcharge on Soden's bill.[33] Certainly Soden kept Wright under surveillance, for in negotiating the 1878 contract with catcher Snyder, Wright told the catcher to name his terms, *"but let them be moderate, and in accordance with the times."*[34]

Elsewhere, economy was the watchword as salaries were cut. Protesting players were black-listed along with those suspected of crookedness. Added to the atmosphere of fear was a challenge by a rival organization, the International League, which sought to establish itself as the major league.[35]

Amidst this gloomy setting, Harry Wright drove his Reds to the 1878 pennant. It was his last major league championship, and it came in a year in which there was little glory or cash to accompany victory. That year the league remained a six-club circuit with three newcomers, Providence, Indianapolis, and Milwaukee, replacing St. Louis, Hartford, and the pariah Louisvilles. Wright's Reds finished with a forty-one and nineteen record, four games up on Cincinnati, which was sparked by a brash rookie, Mike Kelly. The season was a landmark in major league history in that it marked the first time each team in a commercial league completed its full schedule of games.[36]

However, it was another financial flop for all concerned. Even contenders did poorly, as Boston's records show. Its record of the first five years of the league shows mounting seasonal losses: in 1876, net losses were $777.22; in 1877, $2,230.85; in 1878, $1,433.31; in 1879, $3,346.90; and in 1880, $3,315.90. Although managerial austerity, salary cuts, and new stock issues lightened the burden somewhat, it was a discouraging picture. Ranged alongside the modestly profitable Association era, it goes far to debunk the myth of league superiority.

[33] Wright to David McClasky, Cleveland, December 22, 1877. Wright, Correspondence, Vol. VI.

[34] Wright to Charles Snyder, December 15, 1877. *Ibid.*, Vol. VI.

[35] Wright to Chadwick, December 23, 1877 (*ibid.*, Vol. VI); *Daily Globe* (Boston), July 21, 1878.

[36] *Spalding's Official Base Ball Guide*, 1879, p. 108; *Daily Globe* (Boston), September 1, 1878.

During the years 1876 to 1880, at no time did Boston's home receipts match the Association's record of $3,933.93 set in 1875. Furthermore, in the early league years only once did Boston's payrolls surpass the 1875 mark of $20,685. In 1878 the payroll hit $18,814; in 1879 the austerity policy drove it down to $15,759.92; and in 1880 it was down to $14,007.96. If the trend had persisted, Boston salaries would soon have dropped below the seasonal total of the 1869 Cincinnati pioneers.

The economy ax struck at such areas as advertising, down from $1,440 in 1875 to only $873 in 1879; clubroom upkeep, cut from $1,626 in 1875 to $551 in 1880; and travel expenses, down from a princely $6,808 in 1875 to $2,813 in 1880.[37] The drastic cut in travel accommodations so damaged player morale that at one point Wright faced near mutiny. Because of this incident, the Soden administration decided to fire him.

In these years newspapers often ridiculed the league's claim of major league status, and one paper urged clubs from such excluded cities as Philadelphia, New York, Pittsburgh, Washington, and Baltimore to form a real major league. The writer had a point because the league of 1880 was indeed a small-town circuit. Since it had taken on towns like Milwaukee and Indianapolis, the writer sneered, "The League has not sustained the reputation it had three or four years ago. There are clubs in the International Association fully as strong as the League clubs."[38]

Ignoring such taunts, the league directors met in Cleveland and reaffirmed their policy of austere exclusiveness. After unanimously re-electing Hulbert and Young, the delegates voted to oust Milwaukee and Indianapolis as unremunerative. But the directors persisted in their moral boycott of Philadelphia and New York, and voted to admit Troy, Syracuse, Cleveland, and Buffalo; admission of the last two made the league once more on eight-club structure. In pursuing a moral image, the league men continued to oppose Sunday baseball and raised the fine for rowdy behavior to fifty dollars.

[37] Wright, Note and Account Books, Vol. IV.
[38] *The Times* (Philadelphia), October 6, 1878.

In all this the league men were willing to forego profits in the belief that the public must first be convinced that major league baseball was honest. Perhaps after a few years of sackcloth and ashes, the public would reward them by flocking once more to the games. But if such a pattern of thinking appears naïve to modern eyes, let it be remembered that the late 1870's were years of financial depression in America. With little public money available for frills like baseball, the league's policy of biding its time and concentrating on its public image seems more realistic.[39]

While the 1879 campaign failed to brighten the financial picture, at least it gave the public a Cinderella story. For that year, Providence, guided by George Wright, won the pennant. The younger Wright's decision to leave Boston for the newly established Providence team paralleled Spalding's. Like the big pitcher, George had a hankering to manage and a desire to venture into the sporting goods industry. Hence, soon after arriving in Providence, he opened a sporting goods emporium with his friend Henry Ditson on Dorrance Street.

Although the acquisition of stars like George Wright and Jim O'Rourke from nearby Boston gave a manufactured tone to Providence's triumph, the local nine had developed some home-grown heroes. One was hard-working John Montgomery Ward, now the front-line pitcher, who was destined to become one of the great personalities in nineteenth-century baseball. A close student of the game, he continually practiced playing other positions, and in time his prowess rested on his ability as a shortstop. But in 1879, he pitched Providence to the pennant.[40]

That year the Wright brothers found themselves locked in a battle of tactics with the pennant as the prize. At times the sibling rivalry was bitter; once Harry's Reds, on a day off, spent their time at Providence cheering Cincinnati to beat George's team. When the Providence Grays won, they left "with remarkable quietness."

As the season ended, the quirks of the league schedule height-

---

[39] *Spalding's Official Base Ball Guide*, 1879, pp. 92–96.
[40] *Daily Journal and General Advertiser* (Providence, R.I.), April 9, 1879.

ened the tension between the brothers. But in the final week Providence ended the suspense by thumping the Reds in two out of three games, with George Wright scoring the winning run in the clincher. Freed from tension, Providence fans erupted in the greatest demonstration "since Lee surrendered." "They crowed. . . . They shook hands. . . . They held a regular love feast." Men and women alike shouted for joy: "There was a continual fire of congratulations, a continued shaking of hands for very joy. . . . It was worth while to be there, just to see the excitement. It was worth while to catch some of that enthusiasm."[41]

But Providence attendance on the whole left much to be desired. Except for games with Boston and Chicago, the club drew poorly. The total home attendance was less than forty-three thousand, and total receipts of $12,516 certainly failed to cover expenses.[42]

In spite of another year of financial frostbite, the league directors stubbornly held to the course of respectability over profits. At a special February meeting players were warned that suspensions would follow "drunkenness and bummerism." Another Draconian act struck at injured players with the harsh edict of "No pay for no services rendered." However, directors added that "conscientious, earnest, deserving" players would be given special consideration.[43] In all this the owners insisted that their goal was respectability, and it was their firm belief that suffering was necessary to win back a jaded public.

Be that as it may, one may well question this moral interpretation of baseball's plight. With severe business depressions racking the land, many potential fans were out of work. The nadir of the depression was reached in 1878, and a slow upturn followed. If economic conditions offer a better explanation of baseball's troubles than moral shortcomings, nevertheless the fact that the league men chose to define their situation in moral terms was to have a powerful shaping effect on major league baseball as the golden 1880's dawned.

41 *Ibid.*, September 19, 27, 1879.
42 *Ibid.*, October 1, 1879.
43 *Spalding's Official Base Ball Guide*, 1880, pp. 84–90.

6

America's New Heroes

THE PUBLIC IMAGE of the baseball player during this era was schizoid, for while it was being idealized by some, it was being villainized by others. Mass hero worship had not yet raised the player to its pantheon of tin gods, and vociferous moralists frequently damned the athlete as a prime example of debauchery. While conceding that some might be honest, a New York *Times* editor characterized the usual player as a "worthless, dissipated gladiator; not much above the professional pugilist in morality and respectability." This editor said that an individual, in considering his life's work, should choose any calling rather than "hiring oneself to win matches" for teams claiming to represent our national game. To support his contention, the editor painted a picture of players working in the summer and in the other months "remaining modestly out of sight in those quiet retreats connected with

80

bars, and rat pits, where the sporting men of the metropolis meet for social improvement and unpremeditated pugilism." To rid baseball of its unfavorable image, the writer urged that the game be returned to gentlemanly amateurism, for, "To employ professional players to perspire in public for the benefit of gamblers . . . furnishes to dyseptic moralists a strong argument against any form of muscular Christianity." As for baseball's claim to being our national game, any childish sport, even mumble-the-peg, had as good a claim.[1]

Such criticisms were often expressed in the 1870's, but defenders like Chadwick stoutly argued that professional baseball would outlast its detractors. Such an image, he argued, was an outgrowth of the spectacle's rapid growth, and the weedy growth of professional baseball was rather like the peopling of California during the gold rush era. If civilized law could improve that state, so, too, could the National League improve the state of baseball by housebreaking it for Main Street. Thus did Chadwick applaud the heroic labors of the League directors.

Meanwhile Chadwick sought to introduce professional players to the public. In an 1872 *Guide*, he published a complete list of major league players with names, statistics on height and weight, hometown, and team affiliation. An analysis of this list shows that most were very young, the average player being twenty-five years old, with only two in their thirties. Compared with today's players, they were shorter, only four topping six feet, and most were of eastern origin. The large number of Irish names suggests that many second generation Celts were using the game as a means to attain higher economic status.[2]

Certainly a player's life could be a happy one. Up to 1876, rising salaries enabled most to better their pay, equivalent to that of white-collar workers. But for those who had yet to learn the approved middle-class values of thrift and prudence, the additional income burned holes in their pockets.

[1] *Times* (New York), March 8, 1872.

[2] *Beadle's Dime Base Ball Player*, 1872, pp. 41–44; *DeWitt's Base Ball Guide*, 1876, pp. 18–37.

The image of the player as a swashbuckling, free-spender was enhanced by the flashy uniforms they wore. The Athletics of 1871 wore white shorts and pants, with blue stockings and caps. The Louisvilles entered the League in 1876, sporting white uniforms, white caps, blue stockings, two-toned belts, and the word "Louisville" emblazoned in navy blue across their shirt fronts.[3]

Since gambling was considered a mark of gentility during this era, many young players of the 1870's eagerly sought an introduction to billiards and poker.[4] Also, the idle hours of long railroad trips encouraged card-playing and gambling. Less innocent temptations were presented by gamblers, who were ready with suggestions to fix the outcome of games. Sometimes real necessity persuaded players to assent, because they were often uncertain about when they would receive their salaries. In 1872, Boston delayed its final payments, and in 1874 the Reds took a salary cut when the English tour failed financially. Nevertheless, until 1877, no player had been convicted for throwing games, although rumors suggested it was being done. Back in 1865, one was expelled by the amateur Association for throwing games, but he was later reinstated and continued to play as late as 1874.

In truth, argued the *Clipper*, most of the gambling involved "bets or pools on the games" rather than instances of arranging their outcome; indeed, "there is no sport now in vogue in which so little of the element of fraud prevails as in the base ball arena." Rumors persisted, however, and a Buffalo writer argued that, "Any professional base ball club will 'throw' a game if there is money in it. A horse race is a pretty safe thing to speculate on, in comparison with an average ball match."[5]

But Chadwick believed that pool-selling was the real threat to the image of professional baseball. Yet this form of betting had been intended to correct the evils of direct wagering. Under direct wagering, one person bet with another, but much confusion and argument resulted over who was going to hold the stakes. If no

3 Alfred Spink, *The National Game*, 70.

4 *New York Clipper*, February 12, 1876.

5 *Ibid.*, April 24, 1875; *Beadle's Dime Base Ball Player*, 1875, pp. 55–56.

third party appeared, a loser could avoid honoring his bet. To correct the problem, pool-selling developed in "pool rooms," which were conviently located near a ball park. Since pool-sellers held all bets, it was also possible to know the exact amount being wagered on each team.

In 1877 the Boston *Daily Globe* gave an illuminating description of pool-selling. Usually rooms catered to small betters and sought a reputation for sound "business principles." A roomkeeper got a commission for keeping records, for making out the tickets, and for insuring the payment of bets. A reputable room kept tabs on customers, and the operator zealously sought a reputation for being honest.

In selling the pools, the operator ran an auction several days before the game. "How much am I bid?" was the recurring question at such an affair. To the highest bidder went the right to name his favorite team, after which the opposing team was put up for bids. If bets on the second team did not approach the odds sought by the highest bidder, he might withdraw his wager. Naturally, such a system worked best when two well-matched teams were scheduled or when one of the bidders had inside information about a game's having been "fixed."

By 1877 the popularity of pool-selling was challenged by a new British system called bookmaking, but the pools remained popular. In 1877, Boston had eight rooms, and the New York rooms took in as much as $70,000 for key matches. Not surprisingly, the rooms were headquarters for all kinds of gamblers, "a conglomeration of humanity such as scarcely any other place in the world could call together."[6]

Since rumors of fixed games led nervous betters to suspect miscues on the playing field, they often vented their fears at the park with "the vilest obscenity and profanity in their comments on those errors of play which damage the chances of winning the bets."[7] By 1876 this byplay added a new dimension to the baseball

[6] *Daily Globe* (Boston), July 24, 1877; *Beadle's Dime Base Ball Player*, 1873, pp. 46–47.

[7] *Ibid.*, 1873, pp. 46–47.

spectacle, but the League directors wanted no part of it, and after the celebrated Louisville "fix," they sought to harry gamblers from the parks.

But if fast-money men dented baseball's moral armor, so, too, did lurching drunken players. Because of them, the powerful temperance movement verbally tarred all professional players. Indeed, Chadwick and others ranked drinking equal with gambling as a threat to the game, and in time it was listed as the number-one problem.

Some of the best players came under the influence of liquor in this hard-drinking era. Young Adrian Anson sheepishly recalled some of his early escapades in and out of saloons. When the "beer was in and the wit was out," he became involved in embarassing scrapes. While "refreshing the inner man" at "a German saloon," he once got into an argument over who was the best pugilist in America. To no one's surprise, the argument led to a fist fight, after which a subdued Anson was handcuffed and taken to jail. After a friendly club director secured his release, the impulsive Anson celebrated his liberation at another saloon. However, the spree ended when the tipsy player encountered the girl that he had planned to make his wife. It was Anson's mistaken contention that the League's tightened discipline put an end to such sprees.[8]

Of course, baseball had its attractive side, and some players enhanced their image by their Horatio Alger-like successes. Among those players who had built respectable middle-class careers on the side were sporting goods entrepreneurs Spalding, Reach, and George Wright. Others, like Jim O'Rourke, Jim White, and John Ward, studied law during their off months. Many others worked at respectable trades: Harry Wright continued to dabble in the jewelry trade, but found more profitable side lights in pushing his patented score card, lobbying in baseball councils as a representative of the Mahn ball manufacturers, and lobbying for a turnstile company.[9]

[8] Anson, *op. cit.*, 67–68.

[9] Wright to Cammeyer, November 12, 1877. Wright, Correspondence, Vol. VI. Also, Wright, Note and Account Books, Vol. VI.

Meanwhile, the game's livelier style of play appealed to crowds. Above all the new style was fast, competitive, and dangerous to the player. So dangerous, indeed, that by the 1880's the average playing career was short, rarely exceeding six years.

Among the most injured were pitchers and catchers, and few pitchers were more accident prone than George Zettlein. He was hit hard and often by batted balls; once a reporter saw a line ball hit him with such force on the forehead that the ball rebounded sixty feet. Somewhat stunned, Zettlein "shook his head, took a drink, and again went to work as if nothing had happened."[10]

However, since catchers had no masks or protective padding, they were particularly vulnerable. Only the fact that they played far behind the batter saved most from frequent injury. Nevertheless, in 1875, Jim White, scorning all primitive protective devices, introduced the modern style of catching close behind the batter. Most bore the pain of bruises and broken bones stoically, but late in the decade George Wright introduced a patented mouth protector, guaranteed not to have "any disagreeable taste," as one of the first protective devices.

Jeers greeted the introduction of the first catcher's mask when Harvard catcher James Tyng used a friend's patented gear in a game against the Boston Reds. Tyng took a merciless ribbing from players and fans, and Boston catcher Jim White did not help at all when he tried it on and discarded it in disgust because it obstructed his vision. Later Spalding described the innovation as resembling a fencer's mask.[11] Nevertheless, this piece of catchers equipment soon gained much popularity, and two years later Peck and Snyder's sporting goods store was selling them for three dollars each, claiming that some of the "prominent catchers" of 1877 were using them. "They are made of wire and cushioned with soft leather . . . filled with the best curled hair. They are light and easy to adjust."[12] Of course, some purists still regarded users of protective equipment as cowards or hypochondriacs; one reporter

[10] *Tribune* (Chicago), February 10, 1871.
[11] Henry Chadwick, *The Art of Fielding: With a Chapter on Base Running*, 18–19; Spalding, *op. cit.*, 475–84.
[12] See advertisement in *DeWitt's Base Ball Guide*, 1878.

sneered, "There is a good deal of beastly humbug in contrivances to protect men from things which don't happen. There is about as much sense in putting a lightning rod on a catcher as a mask." This argument had merit so long as catchers played far behind the batters, but in 1879 the rules committee outlawed the foul bound catch. Since catchers could no longer put a batter out by catching his foul tip on the first bounce, out went their chief excuse for playing so far back.[13]

Chadwick gave his powerful support to the use of gloves by catchers saying, "The catcher will find it advantageous, when facing swift pitching, to wear tough leather gloves, with the fingers cut off near the joint, as they will prevent his having his hands split and puffed up." Soon came the first chest protectors, and again users faced much ridicule.[14]

Other players using protective equipment were kidded more than catchers. In 1875, Spalding saw the New Haven first baseman wearing a flesh-colored glove and asked about it. With embarassment the first baseman showed a kid glove with a round opening for ventilation. Since the fans were contemptuous of the player's affectation, Spalding prudently waited until 1877, before using a protective glove, when he was in his last season as a player. Boldly choosing a black kid glove, he added layers of padding until he could no longer feel the sting of a thrown ball. Although Spalding was surprised at the tolerance of the spectators, most players shunned the use of the early gloves until the 1890's.[15]

But if public sentiment discouraged the use of protective equipment, the rulemakers tried to eliminate some of the game's dangerous aspects. Correctly identifying pitching and batting as the chief danger spots of the game, the rules committee tried hard to strike a balance of safety, which would not detract from the game's attraction. Since pitchers were able to throw wild pitches with im-

[13] *Courier-Journal* (Louisville), April 1, 1877; *Spalding's Official Base Ball Guide*, 1877, chapter on "catching."

[14] *DeWitt's Base Ball Guide*, 1876, pp. 18–37; George Wright, "Sketch of the National Game of Baseball," *Records of the Columbia Historical Society* (ed. by John Larner), XXVII, 84–85.

[15] Spalding, *op. cit.*, 475–84.

punity, the rules were changed to make umpires call bad pitches "balls." This comforted batters somewhat, but they continued to enjoy the privilege of requesting a pitcher to throw to a high or low strike zone. Since only pitches to one's chosen zone counted as strikes, the batter was ordering the pitcher to pitch to his batting strength.[16]

Yet, in the 1870's, pitchers were gaining new advantages. After 1872, they were allowed to pitch overhand. This put batters at a disadvantage, since they were facing swifter pitching from a distance of only forty-five feet. The shift from underhand to overhand pitching affected a lot of pitching careers. In the early 1870's underhand masters like Spalding, Tom Bond, and Dick McBride were popular underhand pitching heroes. But styles and appreciations changed fast; in 1877, curve-ball pitchers were in demand, despite charges from purists that they were dangerously wild. Indeed, some questioned the reality of a ball curving until an 1877 experiment in Cincinnati lent supporting evidence.[17] Nevertheless, the *Clipper* continued to urge young pitching hopefuls to develop a good fast ball and change of pace.[18]

During this decade a pitcher was not penalized for striking a batter with a pitched ball. In 1875, however, Wright campaigned for some kind of penalty; at least call it a "ball," he urged.[19] Soon afterwards rule makers did just that and ordered an umpire to fine a pitcher if he believed that a pitcher was deliberately throwing at a batter.

Since the National League dominated organized baseball, it allowed its rule makers to radically alter the style of play. Uniformity was a major goal and was evidenced in such league decisions as employing a paid corps of umpires, adopting uniform playing schedules, standardizing the division of receipts, and making players purchase and maintain standardized uniforms.

A more uniform style of batting followed a league decision which

[16] *New York Clipper*, April 15, 1871.
[17] Morse, *op. cit.*, 26–33; *North American and United States Gazette*, (Philadelphia), August 4, 1871; *ibid.*, December 8, 1877.
[18] *New York Clipper*, December 8, 1877.
[19] Wright to A. F. Childs, March 31, 1875. Wright, Correspondence, Vol. VI.

abolished the fair-foul hit in 1876.[20] This decision ended the playing careers of Dick Pearce, the inventor of the fair-foul hit, and Ross Barnes, who used it to become the professional association's perennial batting champion. This "tricky hit" was "produced by striking downward at the ball, blocking it in front of the home base, from which point it bounded off into foul ground." Although some fair-foul experts now turned to the bunt as a substitute, many never adjusted to the loss of their favorite tactic.[21]

Those spectators who liked innovations were pleased by the never ending flow of new tactics, which were introduced by many inventive players, who changed the style of the spectacle. Outfield play was revolutionized when Harry Wright developed the technique of backing up fellow fielders in fielding hits; also, it was Wright who taught fielders always to throw to the base ahead of the runner. After the innovation received acceptance, a reporter said, "it is a poor outfielder who does not cover twice the amount of ground."[22]

Meanwhile, George Wright reportedly introduced the trap-ball trick, which was finally outlawed by the modern infield fly rule.[23] Joe Start, a great first baseman introduced the modern tactic of fielding his position by playing off the bag toward second base, which allowed him to field balls that would otherwise become base hits. Another change in the game's style of play was initiated by catcher White's rash decision to play directly behind the batter; he was motivated by his belief that a pitcher would be more effective if the catcher provided a target.[24]

Changes in the kinds of bats and balls were less dramatic, but the league's decision to give Spalding the monopoly for making the official ball at least brought uniformity to a very annoying aspect of the sport. Under the old association balls were supplied by several small firms, and the only requirement was that they be five and one-quarter ounces in weight and nine and one-quarter

---

20 Morse, *op. cit.*, 32–33.
21 *New York Clipper*, January 6, 1894.
22 *Courier-Journal* (Louisville), February 11, 1877.
23 *Spalding's Official Base Ball Guide*, 1896, 160–62.
24 *DeWitt's Base Ball Guide*, 1876, pp. 18–37.

inches in circumference. The differences among those balls were
due to the association's failure to specify other qualities. Thus,
some teams used red, as well as white-colored, balls; some used
the double-covered ball that was introduced in 1873, and others
did not. Instead of ruling on these differences, the Association
simply let the home team choose its favorite ball. Hence, prior to
1875 several manufacturers claimed to produce the official ball, but
in 1875, the Ryan dead-ball was ruled the official ball.[25]

Although the Spalding monopoly eventually quieted the official-
ball controversy, purists criticized the Spalding ball for being too
lively. The league's forcing its usage, however, did put an end
to some quaint stratagems of the association era. For example, in
1874 some teams tried to beat Boston with the strategy of using
very lively balls, but after two successive "elastic ball" defeats, the
Reds adapted themselves to the ball's qualities, and defeated the
next team that tried to use the tactic. When Brooklyn tried to re-
verse the strategy with a "dead Ross ball," the Reds batted equally
hard.[26]

Actually the dead ball of the 1870's was suited to the parks of
that era. In 1871, Chicago's fences were located an average distance of 375 feet from home base, and the *Tribune* claimed that
it was as big as any park owned by the members of the association.
But the changing style of play and the demand for better seating
capacities quickly made these small parks obsolete. Years later,
recalling Chicago's association park, Alfred Spink wrote, "This
team played its games on the grounds located west of State and
south of Twenty-second street, a rough board enclosure with a
grandstand not near as pretentious as those owned now by the
poorest Chicago City League team."[27]

Certainly the National League's decision to pay its umpires did

---

[25] *Spalding's Official Base Ball Guide*, 1878, 24–44; George Wright, "Sketch of the
National Game of Baseball," *Records of the Columbia Historical Society* (ed. by John
Larner), XXVII, 84–85; Peck and Snyder add in *New York Clipper*, June 21, 1873;
Courier-Journal (Louisville), April 1, 1877, for Nick Young's experiences as official
league ball tester.

[26] *New York Clipper*, June 20, 1874.

[27] *Tribune* (Chicago), March 8, 1871; Spink, *op. cit.*, 65.

much to standardize major league baseball as a spectacle. Until then it had been considered an honor to be asked to umpire, and the "honor" was supposedly given to one who knew the rules well enough to make sound judgments. Although the association tried to encourage uniformity of interpretation, it was the league that did most to standardize the decision of umpires by spelling out the rules and the interpretations for them. On the other hand, such a policy made hirelings out of umpires and put them at the mercy of league directors, who later did little to stop the public from villainizing these arbiters.

But in the 1870's the umpire had not yet become the scapegoat of disappointed fans, and the immediate problem was securing well-trained men who would render uniform decisions. After ruling in 1876 that umpires were to be paid five dollars a game, the league next created an official staff of umpires. But this did not happen until the 1880's, and in the meantime the colorful idiosyncracies of some arbiters kept them from degenerating into slavish drones. In the 1870's there was, for example, Billy McLean who worked in Boston and Providence and was noted for a quick-tempered willingness to impose fines. Having once been a professional fighter, he was respected, and he kept in fine physical condition by walking— once from his Boston home to an assignment in Providence, a feat he found possible by arising at four o'clock in the morning.[28]

During the 1870's the baseball interests of urbanites were nourished by newspapers, and an emerging breed of sportswriters kept appetites whetted by their coverage of the games. Of course, newspaper space was not freely given, for it was clear that the marriage of baseball promoters and newspaper publishers was a mutual convenience. For the publisher it meant increased sales, and for the club owner it meant wider publicity at no expense. For the player it came to mean moments of idolization for splendid performances and moments of damnation for slip-ups, but at least it kept him before the public.

In this decade baseball coverage in newspapers reached im-

[28] *Daily Journal and General Advertiser* (Providence, R.I.), August 11, September 27, 1879; Morse, *op. cit.*, 42; Chadwick, Scrapbooks, I, 64, 101.

pressive proportions. At first, newspapers in major league towns concentrated on the home club, but public demand soon prompted them to provide broader coverage. Also patrons in smaller towns were vicariously enjoying the delights of baseball via the sporting pages.

From the start major league clubs enjoyed unsolicited free publicity, paying only for small advertisements. Also guidebooks were published by outsiders, who willingly bore the expense of printing to get their advertisements before the public. These guidebooks widened the scope of the leisure pastime by enabling fans to keep abreast of changing rules and franchises and to follow by statistics and articles the latest deeds of their diamond heroes. Indeed, publishers vied with one another for the coveted honor of publishing an "official" organ. In the 1870's the association gave this accolade to *DeWitt's Base Ball Guide*; under the league, *Spalding's Official Base Ball Guide* held sway. Among newspapers the *Clipper* was acclaimed the leading baseball organ of the era, but with the league's arrival, the Chicago *Tribune* proclaimed itself the official western voice.

Among the emerging sportswriters, Chadwick became the best known, and he played the role of a Moses who was destined to show baseball leaders how to fulfill the game's promise as America's national field sport. To this end he urged owners to emulate England's sporting gentry and players to behave like gentlemen. Notwithstanding his stilted style, his verbosity, and his repetitiveness, Chadwick was a fighting moralist who defended and castigated his baseball brethren. Most of his attacks were directed toward the gamblers, crooks, drunks, and rowdies in the ranks of the players. He also criticized club owners, chiding them at times for mismanagement and for not making the game as great as he believed it could become. While seldom naming his villains, he did identify evildoers by indirection with his tactic of singling out specific managers and players for praise; his omissions left little doubt where the others stood in his gentlemanly opinion.

Since the tall, bearded Chadwick himself wanted to be known as a gentleman, he championed the "respectable" element among spectators. At this point in his career he believed the game to be a middle-class leisure pastime, but later he would welcome its proletarization, although insisting that the game retain its tone of gentlemanly respectability.[29] With a somewhat naïve faith in human nature, he thought that by preaching what was right he could make the game a moral force in American values.

As a prolific writer and editor of guides, Chadwick spiced his ponderous style with colorful bits of baseball jargon. Thus he rebuked loud-mouthed players for their "chin music," reminding them that a professional player "should play his game quietly, to play it up to the best mark."[30] Yet his advice betrayed not only his own status aspirations, but his lack of understanding of the needs of spectators, some of whom regarded this colorful byplay as an interesting aspect of the spectacle.

As dean of writers, Chadwick sometimes chided colleagues for overwriting and "piling on the agony" in their descriptions. For example, he poked fun at a Cincinnati writer for his long paragraph describing George Wright's hitting a single. He said that the account put "yellow-covered novel writers into the shade" by such phrases as, "The King had not worn his royal purple that day and was determined to redeem himself. . . . Every man, woman and child . . . knew that he was the right man in the right place. Not a nerve trembled" as he heard two strikes called. And when he finally hit a "fair foul," there "rose a shout such as never [had] been heard on these grounds before."[31]

However, Chadwick seldom warred on fellow journalists. Indeed, he sought to introduce his fellows to the fans and to organize a fraternal organization of leading sportswriters, which he hoped would work to establish and maintain professional standards. Chadwick's list of good writers included the names of Will Rankin of the New York *Herald*, Carl Joy of the New York *Tribune*, David McAuslan of the Brooklyn *Times*, and Al Wright of the Philadelphia *Sunday Mercury*. Among the younger set of journal-

29 *Beadle's Dime Base Ball Player*, 1875, pp. 56–57.
30 *DeWitt's Base Ball Guide*, 1876, pp. 33–34.
31 Chadwick, Scrapbooks, I, 90.

ists he commended Charles Peverelly of the New York *Daily News,* Chandos Fulton of the Brooklyn *Star,* Dave Sutton of the Brooklyn *Union,* and Will Hudson and John Clark of the Brooklyn *Eagle.*

But in the same article he scolded some for disgracing the "fraternity," and singled out Carpenter of the New York *Herald,* who was currently boarding "at public expense in New Jersey owing to being a too-much married man." He also berated publishers for neglecting baseball coverage, citing the New York *Times.* Certainly Chadwick was qualified to make these judgments, for in the twenty years of baseball reporting up to 1878, he had covered games for every important daily and sporting weekly in the New York area.

As a species of journalists, sportswriters enjoyed greater literary freedom than other staff men. In exercising this freedom, they soon developed a stockpile of jargon for describing games. Many of these descriptive words and phrases were picked up by readers, and soon a language developed that helped to ritualize the game and solidify its devotees. During the decade this language expanded, but by the late 1880's it became stylized and changed little thereafter. This suggests that the game itself changed little after the 1880's. For the state of baseball jargon in the 1870's, one can examine Chadwick's lexicon of baseball slang which was published in 1874 to help British writers cover the contests played during the tour. The lexicon reveals that sportswriters had already coined a number of stylized terms, many of which are still used. The list includes words and phrases like "wild throwing," "muffed balls," "assists," "balks," "bounders," "daisy cutters," "fungoes," "grounders," "line balls," "pop ups," "double plays," "overthrows," "passed balls," and terms describing scoreless games like "blanked" and "white-washed."[32]

Under Chadwick's influence popular sportswriting attained a high degree of development in the 1870's, with writers adopting an exaggerated, colorful descriptive style. To be sure, many articles were verbose and stilted, and chroniclers of that era wrote in the passive voice and gave too much attention to petty detail. Since

[32] Chadwick, *Chadwick's Base Ball Manual,* 1874.

urban and regional loyalties held sway in those days, much baseball writing was extremely partial to the home club's cause. Furthermore, many writers felt free to indulge in outrageous criticisms, second-guessings, and editorializations. However, a trend toward uniformity was also noticeable, and in the late 1870's a typical account began with a lead paragraph giving an essential factual summary. Next, came a tediously descriptive account of the game, often jammed into frighteningly long paragraphs, followed by another summary and a box score.[33]

By the end of the decade writers made box scores, kept statistics on fielding, batting, and pitching performances, and developed the "checkerboard arrangement" of listing weekly team standings. This uniformity, of course, made possible a fan's following a familiar ritual in his reading habits, and thus contributed mightily to the growing popularity of the game. Using the checkerboard standings, for example, a fan could tell at a glance the exact standing of his favorite team and compare its won-and-loss record with those of its opponents. Developed by sportswriter Al Wright of Philadelphia, this device is still used.[34]

Yet individuality was still existent, and in this era several writers developed their own distinctive styles, which were usually erected on an edifice of jargon and exaggeration. After quickly exhausting the creative possibilities of this medium, some journalists succeeded in spicing their accounts with the then popular tall-story yarn. One writer portrayed the players of his home-town team as supermen. The pitcher's ball was so fast that it had to be coated with phosphorous to be seen, but even then it was often ignited by frictional force and consumed before reaching the catcher. Fortunately, the catcher had hands the size of windmills, which he periodically toughened by "breaking up pig iron at the Newburgh Rolling Mills." If a ball was hit, the shortstop, who could "turn thirteen somersaults without spitting on his hands," caught it with hands or teeth. In the field three men, who traveled "on all-fours

33 *New York Clipper*, June 20, 1874. The description of the Boston-Mutual game in this issue is typical baseball writing style of this era.
34 Chadwick in *Sporting Life*, November 15, 1890.

faster than most professionals can run," stood ready. The manager was "all that a father could be to the boys," and the scorekeeper could keep an accurate double entry book with his pocket knife.[35]

Perhaps a more clever example of tall-story humor is this description of Spalding's pitching style by a New York *Star* reporter: "On receiving the ball, he raises it in both hands until it is on a level with his left eye. Striking an attitude he gazes at it two or three minutes in a contemplative way, and then turns it around once or twice to be sure that it is not an orange or coconut. Assured that he has the genuine article . . . and after a scowl at the short stop, and a glance at homeplate, finally delivers the ball with the precision and rapidity of a cannon shot."[36]

While some writers imitated Chadwick's crusading spirit, most used their critical faculties to condemn the local team's lack of strategy and discipline or to berate the umpire. In 1872, a Boston *Herald* man gave an example of this type of petty criticism: "The umpiring of the game by Mr. Chandler was fair and impartial, notwithstanding the growling which was to be expected from a New York club."[37]

Perhaps the crankiness of such reporters was due to cramped press facilities. In 1869 a Washington reporter complained that he had to "squat on the grass," because the press area was "occupied and surrounded by bogus reporters and other dead beats, usurping the privileges of the press."[38] Apparently criticism helped at times, for in 1871 a Philadelphia writer praised the press facilities of the Athletics' new park saying, "The reporters stand will be placed directly back of the catcher, and will be elevated sufficiently to be out of the reach of strong foul balls that may chance that way."[39]

While often behaving like petty, carping critics, the reporters of this era helped to make public heroes out of good players and pay-

---

[35] George Wright, "Sketch of the National Game of Baseball," *Records of the Columbia Historical Society* (ed. by John Larner), XXVII, 84–85.

[36] *Register* (Rockford, Ill.), June 4, 1870.

[37] *Herald* (Boston), May 13, 1872.

[38] *The Evening Star* (Washington, D.C.), June 26, 1869.

[39] *New York Clipper*, April 1, 1871.

ing customers out of many urbanites. By catering to public demand for news about baseball, the sportswriter became an important factor in this rising entertainment industry. Indeed, some might argue that the baseball page has a claim to being a leisure pastime in its own right, because its vicarious thrills and escapist descriptions certainly compensate for some of the grimmer realities of urban-industrial life.

 II. *Baseball's Golden Age*

7

The Age of "Pop" Anson

W 1. THE CHICAGO DYNASTY

ITH THE ONSET of the 1880's, America's economy took an upward turn that brought unprecedented prosperity to National League promoters, and within five years of the belt-tightening austerities of the late 1870's, club treasurers were tallying unheard-of profits.

The lure that baited urbanites to spend free time and money in league parks was the new public hero, the baseball star. In part a product of keen competition among clubs, this hero was also a creation of sportswriters. His appearance led to ever larger crowds jamming ball parks, and in turn this enabled the stars to far surpass the earnings of most middle-class workers. By the end of the decade an elite cadre of superstars were enjoying an affluent style of life that would not be equaled during the remainder of the century.

The prototype of the new hero-player was tall, burly, hard-hitting Adrian Anson of Chicago. In 1880 the twenty-eight-year-old Anson was named manager of the Chicago club, and over the decade his White Stockings won five pennants. Moreover, when failing to win, they finished close behind, and in the twelve-year period from 1880–92, they were never lower than fourth place. Except for the New York Giants, winners of consecutive pennants in 1888 and 1889, no rival approached this record, making it in a real sense, the age of "Pop" Anson.

A giant of six feet, two inches, Anson weighed over two hundred pounds. He was a versatile performer, who could play any position, but he settled at first base. Hitting was his forte, and he captured four league batting titles in his twenty-two seasons of play and only twice failed to top .300.

The son of an Iowa pioneer who loved baseball and shared his son's diamond dream, Anson was encouraged to play ball. Indeed, the proud father took on the task of getting his husky son his first job in professional ball. In this his zeal was boundless: once he wrote the Chicago management that his son was "a hell of a good player," who would do "nothing else but play ball," and who would hit a homer every time and never miss a fielding chance. Although Chicago in 1870 ignored this unsolicited letter of reference, Rockford hired him, and from there Adrian went to the Athletics, where he played during the association era. At last, in 1876, Chicago realized its earlier oversight and signed a contract with Anson for 1876.

Curiously enough, "Babe" Anson was an unwilling member of that team. Stubborn and rowdy in these early years, he signed only because of the money involved and regretted it almost immediately when the Athletics made a better counteroffer. When his request for a release was refused by Hulbert and Spalding, Anson sulked and refused to practice. But while standing by in street clothes and watching the team practice, the urge to play overcame his bitterness. Joining his new mates proved so pleasant that for the next twenty-two years nothing separated him from the Chicago team. He became captain when Spalding left in 1877, and two years later he became comanager. In 1880, he took full field command.[1]

As a playing manager, Anson became one of the first great, popular heroes of baseball. In his uniform he was formidable in appearance right down to his foot-long shoes, which were armed with a cluster of half-inch cleats on each sole. In time his rugged durability inspired fans in all league cities to dub him with names like "Unk," "Pop," "Pappy," and "the Old Man." And as "Anson's Colts," his team came to be firmly identified with its aging captain.

Since they knew him best, Chicago fans made him a home-town hero. Many years later in a poetical recall of his boyhood, Vachel Lindsay included the Anson cult along with other remembrances from Chicago of the 1880's:

> *When I was nine years old in 1889,*
> *I sent my love a lacy Valentine. . . .*
> *Barnum's bears and tigers could astound . . . .*
> *The baseball rules were changed. That was a gain.*
> *Pop Anson was our darling, pet and pride. . . .*
> *The mocking bird was singing in the lane.*

Gruff, tough, and outspoken, the mustachioed hero captivated fans with his proud swagger as he led his Whites onto the field in single file.[2] A baseball Hercules, Anson also shared the naïveté and intellectual weakness of that Greek god, but being a born showman, he celebrated Chicago's hosting the 1888 Republican convention by marching his men onto the field in black, swallow-tailed coats. Such antics titillated fans as much as his brawling, bullying tactics against umpires. Newsmen found him colorful copy, and a *Clipper* man called him the "Rider Haggard of baseball," a big talker who could hold forth on baseball, politics, and billiards. Over the years his frolicsome behavior inspired a sheaf of articles describing real and imaginary feats, which he rarely refuted. Instead, he rode the crest of public adoration and once even appeared on stage in Charles Hoyt's clumsily written farce, *A Runaway Colt.* Although

[1] *The Sporting News,* May 7, 1887; *Sporting Life,* April 9, 1884.

[2] *Globe-Democrat* (St. Louis), March 27, 1884; Vachel Lindsay, "John L. Sullivan, The Strong Boy of Boston," *Collected Poems* (New York, Macmillan, 1931), 93–94; *New York Clipper,* April 13, 1889.

a theatrical flop, the play testified to the depth of Anson worship among baseball fans.[3]

As he grew older, writers jibed about his "senility." Wearied by such talk in 1892, the forty-year-old manager showed up one day wearing whiskers and looking like Rip van Winkle. After enjoying a good laugh, the fans urged him to remove them, but Anson continued wearing them during the game. Later Chadwick called the stunt an act of "grand sarcasm," but "one of the simplest and most original turns of genius yet recorded."[4] Nevertheless, the "old man image" followed him until the end of his playing days.

Against a background of boisterous tomfoolery Anson stood as the baseball idol of the decade. Although he had his serious moments, he had little of the philosophical concern for the game which characterized Harry Wright. Yet Anson, not Wright, became the hero to the crowds, who found escape from their daily routines by chuckling over the latest caper of their ever boyish "pappy."

An imaginative manager in the early 1880's, Anson employed a strategy which helped to revolutionize the style of play. Gathering together a group of brilliant players, he drove them hard and taught them new tactics, like the use of offensive and defensive signals. He experimented with pitching rotation, effectively alternating the fast-ball pitching Larry Corcoran with slow-baller Fred Goldsmith, while winning three straight pennants. And in 1885–86, by alternating John Clarkson and Jim McCormick, he helped land two more pennants.

Anson's teams were heavy hitters, and his speedy base runners, like Mike "King" Kelly and Billy Sunday, captivated fans with their feats of daring opportunism. Unfettered by English conceptions of good sportsmanship, the Irishman Kelly took advantage of ambiguous rules. Knowing that a single umpire's vision was limited, he once ran from second base to home to win a close game from Boston. By 1885 his base-running prowess approached perfection when he scored 124 runs on 126 hits. Small wonder that Chicago fans considered him their superstar or that Boston, with

---

[3] *Ibid.*, June 21, 1890; *Reach's Official Base Ball Guide*, 1896, pp. 142–43.
[4] *Spalding's Official Base Ball Guide*, 1892, p. 100.

an environment teeming with Irish immigrants, coveted his services. In 1887, Boston landed him by paying an unprecedented $10,000 for his contract.[5]

However, the fleetest White Stocking was pious Billy Sunday, who applied some ethics to his base-stealing. The future evangelist advised would-be players to value good judgment more than speed. Study the pitcher and "always get behind the fielder . . . as you then have him at a disadvantage. He is compelled to keep a sharp 'lookout' for the ball which will be thrown in order to head you off, and . . . he will be compelled . . . to turn around in order to touch you out."[6]

It seems paradoxical that the lumbering Anson surrounded himself with so many fast base-runners, but six of his men were very fleet. Once Fred Pfeffer ran the bases in less than sixteen seconds, and his speed was rivaled by that of George Gore, Ed Williamson, Abner Dalrymple, and Kelly.[7]

As manager of these youthful charges, Anson was respected, but unloved by them. Anson was "matter-of-fact, calculating, and practical" in handling his men. Seemingly indestructible himself, he forced his men to be Spartan and to play with bruised fingers or "faces swollen from severe colds." Yet sportswriter Harry Palmer, who passed these judgments, admired the big captain and declared him to be the greatest judge of "ball playing talent."[8] Concurring in this appraisal was Tim Murnane of the Boston *Daily Globe*, who called Anson the "Baseball Bismarck."[9]

A stern disciplinarian, Anson punished beer-drinkers with hundred-dollar fines, and his nightly bed checks had a legendary thoroughness to them. On one such mission he once found a locked room and correctly concluded that a player was covering for an errant roommate. Resourcefully climbing to peek through the transom, the big captain struck a match for a better view. Sud-

---

[5] Anson, *op. cit.*, 104, 122; *New York Clipper*, May 28, 1881, February 27, 1886, February 19, 1887.

[6] *The Universal Base Ball Guide*, 1890, p. 112.

[7] *New York Clipper*, February 27, 1886.

[8] Harry Palmer, *Stories of the Base Ball Field*, 33–35.

[9] *Daily Globe* (Boston), June 9, 1892.

103

denly, a thrown pillow snuffed out the match and knocked him down, but Anson retaliated by fining both occupants. While such Draconian actions antagonized his men, most conceded his impartiality, and the serious-minded knew that they could escape his heavy hand only by sticking strictly to business. Yet sensitive players resented his domineering attitude; not seldom did good men chafe under him, and when stars like Jim McCormick demanded to be traded from Chicago, this caused some critics to question Anson's methods.[10]

Since Anson often quarreled with umpires, league president Young pegged him as a troublemaker. After fining him $110 for misconduct in 1886, Young declared, "Anson is a hard worker and a good fellow, but I suppose . . . he has walked a hundred miles up and down the first base path in mild deprecation of the umpire's decisions."[11]

If, however, his detractors were many and vociferous, so were his supporters, who credited him with luring thousands to league parks. A *Sporting Life* writer wrote, "Anson's magnetism is not stored up in every piece of human mechanism that is found on the ball field."[12] In 1892 the *Clipper* noticed how many active managers and captains had apprenticed under Anson, naming men like Bill Dahlen, Fred Pfeffer, Hugh Duffy, Pat Tebeau, Mike Kelly, George Van Haltren, Bill Lange, Tom Burns, and Clark Griffith.[13]

An end to his career came with suddenness when Chicago released him in 1898. Refusing to retire gracefully, the forty-six-year-old manager failed in the impossible alternative of raising $150,000, to buy the club from Spalding. Embittered by his failure, he left blaming Spalding. In a final effort to stay active, he took a job as manager of the Giants, but since his brusque personality clashed with that of the hot-tempered Giant president, Andrew Freedman, Anson soon quit. With newspaper plaudits ringing in his ears, he retired in 1898 to his pool room and bowling alley, but as a last

---

[10] *Ibid.*, August 12, 1891; *Sporting Life*, July 30, 1884; *New York Clipper*, February 19, 1898.

[11] *Tribune* (Chicago), July 11, 1886.

[12] *Ibid.*, September 13, 1885.

[13] *New York Clipper*, October 31, 1891.

gesture of defiance, he refused Spalding's offer of a lavish testimonial: "I am neither a pauper nor a rich man and prefer to decline. The public owes me nothing. . . . there are times when one hesitates to receive favors from friends. At this hour I deem it both unwise and inexpedient to accept the generosity."[14]

But in 1880 the years of glory were barely unfolding, and Anson's Chicago team stood poised to capture the first of its five flags. As a freshman manager, Anson developed some new stratagems, like having his fielders back each other on all fielding plays. Soon, while his outfielders were depriving opponents of extra base hits, Anson began encouraging base-stealing experiments. The "scientific play" won Chadwick's approval, and he cited "the very efficient field manager" for having the best-coached team in the league.[15]

Hulbert, however, also kept a tight hand on the reins. On road trips Anson dutifully sent his boss coded dispatches, detailing all his plans. The result was that this tandem combination worked wonders by outmaneuvering all opposition, both on the field and at the box office. Dazzled and enriched by Hulbert's success, the Chicago directors voted their public thanks and renewed confidence in his "manly," moral program. Hulbert's response was to offer more success. Soon, league directors voted approval of his latest proscriptions on Sunday ball and liquor sales, enactments that led directly to the expulsion of Cincinnati for violating the new edicts. A Detroit franchise replaced Cincinnati in 1881.

In 1881, Chicago repeated its victory, but by a narrow margin. In criticizing the close victory, local sportswriters attacked Anson's standpat policy and his weakened discipline. A *Tribune* journalist reported that some players spent too much time in saloons and demanded reprisals. But if he had so desired, Anson could have defended himself by blaming a large number of injuries and the new rule extending the pitching distance by five feet.[16] Hulbert made an equally good target because of his decision

14 Anson, *op. cit.*, 302–305, 337–39; *ibid.*, February 19, 1889.
15 *Spalding's Official Base Ball Guide*, 1881, pp. 11–13, 16, 21–22, 24–27.
16 Anson, *op. cit.*, 105–106; *Tribune* (Chicago), June 12, 26, October 1, 2, 1881; *New York Clipper*, August 27, 1881.

to allow the team to play Troy on September 26, a day designated as a national day of mourning for President Garfield. This mercenary action so angered *Tribune* editor Joseph Medill that he withheld coverage of Chicago's games throughout the following season. The ban was relaxed briefly in April, 1882, when the shocking news of Hulbert's own death was reported.

A moralist to the end, Hulbert had a heart attack shortly after he had ordered lifetime suspensions for the ten chronic lushers of the league. He at least lived long enough to see the league enter a profitable era, which his eulogists charitably ascribed to his puritanic policies. But the fact that the bereaved directors were unwilling to grant Hulbert's successor autocratic powers testifies to an atmosphere of relief in his passing from the scene.[17]

Hulbert's death also left a leadership vacancy in Chicago, which Spalding agreed to fill despite his extensive business commitments. Since business came first in Spalding's scheme of things, Anson gained power, and he again chose to stand pat with his strong team. Once again the White Stockings were victorious, but only after a close battle with Harry Wright's Providence Grays. Indeed, two fortunate breaks saved Chicago from defeat: the first came in a late season clash between the two rivals when hard-sliding Mike Kelly knocked the ball from George Wright's hands, permitting the winning runs to score over Harry's futile protests; the second came later in the season when the financially crippled Buffalo team received permission to transfer its last three Chicago games to Chicago in the interest of making more money. Since this action gave the Whites a home-field advantage, Anson made the most of it by winning three games from the heavy-hitting Buffalos to clinch the flag. Once again Wright screamed vain protests, which were silenced somewhat when Chicago beat Wright's team in a postseason series, which was scheduled by a conscience-stricken league committee.[18]

---

[17] *Tribune* (Chicago), April 11, 1882; *Spalding's Official Base Ball Guide*, 1882, p. 86; 1883, pp. 5–11.

[18] Anson, *op. cit.*, 107; *Tribune* (Chicago), May 28, September 26, 27, 29, 1882; *New York Clipper*, September 30, October 7, 1882; Mike Kelly, *"Play Ball," Stories of*

Meanwhile, mounting profits found the league facing stiff competition from a newly established major-league rival, the American Association. This prompted the league to rescind its earlier boycott of New York and Philadelphia. With these cities again represented, opposition stiffened, and Anson's 1883 team, despite the addition of newcomers like Billy Sunday and Fred Pfeffer, were outdistanced by a veteran Boston team, ably managed by John Morrill. Paced by the fast-ball pitching of big Jim Whitney and inspired by old pros like second baseman Joe Burdock, the Bostons surprised everyone, especially the club's tight-fisted president, Arthur H. Soden. The unexpected victory, with its attendant profits, prompted Soden to expand his park to accommodate more fans for the 1884 season. Elsewhere, other standpatters, gladdened by baseball's new prosperity, were doing the same.[19]

With outsiders eager to share in the profits of major league baseball, the league in 1884 faced competition not only from the American Association, but also from the newly established Union Association. To combat the threat, the league sensed that it would have to come up with something new if it hoped to retain its exalted public position. Another colorless champion like the 1883 Bostons might prove fatal, but luck was with the league. That fall the rules committee altered the style of play by conceding the right of pitchers to throw overhand.[20] While this was intended to restore the balance between the pitcher and the batter, recently disrupted by the increased pitching distance, it inadvertently created a new hero in the person of pitcher Charles Radbourne.

Born in Rochester, New York, and one of a family of eighteen children, Radbourne had been a professional pitcher for six years. Possessing a baffling curve ball and an irascible temper, he was a hard man to manage. One writer declared his catcher to be an unsung martyr for putting up with the "erratic, ill-tempered and capricious Lord Radbourne . . . without a murmur," but another

the Ball Field, 28–31; Jim O'Rourke to Harry Wright, September 25, October 12, 1882. Wright, Correspondence, Vol. II.

[19] *New York Clipper*, June 2, October 6, 1883; *Daily Globe* (Boston), July 8, 1883; *Herald* (Boston), August 26, 1883.

[20] *Spalding's Official Base Ball Guide*, 1884, pp. 11–27, 110–111.

claimed that such shortcomings were not unusual among men of his genius. Admitting that "Rad" was swelled-headed, the journalist stated that "this does not detract from his ability . . . for when he does 'let himself out,' there is some excuse for his vanity."[21]

A marked man in league circles, Radbourne was an unlikely candidate for the heroship of 1884. Signed to play with Providence in 1883, he required careful handling by Harry Wright. When Wright resigned to manage the Phillies, he was replaced by the unimaginative F. C. Bancroft, who soon quarreled violently with Radbourne and other players. Indeed, before the 1884 season, Radbourne was approached by Union Association capitalists, who offered him a $2,000 bonus to jump to their circuit. Although Radbourne refused the offer, he had an early-season quarrel with Bancroft, who in turn used Charles Sweeny as his starting pitcher. But Sweeny, too, was temperamental, as well as a drunkard. When Bancroft berated him for an all-day drinking spree, Sweeny packed up and jumped to the Unions, leaving Bancroft no choice but to accommodate Radbourne. Since much of Radbourne's troubles stemmed from rivalry with Sweeny, he boldly announced that he would pitch every game until his team clinched the flag, provided that the directors would lift his suspension and agree to release him at the close of the season.[22]

This they did, and pitch he did, and from July 23 until late September, he accomplished one of the most remarkable pitching feats in major-league history. Altogether he won sixty-two of the seventy-four games in which he pitched, and by pitching thirty-five of his team's last thirty-seven games, he literally carried his team to the pennant. His record of consecutive appearances was heroic for an overhand pitcher; from July 23 to August 7, he appeared in nine straight games, winning seven, tying one, and losing one. After this exhaustive effort he spent an off day playing right field, and then returned to the mound for the next six games, winning all.

[21] *Sporting Life*, September 24, October 29, 1884; *New York Clipper*, February 25, 1885, May 24, 1890; T. P. Sullivan, *Humorous Stories of the Ball Field*, 252–53.

[22] *Sporting Life*, July 30, 1884; *New York Clipper*, May 24, July 26, 1884; *Daily Journal and General Advertiser* (Providence, R.I.), April 29, June 14, July 14, 17, October 6, 1884; *Spalding's Official Base Ball Guide*, 1885, p. 97–98.

After another day of rest, playing shortstop, he launched his strongest drive. Beginning with a game on August 21, he appeared as pitcher in the next twenty games, winning ten before losing one to Buffalo on September 9. The defeat ended a twenty-game winning streak for his team and his personal sixteen-game winning streak. Backed by such heroics, Providence clinched the flag early and finished ten games ahead of Chicago at the end of the season.

Although this splendid performance outshone the deeds of the American Association, whose pennant went to the New York Mets, and the moribund Union Association, it was wasted on the city of Providence. There the Grays drew poorly, with less than one thousand attending even the most crucial games. Nevertheless, Radbourne was rewarded with a bonus, and the thirty-year-old impresario responded by easily beating the Mets in the first official World Series encounter and by withdrawing his request to be traded.

This easy triumph, coupled with the collapse of the Union Association, restored the league's pre-eminence.[23] Since their rivals had been crushed or accommodated, the league directors turned from power politics to a renewed quest of the moral image, which they believed to be the key to public support. To this end they replaced their president, tough A. G. Mills, with the gentlemanly Nick Young. As a figurehead president, Young at least was given power to suspend crooks, drunks, and rowdies in the ranks of league players.[24]

The real drawing power of the league, however, was its player-heroes, who, more than morality, were the measure of its popularity. By 1885, they restored the league's superiority by beating American Association rivals in a series of preseason exhibition games. Helping to maintain this superiority was "Cap" Anson, who was again ready with a powerful team, built around pitcher John Clarkson. Clarkson's ability to catalogue the batting weaknesses of rival players complemented his natural talents.[25] Confident of Anson's evaluation of his rejuvenated team, President

---

[23] *Daily Journal and General Advertiser* (Providence, R. I.), September 8, 22, 27, October 17, 27, 1884; *New York Clipper*, September 13, November 1, 1884.

[24] *Spalding's Official Base Ball Guide*, 1885, pp. 9, 93, 96–98.

[25] Palmer, *op. cit.*, 45–54.

Spalding persuaded his fellow directors to invest thirty thousand dollars in a new ball park, located at Congress and Loomis Streets, an easy, fifteen-minute horsecar ride from the center of Chicago. If the larger seating capacity failed to recoup the investment through baseball attendance, Spalding stood ready with other leisure attractions. Accordingly, the park was outfitted for cycling, lacrosse, lawn tennis, and track.[26]

It was a gamble that paid handsomely, for on the day that Chicago defeated the Giants, a new attendance record was set. However, Anson's return to power was marred by the plucky Browns of the association, who reopened the question of league superiority by tying the Whites in the postseason World Series.[27]

Also undermining the league's stability was the poverty gap between the rich clubs, like Chicago, New York, and Boston, and the poor ones, like Providence and Buffalo. The poorer clubs were forced to recoup their losses by selling some of their better players. In a spectacular deal late in the 1885 campaign, Buffalo sold its "big four," Dan Brouthers, Jim White, Dave Rowe, and Hardie Richardson, to Detroit for $7,000. Since no rules prohibited such sales, President Young ruled that the rejuvenated Detroits must not play the newly purchased players against the pennant contenders.[28] But hard after this came the announcement of Boston's purchase of the entire Providence franchise for $6,600.[29] As a result of the two deals, both Buffalo and Providence dropped out of the league and were replaced by Washington, D.C., and Kansas City, Missouri, franchises. Although the sales prompted league directors to impose a vague rule regulating such sales, they continued to depend largely on political alignments to block the machinations of their fellow directors who sought to purchase pennants.

As it turned out, Detroit became the strongest of the new challengers, but its pitching was weak. During the 1886 season Detroit owner Fred Stearns tried to buy a pitcher, but Spalding's faction effectively checkmated him by persuading the would-be seller to

[26] *Tribune* (Chicago), May 31, 1885.
[27] *Spalding's Official Base Ball Guide,* 1886, pp. 64, 67.
[28] *New York Clipper,* September 26, 1885.
[29] *Ibid.,* December 5, 1885.

not sell.[30] This helped Anson to stave off the Detroits and land another pennant, the fifth of the decade, after his team forged ahead in the final month.[31] Although victorious, Anson's standpat posture was criticized, and a *Tribune* writer suggested that, "A few new faces in the ranks of the Whites will be a refreshing sight."[32]

For a brief time criticisms of Anson were stilled by the flush of pennant victory, but they rang with greater clamor when Chicago lost the World Series to the Browns. Since the series was held on a winner-take-all basis, the defeat cut deeply, and a disgusted Spalding even refused to pay the team's train fare from St. Louis.[33] But if the series defeat convinced Spalding of the need to rebuild, disturbances from some of his prima donnas helped to sour him. Earlier in the year he was forced to offer bonuses of $350 to Kelly and McCormick in order to persuade them to stop drinking heavily. When neither qualified for his temperance award, both complained, which in turn made Spalding furious.[34]

Faced with a serious morale problem, Spalding moved fast, and over the winter he electrified the baseball world by announcing Kelly's sale to Boston for the unheard-of sum of $10,000. Not only was such a sale unprecedented, but its legitimacy posed a knotty problem for league decision makers. In the meantime, however, both Spalding and Kelly were pleased, Kelly because he was to get a $5,000 salary for captaining Boston.[35]

Kelly's release was a vote of confidence in Anson, and the players were told that "so long as Anson is with us he will remain Captain of the Chicagos."[36] Shortly, thereafter, Spalding swung his ax again, and this time McCormick and veteran outfielders George Gore and Abner Dalrymple were sold. Finally, the Chicago president climaxed his work by selling Clarkson to Boston in 1888 for another $10,000. Obviously Anson's task was clear, he must seek

---

[30] *Tribune* (Chicago), August 28, 1886.

[31] *Spalding's Official Base Ball Guide,* 1887, pp. 13–21.

[32] *Wright and Ditson's Base Ball Guide,* 1886, pp. 10–12.

[33] *Tribune* (Chicago), October 24, 1886.

[34] *The Sporting News,* November 20, 1886; *New York Clipper,* July 31, 1886.

[35] *Free Press* (Detroit), February 21, 1887.

[36] *Ibid.,* February 15, 1887; *New York Clipper,* February 19, 1887.

young players and rebuild. This he would do, and although his "Colts" became a colorful team, they never terrorized the league like his old champions. In a real sense, the age of Anson ended in 1888.

2. GIANTS IN THE LAND

Although their work was overshadowed by Spalding's sales, the league rule makers prepared a little excitement of their own for the 1887 season. In an effort to strengthen offensive power, they voted to give a batter four strikes, and if a batter walked on five balls, he was to be credited with a base hit. In defending the move, President Young admitted that the object was to fatten scoring and batting averages, however, in comforting pitchers, he pointed out that the committee also had abolished the batter's traditional right to request a high or low strike zone.[37]

This was small comfort to pitchers who protested the futility of trying for strikeouts[38] or for managers lacking heavy hitters. Also, Detroit had cornered the batting market with its purchase of the big four in 1885. As the brains behind the 1887 Detroit club, Frederick Kimball Stearns, the heir to a lucrative pharmaceutical business, had learned to love baseball while in college. In searching for a socially approved pastime in which to invest his money, he chose major-league baseball. Naturally, the beleagured promoters of Detroit's struggling franchise welcomed such support. At the time of Stearns's arrival in 1885, they were planning to dissolve their club, but canny, young Stearns kept the would-be buyers dangling while he himself dickered for the purchase of the Buffalo sluggers. In doing so, he outmaneuvered buyers from New York, Chicago, and Boston, who also sought the Buffalo foursome. When he followed this coup with the purchase of some key Indianapolis players, sportswriters hailed him as the league's "Napoleon."[39]

Having spent $25,000 to fortify his team's chances, Stearns

37 The four-strike rule lasted only for the 1887 season.

38 *Spalding's Official Base Ball Guide*, 1887, 127–35; *Free Press* (Detroit), February 28, 1887.

39 *Free Press* (Detroit), September 16, 21, 22, 1885; *New York Clipper*, September 26, 1885, February 27, 1886.

rather naïvely told reporters how he planned to recoup. Knowing that Detroiters preferred horse racing to baseball spectaculars, he proposed to take advantage of the league's policy which granted visiting teams a share of each admission. The Detroit club, in short, was to be a parasite franchise, one whose fortunes must come from road revenue.[40]

Once understood, Stearns's rivals easily turned this transparent scheme against him. In the fall of 1886, over his outraged cries, they abolished the old policy of splitting gate receipts on a percentage basis and substituted a fixed guarantee plan. Under the new plan visitors received a fixed sum of only $125 a game; all receipts above this went to the home team.[41] While squelching Stearns, this decision, favoring as it did the wealthy franchises, would only deepen the league's instability by widening the gap between the rich and poor franchises. Yet, such an act certainly mirrored the prevailing ideology of economic individualism, with its "hoe-your-own-row" credo.

An immediate effect, of course, was to seal the economic fate of the Detroit Wolverines at the very moment when its championship hopes were highest. Saddled with a heavy capital outlay, including a payroll of over $36,000, Stearns for a time threatened to jump to the rival American Association. But when this bluff was called, Stearns appealed to Detroit leisure-seekers to support the club. However, only six hundred season tickets were sold by April of 1887, making the prospect of a bad financial beating almost certain.[42]

Nevertheless, Stearns's formidable team returned from spring training in the South in good shape. Nominally under the leadership of the blustering W. H. Watkins,[43] its real strategist was Captain Ned Hanlon. Nearing the end of a brilliant playing career, Hanlon nursed managerial aspirations, which soon came to pass. But in 1887, he and catcher Charles Bennett supplied the tactical leadership that made the club the terror of the league.

[40] *Sporting Life*, November 24, 1886.
[41] *New York Clipper*, December 4, 1886; *Free Press* (Detroit), January 2, 1887.
[42] *Ibid.*, February 28, April 3, 19, 1887.
[43] *Ibid.*, April 3, 1887; *New York Clipper*, December 24, 1887.

Perhaps the most formidable of the brawny sluggers was Dan Brouthers. A powerful six-footer, the thirty-one-year-old first baseman already had two league batting titles to his credit. Before retiring in 1896, he would rank as a superstar, having bettered the .300 batting mark fourteen times. Rivaling Anson in durability, he would continue to play professional ball in the high minors until he reached the age of forty-eight, thus easily discrediting an early judgment that "he was not built right for a ball player." In 1887, he managed at least one base hit or its equivalent in 107 of the 122 games in which he played.[44]

With Brouthers leading a mighty "sequential slugging" attack, the Wolverines usually overcame its pitching weakness. Detroit's 1887 pennant victory owed most to its .343 team batting average, a figure made possible by the plus .400 efforts of Brouthers and Sam Thompson, and by the league rule that credited a batter's base on balls as a hit.

In spite of these Olympian efforts, attendance was as poor as expected, and Stearns greedily accepted the chance to play a fifteen-game World Series with the association champions. With the Browns as the opposition, Detroit took an early lead and crushed the Browns ten games to five, thereby avenging the 1886 humiliation of Chicago.[45]

Having won dual championships, Stearns had little choice but to stick it out for another season, even though his share of the prosperous 1887 season was meager. Nevertheless, he resigned the club presidency at the close of the campaign in order to allow the directors free choice in deciding the fate of the franchise.[46] Although an offer of $75,000 for all of the club's assets was pending, the directors voted to continue operations when the league decided to restore a percentage system of dividing gate receipts for the 1888 season.

Unhappily for the promoters, this pitching-poor team faded to

[44] The Detroit Tribune Publishing Company, *The Detroit Tribune's Epitome of Base Ball*, 22–30.

[45] *Free Press* (Detroit), September 30, October 9, 11, 23, 26, 27, 1887.

[46] *New York Clipper*, July 23, December 24, 1887; *Sporting Life*, June 8, 1887; *Spalding's Official Base Ball Guide*, 1888, pp. 8–11.

fifth place in 1888, which meant that road attendance also decreased. Faced with seasonal losses of $15,000, the directors sold the club in 1888 for $55,000, a price good enough to allow each $50 share of stock to be paid off at $135.[47] At a later date this franchise would become a profitable American League team, but the surrender of the franchise in 1888 was a protest to the league policy of economic individualism, which ran roughshod over the weaker entries.

As Detroit's sun set, another band of giants saw their star of empire rise. Dubbed "Giants" by the New York press and their ebullient manager, the New York team had gained strength steadily since 1883. Its rise owed much to the promotional acumen of its owners, known as the Metropolitan Exhibition Company. Since no rule prohibited anyone from owning clubs in both the National League and the American Association, the company sponsored two clubs. But when New York fans showed a preference for the league, the owners shrewdly planted the best players on the Giant roster. Naturally this angered the association leaders, but they could do little at first to stop it. Eventually they forced the company to surrender its association entry, but not without a great blow to the association's prestige.[48]

Enhancing the Giants' popularity was Jim Mutrie, the colorful field manager. A native of Massachusetts, Jim Mutrie had a brief playing career. After a season with the league's Worcester team, he moved to New York and organized the Mets as an independent professional team. After watching the association's auspicious beginnings, he enrolled the team for 1883 and won a pennant in 1884. However, he was soon convinced that greater cash and glory could come from league affiliation.

When New York fans supported his new Giant team, Mutrie basked in its glory and in the company of the sports celebrities, who used Nick Engel's "Home Plate" restaurant as their headquarters. As Engel's son later recalled, "Mutrie would arrive at

---

[47] *Sporting Life*, March 16, June 1, 1889; *Free Press* (Detroit), October 7, 14, 15, 16, 1888.

[48] *New York Clipper*, June 21, 1884, April 4, September 19, 1885.

the park dressed formally—high hat, tails and all—and parade around the park shouting, 'Who are the people?' Without waiting for a reply, he would scream, 'The Giant fans are the people!' "[49]

Although Jim Mutrie did much for the club, the tactical command was in the sound hands of John Ward. Once famed as a great Providence pitcher, Ward was now by choice and hard work a first-rate shortstop. Impressed by his studious approach to the game, the Giant directors named him captain, and under him the club's fortunes improved steadily.

Because of a salary wrangle, Ward resigned the captaincy in 1888, but he was on hand to give advice to his successor, catcher William "Buck" Ewing. That year the team mounted a slugging attack, backed by the fine pitching of Tim Keefe and Mickey Welch. Of the two, Keefe was more effective, but Welch pitched well despite his love of beer. Indeed, "Smiling Mickey" credited beer for his pitching effectiveness, saying, "Pure elixir of malt and hops, Beats all the drugs and all the drops."[50]

The batting hero was first-baseman Roger Connor, who in 1886 struck "the longest hit . . . ever made in this city." Despite an ugly hand injury sustained during the off-season, Connor set an 1887 league record with seventeen home runs. But in spite of his hitting, he was perennially overshadowed by such Olympian rivals as Anson and Brouthers. Still, to New Yorkers, he was a superstar, and so much so that in 1915 a cub reporter, covering a Connecticut school game, came to understand just how much of an idol he was. Still a hero eighteen years after hanging up his cleats, Connor, a tall man with a handle-bar moustache could make kids "stop in the streets and stand at respectful attention as he drove by in his horse-drawn buggy, making his daily rounds of the public schools."[51]

Adding to the team's awesome image was their tight-fitting "funeral uniforms," designed and sold to the club by pitcher Keefe.

---

[49] *Times* (New York), September 29, 1957; June Rankin, *The New York and Brooklyn Base Ball Clubs*, no page numbers.

[50] *Ibid.*, no page numbers; *Sporting Life*, April 18, 25, 1888.

[51] *Free Press* (Detroit), March 27, 1887; *Spalding's Official Base Ball Guide*, 1886, p. 61; *Daily Mirror* (New York), February 3, 1950 (Dan Parker's column).

The uniform was entirely black, except for the white raised letters that spelled "New York" across the breast.[52]

But even this wealthiest of league franchises was not without weighty problems. Since the mid-1880's, the city's Central Park commission sought to pre-empt its rented Polo Grounds to build a roadway. Up to 1888 the club had fended off the threat by the traditional methods of bribery, but now only a temporary injunction barred the inevitable seizure. Other difficulties included salary squabbles, involving key players like Ward and Keefe.[53]

With the team lagging until July, the team looked like the "same old Giants," but fans seemingly sensed a pennant in the offing. Large crowds repeatedly jammed the old Polo Grounds, and when 13,333 showed up on Memorial Day, even the *Times* was convinced that baseball served a positive function in an industrial society. Describing the enthusiasm of the men and boys "who are confined in offices, shops and factories during the week days, and who have to content themselves for months with reading accounts of games," the writer delighted in the way they "jumped about like colts, stamped their feet, clapped their hands, threw their hats in the air, slapped their companions on the back, winked knowingly ... and from a baseball standpoint, enjoyed themselves hugely."[54]

Later generations of New York fans would take major league championships in stride, but not those of 1888. That fall the city went all out for the team that landed their first league pennant. A benefit at the State Theatre attracted a throng of dignitaries, who paid ten dollars each for seats. At the ceremony Congressman Cummings furthered his own cause by awarding the pennant, but the real entertainment was the speeches by the player-heroes and by the heroes of vaudeville. Dockstadter's Minstrels performed, De Wolfe Hopper did his famous monologue on "How Casey Lost the Game," and Maurice Barrymore gave a recitation. Another highlight came when artist Homer Emmons unveiled a huge drawing of the Polo Grounds. Altogether the affair netted $6,000, twice

[52] *Times* (New York), July 29, 1888; *New York Clipper*, August 18, 1888.

[53] Rankin, *op. cit.*, no page numbers; *New York Clipper*, June 25, 1888; *Times* (New York), April 3, 22, 1888.

[54] *Times* (New York), May 31, 1888.

117

that which was expected, and the sum was divided among grateful players.[55]

Thus inspired, the Giants met the Browns in the World Series and thrashed them soundly, the decisive victory in the nine-game set coming in St. Louis before four-thousand Browns's "mourners."[56]

Nonetheless, some powerful interest groups cared little for the city's pride. It was in February, 1889, that the Giant directors received the shocking news that the city would soon demolish the old Polo Grounds. The suddenness of the move shocked the directors, who believed the matter to be safely tied up in the courts. A last minute plea in the form of an offer to donate $10,000 to city charities for another year's stay was ignored.[57]

For a time the legal defeat caused the directors to consider taking the franchise out of town, but in 1889 there were no beckoning West Coast cities with enticing concessions. Indeed, in 1888 no urban area could match New York's drawing power for spectator sports. Still the thought that the club might make good its threat frightened the mayor, who like his 1957 counterpart, dangled an offer of free land in the Long Island area. Supporting his plea was the *Clipper* editor, who dolefully commented, "The Polo Grounds seems almost like part of the club, and to deprive the club of its grounds is like depriving it of part of its honor."

Among the offers that poured in was one inviting the club to use the Staten Island grounds, formerly occupied by the ill-fated Mets. Another citizen urged the club to build a new polo grounds on the uptown Astor Estate, a site easily accessible by train or boat. In the end it was decided to use the Staten Island site temporarily, while awaiting the construction of new grounds on the Astor property.[58]

Nor did the club's difficulties end with its foster-child status. A full-scale players revolt was threatening major league baseball, and in 1889 two leaders of the players movement were Giants

[55] *Ibid.*, October 9, 14, 15, 1888.

[56] *Sporting Life*, October 10, 17, 31, 1888.

[57] *Times* (New York), February 9, March 22, 28, 31, 1889; *New York Clipper*, February 23, 1889.

[58] *Ibid.*, February 23, 1889; *Times* (New York), February 16, 1889.

Ward and Keefe, who were loudly protesting the league's attempt to put a ceiling on player salaries.

Furthermore, Boston's rise to power could not be ignored. In March, 1889, Boston purchased the Detroit stars and now posed a real threat. Fortunately for the Giants, pitcher Ned Crane carried the team during its Staten Island exile. This slugging pitcher's rise was brilliant, but brief. The team may have been helped also by the flooded field conditions at Staten Island, which were part of the same torrential rains that had produced the tragic Johnstown flood in May. With flooded grounds, the management had boards placed in the outfield to prevent injury to fielders. By accustoming themselves to such conditions, the Giant fielders gained advantages over puzzled visitors.[59]

That year the floods upset the first half of the league schedule. With all clubs facing postponements, the Giants held their own against Boston and in July received a major morale boost with the completion of new polo grounds. On July 8, after twenty-five games at Staten Island, the team returned to Manhattan. On hand to greet them and to view the new grounds were nine thousand fans. But if prosperity returned, other misfortunes dogged the team. In September more heavy rains caused the Harlem River to overflow, inundating the new park. This kept the team idle while Boston kept on playing and winning. So keen was competition at this point that rumor had it that Boston directors were giving cash incentives to pitcher Clarkson.

Not until the very last game was the issue settled. On October 5, the Giants won the pennant by beating Cleveland while Pittsburgh was beating Boston. But if Clarkson had won his game for Boston, the pennant would have gone to Beantown. It was the closest race in the league's fourteen-year history, and an exciting triumph for the 201,662 fans that had watched the Giants throughout the year. Under the circumstances it is understandable that the relieved Giants celebrated the victory by smashing Mutrie's famous top hat.[60]

[59] *Sporting Life*, May 8, June 1, 1889.
[60] *Ibid.*, July 3, September 25, October 16, 1889; *New York Clipper*, June 29,

Afterwards, in a dull World Series, the Giants beat the Brooklyn Bridegrooms of the association, six games to three. Although marred by unseasonably cold weather, the games netted profits of over $12,000, of which each player received a $380 share. Having made themselves an annual profit of $45,000, the Giant owners could afford to be generous.[61]

Yet the brilliant campaign of 1889 marked the end of the golden age of major league baseball. Ahead lay the forbidding prospect of a costly war with the militant Players League. With battle lines already drawn, the Giant owners watched in anguish as key players seceded to join the ranks of the organized players. Two years would pass before the league again would enjoy a campaign untroubled by conflict with a powerful rival, but when comparative stability returned, the structure of major league baseball would be drastically altered. Thus, the profitable 1880's was followed by the austere 1890's a feudal age in which individualistic magnates would try vainly to win back the public, whose tastes in leisure pastimes had undergone new diversification.

July 20, September 21, 28, October 23, 1889; *Spalding's Official Base Ball Guide,* 1890, pp. 38–39.

[61] *Sporting Life,* October 30, November 6, December 25, 1889; *Spalding's Official Base Ball Guide,* 1890, pp. 117–18.

8

The Interlopers

1. THE BEER BALL LEAGUE

A POST-MORTEM REVIEW of National League fortunes up to 1881 reveals that morality is not a guarantee of profits. Aside from slim gate receipts Hulbert's administration left a trail of ruined franchises along its righteous path. Expelled for playing Sunday games and selling liquor, the Cincinnati Club, the most recent sacrifice on the league's moral altar, went the way of past victims like Philadelphia and New York.

The wisdom of Hulbert's Draconic actions is questionable, for by denying major-league ball to these cities, he really was punishing an entire urban area for the sins of a single franchise. Moreover, he jeopardized the league's dominant status, since in many cases outlawed promoters merely established rival leagues as a means of taking advantage of public interest in baseball. By 1878 some of these ventures were succeeding so well that some promoters were ready to risk a rival major league.

Fearful of this threat, league men that year tried to head it off by creating the League Alliance, a kind of mutual protective organization of professional leagues, under the suzerainty of the National League. Membership was open to clubs whose existence was "not inconsistent" with the league's, meaning that none claimed major-league status. Among other privileges vassals were offered an offensive-defensive protective alliance against baseball predators, provided that all members followed league guidelines on matters such as player contracts, black lists, and playing rules. Simply put, the League Alliance was a pooling scheme with the league aiming at nothing less than full control over organized baseball. All insiders were to be granted life; all outsiders were branded renegades.[1]

The National League's inability to punish maverick operators, however, soon convinced others that the alliance was a paper tiger. As early as 1879 the thriving Inter-State League bucked league opposition and planted a franchise in New York.[2] When others found profits in operating outside the alliance, some investors, whose appetites were whetted by dreams of profits that could be made by invading rich black-listed areas like Philadelphia and New York, began talking about building a rival major league.[3]

Among the boldest plotters was an 1881 group, headed by sports-writer O. P. Caylor, which was hatching a plan to build a rival league. Despite security measures, rumors leaked out, and the Chicago *Tribune* sneeringly warned that a "Beer-Ball League" was in the offing. However, when the National League took no counteraction, the intruders pressed on with plans for an organizational meeting.[4]

On November 1, 1881, an enthusiastic group of promoters met in Cincinnati under the slogan "Liberty For All," and with the avowed intention of building a major league. Delegates hailed from

[1] *Spalding's Official Base Ball Guide,* 1878, pp. 1–23.

[2] Robert L. Finch (ed.) *The Story of Minor League Baseball,* 15–20.

[3] *The Sporting Life's Official Base Ball Guide and Hand Book of the National Game,* 1891, pp. 42–63.

[4] *Reach's Official Base Ball Guide,* 1884, p. 18, 1889, pp. 3–10.

Brooklyn, St. Louis, Pittsburgh, Cincinnati, Columbus, and Philadelphia, along with some interested speculators from New York.
Notwithstanding some factional discord, their first day's work
was so impressive that the Cincinnati *Commercial* headlined its
account "The New Deal," and announced the birth of the American Association of Base Ball Clubs.[5]

Mutual business interests contributed mightily to the co-operative spirit, for four brewmasters among the delegates made common cause of their desire to foster the sales of "German tea"
through baseball promotion.[6] Working as a special interest group,
the quartet of Chris Von der Ahe, John Hauck, Harry Von der
Horst, and John Park persuaded the others not to forbid "the sale
of liquors or playing of Sunday games on the club's grounds."
Otherwise the delegates openly copied the league constitution and
saw no inconsistency in inserting tough punishments for drinking
players.

Having pirated a constitution and tailored it to the interests of
John Barleycorn, the delegates moved to tighten the organization.
An arbitration committee worked rapidly on the problem of franchises and solved a problem of two competing Philadelphia franchises by persuading the rivals to merge. However, this same tact
failed in the case of two rival New York franchises, which decided
to bow out.[7] This was a disappointment, for the promoters desperately wanted a New York entry; hence, overtures were made to
the New York Mets, an independent alliance team, which played
151 games during the previous season. But when Hulbert offered
the Mets an opportunity to join the league, the Met directors decided to wait a year and see which way the wind blew.[8]

Shaking off their disappointment, the interlopers pressed on and
named Denny McKnight their first president. His first act was to
issue an invitation to league players to jump to the association,

[5] *New York Clipper*, November 12, 1881; *Commercial* (Cincinnati), November 2,
3, 1881.

[6] *Ibid.*, November 2, 1881.

[7] *Ibid.*, November 4, 1881.

[8] *New York Clipper*, November 12, 1881; *Reach's Official Base Ball Guide*, 1889,
pp. 3–10.

promising them more security. For one thing, he guaranteed that upon being released they would be given severance pay and would be free agents. McKnight also wooed the fans, vowing a good brand of ball and playing up the fact that the association would bring baseball to cities which had been black-listed by the league. Fans were also told that the association would charge a basic admission price of 25 cents.[9] Although the low admission charge had much to do with winning initial support from fans, it later threatened the stability of the circuit.

Fearful now of league reprisals, McKnight openly lectured Hulbert on his responsibility to the baseball public. Attacking the league's selfish policy of barring major-league baseball to the 2,370,000 people in the association's territory, McKnight warned Hulbert that the league was outnumbered and that league territory encompassed only 1,156,000 people. If Hulbert dared to tamper with association contracts, McKnight threatened to hire the league's black-listed players.[10]

With antileague sentiments running high, the association men met again in 1882 to tighten their organization. Although most members of the association wanted peace and backed McKnight in his hope for coexistence, the league was in no mood for conciliation. Already some players were blackmailing league directors for higher salaries by threatening to jump to the association. Thus, league men had to capitulate to keep their stars in line. Hence, when the league tried to use its alliance to keep their rivals from getting players, the new circuit bravely retaliated by creating its own "American Alliance." In the end the association managed to entice a number of aging players to leave the league.[11]

Although fielding only six teams in 1882, the American Association held out and widened the scope of major-league baseball by bringing an acceptable kind of ball game into neglected urban areas. Also, by providing opportunities for untried players, the

[9] *Commercial* (Cincinnati), November 6, 1881; *New York Clipper*, November 12, 1881.

[10] *Ibid.*, January 7, 1882.

[11] *Commercial* (Cincinnati), March 13, 1882; *DeWitt's Base Ball Guide*, 1882, pp. 64–65.

association rekindled youthful interest in professional baseball, and by bringing Sunday baseball and ball-park saloons into areas where the Continental Sunday was acceptable, the circuit helped mitigate some of the drudgery of the six-day industrial work week.

Of course there were weaknesses. Editor Francis Richter noted that the association promoters were generally less competent than their league counterparts, and the 25 cent admission rate, despite its initial success, soon became a liability, especially when player salaries had to be increased. Nevertheless, the association became the league's only "permanent rival of the nineteenth century," and its spirited rivalry triggered the profitable baseball boom of the 1880's.[12]

But in 1882 modest hope was the posture of the worried promoters, whose chief desire was to survive the coming conflict. If the promoters were fearful, the fans were receptive. In St. Louis the fans were impatient in their desire for better accommodations. A group, identifying themselves "Lovers of the Game," wrote to the local paper carping about the pinchpenny practices of Browns's management, and urged them to spend more money to procure better players.[13] The complaint correctly gauged the strategy of the 1882 association promoters: that most were unwilling to invest heavily was evidenced by Louisville, which captured second place with a former semiprofessional team.[14]

Although flooded out of its playing field for several weeks, Cincinnati won the first pennant. Not only did this town suffer the ravages of spring floods, but Pittsburgh fared worse. That year the Alleghenys were washed out of their "Exposition Grounds," and local newsmen predicted that home plate would be inundated through May.[15] Yet, in spite of the natural devastation, all six clubs finished the season. But survival was difficult, because some league players harassed the association by returning to their former

[12] Richter, *op. cit.*, 23–26.

[13] *Sporting Life's Official Base Ball Guide and Hand Book of the National Game,* 1891, pp. 42–63.

[14] A. H. Tarvin, *75 Years on Louisville's Diamonds, passim.*

[15] *Commercial* (Cincinnati), March 25, 1882; *Globe-Democrat* (St. Louis), May 16, 1882.

club, when more money was forthcoming. And others tarnished the association's image by their unruly behavior and sloppy standards of dress.[16]

On the whole, however, the season was a solid success, and the clubs drew well. In the West the combination of beer sales and Sunday ball proved a powerful lure. Overall, every club made money, although in midseason Baltimore changed owners. As an added achievement, some of the untried players, like Charles Comiskey, Bid McPhee, Pete Browning, and Tony Mullane, blossomed into real stars.[17]

Enheartened by such staying power, McKnight boasted that his circuit would widen its front of battle in 1883. In announcing plans to invade New York, he threatened to launch all-out raids on league playing rosters. This was enough to make league men tremble, and the *Clipper* interpreted the league's decision to drop its weak Worcester and Troy franchises as the direct result of association pressure.[18]

In McKnight's latest ultimatum to the League, he ordered all association teams to shun any contact with league teams until recognition was forthcoming. This hurt the Cincinnati Reds, who hoped to take advantage of its championship status by battling Anson's champs in a World Series. Hoping to circumvent McKnight's decree, the Reds' management "released" its players, then rehired them under special contracts. With this subterfuge the team took the field against Anson's men and delighted its fans by winning the opener. The next day Anson's men retaliated, and with public interest mounting, the papers gave the current contest fine publicity. At this point McKnight clamped down, demanding that the Reds desist or lose their franchise. When the Reds dropped out of the contest, it was as if a horse-hide curtain had been dropped between the two embattled leagues.[19] Over the winter the bitter rivals lowered their drawbridges to sally forth in raids upon one

---

[16] *Ibid.*, May 9, October 11, 1882.

[17] *Sporting Life's Official Base Ball Guide and Hand Book of the National Game,* 1891, pp. 43–63.

[18] *New York Clipper,* August 12, 1882.

[19] *Enquirer* (Cincinnati), October 24, 1882.

another's rosters.[20] Because they were not yet committed to the reserve clause which league players hated, the association clubs scored telling blows against their rivals.

Chastened by such raids, the league men asked for an armistice and invited their rivals to confer about peace. Recognizing the weakness of their reserve-clause stand, some league men favored junking it and just missed carrying their point. But in the end the clause stood, and the league even managed to convert association men to its support.[21]

By backing down in the face of tough opposition and carrying the war to the conference table, the league for the first time employed the stratagem that would give them ultimate victory over all rivals for the next twenty years. This willingness to accept a temporary loss of face, while biding their time and waiting for a rival's weaknesses to emerge, was a most deceptive tactic. Time and again, in this and future wars, it would enable the league to strike telling blows.

The mastermind of his circuit's 1882 strategic surrender was A. G. Mills, Hulbert's successor as league president. In the baseball summit conference with McKnight and Elias Mather of the Northwestern League, Mills proposed peace on the basis of a new, tripartite National Agreement, which would have the reserve rule as its cornerstone.[22] In pleading his case, Mills reminded his rivals of the chaos that existed before the 1879 reserve rule was adopted. Up until then, he argued, revolving had reached such a peak that few clubs made money. Now, said he, the present crisis was like that of 1878, with players profiting instead of club owners. The argument had its effect, and all parties conceded the point. Thus, the three leagues decided that players should be reserved at a minimum salary of $1,000 and that they would respect each other's reserve lists by refusing to sign a revolver. To enforce this agreement, clubs from all three circuits were ordered to submit annual reserve lists to a central committee. As a reward for this conces-

---

[20] *New York Clipper*, December 9, 1882.

[21] *DeWitt's Base Ball Guide*, 1883, p. 25.

[22] *Daily Globe* (Boston), July 17, 1891.

sion, Mills announced that the association was to be given major-league status and the Northwestern League the status of a high minor league.[23]

Although the National Agreement was quickly ratified by all three circuits, there were dissenting voices within the association, which suggested the possibility that the players would turn against them.[24] These suspicions were confirmed, when, during the 1883 campaign, rumors of players planning to organize against the hated clause were much in evidence. However, since association men were intoxicated with their newly won status and by another financially successful season, they found it easier to accept Caylor's scornful judgment that the players were too self-seeking to carry out their threat.[25]

The players, however, were not so easily downed. Furthermore, they found support from writers like Richter, who pleaded their case and berated greedy owners for conspiring to hold down their salaries. Indeed, Richter urged them to battle "the . . . caprice of men who have not one-tenth the ability, brains or heart of their victims." The growing support of sportswriters and sports enthusiasts kept the threat alive in 1883 and helped bring on an all-out revolt in 1889.[26]

But in 1883 such alarms were muted by the music of whirring turnstiles. Delighted at the opportunity to pursue profits in a peaceful environment, the association even ignored the rumor that the owners of their flashy, new Met franchise and the league's new Giant franchise were one and the same.[27] The implications of such a combine were easy to ignore in the light of new found prosperity. Especially attractive was the newly enrolled Philadelphia Athletic franchise with its heavy-hitting, base-stealing team. Because of the 25¢ admission rate, this club quickly became the darling of the

[23] *Spalding's Official Base Ball Guide*, 1883, pp. 58–60.
[24] *New York Clipper*, March 17, 1883; *Reach's Official Base Ball Guide*, 1883, pp. 1–26.
[25] Quoted in *Sporting Life*, July 15, 1883.
[26] *Ibid.*, July 22, September 3, 1883.
[27] *New York Clipper*, April 7, 1883.

vociferous Philadelphia fans, who pointedly ignored the league's new entry, the Phillies.[28]

Backed by good hitting and a tight set of disciplinary rules, which barred cigarettes, cigars, and pipes, along with "mashing" the female fans, the Athletics soared into the lead. By Decoration Day its chances looked so good that a howling mob of fifteen thousand, an unprecedented association crowd, stormed the grounds to the delight and consternation of the management. Although this was a high-water mark, large home crowds followed this exciting team until it clinched its championship with a late-season victory in St. Louis. Waiting in front of the telegraph office at home, thousands watched the posted scores, rendering street traffic immobile.

To a modern observer this scene has the mark of the classic case of "pennant fever," and in its individual aspects it produced some zany incidents. A *Sporting Life* writer told of one fan who, worrying himself sleepless over a Saturday defeat, fell asleep in church the next day. Jolted into semiconsciousness by the pastor's rhetorical question, "Where are the nine?" which was spoken in reference to the parable of the ten lepers, the groggy fan yelled out, "Oh, the nine's all right, and if any man thinks the St. Louis [Browns] are going to down them . . . ." At this point a timely jolt from his good wife's elbow squelched a possible memorable utterance.[29]

Although jubilant association leaders touted this team over the league's champion Bostons, a series of embarassing setbacks at the hands of their lowly home-town rivals, the Phillies, prompted the management to withdraw from a scheduled World Series test.[30] Yet this did not stop the association boosters from juggling statistics to show that their circuit was the equal of the league. In a blatant propaganda maneuver the association awarded its batting title to a part-time bench warmer, Tom Mansell of the Browns,

---

[28] *Inquirer* (Philadelphia), April 7, 9, 1883; *Reach's Official Base Ball Guide*, 1883, pp. 46–47, 1884, p. 24.

[29] *Inquirer* (Philadelphia), April 16, June 1, September 24, 1883; *Sporting Life*, April 26, October 1, 1883; *New York Clipper*, June 2, 1883.

[30] *Inquirer* (Philadelphia), October 4, 12, 1883.

because his .383 effort in twenty-eight games topped Dan Brouthers' league-leading .371.[31]

A far more authentic indicator of association growth was its 1883 profit statistics. Every club except the Mets made money, and the Athletics made "a great deal." That year Von der Ahe said that he personally cleared $70,000 at St. Louis. Even Baltimore, despite a poor record, claimed a $30,000 profit. However, a *Globe-Democrat* list trimmed such claims a bit by reporting a $75,000 profit for the Athletics; $50,000 for St. Louis; $25,000 for Cincinnati; $10,000 for Baltimore; an even break for Louisville and Columbus; losses of $3,000 for Pittsburgh; and no figures for the Mets.[32]

2. THE UNION ASSOCIATION

Unhappily for the association, the sunshine of its counting-houses was darkened by storm clouds that had been long ignored. For now, player resentment over the reserve-clause surrender was boiling over, bringing with it a shocking announcement that in 1884 a new major league planned to enter the lists on behalf of the aggrieved players.[33]

This thunderclap burst following a September meeting in Pittsburgh, which announced the formation of the "Union Association of Base Ball Clubs." Among its sponsors was Editor Richter, whose journal declared the union to be the emancipator of enslaved players and the enemy of the reserve clause: *"Resolved*, That . . . we cannot recognize any agreement whereby any number of ballplayers may be reserved for any club for any time beyond the terms of their contracts with such a club."[34]

However, regardless of their humanitarian claims, these intruders were also profit-seekers. Indeed, the secretary suggested that if the two major leagues recognized the union circuit as a major league, it would affiliate with the reserve clause of the Na-

---

[31] *New York Clipper*, October 20, 1883.

[32] *Reach's Official Base Ball Guide*, 1884, pp. 44–54; *Sporting Life*, October 22, 1883; *Globe-Democrat* (St. Louis), January 27, 1884.

[33] *Sporting Life*, September 13, 1883.

[34] *Ibid.*, September 17, October 1, 1883.

tional Agreement. But if it came to war, the unions resolved to make their cause the abolition of the reserve clause.[35]

In the end war came; the unions were branded "wildcat," and the reserve clause was defended as "wise and judicious." National Association clubs were advised to boycott the "mischevious and censurable" outlaw league, which was without "capital or character." The influential *Clipper*, though critical of the National Agreement's defense of their slavish clause, warned the newcomers that the rule was necessary and preferable to the anarchy that existed when players were able to bargain in a free market.[36]

Undaunted by opposition, the union men pressed on with the work of recruiting players and financiers, thus provoking further defensive measures by their entrenched rivals. In shoring up defenses, the allies tightened the reserve rule, redefined the territorial rights of their clubs, forced players under threats of blacklisting to sign iron-clad contracts, and issued strict orders barring member clubs from playing games with the invaders.

But while they directed the war against the interlopers, the league also seized the opportunity to weaken their association allies. By clever persuasion they got the association to expand to a twelve-club circuit in the interest of denying favorable franchise sites to the invaders. By snapping at the bait, the inexperienced association leaders sustained increased travel costs and suffered revenue losses from fewer home games. But this outcome was unanticipated in January, 1884, and the association proudly took on franchises in Washington, D.C., Brooklyn, Toledo, and Indianapolis.[37]

Meanwhile the invaders were masterminded by a wealthy young St. Louisan, Henry V. Lucas, who became a virtual dictator. One of America's new crop of railroad millionaires, Lucas loved baseball so much that he built his own park on the grounds of his suburban estate. Guests invited to "Normandy" where often expected to play a game before partaking of the famous Lucas cuisine. Of

[35] *Times* (New York), September 13, 1883.

[36] *Daily Globe* (Boston), September 23, 1883; *New York Clipper*, September 18, 1883.

[37] *Reach's Official Base Ball Guide*, 1884, pp. 170–71, 1889, p. 12.

course, his baseball experience went beyond this venture. In 1883, he sponsored the "Lucas Amateurs," paying all costs and playing third base. He also backed a modestly profitable semiprofessional team in St. Louis.[38]

Notwithstanding his boyish dedication, he had considerable business acumen. One of his bitterest detractors conceded as much when he called Lucas "the silver tongued chief executive of pirates and wreckers."[39] The free use of his executive talents and personal fortune went far in organizing the unions into a viable team. Although assisted by a quartet of lieutenants, Lucas personally supplied most of the ideas, enthusiasm, and money. But his major weakness was his inability to comprehend the financial worries of his less affluent colleagues.

Throughout 1884, he was the *enfant terrible* of major-league baseball. In his moralistic assault on the reserve clause he delivered his most telling blows when he linked it with slavery. Once he said, "I cannot see how a body of men has the right to dictate what another man shall do. . . . it will not deter me from hiring a player if I want him."[40] Naturally, his detractors, and even Richter, questioned his sincerity and accused him of being just another profit-seeker. But Ted Sullivan, who managed his 1884 team, called him "one of the squarest little men that has been connected with the game," and vouched for his "honesty of purpose."[41]

Sincere or not, his diatribes impressed many players and haunted major-league promoters for the next decade. During the Players Revolt of 1890 his words served as a battle cry, and even today criticism like his is occasionally invoked against the reserve clause.

Led by the controversial Lucas, the unions enrolled eight clubs for 1884—Altoona (Pennsylvania), Baltimore, Boston, Chicago, Cincinnati, Philadelphia, Washington, and St. Louis. Like other invaders, they too plagiarized existing constitutions and playing

[38] *Sporting Life*, May 7, 1884; *Sporting Life's Official Base Ball Guide and Hand Book of the National Game*, 1891, pp. 68–71.

[39] *Globe-Democrat* (St. Louis), October 5, 1884.

[40] *Wright & Ditson's Base Ball Guide*, 1884, introduction; *Sporting Life*, December 12, 1883.

[41] *Sporting Life's Official Base Ball Guide and Hand Book of the National Game*, 1891, pp. 68–71; Sullivan, *op. cit.*, 106, 165–66.

rules. With 128 games scheduled between mid-April and mid-October, the unions ruled that home teams must pay visitors $75 a game, except on holidays when receipts were to be divided equally. But as in past cases, this adoption of the guarantee plan would prove to be the undoing of the weaker franchises.

To lure the public, the unions stressed heavy batting and adopted the lively Wright and Ditson ball. This evoked sneers from the allies, but sneers turned to grimaces when union men successfully seduced players from enemy rosters. All during the winter of 1883–84 there were rumors and denials of runaway players. One report told of Anson's pitching ace, Larry Corcoran, going to the Chicago unions, but it turned out that Corcoran merely used the threat to coax more money from Spalding. Saddened over this experience, Lucas complained, "I thought he was made of more reliable material . . . . Still it may be that I ought not to blame him for I have been informed that Mills, Anson, and Spalding threatened him with everything but death."[42]

New fagots were heaped on the fires of rumor when editor Jacob Morse published the union's *Guide*. In listing the rosters of the union teams, he gave the impression that the new circuit was draining the talent of its rivals. But this was a bold, deceptive front, for a careful examination revealed that most names were either unknowns or has-beens. By February, it was evident that the allied black-listing threat was working, for most of the union raids were failures. Moreover, Richter claimed that by tampering with allied contracts, the invaders lost public support.[43]

But the greatest union weakness was this league's imbalance. For this, one can blame Lucas, because his lavish spending made the St. Louis Maroons into a colossus, which far outclassed all others. Apparently, he gave his artistic inclination full play, never pausing to consider the effects of a boring pennant race on the public interest. His patrician touch was applied to the construction of his park, which he called "the Palace Park of America," and

---

[42] *Globe-Democrat* (St. Louis), January 13, 1884; *New York Clipper*, December 15, 22, 1883; *Wright & Ditson's Base Ball Guide*, 1884, pp. 10–23.

[43] *Ibid.*, 1884, pp. 46–48; *Globe-Democrat* (St. Louis), March 2, 1884.

which he endowed with such extra features as facilities for receptions and lectures. The seating capacity was ten thousand, but time would tell that there were far fewer like-minded patricians in St. Louis.[44]

If most of the other union teams offered more modest accommodations, at least all were housed by March. In Cincinnati the union entry managed to snag the lease from under the association team, thus forcing the Reds to relocate in an abandoned brickyard. This provoked heated rivalry between the two, and at times hired thugs menaced players of both nines.[45]

Opening day found President Lucas voicing defiance to his enemies, promising the faithful freedom from reserve slavery and urging fans to support his "major league." But at home rain washed out his opening day festivities, providing a grim omen for future events.[46] Yet, when the Maroons were able to play, they were mighty good, so good, indeed, that to Lucas' horror fans began to stay away, even though his club won its first twenty-one games in a row. Apparently, most preferred watching the association's Browns, whose pennant scramble was more exciting.[47]

Meanwhile the allies, too, worried and fretted over their enemy's gains, and Mills found it necessary to write letters in order to buck up the faint hearts.[48] A relentless battler, Mills never relaxed, even when it became clear to all that the unions were a paper tiger. In May, Altoona faltered, and when Lucas refused to underwrite its losses, the directors resigned from the circuit. Although Lucas plugged this leak by enrolling a Kansas City club, another seam burst in August when the Philadelphia Keystones quit in the face of $10,000 losses. To fill this breach, Lucas persuaded Wilmington to desert the Eastern League. At the time this club led the Eastern League, but was losing money. Seizing a chance for quick profits, its cynical directors ignored the obvious fact that their departure

---

[44] *Sporting Life*, April 19, 1884; *Globe-Democrat* (St. Louis), March 16, 24, April 7, 1884; Lee Allen, *The Cincinnati Reds*, 29–30.

[45] *Ibid.*, 29–30.

[46] *Globe-Democrat* (St. Louis), March 16, April 20, 21, 1884.

[47] *Ibid.*, May 10, 25, 1884; *New York Clipper*, May 10, 1884.

[48] A. G. Mills to J. A. Williams, undated. Wright, Correspondence, Vol. III.

would undermine its former league. Baiting them was Lucas' siren song of promised subsidies and a special concession allowing them a half-share of all road receipts. Although this was a fantastic offer, it failed to lift the Wilmington fortunes. Within a month they quit because of poor attendance.

Hard after this defection came the collapse of Chicago, which could not buck Anson's team. When Chicago joined the ranks of the defectors in September, the harried Lucas turned to Omaha and Milwaukee as replacements. But after a few days Omaha resigned and was replaced by St. Paul. At the finish only five charter members remained, and a total of twelve clubs had participated at various times.[49]

Seemingly, there was no end to union misfortunes. Newspaper critics maintained a running tirade, charging the unions with such crimes as prostituting the game by using lively balls, inflating batting averages, and tolerating drunkards among its players. Union spokesmen retaliated with their own propaganda and, even in their darkest hours, refused to surrender. In the end, at least, they could say that they finished the season, and the Maroons won the pennant by finishing twenty-one games ahead of second-place Cincinnati.

While waiting for this stubborn rival to topple and die, the allies nursed wounds of their own, especially the association, which lost heavily because of the ill-advised expansion movement. The league did better, losing only its Cleveland franchise. Of course, the real victims were the minor leagues, and the struggle for survival killed six minor leagues.[50]

Shocked at the wreckage of 1884, it was understandable that the allies decided to demand something less than unconditional surrender, rather than risk another year of battle. As for the unions, total losses, running somewhere between $100,000 to $250,000,[51] took the fight out of Lucas' lieutenants. When it looked like his underlings were going to convert the union into a minor league,

[49] *New York Clipper*, June 7, September 20, October 25, 1884; *Sporting Life*, October 29, 1884.

[50] *Wright & Ditson's Base Ball Guide*, 1885, p. 67; *New York Clipper*, June 21, August 16, 1884.

[51] *Sporting Life*, October 22, 1884; *New York Clipper*, October 18, 1884.

Lucas decided to make his own peace with the allies. On advice from Spalding, league directors offered Lucas the opportunity to enroll his Maroons in the National League, provided that he publicly recant his opposition to the reserve clause. This he did, after securing a promise that the allies would not punish any union players. Thus, Lucas' personal surrender crushed the morale of his lieutenants, who disbanded the organization. However, early in 1885 a few of these men met to form the Western League, which would one day become the present American League.[52]

As for Lucas, his personal triumph soon turned to ashes. Branded a turncoat by his former friends, he found himself a pariah among fellow league directors. Indeed, the quarrel over Lucas' fate led to the dismissal of President Mills, who favored crushing Lucas with no concessions. But the directors preferred the stiletto to the battle ax, and when Mills remained adamant, they simply replaced him with the more pliable Nick Young. With Young in the chair, the league peace squad cold-bloodedly junked the faltering Cleveland franchise to make room for the Maroons. This evoked a loud squawk from Von der Ahe of the association, whose Browns must now face a local competitor. However, Von der Ahe was placated when told that the Maroons would be barred from charging a 25 cent admission rate, selling beer, or playing Sunday ball. In St. Louis of the 1880's, any one of these restrictions could ruin a baseball promoter.[53]

Furthermore, Lucas was ordered to pay $6,000 in fines in order to retain the services of several players who had been lured from league rosters in 1884, and as a final act of submission he had to approve of the league's decision to increase the number of reserve players for 1885. Such Machiavellian diplomacy was too much for the *Clipper* to stomach, and a reporter headlined his account of the settlement "THE NATIONAL LEAGUE AND ITS WAYS."[54]

Time would reveal that Lucas' draft of woe was bottomless. After two years of playing cat and mouse with him, his fellow direc-

[52] *Ibid.*, December 27, 1884.

[53] *Ibid.*, December 20, 1884, January 17, February 7, 1885; *Reach's Official Base Ball Guide*, 1885, p. 10.

[54] *Sporting Life*, April 22, 1885; *New York Clipper*, April 18, 1885.

tors goaded him into resigning. Hemmed in by their restrictions, Lucas had spent good money after bad, until total losses of $100,000 convinced him to call a halt.[55]

The victory showed the league to be the master in the art of baseball *realpolitik*. Not only did they vanquish the unions, but they also seriously crippled their association allies. Indeed, that circuit came out of the war only in slightly better shape than the unions. Not only did the expansion movement cost them profits, but a late season revelation, that their 1884 champion Mets team was really a satellite of the league's Giants, cost the circuit much prestige.[56]

The dual ownership of the Giants and the Mets ought not to be regarded as evidence of a sinister league conspiracy against the association, for the fact remains that New York fans preferred the brawling, colorful Giants to the Mets. Indeed, Gotham fans had little chance to see the Mets since they lacked a home diamond until May 13. At last, when the new park was opened, evidence of shoddy construction was everywhere. Perhaps the worst detractor was the use of decaying garbage as field fill. The ground literally stank, and snide reporters quickly responded by calling the park "Mutrie's dumping ground"—a phrase which had a double meaning, because about this time it was noted that the club directors were shunting unwanted players from the Giant team onto the Mets' roster. And no sooner did the victory parade honoring the Mets for their championship efforts end, than the directors announced the transfer of its star pitcher and champion batter to the Giants.[57]

Stunned by this blow, association men tried to punish the Met owners for contract tampering and double-dealing. These actions, however, were not crimes in 1885 (although in time such dual ownership would be branded as "syndicate baseball"), and the Mets' owners refused to pay the $500 fine, and their refusal was sustained in a court of equity.

[55] *Tribune* (Chicago), August 24, 1886.
[56] *Sporting Life*, September 17, 1884.
[57] *Ibid.*, May 21, 1884; *New York Clipper*, November 1, 1884.

However, some good came out of the association's grief, for the incident put its leaders on guard and fostered a spirit of independence. To purge themselves from league influences was the order of the day, and the directors ruthlessly returned to an eight-club circuit by shucking off its weakest teams. In a direct slap at the league the association decided to open its 1885 season a fortnight earlier than the league.[58] Also, clubs, players, and umpires were put on a wartime footing, with each man reminded of his special mission in the common cause against the league. Subsequently, a grim, but colorful, rivalry for profit and prestige would occupy the rivals, and it would also go far to stimulate unprecedented public interest in major-league baseball.

3. "A SALOON WITH A BASE BALL ATTACHMENT"

Stung by humiliation and by financial losses, the association sorely needed a Samson to champion its cause against the league Philistines. As it turned out, such a man was already at hand, his ass's jawbone being his powerful St. Louis team and his own behavior, at times, bearing a resemblance to another part of that beast's anatomy. This man of the hour was Christopher Von der Ahe, "boss president" of the surging Browns. Half-genius and half-buffoon, he was a hard man to evaluate, and those contemporary writers who did usually took an extreme position. To some he was a tragic genius, who built the Browns into the most profitable major-league franchise, only to fall because of fate. But a larger group belittled his wisdom, judged his success as freakish, and credited him only with the intelligence to defer to the true wisdom of his talented manager, Charles Comiskey. Thus to Gustav Axelson, Von der Ahe was merely a lucky beer garden owner who moved into baseball to sell more beer, and who, when his team began winning, took on what was for him a ludicrous role of baseball genius.[59]

Baseball and Von der Ahe met in 1877, when, as a status-seeking

---

[58] *Ibid.*, May 2, 1885; *Reach's Official Base Ball Guide*, 1885, pp. 73–82; *Sporting Life*, May 6, 1885.

[59] Gustav Axelson, *"COMMY": The Life Story of Charles A. Comiskey*, 69.

owner of a combination grocery and beer garden, he joined the St. Louis Sportsman's Association. After investing $6,500 to fit Sportsman's Park for baseball, he tried promoting semiprofessional teams until a big opportunity came along in the form of the American Association. Knowing how much St. Louisans loved the leisureways of the Continental Sunday, he offered them his formula of cheap baseball in extra-large Sunday doses, and with side offerings of beer sales, horse races, and fireworks. This broadened concept of a baseball spectacle quickly turned the St. Louis franchise from a weak sister to a baseball bonanza.

Furthermore, his service on several key association committees belies his ignorance of baseball. Besides urging black-listing of players who sought to "extort . . . excessive salary," he tried to curb the abuse of the free-pass privilege. Also, in 1888, he forecast that baseball would one day be organized under a single twelve-club major league,[60] although he could not envision the disastrous consequences of that move.

Closely following existing standards of American humor, most of Von der Ahe's detractors concentrated on his German background, trying to laugh him off as an ignorant, funny Dutchman. From such critics flowed a stream of anecdotes, still popular among sportswriters, which tried to equate unfamiliarity with English grammar as an indicator of stupidity. They also capitalized on Von der Ahe's physical appearance, especially his big nose. One story told of Von der Ahe's questioning an umpire's decision to call a ball foul after it had already left the park. Said Von der Ahe, "Mr. Umpire, vat is knocked is knocked, vat is ofer de fence is ofer de fence. Go ahead mit der game yet." Although the tale was intended to elicit laughter, the fact remains that his logic became the accepted ruling for such a situation.[61]

To be sure, he brought much ridicule upon himself because of his desire to be recognized as a gentleman sportsman. To advertise himself, he had a life-sized statue of himself built; to advertise his

[60] *Ibid.*, 57; *Times* (New York), August 10, 1888; *Reach's Official Base Ball Guide*, 1888, p. 24.

[61] Sullivan, *op. cit.*, 98, 115–16, 193–94, 204–208.

team, he put its trademark on cheap crockery, linens, and blankets and named apartment houses after his stars.

Just as the association's rising fortunes are associated with this extrovert, so, too, are Von der Ahe's fortunes associated with the day he signed tall Charles Comiskey to a contract. Son of a Chicago politico who scorned athletics, "Commy" sharpened his baseball in college and also met Ted Sullivan, who signed him in 1879 to his first professional contract. When Commy helped Sullivan's team land the pennant, Sullivan kept him in mind, and when Sullivan became manager of the Browns in 1881, he installed Commy at first base. But Von der Ahe also noticed Commy's promise, and when he dismissed Sullivan in 1883, he chose Commy as captain, and a year later, as manager-captain.[62]

As a diplomat-manager, Commy knew how to circumvent some of the capricious orders of his "boss president." Since Von der Ahe would readily fine players for the slightest offenses, Commy averted a serious morale problem by canceling such fines with bonuses for outstanding play. But on the field Commy set his own pattern, which stressed base-running and fielding, along with superb pitching. And the manager's style also stressed the psychology of heckling opponents into blind anger. This bothered purists who, like a *Sporting Life* writer in June, 1883, found Commy's team intolerable: "About the toughest and roughest gang that ever struck this city is the nine of the St. Louis Club. Vile of speech, insolent in bearing . . . they set at defiance all rules, grossly insulting the umpire and exciting the wrath of the spectators."

Nevertheless, this intolerable style helped to win four straight pennants and led Von der Ahe to increase his manager's salary until it reached $8,000 in 1889.[63] Helping Commy to set the style in 1885 was a handsome, but difficult to manage, third baseman with a wild mustache. As a "coacher," Walter "Arlie" Latham was a merciless heckler, who could talk opponents into fits of anger. A controversial figure, whose coaching methods and "free tongue"

---

[62] *Ibid.*, 27–28; *Tribune* (Chicago), October 8, 1885; *Reach's Official Base Ball Guide*, 1900, pp. 48–49.

[63] *New York Clipper*, July 18, 1887; Axelson, *op. cit.*, 58–66; *Sporting Life*, June 10, 1883.

endeared him to local fans, but won him "lots of enemies in the profession," Latham once found himself scheduled for twenty post-season fist fights, including five with a teammate. A vaudevillian player, Latham, whose badgering prowess concealed his ordinary skills as a player and won him a large following of fans, persuaded others to ape his style—that of a "cheerful chatterbox."[64]

But many damned his style as "a blending of audacity and pure cheek" and as being offensive to fans. Certainly, he was a mixed blessing to Commy, especially since he often stirred trouble in the team. Latham's private life was a shambles: his first wife attempted suicide and his second wife sought to divorce him for perversion, assault, desertion, and infidelity. Yet in an age whose middle-class norms demanded a veneer of morality, fans found such behavior as Latham's rather exciting. Through it all, Latham survived his attackers and hung on as player, captain, and umpire until the close of the century—always remaining a popular favorite and a symbol of changing moral standards.[65]

A more solid acquisition in 1885 was Commy's pitching staff of Dave Foutz and Bob Caruthers. To acquire Foutz, Von der Ahe bought the entire Bay City franchise, and to snare Caruthers, he bought out Minneapolis. Yet both proved to be bargains, and in two years the more talented Caruthers was earning $1,000 a month.[66]

Having given careful attention to the ball park, including seeing to the installation of "a ladies' toilet room, a necessity in all well ordered grounds," Von der Ahe summoned his 1885 aggregation and gave them this advice: "See here now, I don't vant some foolishness from you fellows. I vant you to stop dis slushing and play ball. Of you vin de 'scampionship,' I gif you a suit of clothes and a

[64] *The Sporting News*, October 30, December 4, 1886; *Tribune* (Chicago), August 25, 1886; Sullivan, *op. cit.*, 268; *New York Clipper*, December 12, 1896.

[65] *Free Press* (Detroit), October 13, 1887; *Sporting Life*, September 28, 1887; *New York Clipper*, June 18, July 12, 1887; *Reach's Official Base Ball Guide*, 1887, pp. 24–25.

[66] *Daily Globe* (Boston), September 19, 1898; *Globe-Democrat* (St. Louis), October 8, 1885; *Reach's Official Base Ball Guide*, 1888, p. 2.

benefit game extra, and of you don't you vill have to eat snowballs all winter."[67]

Whatever their reactions to the speech, his players tore apart the association in 1885. One writer spoke reverently of the way "they pranced from bag to bag as if they were monarchs of the diamond, treating the weak attempts to stop them . . . with a lofty air of disdain and contempt."[68] In the end the team won by sixteen games over second-place Cincinnati, and in the World Series it took the measure of Anson's champions. By winning the last game of a deadlocked series, the Browns won both the lion's share of the receipts and the world title.[69]

Having seen the restoration of profits and prestige, joy ruled in association councils, and the official *Guide* proudly proclaimed the circuit as "the head" of American baseball. But a combination of events soon darkened the joy. For one, in the common pleas court of Philadelphia, Judge M. Russell Thayer, in holding that membership in a baseball league is "as sacred as any property," forbade the ouster of the traitorous Mets.[70]

In addition to this reversal serious internal discord followed a quarrel between Von der Ahe and President McKnight. The dispute pitted Pittsburgh against Baltimore and centered over which had the right to purchase a St. Louis outfielder. When Baltimore won, the angry Pittsburgh faction, which included McKnight since he was also a Pittsburgh director, accused Von der Ahe of lying. When this dispute led to McKnight's ouster as association president, the Pittsburgh directors deserted to the league.[71]

However, the association's greatest problem was its cheap admission policy. With better players demanding more money, some payrolls went as high as $40,000 in 1886, sorely taxing the 25 cent admission policy. Fearful of what might happen if they were to

---

[67] *New York Clipper*, March 15, 1884; *Tribune* (Chicago), October 8, 1885.

[68] Quoted in *New York Clipper*, February 27, 1886.

[69] *Reach's Official Base Ball Guide*, 1886, *passim*; *New York Clipper*, October 31, 1885.

[70] *Reach's Official Base Ball Guide*, 1886, *passim*; *Sporting Life*, December 16, 23, 1885.

[71] *Reach's Official Base Ball Guide*, 1887, pp. 8, 115–24.

raise the basic admission to 50 cents, the directors instead tried to force a salary limitation plan on the players.

Finally, the virtuosity of the Browns menaced the circuit's stability. Indeed, in 1886, Commy came up with pitcher Nat Hudson, who was almost as good as Caruthers. Under the circumstances the Browns won again with ease, despite some conceitedness among the players. But if the campaign was dull, the club redeemed itself by scoring a clear-cut victory over Anson's men in a bitterly fought World Series. The Browns did it by winning the last three games at home, with the help of partisan fans who made life miserable for the White Stockings.

In the decisive final game with Chicago leading in the late innings, Commy despaired and sought to get the umpire to call the game because of rain. However, since the fans almost rioted, Von der Ahe drove the team back onto the field. With everyone but Commy confident of victory, the Browns tied the White Stockings' score in regulation time and won the game in extra innings on a dramatic steal home by outfielder Curt Welch—a feat known in baseball folklore as the "$15,000 slide."[72]

Under the winner-take-all ruling, the Browns picked up $13,000 from the series, of which sum Von der Ahe kept $6,900 and gave each player $580. With this reward went the plaudits of the hero-worshipping fans, who shouldered the team and its portly president in an emotion-charged parade. After watching the expenditure of so much leisure energy, a reporter suggested that "Base Ball cranks can now turn their attention to working Thoswood's Australian Puzzle."[73]

This was the apogee of association prestige. With sportswriters acclaiming the Browns as the team of the future, even league men conceded their superiority. That fall delegates from the two majors met as equals, to redefine the National Agreement, the reserve clause, and the playing rules. However, association men had yet to learn that their rivals were most dangerous when most submis-

[72] *Ibid.*, 5–7, 18, 34–42; Axelson, *op. cit.*, 90–91.

[73] *Globe-Democrat* (St. Louis), October 24, 1886; *Sporting Life*, October 27, 1886; *New York Clipper*, November 6, 1886.

143

sive. Soon after this meeting, the league took advantage of the Pittsburgh quarrel to lure that franchise into its fold. Enraged at this act, the association men fired McKnight and replaced him with Wheeler C. Wikoff; later a weaker Cleveland team was enrolled as a replacement for the lost franchise.[74]

Back in St. Louis, Von der Ahe, a chief figure in the Pittsburgh affair, now faced the peculiar problems of prosperity. With his patience taxed by high salary demands, he complained that it cost him $9,000 to sign his three pitchers and almost $40,000 to sign the entire team. His manager had difficulty in handling these prima donnas, but if other clubs expected a letup they were disappointed. Once again Commy came up with a brilliant new pitcher in Charles "Silver" King. This infusion of new blood revived the team after its sluggish start and enabled them once again to terrorize the association. Moreover, the fans were still with them; on Decoration Day twenty-five thousand turned out giving Von der Ahe $10,000 for the day and prompting his outburst that he would not sell his team for $200,000; he further exclaimed that "the Browns will stay in St. Louis until baseball ceases to be the national game."[75]

But the coming of fall soured such joy as the Browns fell before the Detroit Wolverines in a fifteen-game World Series, with Detroit taking ten of the contests. Handed a brutal lesson in baseball superiority, Von der Ahe blamed his men and refused to share his $12,500 series melon with them.[76]

Such obstinancy only deepened existing hostility between the owner and his men, and the following spring saw more salary holdouts, followed by the team's refusal to play an exhibition game with the colored Cuban Giants. Since Von der Ahe was convinced that the men refused to play the Cuban Giants out of cussedness rather than from "honest prejudice," he openly scolded his team as "most unappreciative."

[74] *The Sporting News*, October 30, 1886; *Spalding's Official Base Ball Guide*, 1887, pp. 13–31. *Reach's Official Base Ball Guide*, 1887, pp. 8, 25–26, 115–25, 148–64.

[75] *New York Clipper*, June 4, 1887; *The Sporting News*, June 4, 1887.

[76] *Sporting Life*, October 19, 26, 1887; *Spalding's Official Base Ball Guide*, 1888, 45–49; *Reach's Official Base Ball Guide*, 1888, pp. 11–28; *New York Clipper*, November 12, 1887.

Following Spalding's precedent, Von der Ahe dealt with the problem by selling his high-priced stars. In November, 1887, three lesser stars were sold, but in December he electrified the baseball world by sending ace pitchers Caruthers and Foutz to Brooklyn for $13,500. Since Brooklyn had recently purchased the franchise of the moribund Mets, this latest deal shifted the association's balance of power in favor of Charles Byrne and Charles Ebbets's aggressive entry.[77]

This large scale investment in talented muscle called attention to the association's financial imbalance. A wide financial gap separated wealthy franchises like St. Louis and Brooklyn from poor ones like the newly acquired Kansas City team, a franchise discarded by the league as unremunerative. By way of bridging this gap, the association decided in 1888 that visiting teams were to receive 15 cents on each admission or a guarantee of $130, whichever was larger. But this did little to share the wealth.

Meanwhile, the competition for playing talent drove salaries up, until in 1888, the association took the dangerous step of allowing clubs to set a basic admission rate of 50 cents. Far more dangerous was the decision made jointly with the league, to limit player salaries to a maximum of $2,000, for from such actions revolutions are made.[78]

Although enough signs portended trouble in the glen, most preferred to listen to gossip about Byrne's "Bridegrooms," the much married team that dollars had assembled in Brooklyn. Although the smart money favored this team for 1888, in St. Louis, Comiskey, by now recovered from the shock of his boss's bombshell, combed through some thirty rookies seeking replacements.

With Brooklyn pitted against his team, Commy's rejuvenated team grabbed first place in July, lost it briefly, then regained it in August. In the struggle pitcher "Silver" King, a muscular young man toughened by work in his father's brick kiln, saved the team by carrying the pitching and winning forty games. With a seven-

[77] *Ibid.*, September 24, 1887; *The Sporting News*, November 26, December 17, 1887; *Sporting Life*, January 25, 1888.

[78] *New York Clipper*, February 4, 1888; *Reach's Official Base Ball Guide*, 1888, pp. 35–36, 129–50, 154.

game lead by September, the Browns completed their circuit, finishing six games ahead of Brooklyn, and this time Commy got full credit for the job of reconstruction. Indeed, Von der Ahe's erratic behavior made it a costly triumph, for not only did he anger his own men, but he carried on a hot feud with the Brooklyn directors. Naturally, Commy's victory fanned the fires of hatred between the clubs, and when the league champion Giants had easily disposed of the Browns in the World Series, Von der Ahe received insults that not even his $12,000 series profits could assuage.[79]

With proleague organs whooping it up at the Browns's expense, the Giants rubbed it in by using second stringers in the last two games. Thus, even friendly papers were critical of the Browns's monopoly. In the fall meetings, the association directors revoked the St. Louis proposal of the 50 cent base rate and returned to the 25 cent rate. Such anti-St. Louis sentiment also kept association men from grappling with the smoldering problem of player resentment over salary limits, black lists, and reservations. In the end the few ineffective concessions that were made only widened the breach between owners and players and drove the latter into the arms of the militant players brotherhood.[80]

Ignoring the real possibility of a coming player strike, the association remained transfixed by the hot rivalry between Brooklyn and St. Louis. In Brooklyn a grim determination to humble the Browns fired the Bridegrooms, whose manager promised to jump headfirst off the new Brooklyn bridge if his team failed again. Leaving nothing to chance, the owners marshaled public support by naming every day, except Sundays and holidays, ladies'-day. In the end the Brooklyns needed all the good will they could get, because a fire destroyed the park early in the 1889 campaign, forcing makeshift operations. However, St. Louis was finding that all the comforts of home were unable to quiet the hostilities that divided

[79] *The Sporting News,* June 2, October 20, 1888; *Reach's Official Base Ball Guide,* 1888, pp. 175–77; *Spalding's Official Base Ball Guide,* 1889, pp. 79–84; *Sporting Life's Official Base Ball Guide and Hand Book of the National Game,* 1891, pp. 64–68.

[80] *New York Clipper,* February 16, March 16, 1889; *Reach's Official Base Ball Guide,* 1889, pp. 99–100.

the players and their blustering owner. Although at times a near mutiny seemed in the offing, such problems were forgotten when the two bitter rivals met on the field, and these encounters were spiced with mob scenes, official protests, and fist fights.

By September, it became clear that the arbitration committee's ruling on several protested games would decide the winner. Although the Bridegrooms enjoyed a comfortable lead, the Browns closed the gap in the stretch. Needing a last-ditch effort to carry the day, the Bridegrooms took the desperate measure of avoiding their wives, hoping that celibacy might give them strength. In this decision Caruthers was called the chief martyr since he refused even to see his newborn child.[81]

On paper, Brooklyn's last effort looked good enough, but as the Bridegrooms rushed home after October 14, no one was sure who had won. Uncertainty mounted higher as the arbitration committee vacillated, first siding with Brooklyn and then changing its mind. With Von der Ahe's faction reportedly applying pressure, the committee allowed the Browns to play off some postponed games, but when these were lost, Brooklyn was declared the winner.[82]

With the controversy still raging, Brooklyn met the Giants in the World Series. Already the borough manifested the same cocky individualism which so enriched the folklore of the next century. As expressed in the Brooklyn *Eagle*, "The Brooklyn 'B' series continues to expand. We have the biggest Bridge, the biggest Burying ground and the biggest Base Ball club in this blessed land of big things."

For a time it seemed as though Brooklyn would make good its boast, but after losing three of four games, the Giants took charge. With grim alliteration the *Eagle* tried to joke about defeat saying, "Caruthers' 'Curved' Balls Were Frequently, Forcibly, and Ferociously Flagellated," but Giant flagellations fell too frequently to foist off. By losing the last four games, Brooklyn lost the series,

[81] *New York Clipper*, April 6, 1889; *Eagle* (Brooklyn), March 30, April 23, September 16, October 9, 10, 1889.

[82] *Ibid.*, October 15, 1889; *Sporting Life*, September 18, October 2, 23, 1889; *New York Clipper*, September 28, 1889.

although its owners were compensated by receipts of $12,000.[83]

That year all the top clubs drew well, but seething player revolts clouded the association's future. That year the St. Louis revolt was overshadowed by others, especially the Louisville revolt. In a miserable effort which saw them win 27 games and lose 111, the Colonels were harried by an owner who repeatedly berated and fined individual players. When others petitioned in protest, the owner simply increased the fines, precipitating a June strike that led to an official inquiry. To its horror the investigative committee learned that Colonel players already had forfeited $1,435 in fines, leaving many stranded without funds on a road trip. Outraged by the tyranny, the committee eased out the owner and replaced him with a more reasonable administration.[84]

However, a belated righting of an isolated wrong failed to stem the revolt, which now burned through the majors and high minors. Already well-organized players were building their own major league for 1890, a fearful challenge which taxed the unity of the National Agreement forces. But if the league was united and willing, the association remained torn by internal struggles.

By now the Brooklyn-St. Louis feud had deteriorated into an emotional vendetta, leading other clubs to take sides. Instead of choosing a strong president, clubs were forced to choose either a St. Louis or a Brooklyn puppet. When it was obvious that Von der Ahe's man, Zach Phelps, would win, Brooklyn and Cincinnati resigned from the association and joined the ever accommodating league, which willingly booted out two weak franchises to make way for these stronger ones. It was a crushing blow to the association, but the Brooklyn *Eagle* correctly, if uncharitably, rubbed it in with this headline:

ITS SETTING SUN

Nearing the Horizon of
the American Association
Von der Ahe's Base Ball Combine
Reduced to Distressing Straits—"Corporal"
Byrne's Prominent Place in the League.[85]

Torn by this and other wounds, the association watched its own life's blood diminish through multiple hemorrhages. By 1890, Baltimore and Kansas City deserted, and although neither joined the league, their decision reflected their lack of faith in the association's ability to weather the coming storm. In refusing to invest his money into the coming costly war with the players, President Von der Horst of Baltimore put his team in a minor league for the duration, saying, "They'll come out to Union Park to drink beer, dance and have their picnics just the same."[86]

Dazed by the shock of defections, President Phelps summoned the faithful for a reorganization meeting. Although replacements were recruited, they came from small towns like Syracuse, Toledo, and Rochester, along with a weak entry from a remote section of Brooklyn. It was a bitter cup to drain, for it meant the association could hardly claim major-league status. Indeed, so weak was the Brooklyn entry that it collapsed in August, to be replaced by the Baltimore turncoats who sought higher profits.

In 1890 any kind of campaign would have been impossible if the association had not agreed to divide receipts equally. Long overdue, this vital action came too late to rejuvenate the moribund association. With three major leagues competing in 1890, often on the same day in the same town, the association's inferiority became so obvious that leading journals did not even print its box scores.

Perhaps the most painful evidence of association deterioration was in the record of the Louisville team. Thoroughly routed in 1889 and shorn of its few good men, this team won the 1890 pennant. Even so, the partisan *Courier-Journal* conceded that the association's chief mission in 1890 was the training of future big leaguers. In October this team met the turncoat Bridegrooms, winners of the 1890 league pennant, in the World Series. By man-

---

[83] *Reach's Official Base Ball Guide*, 1890, pp. 44–54; *Sporting Life*, June 19, July 10, 1889.

[84] *Ibid.*, July 10, 1889.

[85] *Eagle* (Brooklyn), November 16, 1889.

[86] Fred Lieb, *The Baltimore Orioles*, 20; *Reach's Official Base Ball Guide*, 1890, pp. 12–16.

aging a tie, the Colonels gave the association a moral victory, but unseasonably cold, snowy weather, combined with public apathy, discouraged attendance, causing the series to be a financial frost.[87]

Although Louisville made a modest profit, the other teams of the association suffered a financial nightmare. That year even the *Guide* editor, usually facile in the art of propaganda, was too despondent to rationalize the campaign beyond the honest admission that it was "anything but a brilliant one." Not only did Brooklyn drop out of the association, but the Athletics, after settling a player strike, went bankrupt and saw its assets liquidated under an auctioneer's gavel. Moreover, the enemies of Sunday baseball got in their licks by invoking the wrath of Jehovah and by staging successful prosecutions in several instances.

Only the collapse of the Players League offered hope for the future, for although a summit conference with the league in January offered hope of a new rapprochement, the threat of a war with the league now loomed. The association's hopes hinged on the orderly return of prodigal players from the ranks of the defunct Players League. At the meeting, it was agreed that all men were to rejoin their teams of 1889, but hardly was the ink dry when the league's Boston team decided to keep two men, who had been with the Athletics. After a futile protest the battle weary association men decided to war with the league and sever all relations.

In pressing the war, association strategy called for invading league territory and stealing its players. By purchasing Players League franchises in Cincinnati and Boston, it was able to plant clubs in those towns. In marshaling financial resources, members of the association decided to share all costs and to have each club turn over 55 per cent of its stock to the president.

As part of its strategy the league used the National Agreement as a boycott device and chose the same kind of financial measures. In its propaganda offensive the *Spalding's Official Base Ball Guide* exuded confidence and predicted that the association's action would be the last gasp of a dying organization.[88]

[87] *Courier-Journal* (Louisville), April 20, May 25, October 29, 1890.

Although the forecast came true, at times the lingering association's last gasp had the force of a whirlwind. In pressing the fight, the association reorganized and strengthened all its clubs and planted rival clubs in Cincinnati, Boston, and Philadelphia, in order to challenge the league. Also, the association recruited new financial backers among status-seeking merchants, yet in the end defeat resulted from the conservatism of the promoters. The league moguls were better led, more united, and more experienced. These seasoned baseball administrators were more determined to survive, and above all they were led by Spalding, a true baseball Bismarck, whose realistic diplomacy had been tested in previous wars.

Association leaders should have learned something from Lucas' experience in battling the league. As early as February, 1891, this unfortunate correctly predicted the outcome: "I now recognize that the League has always outclassed . . . the [association] . . . in its financial solidarity and brains. The Association is composed of a lot of schoolboys, and when they become noisy the League was in the habit of spanking them. . . . I think the Association will go to an early grave unless the national agreement . . . takes pity on it."[89]

In the campaign of 1891, Cincinnati was the association's vulnerable outpost. Lacking local financing, Cincinnati maintained itself with contributions from other clubs; Von der Ahe gambled on the great Mike Kelly packing in fans as its manager. But when this hope had faded in August, Von der Ahe sold the franchise to Milwaukee and gave Kelly the privilege of joining another association team.

Kelly, of course, desiring to return to his beloved Boston, signed with the association Red Stockings. His return so overjoyed Boston fans that local papers printed daily communiques of his journey back to Boston. When he rejoined the club in August, ten thousand fans turned out to welcome him.

[88] *Reach's Official Base Ball Guide,* 1891, pp. 131–37, 1892, pp. 8–22; *Spalding's Official Base Ball Guide,* 1891, pp. 14–15, 64; *New York Clipper,* January 24, 1891.

[89] *Daily Globe* (Boston), March 30, 1891; *The Sporting News,* February 28, 1891.

For one joyous week Boston's association team enjoyed an advantage over the rival Beaneaters, but then came the counterblow. The league lured Kelly to the Beaneaters, and the fickle fans not only forgave their idol, but flocked to see him at the league park. He left a team with a comfortable grip on first place and joined one that was five games behind. His arrival, however, sparked an offensive on the part of the Beaneaters, who electrified local fans by winning eighteen contests in a row and landing the league pennant. Needless to say, this feat hurt the Red Stockings, who were reduced to scheduling games over the lunch hour in hopes of attracting customers. Although Boston that year boasted two champions, in the eyes of the fans there was only one team and one Kelly.[90]

More than anything this incident took the heart out of the association men. For a time there was brave talk of resuming the war with new financial backing and even of invading Chicago, but new disasters put an end to these plans. At the fall meeting, Columbus and Louisville resigned in spite of pleas and offers of subsidies. From here the panic spread, prompting others to abandon a lost cause.

At this point a league peace squad moved in to exploit the situation. Corralling Von der Ahe, the league men divulged their merger plan. Playing upon Von der Ahe's often repeated prediction that a twelve-club major-league circuit must come someday, the group told the promoter that the millennium was nigh and that here was a chance for Von der Ahe to be in on the birth of the twelve-club National League and American Association of Professional Base Ball Clubs. Delighted with the offer, Von der Ahe accepted the mission of selling the plan to the association men, and he did persuade Louisville, Washington, and Baltimore to join with him in scuttling the association. However, Chicago and Milwaukee balked and threatened legal action against the plotters unless they bought their interests. Thus, the league gave Chicago and Milwaukee $131,000, twice the sum that they had planned to pay, in order to

[90] *Daily Globe* (Boston), August 20, 23, September 9, October 3, 1891; *Sporting Life*, August 22, 29, 1891.

purchase the assets of the association survivors. As a result Von der Ahe's new partners blamed him for his lack of bargaining skill.

Although the price was high, the league men could exult as of December 7, 1891, for they had bought a complete monopoly of major-league baseball.[91] Living as they did in an age of industrial empire-building, they fancied themselves as captains of a great entertainment industry. As self-styled magnates, they reveled in their handiwork and ingenuity. Pride was the order of the day, and the puppet ruler of the new domain, President Young, could exult: "Many people seem to think that the National League bought peace dearly in paying $130,000 for it, but according to my way of figuring the price was cheap. We will save nearly all of that during the next five years in salaries, with competition removed."[92]

But for Chris Von der Ahe, the marplot magnate, fortune had no more smiles. Cursed with a poor team, abandoned by his talented manager, and branded pariah by league magnates, he found that his side shows no longer packed in fans, and as his money trickled away, he found himself without friends.

Harried by debts and domestic discord, he fought some twenty court battles during the 1890's, including one with his mother-in-law. In a melodramatic episode in 1898, he was kidnapped by private detectives and taken to Pennsylvania to face still another suit. The end of the century saw him stripped of his franchise, isolated from baseball, and deserted by his second wife. His declining days were bitter ones, but were made livable by financial aid from Comiskey, who still remembered that Von der Ahe started him on his big-league career at $90 a month.[93]

91 *Reach's Official Base Ball Guide*, 1892, pp. 8–22; *The Sporting News*, January 6, 1900; *New York Clipper*, December 26, 1891; Richter, *op. cit.*, 23–26.

92 *New York Clipper*, January 30, 1892.

93 *The Sporting News*, November 6, 11, 1899; Axelson, *op. cit.*, 57–58.

9

The Players Revolt

As ONETIME RULERS of major-league baseball, the players were no ordinary intruders, and they deserve special consideration. Indeed, not only did players predate administrators, but the first commercial major league was a players league, and in the eyes of fans who worshipped them, players were first in importance. Yet, in spite of such advantages, it was feelings of status deprivation that drove players to revolt in 1890.

Actually, players steadily lost power ever since the paternalistic gentlemen gave way to the new magnates. Although still fancying themselves to be gentlemen, this new breed was profit-minded, interested in maximizing the input-output balance, and desirous of making players conform to sound business practices. Furthermore, the anarchy of the association era and the ignominy of the Louis-

154

ville scandal had convinced many of the necessity of controlling the players.

Although the reserve rule yoked a player to his club, it was not wholly tyrannical. It helped to stabilize teams, thus providing higher profits for investors and higher salaries for players. But thoughtful players resented this affluent slavery and wanted measures adopted that would balance the power between themselves and the owners.

One of the first attacks on the legality of the reserve clause came in 1882, when Pittsburgh sued catcher Charles Bennett for breach of contract in his refusal to submit to reservation. However, the court ruled in favor of Bennett on the grounds that the clause was lacking in equity. In time other court decisions would follow similar lines of reasoning in refusing to sustain the clause.

Two years later John M. Ward penned a thoughtful letter to the *Clipper* on the subject of reserve-clause abuses. Noting that some Union Association men had been suspended for violating the clause, Ward attacked such action as tyrannical, and claimed that only dishonesty justified expelling a player. He argued that to call something a crime that was no crime under civil law was unthinkable. Reasoning further, he assaulted the legality of the reserve clause, branding it "an *ex post facto* law . . . depending for its binding force upon the players solely on its intimidating effect." Ward wanted players to know that the reserve rule carried no legal or moral obligations and that violation of this rule was by no means tantamount to dishonesty.[1]

To the *Clipper* reader, whose baseball thirst was usually slaked by frothier prose, this was an unusual letter, but then Ward was an unusual player. Born in 1860 in Bellefonte, Pennsylvania, he attended Pennsylvania State College where he won plaudits for his baseball prowess. After a brief seasoning in the minors, he joined the league in 1877 and pitched Providence to the championship in 1879. Then, after his pitching effectiveness faded, he re-

---

[1] L. A. Wilder, "Baseball and the Law," *Case and Comment*, Vol. XIX (August, 1912), 153; John Stayton, "Baseball Jurisprudence," *American Law Review*, Vol. XLIV (May-June, 1910), 380–81; *New York Clipper*, February 14, 1885.

trained himself as an infielder and acquired enough tactical skill to captain the Giants.

An advocate of scientific baseball, Ward taught himself to switch-hit and studied the fine points of base running. In 1888, his book entitled *Base Ball: How To Become A Player* was hailed as "the best and most exhaustive treatise that has yet appeared on the subject." As a field commander, he had refused the captaincy until full power accompanied the post. Given both, he used them wisely, and up to 1889 no man ridiculed his leadership. Indeed, he was a hero to his Brooklyn players team, which gave him a diamond ring in appreciation of his leadership.[2]

Although a recognized superstar, Ward had other interests, and in off seasons he attended Columbia University law school, graduating with honors in 1885. Returning in 1886, he won a prize for outstanding work in political science.[3]

A handsome man, Ward had time for ladies, and in 1887, he astounded the theater world by wooing and winning one of its best-known actresses, beautiful Helen Dauvray, in a gossip-provoking, whirlwind courtship. Unhappily, this was one of his failures, and his 1890 divorce undermined his relations with his chief lieutenant, pitcher Tim Keefe, who happened also to be Ward's brother-in-law.[4]

Why Ward should have wanted to lead a revolt of lesser men than himself is well worth considering, and the cynic looks in vain for some mercenary motive. True, as a well-paid player, he might have worried about the league's imposing ceilings on salaries, but it is equally true that he was a good lawyer, the husband of a noted actress, the pride of a segment of New York Society, a friend of Spalding, and the recipient of repeated offers from the Giant brass to become an administrator. In short, any of these channels could have freed him from a dependence on his salary as a player.

Ward, however, felt a deep sense of mission for his fellow players, who in turn respected and trusted him. True, they did not

[2] *Sporting Life*, July 27, 1887, August 25, 1888; John M. Ward, *Base Ball: How to Become a Player*; *New York Clipper*, October 25, 1890.

[3] *New York Clipper*, December 12, 1885; *Sporting Life*, May 27, 1885.

[4] *New York Clipper*, April 6, 1889; *Sporting Life*, October 19, 1887.

really understand him, and some suspected his aristocratic mannerisms, like his habit of reporting late for practice, which earned all ordinary latecomers the jeering epithet of "Johnny Ward."[5] Yet it is doubtful that any player but him could have guided a players revolt. It was he who organized, in 1885, The Brotherhood of Professional Base Ball Players and read the eloquent preamble which promised: "To protect and benefit ourselves collectively and individually. To promote a high standard of professional conduct. To foster and encourage the interests of . . . Base Ball."

With Ward and Keefe working cautiously, patiently, and tirelessly in the task of recruiting members, the organization by the fall of 1886 could claim 107 members and autonomous chapters in each league city. Later a successful mission also planted chapters in most association towns, thereby adding some 30 more recruits.[6]

Not until late in 1886 did newsmen get wind of the brotherhood, and when the story broke, Ward gave the scoop to *Sporting Life*. There the liberal editor Richter gave the brotherhood warm support and praised its "intelligent and reputable" membership. Richter's loyalty to this cause was evidenced by his earlier support of the unions and his ready willingness to publish Ward's attacks on the reserve clause. In one such essay, Ward had taken the stand that was to be his position throughout the 1890 revolt, which was to praise the generally stabilizing influence of the reserve clause, but to condemn it for introducing such evils as the buying, selling, and lending of players.[7] In pressing this point, Ward showed his keen logic and facile style of writing, and in choosing Richter as an ally, he showed a canny sense of strategy.

As for other leading sports journals, like the *Clipper* and *The Sporting News*, they neither criticized the organization nor failed to applaud its leaders. This struck a hopeful note for Ward, who feared that the magnates would seek to have the brotherhood depicted as a wild-eyed labor union. To blunt such an attack, Ward

[5] *Ibid.*, October 19, 1887.

[6] *Sporting Life's Official Base Ball Guide and Hand Book of the National Game*, 1891, p. 28; *Player's Guide*, 1890, pp. 6–10.

[7] *Sporting Life*, July 20, August 4, 1886.

wrote explanatory letters in order to convince neutral editors that the mission of the brothers was peaceful and defensive: the only enemy was injustice, and the only acceptable crusaders were the "intelligent and well-behaved" players.

Such entreaties had a wide appeal among sportswriters, and when the battle lines were drawn in 1890, only four prominent writers, Chadwick, Caylor, Ren Mulford, and Harry Palmer, were implacably hostile to the player cause.[8] With powerful editors like Richter and Tim Murnane on his side, Ward was enabled to use their papers tellingly as his sounding board, and even today his well-written letters on the subject of the reserve clause and other matters of the economics of baseball are useful.

In such articles Ward struck hardest at the reserve rule, the black list, and the inequitable contract. When the Kelly sale in 1887 dramatized a new form of player exploitation, Ward scored brilliantly with an essay entitled "Is the Base Ball Player a Chattel?" With barbed logic, he pointed out that Kelly was neither consulted nor given a share of the $10,000 sale price. Ward's remedy was not to throw the reserve clause out, but to modify it and similar matters, like the sale of players, to take account of player wishes.[9]

Late in 1887, members of the brotherhood met to petition the league for certain rights, although Ward despaired of success since President Young had publicly stated that he would not deal with a "secret society." But to his surprise the petitioners were greeted civilly by the league committee, who also listened patiently to Ward's proposed "model contract." Afterwards, the players were astounded by the committee's acceptance of most of the proposal, and they left with a written promise that the league would give them a precise statement covering revised policies on contracts and suspension policies.

For their part the players were pledged to abide by a tighter code of discipline, especially covering matters like drinking, gam-

8 *The Sporting News*, December 31, 1886; *Sporting Life*, April 5, 1890.

9 John M. Ward, "Is the Base Ball Player a Chattel?" *Lippincott's Magazine*, Vol. XL (August, 1887), 310–19.

bling, and dishonesty. The league committee was overjoyed at the prospect of players helping to discipline players, but they had been skittish about striking out the salary-ceiling rule. Although the committee had promised to advise the arbitration committee to strike it out, they failed to keep their promise.[10]

But in spite of duplicity, a friendly spirit marked the relations between players and magnates in 1888. To be sure, some magnates grumbled about the need for salary ceilings, but such voices were drowned in the enthusiasm over Spalding's forthcoming world baseball tour. When the entourage sailed in October, not a discordant voice was heard, but no sooner had the boat carrying Ward left, than the league revived the hated salary-restriction plan. In its ukase the league stated that in 1889 no player would receive more than $2,500, and it was rumored that only twenty men would receive that much.

With their leader on the high seas and under personal contract with Spalding until March, the leaderless brotherhood was paralyzed. Although taking heart in Keefe's grim comment, "Won't Ward and the others be mad," there was still the maddening realization that when he did return, it would be too late to launch an effective counterblow.[11]

To his credit Ward kept a cool head. Upon docking, he was met by desperate men, who were ready to strike, but Ward calmed the hotheads and proposed a countermaneuver. On the one hand he proposed that a grievance committee try to treat with the magnates, while on the other he proposed that financial backing be sought for a rebel league to be launched in 1890. In the end the league destroyed hope of a compromise by flatly refusing to treat with Ward's grievance committee.

Discerning the hand of Spalding in the league's stand, Ward delivered an ultimatum: the league must scrap the salary-ceiling plan and cease the selling of players or face a rival players league in 1890. When this was ignored, Ward's men went to work seeking

---

[10] *Free Press* (Detroit), October 2, 1887; *New York Clipper*, December 3, 1887.

[11] *Sporting Life*, December 26, 1888, March 27, 1889; *New York Clipper*, July 7, 1888.

financiers and urging players to invest money in the proposed league. Since the brotherhood could deliver outstanding talent for a rival major league, financiers were interested. After all, a plant could be operated for as little as $35,000 at this time, and the problem of playing talent could be solved by Ward's brotherhood. Thus, as the 1889 season drew to a close, two enemy camps began organizing for a destructive showdown in 1890.[12]

Hostilities commenced in November, 1889, when the players formally parted from their masters. In a public declaration Ward placed the blame squarely on the shoulders of power-hungry magnates, who once "stood for integrity," but now stand "for dollars and cents"; "Measures originally intended for the good of the game have been perverted into instruments for wrong."

After listening to Ward's keynote address, the brotherhood organized the Players League and drew up an eight-point compact, covering the assignment of players to its eight teams. Next, each team was ordered to contribute $25,000 to a central war fund. Although each player was guaranteed a salary equal to his 1888 pay, it was decided that individual club profits above $20,000 were to be pooled and shared equally by all. It was further understood that the first $10,000 of a team's profits belonged to the investors and that the next $10,000 would be divided equally among its players. Still another share-the-wealth provision called for the equal distribution of gate receipts among contending teams, with a small percentage of the receipts earmarked for a general prize fund. As an incentive, this fund was to be divided on a prorata basis among the first seven teams in the final standings. Finally, players were assured fair representation on the league's board, and security measures were taken to prevent stock from falling into the hands of enemy *saboteurs*.[13]

By December the rebel league was a reality. A thorough planner and organizer, Ward left little to chance. On hand at the organizational meeting were the necessary financiers, the presidents of the

[12] *Player's Guide*, 1890, pp. 3–6; *Sporting Life*, July 10, 1889; *Sporting Life's Official Base Ball Guide and Hand Book of the National Game*, 1891, pp. 73–120.

[13] *Sporting Life*, November 13, 1889; *New York Clipper*, November 9, 1889.

Charles A. Comiskey was manager, captain, and first baseman of the St. Louis Browns, 1883–90.

Baltimore versus Giants, 1894 Temple Cup Series.

MacGreevy Collection, Boston Public Library

John A. Ward, of the New York Giants, ready to bat against John Clarkson, of the "Beaneaters," in 1888.

MacGreevy Collection, Boston Public Library

"Big Dan" Brouthers, whose lifetime batting average in the majors was .348, was a star first baseman of the 1880's and 1890's.

*Pittsburgh at Boston, October 3, 1903, the first game of the
modern World Series.*

"Ty" Cobb, who was a player, 1905–21, and player-manager, 1921–26, for the Detroit American League, was one of the fastest base runners in baseball history. Here he practices bunting.

Henry Chadwick, often referred to as "the father of baseball,"
was editor of Spalding's Official Base Ball Guide, *1881–1908. He*
invented the box score, wrote the first rule book, and was chairman
of the rules committee in the first nationwide baseball organization.

Fans sneaking into the Boston American League park on
September 3, 1903.

eight clubs, the umpires, and the managers. A code of playing rules was adopted, which included the innovation of assigning two umpires to referee each game. Since the new circuit aimed at nothing less than total victory, franchises were planted in nearly all National League towns in order to carry the war to the enemy's territory. Part of the strategy included extending the pitching distance to fifty-one feet and clothing umpires in white. Perhaps the color change was intended to symbolize the purity of the crusade, but in any case the new league was a masterpiece of efficient planning. The Players League confronted the National League as its most dangerous rival.[14]

Visibly shaken, the National League looked to its war committee of Spalding, John Day, and John Rogers, men who could be counted upon to employ every weapon of war, including, of course, diplomacy and propaganda. Aware of the high stakes involved, this group began operating even before the players were fully organized. In a joint meeting with its association allies, it passed a resolution to prosecute all players who jumped the reserve clause. However, the unity of these reluctant allies was shaken when the league grabbed up the association's runaway Brooklyn and Cincinnati franchises. A farsighted group, the National League war committee had the ability to see beyond the immediate war to another rule-or-ruin war with the association, one that could complete the grand design of giving the league a complete monopoly over major-league baseball.

In an interview Spalding denounced the brotherhood leaders as "hot-headed anarchists," who were prompted "by a few enthusiastic long-chance capitalists whose only possible interest . . . is the amount of money they hope to realize out of it."[15]

In combating force with force, this committee husbanded its depleted resources. To insure against defections, each franchise was bonded for $25,000, and the visitor's share of each game was raised to 40 per cent. At the same time, propaganda artillery was trained on the fans, who would ultimately decide the outcome.

---

[14] *Player's Guide*, 1890, p. 106; *New York Clipper*, December 28, 1889.
[15] *Ibid.*, November 23, 1889; *Sporting Life*, November 20, 1889.

They were told that all player demands had been met, that the salary ceiling was a dead issue, and that players about to be sold were to be consulted. Cleverly avoiding direct attacks upon the Players League, the *Spalding's Official Base Ball Guide* merely treated it as the tool of power-hungry leaders. Especially did the *Guide* malign Ward as the "chief conspirator," who was employing "terrorism peculiar to revolutionary movements." As evidence, the *Guide* pointed out that the Central Labor Union of New York had supported the players, and Editor Chadwick took a swipe at the younger sportswriters, who failed to understand the National League's pure motives.

Quite evidently, Chadwick hoped to lure the prodigals back to sorrowing and forgiving masters. In his assessment of the coming struggle, he pictured the National League as having sound managerial experience, which took to heart the interests of fans. He hoped that fans would support "the grand Old League," which had rescued the spectacle from degradation and which worked steadily, if not always wisely, "to elevate it and its exponents."[16]

Fully aware of the importance of press opinion in promoting the league's image, Spalding used economic power to neutralize *Sporting Life*. He did this by purchasing the *New York Sporting Times* and installing Caylor as editor. Another writer, Harry Palmer, functioned as Spalding's agent and had the power to hire reporters. *The Sporting News* later charged that Spalding had coldbloodedly killed the *New York Sporting Times*, when it was no longer needed, even though he had been well served by the organ. Other probrotherhood organs were neutralized by threats to withdraw advertisements. This was the case of *The Sporting News*, which had been subjected to a barrage of postcard hate notices and threats to withdraw ads.[17]

Bribery was a favorite league committee weapon used against the Players League. While propaganda raged, league men offered enticements to stars who planned to jump to the players. One sally

[16] *Spalding's Official Base Ball Guide*, 1890, pp. 11–26; *New York Clipper*, June 1, 1889.

[17] Palmer, *op. cit.*, 142–63; *The Sporting News*, May 10, July 19, 1890, January 13, 1894.

snared pitcher Clarkson, who reportedly received $10,000 for defecting. Later, his name and fourteen others were listed by the *Player's Guide* as traitors to the cause, and fifteen others were named as outright defectors. Although Ward feared linking his cause to that of the labor movement, he did not hesitate to brand deserters as "scabs."[18]

Certainly such bribe offers severly tested player loyalties. Spalding admitted that he had offered Kelly a blank check, which that player sorrowfully refused, saying, "My mother and father would never look at me again if I could prove a traitor to the boys."[19]

If the campaign of propaganda and bribery won tactical successes, this was not true of the league's legal attack, for in case after case its legal staff was put to rout by court decisions against the reserve clause. By winning suits initiated by league clubs, Bill Hallman, Buck Ewing, George Gore, Hardie Richardson, Keefe, and Ward achieved victories which bore out Ward's earlier forecast that league contracts would be held lacking equity. Indeed, Ward had staked his Columbia legal training on his belief that the reserve clause would not hold up in the courts.

After hearing Judge M. Russell Thayer's angry denunciation of the reserve clause in the Hallman case in the Philadelphia Court of Common Pleas in March, 1890, the league's legal expert, John Rogers, despaired of further suits. "I have nothing further to say," he told a *Clipper* man, "except that in Pennsylvania our 'reserve' clause will have to be rewritten, or it must disappear from all future contracts."

In New York the Giants fared no better with their case against Ward. There Judge O'Brien of the state supreme court declared that the reserve clause presented "the spectacle of a contract which binds one party for a series of years and the other . . . for ten days, coming into a court of equity against the party bound for years." A U.S. Circuit Court judge in New York's Southern District, ruling against the Giants in the case of Buck Ewing, called the clause

---

[18] *Player's Guide*, 1890, p. 99; *New York Clipper*, November 30, December 14, 1889.

[19] Spalding, *op. cit.*, 295–97; *Sporting Life*, March 11, 1890.

"wholly nugatory" as a basis for a damage suit. Thus in New York state alone, the league's losing court battles cost the circuit $15,000.[20]

Although beaten in the courts and deadlocked in the propaganda battle, the National League at least held its own on other fronts. Fortunately, league men had retained Wright and Anson, two big names among player heroes. From the start Wright had sided with the League, although he respected the rights of those who had joined the players. As he told Tim Murnane, "I don't want any player in my team who is not with me heart and soul." That many gave both to his safekeeping was a tribute to his influence. Of all league teams his Phillies suffered the fewest desertions. Indeed, eager, young George Stallings, rejected once by Wright for lack of ability, now spurned three offers from players teams and begged Wright for another chance. He said that "since leaving your team in 87 it has been my ambition to make my self competent and play under your management again."[21]

Such loyalties hurt the players cause. Knowing Wright's influence, they had sought his services, but were refused. With his Phillies becoming a strong team, this put pressure on the players shaky Philadelphia franchise, the most vulnerable spot in the Players League.[22]

If Anson failed to command such loyalty, at least he retained the nucleus of a good team. Almost a team himself, he held on to three key stars. Another strong point was Charles Byrne's Brooklyn team, which recently had deserted the association. Because of Byrne's proven generosity, most Bridegrooms stayed, enabling Manager McGunnigle to accomplish the unprecedented feat of winning consecutive pennants in two different major leagues.

Elsewhere, loyalties were so rare that mass desertions forced

[20] Stayton, "Baseball Jurisprudence," *American Law Review*, Vol. XLIV (May-June, 1910), 380–81; *New York Clipper*, April 5, 1890; *Daily Globe* (Boston), April 7, 1890.

[21] William Schriver to Wright, November 13, 1889; George Stallings to Wright, December 8, 1889. (Wright, Correspondence, Vol. IV); *Daily Globe* (Boston), March 24, 1890.

[22] *New York Clipper*, July 26, 1890.

President Young to circulate copies of an application form that was offered to "any club member of the National League." Its purpose was to recruit players, who had only to fill in details on vital statistics and previous playing experience in order to qualify for a major-league tryout.[23]

The National League, however, did forge ahead on the financial front. As the 1890 season opened, a pattern of economic war emerged, with the league putting pressure on the players' financial backers, hoping to scare away faint hearts. Since all players teams had capital outlays of at least $50,000, the league strategy was to drive a wedge between the brothers and their financiers, which, it was hoped, would break the back of the rebellion.

Thus the National League concentrated on financial harassments. By withholding publication of its playing schedule until after the players had released theirs, the league forced a box-office showdown of conflicting dates. Frightened by the move, some rebel financiers wanted to revise their schedule, but at an emergency meeting, it was decided to meet the challenge head on.[24]

Since both leagues were competing for the same fans on the same dates, the financial war almost overshadowed the actual playing. With both sides eager to win public support, major-league tickets were never so easy to acquire as in 1890. It was a freeloader's paradise. Both leagues used ladies'-days, and Spalding even instituted a "Professional's Day," which permitted actors to attend free of charge. In Brooklyn, Byrne defended his spate of ladies'-days by rationalizing that it saved him from having to pay money for special police, since fifty ladies were worth as many policemen in insuring good behavior. By midseason Richter accused the National League of making a free show of baseball by placing free tickets in barbershops and saloons. He also quoted a New York *Herald* reporter's investigations, to prove that both sides were falsifying attendance figures. Confronted by the evidence, Spalding admitted that league statistics were inaccurate,

---

[23] For a copy of the application see Wright, Correspondence, Vol. IV.

[24] *Courier-Journal* (Louisville), April 3, June 8, 1890; *Sporting Life*, March 19, 1890; *Tribune* (Chicago), April 28, 1890.

but he insisted that the league was keeping an accurate secret count. Said he, "We have an established business to fight for," and he challenged the brothers to keep up the fight if they could.[25]

At this point Richter realized that such "war to the knife" would likely end with the extinction of the Players League and with the National League's winning "a one league monopoly." Richter thought that such a triumph would disgust the public, but *The Sporting News* editor took a more tough-minded view—the war would purge the spectacle of its weaker elements.[26]

Yet this kind of war was ruining the Players League. In July the *Clipper* reported that the players' Philadelphia franchise was about to collapse. However, the wealthy Wagner brothers saved the day by picking up its loose stock. Elsewhere, National League bribery was creating a climate of suspicion between the players and their financiers, with the latter trembling for fear of big losses. Toward the end of the season the players secretary admitted that since most franchises had cost too much, the poor gate receipts and bad managerial methods were killing the circuit.[27]

But the rebels were getting in blows of their own. In July, Spalding rushed to New York to prevent the collapse of the Giants. It took $80,000, to save the club, which became the virtual satellite of Chicago, since the latter club supplied most of the money.[28]

In August, Judge Cullom of New York, a respected student of baseball, computed National League losses at $201,713, and at the end of the campaign his figure soared to $300,000. Cullom blamed high payrolls for most of the losses and estimated the league's total payroll at $311,964, which included $70,500 in special bonus lures. After the fury of battle was over, *Reach's Official Base Ball Guide* credited the players with outdrawing the league, 980,887 admissions to 813,678.[29]

Just before the nightmare season ended, the players delivered a heavy blow by purchasing the league's Cincinnati club. Ward

[25] *Sporting Life*, July 5, August 9, 1890; *Daily Globe* (Boston), August 9, 1890.
[26] *Sporting Life*, August 12, 1890; *The Sporting News*, May 17, 1890.
[27] *Sporting Life*, November 29, 1890; *New York Clipper*, July 26, 1890.
[28] *Spalding's Official Base Ball Guide*, 1895, p. 123.
[29] *Daily Globe* (Boston), August 21, 1890; *Reach's Official Base Ball Guide*, 1891.

exulted over the coup, saying, "It will not only bring into our league one of the best ball teams in the country . . . but it will give us an ideal circuit." He then proposed an armistice on the basis of major-league recognition for his rebel circuit. The stunned league men replied by inviting the players to a conference in October.[30]

Although many rebels felt secure in their initial victory, Richter warned that they must "win the peace" or lose everything. But even he had failed to divine the machinations of the league diplomats. At the meeting the league men announced their willingness to deal with the players "capitalists" as equals, but not the "renegade" player-leaders.

Now Ward called for a boycott of the meeting, but his "capitalists" harbored growing doubts about their future. This caused a rift, which the league exploited by spreading word of secret meetings between the league and the players capitalists. Soon Ward became suspicious of "dark corner" meetings, and he accused his financiers of "not treating the players in good faith." Sensing a betrayal, he tried to get players to put up the necessary capital to buy out the traitors.

Events, however, were moving too fast for such action. Since most of his financiers had the fight knocked out of them, they were anxious to recoup some of their losses. Along with Editor Spink of *The Sporting News*, many were convinced that they must either compromise or go broke.[31] What remained of the united front broke at the Players League meeting in November. In submitting resignations, Pittsburgh and New York offered to sell out to their colleagues, but the money supply was exhausted. Next, President McAlpin resigned, and although he pleaded outside business obligations, players charged him with stabbing them in the back. However, the real shock came when a director admitted selling his franchise to the league, because of his "ungrateful players." What little good will remained disappeared when Buffalo and New York defaulted on their remaining salary payments.

Meanwhile, Secretary Bruenell's report stated that Boston alone

---

[30] *New York Clipper*, October 11, 1890; *Sporting Life*, October 4, 1890.
[31] *The Sporting News*, October 18, 1890.

made money. Otherwise, the Players League's seasonal losses totaled $125,000, to which could be added another $215,000, which had been spent on plants and equipment, and $45,000 for legal fees. Of course much of the capital outlay was recoverable, and some satisfaction could be drawn from the league's estimated $231,000 losses. But the big losses were too much for the players' magnates, and the annual meeting soon rang with accusations of treason. In the end Ward wearily admitted that the Players League was dead.[32]

Magnanimous in victory, Spalding assured the beaten players that there would be no reprisals, not even for Ward. Having won the victory, the league committee now revised the National Agreement. Using disguised terminology, the salary-ceiling law was made more palatable, and instead of the hated reserve clause, contracts now held an "option to renew" clause.[33]

Since by January most of the players capitalists had sold out, Ward, Richter, and some others held a wake for the brotherhood at Nick Engel's saloon. Although disillusioned, nobody was crushed, as was implied by Ward's cynical toast: "Pass the wine around, the League is dead, long live the League."

Richter replied, "Base ball will live on forever. Here's to the game and its glorious future." But in league councils celebrations were omitted, because victory had been expensive, and the league was now facing the very real possibility of a new war with the association. However, *Spalding's Official Base Ball Guide* contented itself with a satire on the players' defeat:

> *Backward, turn backward, O Time in thy rush,*
> *Make me a slave again, well-dressed and flush!*
> *Bondage come back from the echoless shore,*
> *And bring me my shackles I formerly wore.*[34]

In summarizing the Players League season, Ward praised Boston as a model of loyalty and efficiency. It was this formidable team which captured the pennant under easygoing Mike Kelly's direc-

---

[32] *Sporting Life*, November 29, 1890; *Spalding's Official Base Ball Guide*, 1891, pp. 15–18.

[33] *Ibid.*, 1891, pp. 49–64; *Sporting Life*, December 20, 1890.

[34] *Ibid.*, January 24, 1890; *Spalding's Official Base Ball Guide*, 1891, pp. 44–45.

tion. But Ward might have mentioned his own brilliant, and unexpected, success in winning second place for his Brooklyn
"Wonders."[35]

But by inference, Ward's words of praise suggested that other
teams were less than loyal. Indeed, with its initial financial backing and its strong teams, the circuit should have held out. However,
the ever rational Ward probably counted too much on the loyalties
and determination of the players and their capitalists.

On the other hand, Spalding knew from the start that most players were self-seeking individualists, and he used this insight brilliantly in driving the fatal wedge between the players and their
financiers. As a result the league kept both its salary-ceiling rule
and its reserve clause. As for the latter, it continued to be an extra-
legal imposition. That the league got away with its continued use
was due to the fact that players had forfeited their power, and
fans had concurred in the "legal sin" by showing a "popular interest" in baseball, "which overshadows presidential elections."
Thus, Spalding's genius was his understanding of baseball and his
intuitive knowledge that a democratic form of control could never
have made a million-dollar leisure pastime out of the game.

This lesson Ward had learned the hard way, although he never
fully resolved it with his more liberal philosophy, he did admit
that players must recognize that "baseball is a business, not simply
a sport." A player, after all, is a hireling, and his salary is geared
to his muscles and skills; "it is for his own interest to keep himself
in the best of condition, and study how to get the best results."[36]

[35] *Sporting Life's Official Base Ball Guide and Hand Book of the National Game,*
1891, pp. 80–87; *New York Clipper,* December 20, 1890.
[36] Stayton, "Baseball Jurisprudence," *American Law Review,* Vol. XLIV (May-
June, 1910), 374–80; *New York Clipper,* December 26, 1896.

10

Baseball's Cast of Characters

1. THE HEROES

Bᵧ THE 1880's, baseball's unrivaled popularity portended a bright future for the sport. Hence, it was realistic to speak of major-league baseball as a career field that could accommodate 240 skilled workers in the two leagues. But to aspiring young men with visions of high salaries and the adoration of fans, becoming a player was far more than a mere job. Indeed, the lure of a big-league career was a siren call to American youth, who dreamed of someday holding a job that would remunerate one for just having fun. That so many lads would struggle for the few available openings was bound to affect the style of play.

Certainly, Chadwick's forty years of watching the American baseball scene qualified him as an authority on the game's changing style, and in the 1880's he unhesitatingly pronounced the new style as being superior. Recalling the old-timers of the 1840's, Chadwick admitted that the moderns were faster and better skilled. Over-hand pitching, he thought, made the difference, because it demanded more strength and more courage, especially the latter, because of the increased threat of injuries.[1]

But in spite of the dangers, every year saw a fresh crop of apple-cheeked youths seeking positions on the rosters. Most of these neophytes came from minor-league training grounds; however, these unstable circuits were but one source of supply. Another source was the sand-lot route to some amateur league, or, perhaps, to a college league. From there a talented lad might go directly to a major-league club. The most brilliant prospects, called "phenomenons," were greedily snared by managers on advice from scouts or "touts." But getting noticed was just a beginning, for staying on was tough, and battlewise men, like Harry Wright, knew that most "phenoms" were flops.

Those athletes who made a team and stayed on did so for a variety of motives. Some took a casual view of their baseball career, regarding it as a mere step toward a more permanent goal. For example, young Harold McClure did not wait for time to take its toll, but bowed out because he knew that baseball was a fickle career. Since "the least injury will deprive a man of his living, a player ought to be following some other pursuit."[2]

In assessing the ambitions of ballplayers, the *Clipper* counted few men with outside aspirations. Among those keeping their powder dry was Ward, McClure, and Jim O'Rourke, who spent their spare time reading law. Others studied for the pharmacy, and "Doc" Bushong practiced dentistry. Among the marginal careerists was "Bassett of Indianapolis . . . a college man who writes." Another class included aspiring young merchants, like Tim Keefe, who sold real estate on the side, and John Morrill, who worked for a brokerage firm. And moving into the trades, there were several printers and some farmers. Finally, after citing the praiseworthy ambitions of five others, the writer concluded by lumping all others into a kind of catch-all proletariate class of ne'er-do-wells and

[1] Henry Chadwick, *The Art of Fielding: With a Chapter on Base Running*, 16–17.
[2] Harold McClure to Wright, January 28, 1884. Wright, Correspondence, Vol. II.

loafers. Nor was the writer impressed by those who played winter ball in the South, since in his Yankee opinion, such leagues were a disgrace both to the profession and the spectators.[3]

Opposing this view was Manager Ted Sullivan, who stoutly avowed that most players were thrifty and prudent, but this contention was not supported by observers like Wright and Chadwick. Much of Wright's winter mail came from prodigals, who had blown their pay and who wanted advances on their future salaries for such purposes as "meating" a board bill or paying off debts. Meanwhile, as editor of *Spalding's Official Base Ball Guide*, Chadwick often chided league players for not budgeting properly.[4] Another reporter, Harry Palmer, described the typical player as a devil-may-care character, who was careless of both his health and his money and viewed life as being "full of good things." This average athlete spent his playing days "like a prosperous young merchant," throwing his money away on idle pursuits and searching for laughs. Palmer noted that some players were arrogant and conceited, but he added that most were genial, and he crowded his book with anecdotes of the ballplayer's fun-loving way of life.

Although most clubs forbade drinking, many players comforted themselves with booze and "German tea." Knowing that most baseballers had acquired only a limited formal education, Palmer was not surprised at their superstitious, uncritical view of the world. For example, Palmer cited Pete Browning, a redoubtable hitter, who credited his success to his habit of touching third base each inning. But if Palmer himself disbelieved such childlike interpretations, he marveled that in an age of frequent railroad accidents none of the much-traveled players had been involved in a major accident. Nor did club owners concern themselves over such a possibility; indeed, not for another seventy years did owners bother to plan for these exigencies. To be sure, there were minor traveling accidents, but most of these resulted from practical jokes, and Palmer cited incidents of players being knocked out of sleeping

[3] *New York Clipper*, November 19, 1887.

[4] Sullivan, *op. cit.*, 206; *Spalding's Official Base Ball Guide*, 1885, pp. 98–99; Joe Mulvey to Wright, February 16, 1884, and J. Remsen to Wright, February 14, 1884. Wright, Correspondence, Vol. III.

berths and of rookies being told to rest their arms in the convenience hammock of the upper berths—advice that was certain to yield stiff arms.[5]

For many players with rural backgrounds, the adjustment to city-ways was difficult. Not surprisingly, many made spectacles of themselves, and in 1889 a reporter compiled a list of their boorish acts. In one case a manager reportedly released a player for eating with a knife, and other cases told of players drinking the contents of finger bowls. Although decorum was a relative thing to some managers, others were easily outraged. Some flew into tantrums when players merely piled food scraps in soup bowls or used spoons to eat pie. Most managers, however, depended on the mocking contempt of other players to educate their rustics to the ways of urban etiquette. Under such pressure, most learned fast, conformed quickly, and took revenge by picking on the next newcomer with similar shortcomings.[6]

However, some social pressures boomeranged, and in many cases they resulted in innocent players becoming drunkards. Indeed, by the 1880's the boozing ballplayer was a prime target of the temperance people. Since these moralizers were ever ready to draw a scientific correlation between drinking and physical deterioration, ballplayers soon became prime case studies. Too easily convinced by such claims, sportswriters were quick to castigate guilty players. In the West, *The Sporting News* belittled stars like Kelly and McCormick as incorrigible lushers. The same paper told how drink had ruined the career of Pete Browning in 1886, although that star enjoyed several fine seasons thereafter. However, *The Sporting News* was baffled by the case of Curt Welch. Although Welch habitually concealed a stock of beer behind the billboards at Sportsman's Park, he continued to make "those circus catches for which he is renowned."[7] But only rarely were such exceptions introduced. Usually crusading reporters went further afield, like the Cleveland writer who attacked tobacco chewers and

[5] Palmer, *op. cit.*, 55, 70, 119–27; *The Sporting News*, February 11, May 5, 1888.
[6] *Ibid.*, February 9, 1889.
[7] *Ibid.*, October 25, 1886, May 14, 1887, February 11, 1888, June 8, 1889.

attributed their "dulled perceptions or even stiff arms" to the use of such "narcotics."[8]

Under such pressures most clubs adopted strict rules of personal conduct, and Boston's strictures against dissipation, loitering in saloons, consorting with gamblers, keeping unreasonable hours, and gambling were typical examples. Since the Boston code also expected players to report each day and carry out orders cheerfully, few moralizers could demand more.[9]

Aside from such impositions, players also faced financial crises that were not of their own making. Early in the decade many clubs continued to renege on promised payments, leading one reporter to protest "the unfair contemptible character of the present League contracts," which guarantee the greatest share to the management, and the "players themselves very little."

Although rising prosperity ended this kind of tyranny, directors always tried to hold down salaries. Support for this policy came from the official league guide, which complained about unreasonable salary demands. Players were compared with ten-dollar-a-week laborers; a $2,000 salary was held to be sufficient for "workers" who labor only three hours a day at pleasant employment.[10]

Apparently, the above attack was a trial balloon, aimed at testing player reaction to a salary-ceiling law. And in 1885 such a law was enacted, setting $2,000 as maximum pay and outlawing all bonuses, except those for necessary travel pay. Luckily for the players, however, many managers feared that poor salaries would lower a team's morale to the point of encouraging players to strike or jump to rival leagues. Hence, the law was honored in the breach.

Indeed, the rule not only angered players, but it fostered the brotherhood movement. Helping to fan the fires of revolt were reported incidents of stinginess on the part of owners. At St. Louis, Von der Ahe alienated his men by insultingly refusing a wife's request for an advance on her husband's salary, and in Pittsburgh, hard-working Jim Galvin, a star pitcher, recounted a tale of broken

8 *Globe-Democrat* (St. Louis), May 5, 1884.
9 *New York Clipper*, April 9, 1887.
10 *Ibid.*, September 17, 1881; *Spalding's Official Base Ball Guide*, 1884, pp. 41–45.

promises that belied the myth of hard work yielding its just re-wards. In 1891, Galvin's boss promised the pitcher incentive pay for extra work, but then reneged. Although the incident cost Galvin $500, it was not the first time that he had been "thrown down." Once before he had been promised a "brown stone front on a good street," only to have the owner forget about it.[11]

These and other complaints underscored the insecurity that was a player's lot in the 1880's. If he was sick, injured, or tempo-rarily ineffective, the athlete's pay was cut off indefinitely. Of course, the same was true for any ordinary worker of the times, since the principle of payment for services rendered was very much a part of American ethics. Indeed, few players questioned this rule, yet the grim realization that salaries would be halted while recovering from injuries probably encouraged many to shrug off impairments that would sideline modern players.

Certainly, the decade had its share of Spartan heroics. In 1881, Bob Ferguson of Troy played five innings with a fractured wrist.[12] In 1885, Radbourne had his chin cut open by a line drive, but con-tinued to pitch.[13] Nor were these isolated examples—with over-hand pitching, batters faced serious injury every day. Buck Ewing discovered this when he was struck by a Detroit pitcher: "I saw him squeeze the ball and imagined he was sending me a curve. . . . Instead . . . it was a fast, straight ball, and I stopped it with my head. I dropped over the plate, conscious, but unable to move. I knew all that was going on . . . but I didn't seem to be 'in it' at all."[14]

Indeed, the very rules of the game conspired to force players to keep playing, in spite of injuries. Substitutions were limited only to cases of serious impairment, and the opposition had the right to decide what was serious. As a tactical measure, most teams refused to concede any injury as being serious, especially those involving catchers. In 1885, Chicago precipitated a row by refusing to let

[11] *Globe-Democrat* (St. Louis), December 19, 1884, October 18, 1885; *New York Clipper*, September 19, 1891.
[12] *Ibid.*, July 2, 1881.
[13] *Globe-Democrat* (St. Louis), May 17, 1885.
[14] *New York Clipper*, March 26, 1892.

the Phillies replace a catcher who had broken a finger. Although the finger was "swollen to about twice its natural size," Anson said it was "nothing." In the end the Phillies replaced the ineffective catcher anyway, but this drew an official protest from Spalding.[15]

So ruthless a code left scant room for humanitarian consideration. In 1880 a Boston player severely injured his ankle on a base spike, but when the Chicago pitcher moved to help him, Anson ordered him back to his post. Chicago men, too, had to shrug off hurts. In 1885 the team continued playing, despite colds, sore arms, and bad ankles.[16] When Larry Corcoran's sore arm threatened to end his brilliant career, Spalding reminded him that useless men would be replaced. When Corcoran protested, Spalding called him "a little sniveler."[17] Since few players had alternative careers to pursue when dismissed, the decade was rife with tales of destitute has-beens, who could not overcome their rejection. Some, like pitcher Fred Goldsmith of Chicago, attempted repeated "comebacks" and submitted to exotic medical treatments, like the blistering "moxa treatment," reputed to restore dead arms.[18]

Only rarely did a humanitarian voice rise in protest. Almost unprecedented was a *Clipper* suggestion that clubs might consider paying hard workers who were injured in line of duty. The writer believed that the plan would pay dividends by encouraging men to make extra efforts.[19]

Since the conditions for survival were fierce, it was not surprising that the year 1887 found only two men with records of continuous league service with the same team. Moreover, the number of ten-year veterans was small, and catchers' careers were usually far shorter than those of other players. An exception was Detroit's Charles Bennett, but his record of durability came at the expense of battered hands: ". . . he has not a whole or straight finger in the lot. Every joint is swollen and misshapen."[20]

15 Chadwick, Scrapbooks, II, Article dated August 28, 1885.
16 *Herald* (Boston), May 6, 1883.
17 *Sporting Life*, July 22, September 9, 1885.
18 *The Sporting News*, April 23, 1887.
19 *New York Clipper*, April 22, 1882.
20 *The Sporting News*, January 29, November 12, 1887.

Aside from physical dangers and predatory promoters, there was the threat of black-listing. Since it could be applied to many offenses, from drinking and training violations to jumping to a rival league, players hated and feared the weapon. Although black-listing was usually effective in keeping men in line, it was rarely defied; once, however, because several association teams overworked it by black-listing too many training rule violators, these pariahs got together and formed their own team, "The Black-listed," and made money. They did so well that the association decided to reinstate them.[21]

If managers and owners could be cast as slave drivers, players could certainly be cast as affluent slaves. Not only was the pay high for the times, but there was always the dazzling prospect of becoming a public hero. Already many were idolized for their skills or some personality attribute. This was obviously the case of one-armed Hugh Daly, a fair pitcher, who was the darling of fans for his gamecock battling against umpires and rival players.

Still another pride of lionized players was enshrined as heroes because of their durable efficiency. Heading this group was Joe Start, who retired in 1886 after twenty-eight years with the best baseball teams in the land. Called "Old Reliable," Start had a unique career that spanned the three stages of the rise of major-league baseball. Another member of elite baseballers was Ezra Sutton, whose career bridged the NAPBBP era. But as the decade wore on, the aforementioned men gave way to new Titans like Anson, O'Rourke, Galvin, Connor, Ward, and Brouthers.[22]

A splendid performance was a sure way to capture the hearts of fans. Radbourn skyrocketed to fame by his one-man pitching heroics of 1884, and in short order other pitching heroes like Clarkson and Keefe joined him. Batting prowess was admired too, and fans of the 1880's seemingly liked big, burly sluggers, such as Anson, Brouthers, Connor, and Dave Orr. Fans also deified skilled managers like Wright, Anson, and Comiskey, who was boosted to

[21] *Globe-Democrat* (St. Louis), June 28, 1885.

[22] *Sporting Life*, September 3, 1885; *New York Clipper*, January 27, 1884; *Wright & Ditson's Base Ball Guide*, 1885, pp. 43–45.

the point where he was able to cash in on his endorsement of "Menell's Penetrating Oil" as a panacea.[23]

But the changing style of play also made heroes out of base-stealers like Harry Stovey, Billy Sunday, Latham, and Kelly. Sunday, indeed, never forgot the electrifying impact of his steals, and years later he slid onto the stage, to spice up his vaudevillian sermons. However, if Sunday was a hero to the Sunday school set, Kelly was aggrandized by those who liked rakish behavior. His slugging dash endeared him to many, and he knew the value of getting his name in print. Once he told a pal that he did not care what was said about him, so long as it was said. As Kelly explained to a group of his mates, "See what they say about the old man. I don't observe any reference to . . . my colleagues. I am the 'only player.' Why don't some of you dubs break a window and get yourselves talked about?"

As king of players, Kelly knew what the crowds enjoyed, and he was always ready to entertain them. While running the bases, he would sometimes feign lameness, then suddenly recover and dash for the next base. When playing in the outfield, he enlivened dull contests by playing up to Irish-Americans in the bleachers, or "Kerry Patch," as this area was called in St. Louis. On occasion he would taunt them, by pretending to be an Orangeman and whistling "The Boyne Water."[24] Once, he amazed them by trudging to his soggy outfield post carrying a heavy board, and then, while his fellow fielders slipped and slogged, he remained high and dry, in spite of catcalls and mud balls from the fans.

Unfettered from the prevailing Protestant taboos on drinking, Kelly loved to tipple and told a writer that ale and wine was good for a player. This made him the bane of his managers, but years later, however, as manager of Cincinnati, he found himself in their position. Once, when one of his players, a reformed drunk, made several errors during a game, Kelly gave him money to get drunk, saying, "When sober you're the rottenest ball player I ever saw."[25]

23 *The Sporting News*, June 4, 1887.

24 *Ibid.*, April 2, 1887; *Reach's Official Base Ball Guide*, 1895, pp. 84–86.

25 Kelly, *op. cit.*, 48, 68–71; *Daily Globe* (Boston), May 24, 1897.

Seldom serious, Kelly wrote his autobiography, which revealed the sunny attitude that appealed to many. In making him their superhero, many fans probably found in his antics a vicarious freedom, which was otherwise attainable only in their dreams. After all, by identifying themselves with Kelly, they could play out some of their own frustrations and strike out against their peers. Indeed, Kelly once took the measure of the President of the United States. Invited with the rest of his mates to shake Grover Cleveland's hand, Kelly turned Cleveland's gesture of friendship into a painful ordeal by squeezing until he winced, after which his mates followed suit.

A baseball Elijah, Kelly was raised above the company of mortals in 1887, when Boston purchased him for the incredible sum of $10,000. This deal became the baseball story of the century, and papers carried articles about it for weeks. At the time Kelly was so popular that a picture of his sliding into second base actually rivaled "Custer's Last Stand" in Boston saloons. When his sale was announced, J. E. McCann's poem, "Beautiful Mike," ran six stanzas, with each more lavish than the preceding one. Forced on the defensive, *The Sporting News* defended the sale of this western star by rhapsodizing over the sale price: "Ten thousand clear in Puritanic Gold."[26] However, when the hullabaloo died down, there was no doubt that the fans had chosen their superstar.

2. The Chorus

The public furor over the sale of Kelly testifies to baseball's popularity among its partisans, or "kranks," as they were called. To be sure, Manager Ted Sullivan claimed to have invented a new word, "fan," to describe some of the more rabid baseball buffs, but, if this is true, it was small comfort to those counted in the class, for both terms referred to a form of insanity, or, at the very least, to the loud, raucous behavior of these leisure-seekers.[27]

If innocence of social psychology kept writers of this day from

[26] *New York Clipper*, February 19, 1887; *The Sporting News*, March 5, 1887.
[27] Sullivan, *op. cit.*, 254; Mitford Mathews (ed.), *A Dictionary of Americanisms on Historical Principles*, 583.

analyzing fans, this did not deter Thomas Lawson. His "book," round like a baseball and bound in a horsehide cover, sold for 25 cents under the title of *THE KRANK: HIS LANGUAGE AND WHAT IT MEANS*. Inside, with sardonic style, Lawson portrayed the characters who haunted the Boston park in such great numbers. Their chief characteristic was their prying curiosity about all points of baseball, including players, umpires, reporters, and other kranks. According to Lawson, the species had evolved only in America of the 1870's. Generally of masculine gender, since "the Kranklet is at present only partially developed," the kranks would almost never let their interest stray from baseball. During the winter they survived on a diet of "strong newspaper articles on deals." Not being content to "know it all," they also wanted to "tell it all."

Because of this characteristic, kranks were incorrigible nuisances, who would annoy fellow horsecar passengers en route to a game. Bucking the line at the ticket window, they would impose themselves on both ticket seller and gatekeeper, with requests for inside "dope." Once inside the park, they would head for the newspaper pen to badger the writers. From there they would move to the front row seats, where they accosted the battery, pressing to know whether the score card is correct and whether certain athletes would play that day. During the course of a game they would tirelessly shout advice to players and scornful epithets to umpires. Between innings they would argue with other fans over points of the game and the accuracy of their scorekeeping.

Since being familiar with the kranks' language was essential to understanding them, Lawson compiled a lexicon. In the lexicon the umpire was the "tenth man" or "the robber," and if one presses on, he will find other phrases that are still used. To the fan of the 1880's the bat was the "willow" or "ash." "Pushing the air," was to strike out. Home-town batters were told to "lace it out," and fielders were referred to as "circus catchers." If a player missed a catch, it was because of "butter fingers" or that the ball was "too hot to handle." Pitchers were told to "back up" fielders, and runners were "nailed" by good throws. The "bleaching boards" were seats for kranks who were not intimate with the doorkeeper of the grandstand, which was a wooden structure divided into seats, "just large enough for three-quarters of a Krank." Of course, Victorian decorum demanded a segregated area for the "fair Kranklets." Reporter Lawson, however, was less humorous in his description of fans' invading the press area, and he scolded them for thinking that it was a place for smoking, gossiping, and playing "tick tack" tunes on "finger exercising machines."[28]

Some fans were more prominent than others, and one such fan was the celebrated General Arthur Dixwell of Boston. Personally wealthy, he rewarded players for outstanding feats and boosted the minor leagues with his award of the coveted Dixwell Trophy. More sophisticated than Lawson's "ideal type," he was a character, and, when excited, he would scream "Hi! Hi!" which led to his nickname of "Hi! Hi!" Dixwell.

If many kranks behaved like boys, few were able to unnerve gatekeepers with the ingenuity of some urchins. In Boston, one gang challenged the most clever security measures for weeks, until someone discovered that their secret entrance route was a large drainpipe.[29]

However, the color of fans' money, rather than their personality types, was of chief interest to promoters. By 1885, throngs of 10,000 and more were common, and owners were awed and delighted to see attendance records rise. In 1886 the Giant fans set an attendance record of 20,709 at the Memorial Day game, but this record was broken on the same day a year later with a 30,000 turnout. If the rising tide of public interest fattened the purses of owners, it also created headaches. One of these headaches was a quasi-moral problem created by the league's barring the association's practices of Sunday ball, cheap admission rates, and beer sales, which really attracted the urban fans. Although some league promoters were ready to chuck morality out the window, league directors decided to continue the ban on Sunday ball, beer, and 25 cent admission rate. The Phillies, however, were allowed to

[28] Thomas Lawson, *The Krank: His Language and What It Means*, 1–64.
[29] *Sporting Life*, March 21, 1891; *The Sporting News*, June 16, 1888.

charge twenty-five cents, because of keen competition from their association rival.

Policing unwieldy crowds, with their trouble-making elements, also challenged promoters. Cincinnati owners discovered that the overuse of bouncers frightened away paying customers. But on the other hand, to ignore hooligans was to run the risk of a tirade from some moralizing editor. This happened to the Phillies in 1889, and the owners were warned that the "better class of people" will not tolerate the antics of "That class . . . which does not know how to behave itself."[30]

For a time owners clung to a gallant, if not naïve, notion that the presence of ladies would help to keep order. *The Sporting News* stated, "The presence of the fair sex . . . not only adds beauty to the scene, but . . . has a good effect upon the crowd." Supposedly, the men become less excited and "more choice in their selection of adjectives." Such a myth led owners to institute ladies'-day, and in 1885, Brooklyn won the admiration of the *Clipper* by making every day, except holidays, ladies'-day.[31] However, in a short time the belief in this female prowess was doubted. Indeed, some ladies were found to cramp the style of inoffensive male fans with their prudish protests against cigar smoking and tobacco chewing. For a brief time in Philadelphia, they had their way, when Manager Wright stationed a policeman to curb smokers and mashers.

Prudish surveillance, however, overlooked baseball's function as a relaxing leisure pastime. Fortunately, some astute owners grasped this oversight, and decided to let well enough alone, even to tolerate an occasional mob scene. Nevertheless, they did truckle to the protests of the do-gooders, probably because they themselves were prisoners of middle-class values, which held that the national spectacle ought to be character-building.[32]

Finally, promoters learned that the business of selling leisure meant listening to critical comments from supporters. Almost any policy change, like raising the price of a score card to 10 cents,

[30] *Sporting Life,* May 13, 1883; *Public Ledger* (Philadelphia), July 18, 1889.
[31] *The Sporting News,* December 11, 1886; *New York Clipper,* April 18, 1885.
[32] *Public Ledger* (Philadelphia), July 18, 19, 1889; *New York Clipper,* July 23, 1887.

might bring a barrage of criticism. Then, too, there were fans who were always ready to tell a manager how to run his club. In this decade Wright acquired a swollen file of letters, both praising and condemning his actions and those of his captains.[33]

Although some fans were unruly and even dishonest, like one who set himself up as gatekeeper and pocketed his take, or another who built and rented elevated seats on his property which was just outside the Detroit fence area,[34] at least the majority were co-operative. Given a champion club, or even a fighting runner-up, most fans were generous in their support; indeed, a pennant winner in any major-league town of the 1880's always received parades, lucrative benefits, and gifts from hero-worshipping fans.

3. THE VILLAINS

If plunking down his silver piece entitled a fan to make tin gods of baseball heroes, the same act qualified him to make devils of others. But why they chose to add umpires to the company of the damned requires more consideration. By the end of the 1880's the baseball umpire, that rational symbol of orderly conduct, had become a universal symbol of hate. Moreover, by 1890 it had become evident that neither king's horses nor men were able to rescue him from ignominy. Indeed, the surprising thing was that the owners and directors wanted it that way, for they had discovered that villains, too, could be profitable.

That the fans of this era found relaxation and fun in villifying umpires is an interesting American folk phenomenon. For insights into its origins one can acquire a useful perspective from a modern sociological work entitled *Heroes, Villains and Fools*. According to the author, Orrin E. Klapp, Americans of this era were more certain of who their villains were than we are now. To them, black was black and sin was sin, because their self-confidence had not yet been shaken by moral and ethical relativity. Thus, if Americans of the 1880's had fewer villains than we, at least they agreed as to

[33] *Tribune* (Chicago), June 20, 1886; Will Ursher to Wright, 1889. Wright, Correspondence, Vol. III.
[34] *New York Clipper*, August 13, 1881.

who was villainous. Today, we tend to humanize our villains and our heroes, and we expect heroes with feet of clay and villains with vestigial wings.

In writing about these early American villains, Klapp lists five different orders, including one called "status abusers and arrogators." Within this order is a genus called "oppressor types," and beneath this a species of "moral persecutors," who had a nasty habit of misusing power.[35] This is precisely the way fans of the 1880's regarded umpires. In their eyes he was a threat to the hopes of the home-town team and to the splendid performances of their heroes. Since both had their off days, it was convenient to have a moral persecutor like an umpire to blame. Hence, the umpire became a sacrificial lamb, who as a villain served as a safety valve for the frustrations of fans. As such, he actually helped restore their morale, since he was viewed as the cause of the frustration.

If this diagnosis explains the creation of the villain umpire, it must be pointed out that pioneer baseball promoters never intended for umpires to become scapegoats. They saw him as a gentleman's gentleman, and they believed that appointing an umpire was a way of honoring their most knowledgeable members. Since Chadwick was determined to maintain this image of the early-day umpire, little was done to professionalize the status of umpires until the advent of the National League.[36]

The league brought both an end to Chadwick's policy-making influence and a beginning of a professional status for umpires. From its birth the new regime had sought to systematize umpiring, and one of its first steps was to pay an official $5.00 a game. In 1879 the league ruled that all umpires had to be chosen from an official list, but it was the rival American Association in 1882 which adopted the first full-time staff. Anxious to end bickering over the selection of umpires, the association plan scheduled three umpires to referee all its games, and each was to be paid a salary of $140 a month. Another badge of this new status was the clothing—blue

[35] Orrin E. Klapp, *Heroes, Villains, and Fools,* 50–67.
[36] *Chadwick's Base Ball Manual,* 1870–71, pp. 56–63.

coats and caps that created an image which was to persist in folklore.[37]

That year the prospects of entering the new profession attracted many, including a number of "played out ball tossers." Fearing that such positions would be filled with political appointees, the Chicago *Tribune* warned major-league leaders to exercise care in their selections. Because of the politicking that was going on, the league in naming its first staff in 1883, finally gave the four $1,000-a-year posts to a quartet of unknowns. Tenure, however, was denied these first professional umpires, and the protests of four clubs could secure their immediate dismissal. Under the circumstances this quartet suffered maltreatment—only one finished the season. One of the unfortunates, A. F. Odlin, of New Hampshire, admitted that he could·not take the abuse of the crowds; in the face of "customary and inevitable howls of disapproval," he became "more or less nervous" and was unable "to exercise accurate judgment."[38]

Meanwhile, the rapidly changing style of play brought further confusion to fans and increased strain on the umpire. In this decade hardly a year passed without some change in rules regarding balls and strikes. Also, the new pitching style brought many tricky deliveries and the problems resulting from overhand throwing. Since the rules often failed to define a legal pitch, it was the umpire's duty to rule on the legality of a pitch or a tricky motion by the pitcher. Batting tactics, like the bunt and hit-and-run, along with fielding and base-running changes, brought new headaches to working umpires. To say that these were rough times for umpires is an absurd understatement, and preseason seminars, planned to orient umpires to changing rules, failed to secure uniform interpretations or to clarify ambiguous rules.[39]

Not surprisingly, league officials faced a mounting number of offenses against their umpires. By the mid-1880's it became evident

[37] *New York Clipper*, February 10, 1885; *DeWitt's Base Ball Guide*, 1883, p. 18.
[38] *Tribune* (Chicago), October 8, 1883; *New York Clipper*, March 10, June 8, 1883.
[39] *Sporting Life*, April 22, 1883; *Spalding's Official Base Ball Guide*, 1896, pp. 160–62.

that the popular villification of these officials was getting out of hand. Certainly, nothing illustrated more clearly the despised status of the umpire than the number of outrages against his person. In 1884, Baltimore installed barbed wire to discourage mobbings by fans. That same year a mob assaulted league umpire Gunning, because he called a game a tie on account of darkness, and a Philadelphia mob turned on Umpire Billy McLean. In the latter incident, ex-boxer McLean was goaded beyond endurance by taunts, and he threw a bat at a group of fans. Within minutes he was besieged, and it took a police escort to rescue him. The following year, the fiery Billy again needed a police escort to escape a mob.

During the 1880's, umpires found players only slightly less menacing than mobs. Several times umpires were attacked by players, and in 1884, Umpire Gaffney suffered a cut eye in a fight with John Ward. Since Ward apologized and took Gaffney to a surgeon, he received only a fine and a brief suspension, but this incident prompted league men to invoke $200 fines for future offenses. Yet the reluctance of a club owner to "throw the book" at a player was evidenced a year later, when a player's apology excused him for having struck Umpire Dick Pearce.

The number of abuses led some to analyze the umpire's role. In 1886, Umpire Joseph Ellick, writing in *Lippincott's,* blamed the "kicking player" who was "anxious to save face in front of a home crowd." Such a man gave a crowd its "cue for kicking." Thus aroused, crowds easily became mobs that were anxious "to kill you and wish you an unpleasant time in the next world." Others soon conceded the validity of this thesis. Indeed, players were good needlers, and many were encouraged by owners, who willingly paid their fines. In 1886, Umpire Ben Young cited Comiskey as "a most aggravating player," especially when he worked his trick of pretending to converse with a player within an umpire's earshot. Usually, Comiskey's private conversations became barrages of insults directed toward the umpire.[40]

---

[40] *Sporting Life,* October 8, 1884, March 18, 1885; *The Sporting News,* November 6, 1886; *Globe-Democrat* (St. Louis), April 27, 1886.

Although it is apparent that the security of umpires could have been guaranteed by co-operation from league officials, owners, and writers, at no time during the 1880's was this co-operation forth-coming. This strongly suggests that some found umpire-baiting to be profitable. Although the league sided with umpires and tried to appease them with pay increases and more power over players, the mere possession of either was not meaningful. In the parks the individual owners ruled, and some sought the profits coming from the degradation of umpires.

Certainly, Von der Ahe saw no reason to restrict umpire-baiting. Indeed, he encouraged it by paying his men's fines. As a result, St. Louis was a tough assignment for umpires, but for Von der Ahe it meant increased profits from fans who liked this kind of by-play. Other owners favored a policy of letting players blow off steam at the umpire's expense. A *Boston Courier* writer defended the latter position with the argument that umpires "are too fully equipped with the foibles of our common flesh to assume the business of . . . repressing the hasty passions of others. What's the use of coining a player's unpremeditated damn into dollars and cents?" With writers urging umpires to accept some abuse as a normal part of the spectacle this attitude was difficult to overcome. After his ouster in 1887, an umpire confessed that league president Young accepted this point of view and had actually advised him to give "the closest and most doubtful decisions to the home club."[41]

Strong endorsement for this point of view came from Spalding, who argued that in despising umpires fans merely exercised their democratic right to protest against tyranny. Others agreed, and in the 1890's, when a group of umpires tried to protest the ambiguity of certain rules, they were told that they were "employees" and were not to question their superiors. In the 1890's, players like John McGraw and Ned Hanlon argued that fans favored the rowdy, umpire-baiting style. Hanlon told umpires to remember that players "are not school children, nor are umpires school-masters. . . . Patrons like to see a little scrappiness in the game, and would be very dissatisfied . . . to see the players slinking away like

[41] *Sporting Life*, October 29, 1884; *New York Clipper*, September 17, 1887.

187

whipped schoolboys . . . afraid to turn their heads for fear of a heavy fine from some swelled umpire."[42]

Given such encouragement, the fans villified umpires to the surprise of no one. In the 1880's and 1890's, mob incidents increased, and scarcely a season passed without multiple firings and resignations of umpires. By the 1890's, the practice of players' reacting to umpire decisions was so ritualized that the Brooklyn *Eagle* sarcastically urged players to practice the art:

> *How does the busy base ball player*
> *Improve each shining minute?*
> *He plagues the umpires all the day*
> *Because there's glory in it.*[43]

Sportswriters of this era also were delighted with the umpire scapegoat. Seizing the villain with gusto, they poured out reams of half-humorous and half-serious abuse. Even thoughtful editors, like Tim Murnane, were not above headlining a local defeat, "UMPIRE'S GAME." A *Clipper* man introduced the umpire as "the mortal enemy" of players and fans, "whom it is the proud privilege of every man seated . . . to hiss at and 'bullyrag' and abuse when he does not especially favor the local club." *The Sporting News* stated that one who umpires "must have a deformed head."

One of the most sadistic enemies of umpires was Joe Campbell of the *Washington Post*. In his headlines he included such tidbits as women spectators pursuing an umpire and smiting him "with their parasols." In his story he frequently railed at umpires; once he called "Umpire McFarland, the yellowest piece of bric-a-brac that ever disgraced Nick Young's staff of indicator handlers."[44]

In this era other writers found salable themes in the national rite of umpire-baiting. In 1888 the *Clipper* noted that John Philip Sousa had written the music for a comic opera, one which had a theme built around the evil designs of an umpire. Written by a Washington newsman, the plot pitted clean-cut Eli Yale, a Giant

---

[42] *Ibid.*, May 25, 1895; *Sporting Life*, April 10, 1897.

[43] *Eagle* (Brooklyn), July 26, 1890.

[44] *Washington Post*, July 26, September 13, 1897; *Daily Globe* (Boston), July 11, 1892, August 9, 1897; *New York Clipper*, November 27, 1884.

pitcher, against villainous Umpire Moberly, who lusted after the heroine, Angela. Moberly also planned to cheat Yale's Giants out of the pennant. Embellishing this tired plot were songs with fetching titles like "He Stands in the Box With the Ball in His Hands," "The Umpire and the Dude," and "An Umpire I, Who Ne'er Say Die." Knocking umpires also brought out the poet in some sportswriters, but few matched this 1886 effort:

> *Mother, may I slug the umpire,*
> *May I slug him right away,*
> *So he cannot be here, mother,*
> *When the clubs begin to play?*
> *Let me clasp his throat, dear mother,*
> *In a dear, delightful grip,*
> *With one hand, and with the other*
> *Bat him several in the lip.*[45]

Helpless against such abuse, umpires watched sportswriters cement their image as moral oppressors. If they fought back, as Umpire Dunnigan had in 1886 by beating up a reporter, they lost their jobs. Sometimes they lost more. In 1884, Umpire Al Jennings tried to beat up a Washington writer for his insults. Arriving at the newspaper office, the umpire ran afoul of the paper's formidable sports editor, who beat him with a paste pot and threw him out.[46]

Even without paste pots, reporters had the upper hand. In this era headlines frequently charged umpires with "robbery," "daylight crime," and the uglier charge (because it suggested cowardice) of "home umpire." So frequent were such attacks that in 1890 *Reach's Official Base Ball Guide* begged reporters to at least stop calling their decisions examples of robbery.[47]

It is a tribute to some umpires that in so hostile an environment they adapted and did not go the way of the passenger pigeon; indeed, a handful of thick-skinned arbiters found unique ways of existing in the perilous habitat. In this age John Gaffney outper-

[45] *Tribune* (Chicago), August 15, 1886.
[46] Chadwick, Scrapbooks, II, 69.
[47] *Reach's Official Base Ball Guide*, 1890, pp. 38–40.

formed most others in storing up merit and longevity, thereby winning the thorny crown of "King of Umpires." With little playing experience, he joined the league staff in 1884 after a brief career in the minors. Called on to referee a crucial game, he nervously dressed alone in a remote corner of the dressing room, when an outspoken player, oblivious of his presence, blurted, "What do you think Nick Young has gone and done? He's sent down to the rural districts of Worcester . . . and got a hayseed to come here and umpire. . . . He'll be lucky if he gets out with his life."

However, Gaffney, a tireless, imaginative, and efficient worker, belied the grim forecast by hanging on throughout the century. Although suspended for drinking and constantly heckled, he accepted his status as villain as part of the job, consoling himself with the questionable assurance that only the riffraff gave him trouble. Moreover, he did much to stabilize the profession. It was the beating he took from Ward that moved league officials to impose heavy fines for such offenses. Furthermore, he had a direct influence on the field. One manager credited him with real imagination in deciding what to call a fair ball which turned foul as it soared out of the park. Gaffney's decision was a model of common sense; like Von der Ahe, he believed that once the ball was out of the park it passed out of his jurisdiction, and ruled accordingly. Soon his solution to this problem became official.

In 1888, journals also took serious notice of Gaffney's "system" of umpiring. Until then an umpire either worked behind the pitcher or the catcher, but since both posts were advantageous, Gaffney chose to referee from behind the catcher until a runner reached base, whereupon the went behind the pitcher. Impressed by this logic, the league officials urged others to try it, and for a time it was the "rage." As a result, Gaffney in 1888 found himself the highest paid umpire with an annual salary of $2,500, plus expenses.

To be sure, some of his ideas were unrealistic. He thought that the "kicking problem" would be solved if the league were to make players pay fines directly to the offended umpire. Although he was probably correct in assuming that no player would want to enrich

190

an umpire, he failed to take account of the club directors who used the league's fine fund to finance their annual Gargantuan banquet.

When asked for the secret of his success, Gaffney said that he constantly studied the rules, that he followed the ball "with all possible dispatch," that he tried to be calm in dealing with players, and that he studied different styles of base running. Also, he was sparing on fines, and boasted that in seven years he had fined a total of only $300.[48]

Although Gaffney was king, there was still room for nobles, and Gaffney's closest rival was doughty Bob Ferguson. Well known as player and manager, Ferguson was aloof, conceited, and stubborn—the archtype of the dictator-umpire. His refereeing philosophy was tough-minded and a polar opposite to Gaffney's. As he put it, "Umping always came as easy to me as sleeping on a feather bed. . . . Never change a decision, never stop to talk with a man. Make 'em play ball and keep their mouths shut, and never fear but the people will be on your side and you'll be called the king of umpires." If such a philosophy darkened the image of umpires, at least it enriched Ferguson. In 1886, he demanded $1,500, or $500 more than any other umpire. When asked why, he proclaimed that he did not care what others got, he was worth more.[49]

Ranged between these extreme types were some interesting intermediary personalities. One of the more intellectual umpires was Ben Young, whose promising career ended in death in a railroad accident, while en route to an assignment. In 1887, he had pioneered in the formulation of a professional code of ethics for umpires and had drawn up a ten-point plan for improving the status of umpires. Among other points, he wanted umpires to work in both major leagues, to be given a year's tenure, and to be protected by club owners from insult and assault. In return Young thought that umpires should avoid saloons and the company of players. While not adopted at that time, these points are embodied in rules today.

Like Young, Bob Emslie sought to uplift the profession. He

[48] *The Sporting News*, July 4, 1891; *Sporting Life*, August 8, 1888; *New York Clipper*, May 12, 1888, February 13, 1892.

[49] *Free Press* (Detroit), June 5, 1887; *New York Clipper*, January 2, 1886; *Sporting Life*, March 24, 1886.

concentrated on the re-education of newspaper reporters, urging them not to make "false excuses" to explain local defeats: "If we can only have base ball reporters whose partisanship was mild enough to treat us all alike the game would be greatly benefited in the end."[50]

In this age, however, such a millennium seemed far off. During the 1890's, abuses increased, and umpires were cursed, bombarded with beer bottles and rotten eggs, and subjected to beatings. The blackest year was 1897, and in August, President Young was losing sleep over the problem. At the time two had resigned, one until "the business gets semirespectable," two had been injured, and one had been arrested.[51]

If Young lost sleep over the problem, one can imagine the nightmares of the working umpires. Two from this era, John Heydler and Tom Lynch, later became National League presidents, but both admitted that the mere recollection of their "umping" careers made them shudder. To be sure, conditions would improve in the years after 1900, and umpires of today scarcely believe such tales. It was a tough life, too, for Americans who lived through the depression-racked 1890's, and for them the umpire was a cathartic outlet for pent-up emotions. Nor did fans do it all, for they were egged on by profit-minded promoters and writers.

For the working umpire who had battled through these years and learned to bear up under such an onus, at least there were some compensations. According to Tim Hurst, who was as handy with a quip as with his fists, he tolerated this dog's life because "You can't beat the hours."[52] Also, few umpires complained about the $1,500 salary for seven months' work.

4. THE CRITICS

From another point of view, the villification of umpires was a negative aspect of the evolution of sportswriting. During the 1880's the popularity of this literary form grew so rapidly that it

[50] *Sporting Life*, November 30, 1887, September 6, 1890, October 24, 1896.
[51] *Daily Globe* (Boston), August 9, 1897.
[52] *Sporting Life*, March 9, 1901; *New York Clipper*, December 29, 1884, February 22, 1896.

forced most sizable dailies to adopt the use of sports pages. In catering to the public appetite for baseball news, publishers created a new kind of specialist, the sportswriter. It was this craftsman who, having discovered the public hunger for such fare, now vied with his colleagues in grinding out stylized accounts, studded with hackneyed phrases, for the consumption of fans whose intellectual demands were modest.

In the history of American leisure one might argue that their greatest contribution was the creation of an artificial form of baseball, something that could be vicariously enjoyed by people who could not get to a major-league game. Still another function was their reminding, along with other sports specialists, urbanites of the changing of the seasons, since the city environment cut off its people from the agricultural cycle. Be that as it may, it is enough to say that the modern eclectic sports page was clearly recognizable by the end of the nineteenth century—in today's sports columns one finds the same clichés and style of writing.

However, writers of this era disagreed as to the extent of their influence. For one, Chadwick believed that the sportswriter's influence was great and should be used to uplift the spectacle by "every gentlemanly exemplar." But in the 1880's, Chadwick believed that some of his younger contemporaries were hurting the spectacle with their carping criticisms. Yet this point of view was scorned by writers like O. P. Caylor. Certain writers, he gibed, have egos that need daydreams to sustain them, especially, "those who actually imagine that the success of the game is raised or lowered by the leverage of their pen, with their ego as a fulcrum."[53]

Regardless of writers' quarreling over their own importance, many publishers were convinced that a good baseball page could sell papers. One who held this view was Francis C. Richter, who in 1883 founded *Sporting Life*. A keen observer of reading tastes, he noticed that many urbanites, when opening newspapers, turned first to the sports page and then to the financial section. This convinced him that big-city publishers could profit by increasing their baseball coverage. This he did, and within a year his sporting

[53] *Ibid*, April 28, 1888, April 27, 1889.

journal had twenty thousand readers, and within three years the circulation rose to forty thousand.[54] By 1890, he was able to increase the price of his paper to 10 cents and the number of pages from eight to sixteen.

Meanwhile, editors of city dailies were doing the same. In 1887, Harry Wright was offered a free-lance rate of three dollars a day by the editor of the *Philadelphia Record* to supply daily reports of his team's progress during spring training. Admitting that practice games meant "nothing," he nevertheless wanted "the score of each five inning practice game [which] will be greedily scanned by the enthusiasts here."[55]

By the end of the decade other editors were following suit, and competition grew keener when Joseph Pulitzer bought the New York *World* in 1882 and organized a separate sports department. Soon all kinds of gimmicks were used to lure the fans. The Detroit *Free Press*, for one, handed out illustrated, pocket-sized major-league schedules as inducements, and others quickly employed similar lures.[56]

Impressed by Richter's success with *Sporting Life*, the Spink brothers of St. Louis launched *The Sporting News* in 1886 as a western baseball weekly. In competing with thriving eastern rivals, the brothers relied on their belief that Midwesterners had a deep and permanent interest in baseball. From the start, the Spinks catered to Midwestern suspicions of eastern influences on sports, and they were not above dropping editorial digs at alleged wickedness and sexiness in some of the eastern papers. Piously, the brothers pledged that *The Sporting News* would always be "fit to enter the home of any man."

In particular, *The Sporting News* attack was aimed at the *Clipper* and the *Police Gazette*, since both spiced their offerings with sexy stories. However, *The Sporting News* could have avoided such a moral posture, especially since it was an attractive paper, with eye-catching makeup, thoroughly dedicated to baseball. In

54 *Sporting Life*, May 28, 1884.
55 H. M. Gillam to Wright, March 15, 1887. Wright, Correspondence, Vol. III.
56 Frank L. Mott, *American Journalism: A History of Newspapers in the United States Through 250 Years, 1690–1940*, 434, 443.

bidding for the title of "bible of baseball," the Spinks extended coverage to include most of the minor leagues, and although it took notice of other sports, baseball always drew top billing. Such dedication was rewarded, for after 1890 the *Clipper* decided to move in the direction of increasing theater coverage, and *Sporting Life* spread itself thin by giving much attention to fads like the bicycle boom of the 1890's.

But in the 1880's these three journals competed spiritedly for top billing. For a time the *Clipper* led, especially under the imaginative leadership of Will Rankin. By staffing a number of "baseball centers" with competent observer-writers, the *Clipper* vitalized its coverage and blanketed the major-league world. Not content with mere reports of scores, these centers poured forth a stream of lively gossip on the doings of baseball's characters, thereby satiating the public demand for rumors and "inside dope."[57]

Competition also invaded the world of the official guides. With the coming of the American Association, *Reach's Official Base Ball Guide* became an authoritative voice and immediately challenged *Spalding's Official Base Ball Guide*. Published by Reach's sporting goods house, this journal was well served by editors Caylor, James Williams, and George Munson. This journal even managed to survive the demise of its parent association. But such was not the fate of other official guides. *The Player's National League Official Guide* died with the collapse of the brotherhood movement, and that stepchild of the Union Association, the *Wright & Ditson Base Ball Guide*, carried on with diminishing success following the union collapse. By 1890, it was evident that the greatest success in the battle of the guides belonged to *Spalding's Official Base Ball Guide*. Faithfully edited by Chadwick, it proved so sturdy that he allowed two of his earlier foundlings, *DeWitt's Base Ball Guide* and *Beadle's Dime Base Ball Player*, to expire peacefully.[58]

The public's enormous appetite for baseball fare also created a solid career field for writers, many of whom answered the call because of the excitement and stylistic freedom that could be enjoyed.

[57] *The Sporting News*, September 15, 1888; *New York Clipper*, March 19, 1892.
[58] Ernest Krotz, *Collector's Guide to Baseball Publications*, 5–25.

To be sure, few became rich, and even Chadwick insisted that all of his prodigious labors earned him only a modest living, estimated at $1,400 a year in 1900, or considerably less than the salary of a good player. That he spoke the truth is borne out by the research of the late Frank L. Mott, the historian of American journalism. Although his findings showed that journalistic salaries doubled in the 1880's, top baseball reporters received $15 a week less than police reporters and $25 a week less than general-assignment men. Since top baseball writers ranked lower, they were probably attracted by the glamour of the life, which helped sportswriters bear up under unkind characterizations, like that of President Eliot of Harvard, who called journalists "drunkards, deadbeats, and bummers."[59]

Yet sportswriters seemingly enjoyed their life. Sustained by the camaraderie of their fraternity, they enjoyed press-box privileges, which they jealously guarded. If their press boxes were invaded by outsiders or encroached upon by economy-minded promoters, the writers fought back viciously in defense of their domain. In 1882, Detroit sportswriters pressured the Detroit Club to exclude "butterfly reporters," who were stealing their seats and swapping lies "about conquests of simple girls and silly women." Their battle cry included a new definition of a sports reporter: "No man is a reporter who is not engaged in reporting."[60]

To validate their status and to preserve their domain, major-league writers met in Cincinnati in 1887 and formed The Reporters National Association. With George Munson as president and Chadwick as vice-president, this new organization pledged itself "to promote the welfare of the National Game" by improving the official scoring of games and the collection of playing statistics. To further the cause, annual meetings were scheduled, and all writers in good standing were urged to join.

Two years later this association created a Scorer's League for reporters who served as official scorers of major-league games. Although the practice of using local reporters as official scorers was

---

[59] *The Sporting News*, November 10, 1900; Mott, *op. cit.*, 489.
[60] *Free Press* (Detroit), July 4, 1882.

a traditional one, the group was concerned with the lack of uniform procedures. Indeed, in 1887 the Detroit *Free Press* had denounced the "seventeen different varieties of scores" that were in use and blamed the individualism of the Boston scorers for the sad state of affairs. Hence, the league regarded itself as a watchdog agency working for order and uniformity in the area of baseball records.[61]

Advancements in communications technology also fostered the trend for uniformity in reporting games. In this era the need for efficient schemes for telegraphing accounts led to an ingenious scheme for uniform reporting known as the Orr-Edwards Code. In using it, a reporter began by giving symbols for weather and attendance reports. After this came a detailed summary of the main points of the game, followed by a "detailed table," including line score, summary, and the record of each player.[62]

The same trend for uniformity crept into the colorful style of baseball reporting. Like their forerunners of the gentleman's era, the reporters of this era loved jargon and puns. A labored example of the latter appeared in *Sporting Life* and described how a runaway dog held up a game. In his account the writer called the dog the "canine," and "the phantom barque." As for jargon, most of the present-day lexicon was completed and overworked by 1890.

But if the mental reservoirs of sportswriters were running dry by 1890, so, too, was their freedom to criticize. By the end of the decade club policies were encroaching upon freedom of expression, making reporters truly intellectual prostitutes. Commenting on the Kelly sale, as a case in point, a *Free Press* writer showed that reporters first had criticized Anson and Spalding, but quickly retracted their condemnation and praised the brilliance of "old Anse" and "Col. Spalding."[63]

Happily, a handful of plucky writers dared to buck this literary drift toward drab, stylized uniformity. However, their efforts were more the result of the personalized, emotion-bound style of journalism then prevalent, rather than the result of their own personal

[61] *Reach's Official Base Ball Guide*, 1888, pp. 37–39; *ibid.*, 1889.
[62] *The Orr-Edwards Code For Reporting Base Ball, 1890.*
[63] *Free Press* (Detroit), July 7, 1887; *Sporting Life*, April 2, 1884.

courage. It was characteristic of sportswriters of this age to become emotionally involved in their reporting. After all, regionalism and urban rivalries were strong influences at that time, and, not surprisingly, writers took victories and defeats more personally. At times deep personal involvements invoked real pathos, like the time an unknown Cleveland writer poured out his frustrations with these words: "There was not a man in the audience yesterday who did not feel like going home and kicking his pet poodle all over the house. It was one of those games that keeps a man four inches from his seat for two hours, at the same time wishing that he could thump the nearest small boy."[64]

With local sentiments running so high, one can appreciate the fears of a Detroit reporter who was questioned at the telegraph office by a muscular clerk, who demanded to know whether he was the writer who had called Boston "the bum team from Beantown?" When the writer squeaked a timid, "Yes," he was relieved to have the clerk extend a friendly hand and bellow, "Shake."[65]

Since journalistic standards called for aggressive attacks on rival papers, baseball writers were expected to take the offensive. This most of them did, and the "Notes and Comment" columns of the leading journals often became dueling grounds, in which charges of gullibility were the weapons. In 1889, Richter urged an end to the practice, scolding the "Industrious baseball faker" for foisting tales of "driveling Idiocy . . . upon a long-suffering public. . . . Nothing is too absurd or improbable for these . . . ink-slinging camp followers." Yet up until that time his own gossip columns gave no quarter: "The office boy who 'does' the baseball . . . [for the Cincinnati *Enquirer*] ought to look before he leaps. . . . How much would the office boy like to wager that Sneed is manager of the Nashville Club?" In another savage sally, Richter's paper struck at the Chicago *Mirror of American Sports* for allegedly pirating news from *Sporting Life*: "Its only spark of originality . . . is the billiard department, and that is simply owing to the fact

64 *New York Clipper*, May 20, 1882.
65 *Free Press* (Detroit), October 20, 1887.

that it is owned and controlled by a Chicago table manufacturing company."[66]

In those days nobody, not even the mighty Chadwick, was above criticism. At this time *The Sporting News* tried hard to debunk his claim to being the father of the game, as did Will Rankin, a pretender to the title, who argued that baseball was forty years old before Chadwick wrote. Chadwick not only weathered these attacks, but before the decade was over, he had his own column in *The Sporting News*. With the king no longer fair game, that paper trained its guns on Caylor, calling him that "cadaver, that cross red mongrel."[67]

But energetic, Oliver Perry Caylor was quite able to defend himself with style. Born in Ohio in 1849, he acquired an educational background that was superior to those of most of his contemporary reporters. He finished first in high school and later became a Cincinnati lawyer. Having tasted the joys of newspaper work, however, he abandoned his law career to become a Cincinnati reporter. While with the *Enquirer*, he covered his first baseball games, but it was another five years before he embraced the game. In 1882, he helped found the association's Cincinnati Club, and after a brief fling as its manager, he turned to editing *Reach's Official Base Ball Guide* and to free-lancing for several Cincinnati papers. Falling out of favor in Cincinnati, he left town, nursing grudges. Drifting to Carthage, Missouri, he bought his own paper, sold it at a profit, and continued his restless ways. In search of bigger game he journeyed to New York and became editor of the *Sporting Times and Theatrical News* for a time, but failed to halt its decline. After this followed more literary failures, including a try at founding a western sporting weekly and an unsuccessful novel. Embittered by reverses, he finally settled down in a secure, mundane career as baseball editor of the New York *Herald*, which left him with time to write for the established sporting weeklies and to serve as official scorer for the Giants.[68]

[66] *Sporting Life*, June 2, 1886, July 31, 1889.
[67] *The Sporting News*, July 6, October 26, 1889.
[68] *New York Clipper*, May 13, October 29, 1881, March 20, 1886; *Sporting Life*, June 26, 1889; *Reach's Official Base Ball Guide*, 1897, pp. 109–10.

Possessing a witty, cutting, and sarcastic style, Caylor wrote articles that made lively reading for those who were not the object of his attention. Always an independent thinker, he tried in his own way to elevate the image of major-league baseball in general, and baseball writing in particular. In pursuing his will-o'-the-wisp objectives, Caylor cast himself in the role of iconoclast. Thus, instead of bluntly attacking the association's grandiose plan of using an all-star staff of umpires to "solve" the umpire problem, Caylor waited until he was able to report that every member of the vaunted staff had been mobbed by fans. Then he drove home his message— ". . . paying a man a big price will not make him infallible or shield him from the injustice of an over-exacting public." By overselling its staff, the association, he charged, damaged the new profession by encouraging prima donnas. He singled out Umpire Ferguson, who was touted as "Robert the Great," but who was referred to by fans as "Robber the Great!"

Writing in the *Clipper* in 1885, Caylor warned that association complacency was comforting their league rivals, and it was he who broke the story that the same group of directors controlled both the league's Giants and the association Mets.[69] A staunch opponent of monopolistic baseball, Caylor could not bring himself to support the Players League, and he lent his pen to the opposition.

When not criticizing the baseball bigwigs, Caylor continuously attacked his colleagues. He was especially good at mocking reporters who could not see beyond the bounds of their own city. In mocking the chamber-of-commerce style of writing of an 1883 Detroit reporter, who boosted his team's recent entry into the league, Caylor pictured the city as being bonded to raise money to give each godlike player "a house and coach and four." Also, he taunted, each will get clean shirts, socks, "a toothbrush with instructions how to use it, a box of soap and towels . . . a first reader. Men have offered themselves as tutors, and Derby, who can spell, will run for Congress. Mayor Thompson has issued an order requiring the citizens to raise their hats when passing the

[69] *Sporting Life*, September 5, 19, 1888; *New York Clipper*, December 19, 1885.

honorable aggregation, school children will sing 'The Conquering Hero' when one of them approaches."[70]

Among Caylor's greatest admirers was Chadwick, his friend of twenty years. Although Caylor's reputation was second to that of Chadwick, the older man liked his style. When Caylor died in harness in 1897, Chadwick wrote of his friend's dedication, telling how on the very eve of his death Caylor had asked for copies of eastern papers so that he could answer his critics, who were speaking of his "approaching death." Further tribute came from a *Herald* colleague, who described as "pathetic in its boldness," Caylor's fight to stay alive: "The struggle was one-sided, but on his part . . . heroic. Before he left the city for the West and hoped for recovery he went to the ball grounds . . . accompanied by his wife, and though scarcely able to reach his old seat . . . his courage never faltered."[71]

Matching such independence of spirit was Richter, who thought long and hard on how to improve the spectacle. His productive career lasted until the eve of the First World War, when death ended his weekly brain child. But his influence was at a peak in the 1880's, when he proposed his famous "Millennium Plan" as a solution to major-league exploitation of the minors. Confident that his revolutionary scheme would solve problems like unstable franchises, major-league rivalry, and the exploitation of minors, he sought to equalize player salaries and to eliminate the sale of players. With pardonable pride he touted his plan as "grand in conception, comprehensive in scope and tremendous in wide-reaching ramification; and yet withal it is so simple and direct in action."

In December, 1887, he outlined the plan. First, he suggested that the National Agreement be revised to end the cold war dividing the two big leagues. To do so, he advocated that all professional clubs join in a confederation for their mutual aid and protection. Those designated as minor leagues were to have player-reservation rights along with the majors. This, he believed, would stabilize

[70] *Ibid.*, July 21, 1883.
[71] *Reach's Official Base Ball Guide*, 1897, 109–10.

201

minor leagues and give young players more seasoning. Yet, because the plan would allow the majors to draft a limited number of minor-league stars each year, the interests of both would be served. For the fair administration of this plan, he proposed that an arbitration committee be established and be composed of major- and minor-league administrators.

More controversial was his idea for equalizing the strength of big-league clubs. In this his plan was for the leagues, not the clubs, to reserve the players. By allowing a club to reserve only one player, presumably a captain, wealthy clubs would no longer be able to buy pennants. All other players would be graded by their skill, teamwork, moral conduct, and an annual lottery would be conducted every year in both major leagues for the purpose of selecting each team's line-up for the coming year. The luck of the draw would not only equalize the strength of teams, but would silence newspaper criticism of managers and directors.

Under this scheme players would also be paid according to their classification, with a maximum salary of $2,500 for pitchers and catchers in the top class. The best infielders would draw a maximum of $2,200, and top outfielders, $2,000. However, Richter also proposed incentives, including a 20 per cent bonus for each member of a pennant-winning team, and prorated percentages for members of first-division clubs.

The plan even took care of the wallflowers who failed to get picked. Such men would be placed in a special category, from which would be formed teams that would play exhibition games with regular clubs. Their pay would come from the receipts of these games.

After broaching the plan during the 1880's, Richter seemed content to watch the debate which it provoked, which was considerable, but in the end the scheme was shelved as visionary. Wealthy promoters, instead, preferred free-enterprise and did not take kindly to socialistic agitation.[72] Except in times of crises, free-enterprise was gospel for major-league operators, and this is still the case today.

[72] *Sporting Life,* September 7, December 14, 1887.

Overshadowed by literary giants, like Chadwick, Caylor, Richter, and the Spinks, were lesser innovators. One, Clarence Dow, an able, young Boston writer, recognized the importance of reliable statistics, and by the 1890's, he was acclaimed as the ablest statistician.[73] In 1888, Ernest L. Thayer, of the *San Francisco Examiner*, penned his famous poem, "Casey at the Bat." And, De Witt Ray, of the New York *Sporting Times and Theatrical News*, made his contributions to the growing storehouse of baseball humor. One of Ray's most effective techniques was the fictitious interview. Once he spun a yarn about a crooked umpire, who was determined to save the money that he had wagered on one of the teams. With two out in the ninth, his favorites needed two runs to tie, and an eager player very nearly ended the umpire's hopes by sliding past second base and being tagged out. But since the player had left his pants hung up on the second base spike, the umpire decided to call him safe, because he was out of uniform, and the rules demanded players be in uniform at all times. When an opposing player protested, the umpire appeased him by calling the pants out, but leaving the runner safe. This set the stage for the umpire to give the next five men their bases on balls and, thus, win the bet.[74]

It was the voracious mass consumption of colorful tall stories that helped to make major league baseball a dynamic leisure pastime. In this way these yarn spinners found a place in the spectacle's cast of characters, along with the player-heroes, the chorus of fans, and the villainous umpires.

[73] *Reach's Official Base Ball Guide*, 1894, p. 54.
[74] N. Fred Pfeffer (ed.), *Scientific Ball*, 74–75.

11

Baseball Comes of Age

I T IS SOMETHING of a paradox that baseball's "blue season," as President Hulbert once called the winter months, is the time when revolutionary changes in the style of the spectacle are effected. However, since military doctrine is refashioned during postwar eras, it should not surprise fans that baseball doctrine is also reshaped during the offseason, for traditionally the winter months are the time for the annual major-league meetings, the time for "addle heads and thick-skulled malcontents" to get together and seek ways to alter the sport to their advantage.[1] It is during the dry minutes of these yearly meetings that one may hear the innovations suggested which will influence the pattern of baseball the ensuing season.

[1] William Hulbert to Harry Wright, February 22, 1878. Wright, Correspondence, Vol. II.

During the 1880's the most eagerly awaited report was that of the committee on playing rules. This group usually acted on the basis of observations and criticisms of the previous season's play, and, for the committee's harried members, free advice was plentiful and came from such sources as players, umpires, owners, reporters, and fans. It was also welcomed advice, and in this era the committee responded readily to grass-root suggestions. Such receptivity helped to make the 1880's a time of stylistic change, which in turn helped to bring the spectacle to a rapid maturity.

To be sure, many of the committee's decisions were impulsive, shortsighted, and ridiculous, but this was an age of experimentation—a period marked by the introduction and rejection of new ideas. Since the major-league spectacle was new, tradition did not fetter the rules committee, which felt free to test new ideas. Thus, the committee often practiced radical surgery, and unhesitatingly cut away elements that were held sacred during the bygone gentleman's era, replacing them with stylistic grafts that are easily recognizable to modern observers.

Especially did the committee members focus their attention on the problem of imbalance between pitching and batting. In 1881, the committee penalized the pitcher by increasing the pitching distance from forty-five to fifty feet, but pitchers did retain a big advantage—that of being permitted to move freely about in a large rectangular "box." Indeed, some foxy pitchers employed a deceptive running delivery, which confounded many hitters. Furthermore, no rule prevented pitchers from concealing the ball before delivery, and they were also allowed seven bad pitches (balls) before a batter could take his base.[2]

It is not surprising, therefore, that so many baseball contests of the early 1880's were pitchers' games. However, this gave the spectacle such an unbalanced aspect that President Eliot of Harvard recommended in 1884 that baseball be excluded from the modern interscholastic athletic program: "I think it is a wretched game. . . . There are only nine men who can play a game . . . and out of the nine there are only two desirable positions—pitcher and

[2] *Spalding's Official Base Ball Guide*, 1881, pp. 16, 62–81.

205

catcher—so there is but little chance for the youth to gratify his ambition."[3]

Not only did Eliot's criticism apply to the major-league spectacle, but pitchers seemed reluctant to remedy the game's imbalance. As a group, they were ever receptive to new tactics that might frustrate batters, like overhand pitching, which was first barred by the rules. However, sidearm pitching came to be accepted by 1883, resulting in a new rule that allowed pitchers to throw in any manner except overhand. Having won the right to throw the ball in this manner, pitchers soon smuggled in the overhand delivery, in spite of the opposition from the rules committee. To combat the heresy, association umpires were ordered to penalize violators in 1884, but the league decided that year to legalize overhand pitching. The following year, the purist defenders of the old game made their last stand by persuading the committee to impose a one-month trial ban on overhand pitching. When the experiment failed, it marked the end of further efforts to restrict this delivery, and with the capitulation of the league, the association was forced to follow suit.[4]

The new pitching freedom prompted purists to predict dire results. Among the worriers was Tim Keefe of the Mets, who thought the new delivery would injure pitching arms. Also, he argued that "a high thrown ball is not so deceiptive [*sic*] or so hard to hit as a ball delivered from below the shoulder." Another observer, George Wright, opposed the change because he was afraid catchers would "break up" under the punishing strain of increased speed.[5] But the introduction of protective armor soon banished this fear, and the utilization of trainers skilled in the arts of massage helped minimize Keefe's worries.

Thus, by 1886, it was apparent that the pitchers had gained a great advantage, so great that the joint major-league rules committee sought new ways to restrict the pitcher. Eventually, they

---

[3] *Globe-Democrat* (St. Louis), April 12, 1884.

[4] *Spalding's Official Base Ball Guide*, 1883, pp. 29–30, 1884, pp. 29–34; *Reach's Official Base Ball Guide*, 1884, pp. 155–69; *Sporting Life*, June 17, 1885.

[5] *New York Clipper*, December 15, 1883; *Globe-Democrat* (St. Louis), April 7, 1884.

came up with a rule that required the pitcher to hold the ball in front of himself before delivery, which restricted the pitcher's movements within the box and which reduced the size of the box. Since the pitcher now had to keep one foot on the rear line of the box while winding up, this prevented him from employing such tactics as the deceptive running delivery and the hidden ball.

In molding a modern style of play, the rules committee did not fear breaking with the past. Although it was traditional for batters to have the privilege of requesting a high or a low strike zone, this prerogative was summarily withdrawn in 1887, and the new strike zone was defined as being between a batter's shoulders and knees above the plate. At the same time the committee reduced the number of called balls necessary for a batter to take a free base to five. If this ruling approached present-day regulations, another decision of the committee sent baseball far off in another direction. Up to 1887, requiring three strikes for an out was one of the most revered rituals in the spectacle, but in 1887 the committee decided to give a batter four strikes. Having helped batters in this manner, the committee also decided to give him credit for a base hit for each base on balls. Furthermore, if a pitcher hit any part of the batter or his uniform, the batter was to be permitted to take a free base, providing he made an honest effort to dodge the missile.

These precedent shattering innovations lasted but one season. In 1888, the three-strike rule was restored, and the batter once again had to hit the ball to receive credit for a hit.[6] From this point onward the committee moved in the direction of the present-day style, and in 1889 the formula of four balls and three strikes was adopted, along with a rule making a sacrifice hit nonchargeable as a time at bat.

Other lasting patterns arose from the farsighted 1889 conference. At George Wright's suggestion, the batter was to be permitted to run past first base without being tagged out upon returning to the bag. Also, if an umpire believed that the batter was deliberately fouling off pitches, he might declare the batter out. In another step

[6] *Spalding's Official Base Ball Guide*, 1887, pp. 76–79, 127–35, 1888, pp. 80–86; *Reach's Official Base Ball Guide*, 1887, pp. 25–26, 148–64, 1888, pp. 156–63.

toward the modern style of using part-time specialists, managers won the right to make substitutions, although at first only one substitute was allowed per game, and he was to enter the game only at the conclusion of an inning.[7]

Viewed in retrospect, 1889 was a year of lasting stylistic innovation. To be sure, some imbalance between the pitcher and batter still persisted, which would result in the 1893 extension of the pitching distance to the present-day sixty feet, six inches. But except for this and the introduction of the now-familiar, pentagon-shaped home plate in 1900, the game of the golden age had come to resemble the contest with which we are now familiar.

Of course, constant tinkering with the style of the game provoked many arguments. That the changes were generally for the good of the game was Chadwick's opinion. Writing in 1889, he marveled at the prowess of the overhand pitchers and found the new style both exciting and challenging. He noted that the pitchers, far from merely exercising brute strength, had developed an increasing amount of cunning and resourcefulness. Especially did he like their changes of pace and their spot pitching, for such deceptions not only taxed the batter's balance and timing, but often forced him to hit to the wrong field.[8] Yet, because pitchers could no longer employ the running delivery (as Radbourne did so successfully in 1884) or conceal the ball, Chadwick was convinced that batters had gained enough advantage, and he praised the work of the rules committees of 1887 and 1889.

Of course, baseball style also changed as a result of individual innovations made on the playing fields. Pregame batting practice was one example; eventually it became so much a part of the spectacle that many fans came early just to watch the demonstration. According to Chadwick, this was another of Harry Wright's fertile ideas. While managing the Phillies, he required each man to hit twelve balls as part of a pregame exercise program. While this was going on, "fungo" hitters stood farther down the base lines and drove fly balls to outfielders. Chadwick praised this crowd-pleasing

---

[7] *Spalding's Official Base Ball Guide*, 1889, pp. 101–27, 1890, pp. 31–33.
[8] *Ibid.*, 1889, pp. 45–51; *Reach's Official Base Ball Guide*, 1891, pp. 3–4.

program as highly conducive to "scientific" batting, and he noted that it was far superior to the old custom, whereby teams simply warmed up with a little ball tossing prior to a game. But if by scientific batting, Chadwick meant less brute slugging,[9] he was to be disappointed, because in time pregame batting practice would whet the public appetite for more slugging.

Another popular innovation was the growing practice of "coaching" from along the side lines by captains and managers. In time this practice took the form of heckling the opposition and stealing their signals and tactics, which so delighted the fans that it was quickly adopted by baseballers everywhere. Indeed, so widespread was the practice that a Boston writer in 1886 demanded remedial legislation: "A disreputable feature of base-ball is the hooting, howling, and yelling of coaches to disconcert . . . other players in the field. It is no part of the game. For men to stand . . . as near the lines as possible, and yell like Indians . . . should be frowned upon." Especially was the writer annoyed by such exhortations by coaches as "He'll muff it!" or "He can't throw it."

By this time "jockeying" was so appealing to fans that it could not be totally banned. By 1888, players, like Latham, were so popular with fans that to curb the coaches might greatly affect attendance. Thus, realistic rule makers of 1887 chose, instead, to restrict, and they did so by establishing fixed coaching lines and confining the coaches to these boundaries. In this way the coaches remained, and their distracting tactics were somewhat curbed.[10]

The effects of these alterations upon baseball were partially revealed in a series of six drawings of major-league scenes that appeared in *The Illustrated Graphic News: The Great Western Pictorial Weekly* in 1886. Based on photographs taken by a pioneer in the art, these drawings portray the major-league style of the golden age. In one of the scenes, a Cincinnati batter wields a heavy bat, not rounded off at the barrel as those of today. He is dressed in a uniform similar to those of the present, but his cap resembles

[9] Henry Chadwick, *The Art of Base Ball Batting*, 38–39; New York Clipper, September 17, 1887.

[10] *Tribune* (Chicago), August 15, 1886; *Spalding's Official Base Ball Guide*, 1887, pp. 127–35.

those worn by soldiers during Civil War, and his high-topped cleated shoes differ from the low-cut ones of today.

The same scene shows the catcher wearing a mask, but his protective gloves, worn on each hand, resemble modern dress gloves. Behind the catcher stands the umpire, wearing a dark suit, protective mask, and a light-colored cap. At this time neither catcher nor umpire wore a chest protector.

In another scene a visiting Louisville player is at bat, while the next scheduled batter waits his turn at the end of the players bench. Lacking the privacy of the modern dugout, this long wooden repose was located near the grandstand, with only a low fence between them. At this close range the visitors were vulnerable to missiles like bottles and spittle, not to mention curses and insults.

Cincinnati first-baseman "Long John" Reilly moves toward the fence to catch a fly ball in another photograph. His bare hands remind us that fielders' gloves were not then widely used.

Another sketch shows the playing field, enclosed with a four-foot wooden fence, which was intended to discourage mobs. The entire ball park is encircled by an eleven-foot board fence. Spectator accommodations are also revealing. The expensive pavilion area has a roof supported by wooden beams to shield the more affluent fans from the sun, while average fans sit under the sun on the less expensive "bleaching boards."

Outside the park, clusters of wires heralded the advent of the new age of electricity.[11] Those strung into the park were telegraph wires, and in the 1880's most parks were serviced by telegraph companies. For some clubs, this service proved to be a profitable side line, especially since rival telegraph companies would bid for the service. In 1886, although the Browns had sold monopoly rights to the Baltimore and Ohio Company, a rival, Western Union, smuggled a man inside, who hooked in and operated nearly the entire game before Superintendent Solari caught him and "bounced him with his instrument from the grounds." Such fierce rivalry for the telegraph concession suggests that these companies found that

[11] *The Illustrated Graphic News: The Great Western Pictorial Weekly,* June 19, 1886.

their offices were becoming surrogate ball parks for many fans.

For fans who wished to avoid the ordeal of pregame ticket lines, tickets were sold at various spots in town. Most of the sites were male haunts, like cigar stores and billiard halls, and although ladies could pick up tickets at a few drug stores, for the most part the game of the 1880's was a masculine leisure pastime. Indeed, Victorian sensibilities were shocked in this decade when a Mr. Freeman sponsored a professional "Female Base Ball Club." Like baseball Magdalenes, these girls were denounced as virtual whores, guilty of the additional crime of prostituting the game. Richter's attacks were heavier than stones when he accused the girls of behaving in such a manner that Georgia ladies would not ride the same train with them, or when he wrote, "The female has no place in base ball, except to the degradation of the game. For two seasons . . . [people] . . . have been nauseated with the spectacle of these tramps, who have been repeatedly stranded and the objects of public charity."[12]

As a mirror of dominant national values, the major-league game not only reflected social mores, but also the dynamic sentiments of our national faith in machinery and gadgets. In regards to the latter, some dreamed at this time of making baseball a twenty-four-hour-a-day possibility, and to this end they worked on making night baseball a technical reality. In 1883, Fort Wayne, Indiana, experimented with night baseball, and that year, too, the Jenney Electric Light Company, of Quincy, Illinois, repeated the experiment, using lights strung on fourteen poles erected about the park. Notwithstanding two power failures, the persistent problems with outfield flies, and the loss of new baseballs, the *Clipper* approved of the idea. Although the company repeated the experiment with greater success and although others also proved that night baseball was technically possible in the 1880's, the innovation was not widely adopted until the next century.[13]

Even though the prospects for night baseball were poor at this time, the same could not be said for Sunday baseball. The advo-

---

[12] *Globe-Democrat* (St. Louis), April 11, 1886; *Sporting Life*, December 24, 1884.
[13] *Sporting Life*, June 10, 1883; *New York Clipper*, June 2, 1883.

211

cates of Sunday baseball fought hard, and they were opposed by equally zealous defenders of the sanctity of the Lord's day. Since both camps were strong and unyielding, the fight continued far into the twentieth century. In taking its stand on this controversial issue, the National League first chose to side with the angels, and, in 1880, Hulbert peremptorily stripped Cincinnati of its franchise for playing Sunday ball. Although the Cincinnati owner protested, stating that his action was in the interest of making more money, Hulbert refused to reconsider his action. Nevertheless, as future league leaders soon discovered, this Cincinnati promoter had realistically gauged the changing values of the fans. With immigrants bringing the "Continental Sunday" into towns like Cincinnati and St. Louis, Protestant values eroded rapidly. Although the league ignored this important change, the association did not, and its directors discovered that their toleration of Sunday ball paid handsome returns.

For giving its members the right to decide themselves on the question of Sunday ball, the association was denounced by its rival as immoral and corrupt. But such epithets were soon muted by the whirring of Sunday turnstiles in association towns. Especially did western fans support the Sunday game, and in western towns the proponents of Sunday ball scored their first victories against the moralizers.

However, defenders of the Puritanical Sunday employed old watchwords in mounting their defense. Since such axioms matched the sympathies of many ruralites, whose backgrounds included a rural-Protestant orientation, the Sabbatarians were able to defeat the spread of Sunday ball into the East, and then they launched a counteroffensive in the West.

From 1883 onward, a battle of words raged between the two camps, with one side advocating the logic of science and secularism and the other exhorting the logic of the Good Book. The conflict resulted in strange alignments. No doubt most observers of baseball expected the upright Chadwick to side with the opposition, but he had long been a city dweller and could not abide the twisted logic of New York Sabbatarians, who would allow commercial dens like Coney Island to do business on Sunday, but would forbid Sunday baseball. Nor did he attack the association's Brooklyn team for transferring games outside the borough in order to escape the anti-Sunday ball ordinance, for, in 1889, Sunday games drew well and reflected a strong popular demand.

While the controversy continued, both camps readied their propaganda artillery. In St. Louis, where the Browns profited from Sunday ball and beer sales, churchmen in 1885 plotted to end the practice. According to a clergical report, intended to show that piety was waning, a Sunday survey tallied only ten thousand churchgoers, while on the same day, twenty thousand crowded the ball parks, another twenty thousand gathered at the beer gardens, and five thousand assembled to hear two lectures by Colonel "Bob" Ingersoll, the great agnostic.[14]

But if changing values were against the Sabbatarians, local laws were not. Thus, a favorite ploy of the antis was to prosecute the management of the club for violating some long-forgotten ordinance which banned work on Sundays. Usually this was effective, but at times it backfired. In Columbus, Ohio, in 1884, when Sunday ball was banned on these grounds, the clubs retaliated by securing an injunction against horsecars operating on Sundays, which cut deeply into church attendance. In other towns, club owners struck back by enjoining theaters from operating on Sunday, a practice which drew anguished howls from the theater crowd. Since the *Clipper* served both the theater and the sports publics, such a ploy placed the paper in an awkward position. Pressed hard, this journal finally supported the theater, arguing lamely that baseball crowds were more "promiscuous" than theater crowds.

Because of the boomeranging effects of such a weapon, the moralizers fought for laws that would be applicable only to baseball. In 1887, they secured the passage of a state law which threatened the Brown's operation, and in that same year two other association clubs felt the sting of new legislation.

However, moralizers in St. Louis received a sharp setback when

[14] *Tribune* (Chicago), October 5, 1880; *Sporting Life*, December 31, 1884, May 20, 1885.

213

a state supreme court judge ruled against the law. Basing his opinion on his belief that Sunday baseball was not work, but "a reasonable sport and the use of nature's powers," he refused to apply the new anti-Sunday work law against major-league baseball in St. Louis.[15] It was this decision which indirectly ushered Sunday ball into the league, for under the terms of the association's 1892 surrender, the four association defectors were to be allowed to play Sunday games at home. In explaining this change of heart to a reporter, Von der Ahe explained that money, not morality, dictated the league's new stand. The league was now aware of the changing tastes and desires of urban people: "Pittsburgh has been losing money long enough, and they want a few thousand of those nice Sunday dollars. Then there is Cincinnati with its wooden shoe population. You might as well put the average Dutchman in jail as deprive him of his game of ball and glass of beer on Sunday."

Drawing upon his long experience in Boston and Philadelphia, Harry Wright countered these rationalizations with his notion that the money from Sunday games did not justify the moral struggle. Although admitting that he held scruples against Sunday ball, Wright argued that the big Sunday crowds merely siphoned attendance from Friday, Saturday, and Monday games. Over the long run, then, spectacular Sunday crowds failed to raise annual figures enough to warrant engaging in legal and moral controversies.[16]

Nevertheless, outside of the western strongholds like St. Louis, the moralizers were effective. In an 1890 Maryland decision a judge held that since professional baseball "can be construed as nothing else than work," anti-Sunday work statutes could be used against Sunday baseball promoters. Moreover, a series of Cincinnati crusades so discredited Sunday baseball in that city that by 1891, Manager Kelly of the Reds found himself in court on three separate occasions as a violator of the Sabbath. But in each instance friendly juries refused to find the baseball hero guilty.

Of course, Sabbatarians sometimes drew fire from religious

---

15 *New York Clipper*, July 5, 1884, July 23, 1887; *Sporting Life*, July 20, 1887.
16 *New York Clipper*, January 23, 1892.

groups, which held that workingmen needed diversions. Apparently, the Roman Catholic Church better understood this basic need of man; in any event, the church was a strong urban religion at this time, and it did lend support to the advocates of Sunday ball. Thus, as early as 1887, the *Catholic Watchman* of Cincinnati gave its blessing to Sunday ball, "both as a measure of health and morals."[17]

This play of force and counterforce, however, merely served to provide rallying points and to enroll in the hostile ranks those trenchant minds which such controversies always provoke. In retrospect, the 1880's merely witnessed the opening round in a moral war, which would be fought well into the present century.

If changing American morals could alter the spectacle of baseball, so, too, could changing American technology. In an age of machine- and gadget-mindedness, major-league club directors were ever eager to adopt the latest baseball gimmicks. By 1890, *Reach's Official Base Ball Guide* was able to display an impressive array of baseball equipment, which was designed to help players achieve success. For example, an 1889 advertisement offered the harried catcher a "heavily-padded mitten," to prevent "broken and stoved up fingers," masks, and several types of inflated chest protectors. In supporting the use of these aids, the Reach firm cited league catcher Charles Zimmer's feat of having caught 125 games in a single season, a feat "beyond belief," but possible only because he used the available equipment.

That same year the guides advertised their modified gloves, which they claimed to be used by most defensive players. Naturally old-timers sneered at the new devices; even George Wright, who forgot for a moment that his firm made many of them, in 1888 demanded that the rule makers limit the size of fielders' gloves, because they place batters at a disadvantage.[18]

But far from being reversed, the trend continued, and, in 1890, Harry Decker, a former major-league catcher, perfected his

[17] *Ibid.*, September 24, 1887, July 26, 1890; *Sporting Life*, June 20, 1891.

[18] *Reach's Official Base Ball Guide*, 1890, pp. 35–36; 1891, *passim; New York Clipper*, August 18, 1888.

"Decker Safety Catching Mitt," the forerunner of modern mitts. By the end of that year, Spalding controlled its sales and promotion, and the "decker" quickly became a common term for all big mitts.[19] In time the trend would also affect the size of fielders' gloves, although during this century they remained small and on the order of dress gloves.

An ever growing public demand for the varied artifacts of baseball was a bonanza for sporting goods entrepreneurs. In 1882, the *Clipper* estimated that fifty thousand balls were sold along with thirty thousand cords of bat lumber. And in 1891, Reach, now part of the Spalding trust, actually complained about the number of baseballs used and lost by major-league teams. But, lest the reader doubt Mr. Reach's sanity, let it be known that his company customarily supplied balls free of charge to the association clubs. Understandably then, this old-timer of 1891 wondered how eight association clubs could use eighty dozen balls in spring training and wondered further whether players were eating them.[20] By way of comparison the *Clipper* in 1882 once expressed its astonishment that a team could have used three balls in one game.[21]

In the 1880's, bats and balls, those necessary parts of the spectacle, varied in quality and cost; the cheapest bat or ball sold for as little as 5 cents, while the finest of either cost 75 cents. To satiate a voracious public appetite for cheap bats, Spalding offered to purchase 100,000 wagon tongues, to be lathed by mass-production techniques into his folksy "Wagon Tongue Brand Bats."[22] Meanwhile, new machines were manufacturing baseballs by the thousands, and, in 1883, Reach described his assembly-line techniques. Cheap balls were made entirely by machinery, each taking but ten minutes. Of course, official balls took longer to fashion and involved several integrated operations, including hand stitching with catgut thread. A trained crew of specialists, stitching away on a ten-hour shift, could produce twenty-five dozen first-class balls a day. Although Reach bragged that his best balls were made

19 Harry Decker to A. J. Reach, March 18, 1889. Wright, Correspondence, Vol. IV.
20 *New York Clipper*, July 21, 1883; *Daily Globe* (Boston), April 12, 1891.
21 *New York Clipper*, September 2, 1882.
22 *Spalding's Official Base Ball Guide*, 1888, advertisement.

in a manner that was virtually perfect, teams continued to complain that some of the balls became soft and unusable after only a few hard knocks.[23]

At the price of a few complaints, however, there were fortunes to be made in the sporting-goods business of the 1880's. At the beginning of this decade, it was an open field with sizable firms like Reach, Spalding, Wright and Ditson, and Peck and Snyder competing with others like Rawlings Brothers of St. Louis, Buckley and Decker of Chicago, and the Charles Morris bat firm. At this time some specialized in one product, such as Buckley and Decker in catchers' mitts and Morris in bats. Anxious to corner the bat market, Morris once wrote Wright asking him to attest to the fact that Morris bats "increased the batting." Hopefully, Morris wondered if Wright might bring himself to testify to the fact that Morris bats decreased the strike-out rate.

Although Wright remained skeptical of such claims to mana in bats, he once invented a bat flattened on one side, which he believed would facilitate bunting. But a wilder notion came from Emile Kinst of Chicago, who developed a curved-barrel bat, shaped like a question mark, which he expected to put a deceptive spin on a batted ball, thus adding to the uncertainties of ball games.[24]

Unhappily, for the small-fry producers, the sporting-goods industry, like so many other industrial enterprises of the day, quickly came under monopolistic controls, which destroyed the free market. In the early 1880's, it appeared as if Reach might become the octopus of the industry, although the newly created Wright and Ditson firm, with its patents on the Thayer catcher's mask, looked formidable. But in struggling to expand, both of these rivals found themselves dwarfed, and then devoured, by Albert G. Spalding's dynamic enterprise. In a real sense, Spalding shouldered his way into the company of the self-made "captains of industry," and he did it with his superior organization, imagination, and ruthlessness.

In 1881, "A. G. Spalding & Brothers" occupied a modest build-

[23] *New York Clipper*, January 20, 1883, August 30, 1884.

[24] *The Sporting News*, February 2, 1889; *Sporting Life*, July 5, 1890; Chas. Morris to Wright, May 25, 1889. Wright, Correspondence, Vol. II.

ing in Chicago, and at this time Spalding seemed content with his interest in the Chicago team and in running his small factory in Hastings, Michigan. But as the years rolled along, the small firm grew, and in 1884, Spalding opened offices in New York and secured control of a leading turnstile manufacturing concern. In a bold 1887 advertisement he announced that his firm now had branch offices in twenty-three American cities.

However, the shockingly unexpected announcement came in 1889, when a journal announced Spalding's acquisition of Reach's firm. According to *Sporting Life*, the merger was accomplished secretly, but its explosive effect was to make Spalding's "the chief sporting goods house in the world."[25]

In building his empire, Spalding capitalized on his rivals' lack of expansion capital. By buying their stock, he came to dominate many, but another of his tactics was to make them dependent on his firm by subletting his own production of certain items to them. This was the case of Reach, who was handed a contract to produce almost all of Spalding's baseballs. However, it so taxed Reach's facilities that he was first obliged to borrow capital from his rival, and eventually forced to sell out to his rival. At the time of the sale, in which Reach received $100,000 and an executive post with Spalding, a community of interest already existed between the rival firms.[26]

Meanwhile, the death of Henry Ditson, late in the decade, gave Spalding a shot at another rival. At Wright's request, Spalding bought up Ditson's interest, which paved the way for his future control. With the destruction of his competitors, Spalding was able to complete his grand design. Taking advantage of the favorable corporation laws of New Jersey, he established headquarters there and capitalized his sporting goods empire at $4,000,000. Since this was being accomplished in 1892, one can understand why, after his work with the league in the brotherhood war and the association

---

[25] *New York Clipper*, March 26, June 25, 1881, April 12, 1884, April 13, 1886; *The Sporting News*, May 14, 1887.

[26] *Sporting Life*, September 4, 1889; Bartlett, *op. cit.*, 147.

war, he chose to retire from the league councils on the grounds that he was "entitled to a rest."[27]

In pulling out of major-league baseball for the time being, Spalding probably did so because he was jaded over his experiences with his world baseball tour of 1888–89. Anxious to promote major league-baseball, and, no doubt, the name of his sporting goods firm in every continent, this baseball missionary led two teams in a $50,000 round-the-world tour.

If he expected the quick acceptance of baseball at home or abroad, he was mistaken. At home he drew the wrath of the ball-players' brotherhood, which accused him of taking their leaders out of the country, while the league performed its dirty work. Moreover, club owners and managers, whose men were under contract to Spalding, bitterly resented Spalding's failure to return the men in time for spring training.

Abroad, Spalding drew respectable crowds in Australia, but in Hawaii he drew a cipher: "like interrupting a funeral with a circus," as Mark Twain later said. In the Mediterranean region the entourage did no better. Indeed, the stunt of playing a game in the shadows of Egypt's pyramids failed to interest the natives, although it did excite the jeers of American commentators.

In Italy, Spalding's attempt to use another monument of Western Civilization as a backdrop drew even stiffer opposition. When Spalding's agent tried to "book" the Colosseum for a game, with Caesar's monument as a backstop, working archaeologists were horrified, and the Italian government, "scandalized by the suggestion of this sacrilege," refused. At this point Spalding tried to buy his way in by offering $5,000 to Italian charities, but this crass attempt only elicited a stiffer rebuke.[28]

Although the anthropologically hopeless attempt to plant an American field sport in lands where leisureways differ from ours is perhaps the biggest theme of this episode, one can gain further insights into the game's changing façade by analyzing the effects of

[27] Spalding to Nick Young, April 14, 1891. Published in *The Sporting News*, April 18, 1891.

[28] *Ibid.*, February 9, 1889; *Sporting Life*, February 20, 27, 1889; Anson, *op. cit.*, 140–285; Spalding, *op. cit.*, 175, 229–33, 251–65.

Spalding's baseball tour. For example, in the grumblings of American baseball promoters, whose spring training programs were in-
terrupted by Spalding's meddling, one can discern a deadly serious,
businesslike attitude toward the conduct of major-league baseball.
Behind this lies a revolution in the administration of major-league
clubs, a movement in the direction of profits, orderly administration, and efficient input-output financial practices.

Back in the 1870's the gentleman promoters felt little compul-
sion to harness such tactics of business enterprise to their hobby.
But in 1886, Richter counted only one gentleman-sponsor in the
National League, the others had been replaced by profit-conscious
businessmen.[29] Indeed, by then profits were rolling in, with league
clubs like Chicago, Boston, and New York netting annual profits
of nearly $100,000 each during the years of 1885–89. This was a
remarkable reversal from the austere days of the late 1870's or the
slim profits of the early 1880's, when a $20,000 profit was con-
sidered good.

It was the new profit potential, then, that prodded the new
breed of major-league owners into altering the spectacle by en-
larging the ball parks and by bureaucratizing the ball clubs with
the introduction of experts like front-office men, groundkeepers,
trainers, and concessionaires.[30] Although many of these activities
were unbeknown to the fans, this was not true of concessionaires,
who in the 1880's introduced baseball's classic lunch of Frank-
furters and soft drinks. But innovations like streamlined playing
rules, modernized parks, and professionalized administrative staffs
came not from profit-seeking alone. For example, the competition
from rival major leagues kept National League owners receptive to
changes, especially those which would shunt fans their way.

Another example was that the ideology of the 1880's put a great
value on business enterprise, as expressed in administrative efficiency and in the requirement to be "up to date." Above all, the
business ethos of the day exhorted one first to be a financial suc-

[29] *Sporting Life*, June 6, 1886.
[30] For an expanded treatment of this aspect, see David Q. Voigt, "CASH AND
GLORY: The Commercialization of Baseball as a Sports Spectacular, 1865–1892"
(unpublished doctoral dissertation, Syracuse University, 1962), 504–54.

cess, and then a gentleman. In adapting to this new posture, major-league promoters modeled themselves after the captains of American industry, whose empire-building exploits made them messiahs of the new economic order.

In 1892, by dint of vicious in-fighting, the National League owners, having buried all rivals, laid claim to a monopoly of major-league baseball. No longer could one refer to them merely as owners, for now they chose to be known as magnates, and they mistakenly interpreted public curiosity in their exploits as adulation.

At the peak of their pride in 1892, they thought that they were leaving a primitive decade of baseball organization, and they fully expected to lead their million-dollar entertainment industry into more profitable uplands, in which business enterprise would enable them to reap more wealth. But how could they know that the future would show that the decade only just passed was in reality the golden age of major-league baseball? Indeed, never would the game change so dramatically, so rapidly, or so successfully. To be sure, the game would continue to bloom as a major commercialized field sport, and at times it would top the profits of the 1880's. But measured in terms of realistic adaptation and bold innovation to the needs of its public, the golden age was over.

Henceforth, like the hero who won most of his laurels in his youth, major-league baseball would take on a "proper" aspect—a stable, ritualized existence in an ever changing society.

III. *Baseball's Feudal Age*

12

The Baseball Barons

F OR THE BASEBALL MEN who had just engineered the greatest victory in major-league history, Christmas, 1891, was a joyous one. By perseverance in battle and cunning at the conference table, they had organized major-league baseball into a super trust called "The National League and the American Association of Professional Base Ball Clubs." Having styled themselves as baseball magnates, they compared themselves with the great industrial organizers of the day, such as Rockefeller, Carnegie, and Frick. Convinced of their own importance, they would soon expect sportswriters to cover their movements as assiduously as those of the players. Indeed, for a time they even convinced themselves that they were as important to fans as the players. Such egoism would take time to dispel, and enough time to prompt one to say that at no other time would club owners be so celebrated as during the 1890's.

But, as the decade wore on, it became obvious that this new empire lacked an emperor. To be sure, Nick Young was the president, but his role was limited to that of being a caretaker, treasurer, and record keeper. Having neither the authority nor the *charisma* to be a policy-shaper, Young was the perfect figurehead. Consequently, the territory of the baseball realm was actually ruled by the individual club owners, each serving his own interest in his own fief. In time they would enter into fierce conflict with each other, thus completing the picture of major-league baseball's feudal era.

If the magnates had only paused to heed the warnings of prophets like Frank Bruenell, they might have tempered their joy with wisdom. Bruenell warned that the public would not submit to their "commercial Jesuitism," and John B. Foster added that the new breed of magnates must decide whether major-league baseball was to be a sport or a commercial exhibit.[1]

Being human, and imbued with pride, the magnates understandably ignored such prophecies and, instead, chose to read of their triumph. One editor calculated the worth of the new league at $1,000,000 and estimated that the annual players' payroll would come to $420,00, with $140,000 for annual travel expenses. At the same time it was pointed out that the baseball empire extended, under the new National Agreement of 1892, to the minors, which were now satellites of the "big league." And even higher notes of optimism came from President Young's office; in his message of July, 1892, Young called the league "an unqualified success" and predicted that all clubs would profit.[2]

However, the magnates liked to read about themselves, and during the 1890's the fans came to know these chieftains rather well. Best known, of course, was Young, but others were prominent in their own lairs. In 1892, Louisville was ruled by Dr. Stuckey, who soon sold out to Barney Dreyfuss and newsman Henry C. Pulliam. Washington was the patrimony of the Wagner brothers, who were wealthy associates of the Armour meat-packing firm. In Cleveland another set of brothers, Frank de Haas and Stanley Robison, local

---

[1] *Sporting Life*, December 19, 1891; *New York Clipper*, January 30, 1892.
[2] *Sporting Life*, December 26, 1891, July 23, 1892.

streetcar tycoons, dreamed of making their franchise the power of the West. Pittsburgh was controlled by W. W. Kerr and Ashley Lloyd, although later Dreyfuss, of Louisville, would buy his way into the Pittsburgh club.

Better known were the rest of the magnates. Boston's director, A. H. Soden, was called "the Dean of the National League." In Chicago, as Spalding faded into the background, Jim Hart emerged as a strong leader. Philadelphia remained in the firm hands of Reach and John Rogers, with the latter wielding the greater power. In Brooklyn, Charles Byrne, "the Napoleon of Base Ball," ruled this former association franchise as a respected league power. In Baltimore, Harry Von der Horst and Ned Hanlon controlled the franchise, while St. Louis remained in the hands of the discredited Von der Ahe.[3]

A controversial figure was John T. Brush, the Cincinnati magnate, who in 1898 would dictate his famous resolution on player discipline. So harsh and restrictive were his demands that he came to be called "puritanical" and "the apostle of Chesterfieldian base ball." Unpopular in the East, Brush traveled west and gained control of the western coalition of league politics. To his disciples he was regarded as "the ablest man in base ball."[4]

Most controversial of all the barons was the sinister Andrew Freedman, who wrested control of the bankrupt New York Giants in 1895. A brilliant realtor-politician, Freedman was associated with the Tammany group and was worth an estimated $500,000. Reportedly, in 1895, he paid $50,000 to acquire this moribund franchise, which had been so jolted by the brotherhood war that its existence required subsidies from league clubs. With Freedman in, the Giants returned to home rule, but the brusque Freedman made so many enemies that some New Yorkers wished the Giants had remained bankrupt. From the start he was determined to make the Giants a profitable club, and he completely disregarded the obvious fact that his brother barons had similar ideas. In his first

---

[3] *The Sporting News*, December 10, 1892; *Reach's Official Base Ball Guide*, 1896, pp. 162B–62C; *ibid.*, August 8, 1891, January 1, 1898.

[4] *Sporting Life*, May 7, 1898, March 18, 1899.

year as president, he made wild offers to buy established stars, and when he was rebuffed, he insulted his colleagues. That same year he angered Baltimore's president by publicly calling the Orioles' victory a "fluke." In short order, he was carrying on vendettas with critical sportswriters and players. Although a pariah to the other magnates, he was constantly supported by the local stockholders, which led him to carry his war straight to his colleagues. Perhaps his most celebrated countermaneuver was his deliberately weakening his team in a vindictive effort to prove that his fellow magnates could not prosper without the revenue of large and satisfied New York crowds.[5]

Although Freedman's actions led his detractors to regard him as a robber baron, some of his points were well taken. For one, he openly urged his fellow magnates to admit that baseball was a profit-making spectacle and then to run it as such. This, he argued, meant getting rid of Young and appointing a strong president who would cast out the weaker franchises in the interests of profits-above-all. In 1899, he proposed a genuine trust organization for baseball to be composed of the "most powerful and wealthy" franchises. He said that these clubs should be planted in the most lucrative cities, staffed with good players, even if this meant annual redistributions, and fully capable of defeating any rival circuits. This was his tough-minded answer to the shortsighted interest groups, whose petty intrigues for limited gains characterized the conduct of big-league affairs during the 1890's. But such boldness only angered his colleagues, who not only ignored his suggestions, but found solace in mocking Freedman as a "God-damned Sheeney."[6] No doubt it was such bigotry that caused Freedman to overcompensate and to imagine himself unjustly villified. However, two magnates, Soden and Rogers, appreciated the value of his insights and applauded his attempt to apply realistic economics to baseball promotion. If some saw him as a "modern Achilles

[5] *The Sporting News*, December 30, 1899; *ibid.*, January 26, October 19, 1895, August 26, 1899.

[6] *Sporting Life*, November 25, 1899.

sulking in his tent," others, including informed fans, recognized him as an informed prophet.[7]

Yet the image that remained was the picture of Freedman as the "Talleyrand of Baseball," the robber baron who was "the most cordially detested man ever identified with the National game." Because Chadwick had felt his wrath, he fostered this picture; so, too, did Spalding, who tried unsuccessfully in 1901 to force Freedman out of the league. Together these influential patriarchs coined the term "Freedmanism" and applied it as the "incarnation of selfishness supreme" and as the "destructive element" of "our national pastime."[8]

In retrospect he was far from being a monstrous threat to baseball. Judged by business standards of the day, Freedman's trust idea was farsighted and was based on the assumption that major-league baseball was business. His proposal for making the spectacle profitable included the idea of tight control over player salaries, the redistribution of player talent, and the regimentation of minor leagues as sources of new talent. In comparison with his forthright plan, the individualistic administration of big-league baseball during the 1890's seemed divisive and suicidal. That Freedman despaired and left baseball in 1902 was due to a combination of factors, including his antagonistic personality, a threatened players' revolt, and the rise of the American League as a countervailing threat. But most of all, his suggestions ran afoul of America's "age of reform," which took a dim view of trusts. Furthermore, his plan ignored baseball's gentlemanly heritage, which resisted the notion that baseball was strictly a business venture. Not only did this image remain among many promoters, but it dominated the thinking of most fans, who continued to consider the game as a competitive sport.

By playing upon baseball's gentlemanly heritage, John T. Brush became Freedman's chief antagonist. A lean, ascetic-looking man, Brush gained notoriety by his extremist approach to player

[7] *The Sporting News*, January 27, 1900; *ibid.*, December 15, 1900.
[8] *Ibid.*, August 6, 1898; Spalding, *op. cit.*, 302.

discipline. Convinced that players were getting out of hand by bullying umpires and making free use of foul language, Brush made it his mission to banish such affronts to Victorian sensitivities. In 1898, he persuaded his fellow magnates to adopt the "Brush Resolution," a punitive attack on "obscene, indecent and vulgar language." Goaded by Brush into puritanic fervor, the magnates endorsed the twenty-one-point resolution, which would punish players with expulsion for such indiscretions as umpire-baiting and "villainously filthy language."

Obviously, such a purgative was worse than the ailment. In mounting rational opposition, Director Fred Robison of Cleveland warned that the courts would not sustain such punishments. Although Brush's faction refused to withdraw the resolve, no one dared to cast the first stone. Finally, in 1899, the first case was brought forth, but the accused drew only a rebuke. After that the rule remained a dead letter and a monument to the petulance of baseball's feudal era.[9]

Although sharply divided by the ideologies of "Brushism" and "Freedmanism," baseball's barons found other causes for warring among themselves. Anxious to justify themselves, nearly all of the barons aired their dirty linen in the papers, thus affording fans of the 1890's further insights into the feudal age. One such issue, reflecting the struggle between rich and poor franchises, took the form of hot arguments over the division of gate receipts and the payment of the league's war debts. In this struggle the impoverished faction, known as the "little seven"—Baltimore, Brooklyn, Cincinnati, St. Louis, Cleveland, Washington, and Louisville—succeeded in forcing a fifty-fifty division of gate receipts. In another "soak the rich" move they managed to place the heaviest burden of the league's debt on the shoulders of the "big five." Also, this faction fought and won the right to play Sunday ball. Overall, the politics of poverty led to sharp leadership clashes, both among and between the two factions. So vicious were the embroilments that an eastern magnate complained to a reporter, "We

---

[9] *Spalding's Official Base Ball Guide*, 1898, pp. 195–98; *New York Clipper*, March 12, 1898, May 20, 1899.

can't trust each other." He denounced the methods of his unwanted "business partners" as despicable and treacherous, adding, "If I were out of base ball I would cut them dead. . . . I regard my connection with them as degrading."

In this age of weak central control almost any issue touched off savage infighting among the barons. Annually, there were battles over the re-election of Young, the appointment and activities of umpires, scheduling, rule changes, salaries, the fate of unremunerative franchises, and a raft of other issues. Amidst this atmosphere of bickering, the league somehow muddled through, but the dreary spectacle wearied many men, including Spalding, who yearned for a return to the gentleman's era, when men of breeding could "caucus" instead of "combine." Spalding added, "In the old days of the League it was looked upon as a disgrace to enter into a pledged 'combine' before a meeting, and the sooner the present League magnates get back to the old custom the better."[10]

Outsiders, equally fed up with the endless ax-grinding of the barons, voiced protests. In 1898, Richter said that a disgusted public was boycotting major-league baseball, and he blamed the magnates for "killing the game"; they "should either reform, reorganize or retire—anything to save the National sport from cold-blooded murder in the house of its so-called friends."[11]

By this time players, too, were seething, and their list of grievances was long. But with typical disregard for the handwriting on the wall, the magnates of 1899 treated themselves to a sumptuous banquet, with courses served over a six-hour period, and blandly announced to reporters that the cost of the affair had come from accumulated player fines.[12]

Naturally, some players were ready to rebel, and over the years Fred Pfeffer, a veteran of the brotherhood war, twice supported plots to break the magnates' grip through rival leagues. When both attempts failed, Pfeffer was branded a "revolutionary" and was expelled. But the fear that he might go to the courts led to his

[10] *Sporting Life*, December 29, 1894, August 8, November 21, 1896, April 8, 1899; *Reach's Official Base Ball Guide*, 1895, p. 120; *Washington Post*, May 27, 1897.

[11] *Sporting Life*, March 6, 1897, August 20, 1898.

[12] *Ibid.*, November 20, 1897.

231

reinstatement, although he was fined and exiled to hapless Louisville with his salary frozen at $2,000 per year.[13]

As financial records show, the fans were not enthusiastic over the twelve-club monopoly. Although Director Soden of Boston had hoped to better the $300,000 profits which came to him during the golden age, he admitted in 1892 that baseball profits were less than they had been in 1882.[14] And as the decade progressed, profit figures everywhere were less than those of the late 1880's. In 1898, John Rogers of the Phillies released financial figures for the decade, which showed a steady decline since 1885; indeed, the $49,000 gross receipts of 1898 were second only to the low figure of $47,000 of 1891, the year of the vicious association war. These statistics were significant, because the Phillies were members of the wealthy "big five," although by special concession they were permitted to charge a basic admission rate of 25 cents.[15]

For the rest of the league the financial picture is incomplete, and it is significant that the leading journals were given little data as the decade moved along. Yet some comparative figures exist for the 1892–94 period. In 1892, the first year of the monopoly, clubs labored under the burden of an unpopular split championship season and under the added burden of having to pay a percentage of home receipts to the league's war fund. In that year the Giants lost over $30,000, a disaster abetted only by subsidies from rival clubs. The following year, because the league finally liquidated the debt incurred in buying out the association, President Young jubilantly announced that clubs were making money once more. But profits were modest, and the Phillies led all with a $50,000 profit. Such earnings, however, owed much to the drastic salary cuts that were imposed by the magnates. Furthermore, only four clubs made profits of as much as $15,000, showing a widening rift between the haves and have-nots. Over the years the gap widened further, and although the league attracted 2,883,631 fans to its games in 1897, most of the receipts went to five or six clubs.

---

13 *Reach's Official Base Ball Guide*, 1896, p. 120.

14 *Sporting Life*, August 8, 1891, September 10, 1892.

15 *Ibid.*, December 24, 1898.

Nor did the rule giving clubs a share of receipts on the road help the poorer clubs recoup, because fans showed a marked preference for teams like Boston and Baltimore. Others consistently drew badly, with the Phillies and Washington as the poorest attractions away from home. Finally, the twelve-club league, with its increased travel, added further expenses to all clubs.[16]

The closing years of the decade witnessed a further decline in profits; in the war year of 1898, Boston grossed $50,000, but only five others profited. In 1899, attendance fell off 500,000 more, and John T. Brush admitted that by cutting his salary list to $40,000, he was girding for further losses in 1900. At last, in 1900, the league returned to an eight-club circuit, dropping the perennially profitless Cleveland, Louisville, Washington, and Baltimore franchises. But even this drastic surgery remedied little, for that year attendance fell off even on the popular holiday dates. That year the Robison's mortgaged their St. Louis holdings in order to borrow money.[17]

Offsetting this alarming trend was the barons' success in holding down player salaries. Indeed, during the decade this cause was the only thing they agreed upon. As early as 1893, their united action made salaries of $3,000 or more (all fairly common during the golden age) legends of the past. Not only were salaries slashed to the bone, but players who were playing under three-year pacts, which called for high figures, were forced to renegotiate at lesser sums. Also revived was the old austerity tactic of releasing an entire team before the expiration of their contracts. Quite typical of the new hard-line policy was this terse front-office note handed to Manager Wright of the Phillies: "There will be no extra agreements with anybody next year. Maximum salary will be 1800 for '94."[18]

---

[16] Wright, Note and Account Books, 1892, Vol. VII; Wright, Correspondence, Vol. IV; *ibid.*, Vol. IV, October 14, 1893, October 6, 1894, October 13, 1900; Celler Committee, *Notes on Organized Baseball*, 37, 138; *Reach's Official Base Ball Guide*, 1894, p. 4.

[17] *Sporting Life*, September 8, November 24, 1900.

[18] *New York Clipper*, January 2, July 23, 1892; Wright, Note and Account Books, Vol. XVI; *Sporting Life*, October 28, 1893.

In justifying their hard-line tactics, the magnates announced to all that they were following a time-honored policy of no play, no pay, and that profits came before pay: ". . . the capitalists will insist on first getting a fair return on their investment, say 6 or 8 per cent."[19]

Powerless to resist, and with no rival major league as an alternative, the players submitted to the yoke. To neutralize public sympathy, the magnates made skillful use of propaganda, telling fans that reduced salaries will make for better spectator accommodations. Cast thus in the role of serfs and blamed indirectly for the poor spectator accommodations, the players could do little other than register anonymous complaints with sympathetic reporters. But such plaints failed to stir organized opposition against the salary-limit law, and by 1894 the $2,400 ceiling was firmly established. By way of rubbing salt into the wound, sportswriters delighted in contrasting the existing salaries with the affluent days of the 1880's. Now, only rarely did a superstar breach the united front; in 1896, star pitcher Amos Rusie, after staging a yearlong holdout, won himself a $3,000 pact, but there were few Rusies. Most players were so apprehensive of the many minor leaguers, who were ready to take their jobs at a starting salary of as little as $600, that they bowed to the *status quo*.[20] Not surprisingly, by the end of the decade low payrolls were taken for granted; in 1899 the Baltimore payroll totalled $39,000, with $10,000 of it going to manager-promoter Hanlon. As for the rest, four superstars each drew slightly above $2,400, eleven drew less, with seven of these getting well below $1,500. Elsewhere, it was the same story, and, if anything, the larger squads of this decade merely added to the austerity. Thus, Boston paid two superstars slightly more than $2,400, gave eight more the limit, and the rest received much less. Compared with the big paydays of the 1880's, when payrolls of $60,000 and more were divided among smaller squads, these were lean years, indeed, but the 1890's were also years of industrial depression. Furthermore, the managerial philosophy of this era

[19] *Sporting Life*, February 20, 1892.
[20] *Ibid.*, November 13, 1897.

called for profits, and one sure way to modest profits was to cut the expense of salaries.[21]

In other ways, too, the magnates sought to adapt to the economy of scarcity. Some enlarged their parks to admit more fans, but usually this capital investment was forced upon them by stringent city ordinances requiring a minimum of fireproof protection. At this time *The Sporting News* reported that if measured in terms of annual investment, there were three categories of clubs. Cheap major-league clubs like the 1899 Cleveland team might be operated for as little as $45,000 a year; average clubs cost $66,500 annually; and elite clubs like Boston cost about $95,000. Hence, by putting his business acumen to work, the average club owner was able to suck blood out of his stone. In 1898, to run an "average" club, one had to pay about $39,600 in salaries for eighteen men, approximately $18,000 to the league for administrative costs, about $17,500 for ground-keeping, nearly $13,285 for travel, $4,000 for the manager's salary, and $1,000 for insurance.[22]

Cutting costs meant cutting corners, but there were fair and foul means of doing this. During these years many cried "foul" at those who were supposedly using their friendship with Jim Hart, the league's schedule maker, to obtain a nice gerrymandered schedule, which would lessen railroad and hotel costs. Eventually, the guillotining of the league's four weakest franchises in 1900 silenced the complainers. On the other hand, a "fair" way of cutting corners was to lobby for the 25-cent admission price, which in 1900 was granted to several league clubs. Still another approved way of saving money was to employ bench-warming players as ticket takers or gate watchers.[23]

Naturally, managers were under strict orders to economize. In these years honest Harry Wright was ordered to strain his already fading eyesight by keeping a minute record on the condition of each baseball owned by the club. Since this included practice balls, Wright now offered free admission to any "urchin" who returned

[21] *New York Clipper*, February 11, 1899; Voigt, *op. cit.*, chapter 14.

[22] *The Sporting News*, April 10, 1897, November 12, 1898, February 4, 1899.

[23] *Reach's Official Base Ball Guide*, 1901, p. 100; *The Universal Base Ball Guide*, 1890, pp. 117–19; *ibid.*, April 7, 1900.

a practice ball batted out of the park. Also, at owner Reach's behest, Wright used cheaper Reach "rocket" balls for practice. That other clubs also were ball conscious is evidenced by an eyebrow raising comment in *Reach's Official Base Ball Guide* which demanded to know how Cleveland could have spent $390 for balls in a single season.[24]

Newspapers in this nickel-nursing era also weighed in with economizing advice. When Boston fell victim to ticket counterfeiters, a reporter suggested that they emulate the St. Louis security system by locking tickets in fireproof tin boxes until the very day of their sale. When ready to sell the tickets, they used an efficient numbering system, which enabled them to check on the sale of all classes of tickets. Since ticket sellers must use the numbers in filling out reports, these numbers, when checked with turnstile counts, provided effective security checks. An equally strict eye was trained on the distribution of "Annie Oakleys" (free tickets) and the daily sales of concessionaires or the ball-park saloon. At the end of the game the front-office secretary prepared his formidable and complex report of receipts from all sectors of the spectacle. A strict policy on disbursement forbade any money being paid to anyone except by a voucher signed by the secretary.[25]

Of course players came under strict surveillance, and most barons directed their managers to draw up and enforce strict codes of conduct. Among the more Draconic was Dr. Stuckey's eleven-point code, which governed player behavior both at home and on the road. Almost as dictatorial was Pittsburgh's ten-point code, which ordered substitutes to serve time on the gate and which also tried to end "practical jokes." Both codes forbade players to complain directly to the owner, and insisted that all complaints go through a "chain of command," beginning with the captain or manager.[26]

Over this decade only two managers, Ned Hanlon of Baltimore and Frank Selee of Boston, managed to retain their posts. Since

[24] Wright, Note and Account Books, Vol. XVI; Peter Craig, *Organized Baseball*, 205–206; *Reach's Official Base Ball Guide*, 1896, p. 136.

[25] *New York Clipper*, July 9, 1898; *The Sporting News*, June 3, 1899.

[26] *Sporting Life*, April 2, 1892.

only they won pennants, their tenure was assured, but for the other managers it was a case of win or else. Since past reputations counted little, even the great Harry Wright found his last years soured by increasing interference from the testy John Rogers. In 1892, Wright accepted a humiliating $2,000 contract, and after another year at the same pay, he was dismissed. Although Wright's friends immediately secured for him the post of chief of umpires, he had no executive power; indeed, several magnates protested the added expense of having him on the league payroll. When Wright died in 1895, the shabby handling of "Harry Wright Day," a day on which all magnates agreed to set aside receipts for his widow, testified as to how far the new breed had departed from the values of the gentleman's era.[27]

At this time many economy-minded magnates employed player-managers. But laboring under multiple roles and front-office pressures taxed the effectiveness of most of them. Taskmasters like Freedman went through a series of player-managers, discarding them freely when they did not perform according to expectations. One of Freedman's most famous victims was the doughty Anson, acquired on the rebound from Chicago. However, since Anson believed that the manager ought to be autonomous on the field, he lasted only three weeks with Freedman, for in this age, the cult of the magnates brooked no competition from rival heroes, and thus, Anson, Wright, and Comiskey all found themselves jobless.

Perhaps the most enduring mark etched by enterprising magnates on major-league baseball was the "syndicate" approach to baseball organization. Stripped of its high-toned title, this scheme was nothing more than the pooling tactic used by big businesses to insure profits. In applying it to baseball, most magnates, one must remember, were also petty entrepreneurs, who ran local enterprises like breweries, traction companies, real-estate firms, and similar businesses. Since running a major-league club was as close as most of them came to participating in a nationwide enterprise, they sought enhanced status by displaying their knowledge of the

[27] Wright, Note and Account Books, Vol. VII; *Spalding's Official Base Ball Guide,* 1895, p. 124.

scheme in baseball. Although previously employed with some success by the 1883 Giants, which also controlled the association Mets, it had fallen into disrepute. However, the baseball wars of the early 1890's put heavy financial pressures on certain owners, who tried to recoup by widening their sphere of influence. Thus, in 1891, Von der Ahe controlled two franchises, St. Louis and the moribund Cincinnati club. Meanwhile, the embattled league attempted a similar scheme in which four of its clubs moved to succor the hard-pressed Giants. In performing this rescue operation, some barons were intrigued by the profit possibilities that might result from a more systematic application of the pooling technique. At first, the idea of investing in another club in order to assure oneself of a better chance at profits was done surreptitiously, but late in the decade some investors boldly announced their intention to operate two franchises simultaneously. One celebrated example of pooling came in 1898, when Ferdinand Abell of Brooklyn joined with magnates Von der Horst and Hanlon of Baltimore in an open merger of their two franchises. Since Baltimore was losing patronage, the magnates hoped to make money by transferring Baltimore stars to Brooklyn. Accordingly, the merger was completed with Hanlon and Von der Horst assuming executive powers. The move linked Brooklyn and Baltimore with an interlocking board of directors, and although both teams were to be run independently, Hanlon was able to stock the Brooklyn team with his pick of both rosters.

Not only was this move openly discussed, but Hanlon even renamed the superteam the Superbas. This left Baltimore with the leftovers, but under combative John McGraw, who concealed a few stars for himself, the Orioles proved embarrassingly strong. Thus, in the 1899 race, McGraw gave a good account of himself to the embarrassment of Hanlon, who at one point seemed on the verge of intervening in Baltimore policies in order to assure Brooklyn of the flag. Such a brazen move on Hanlon's part excited hot criticism of the syndicate approach and further discredited the magnates.[28]

Meanwhile, a western experiment in syndicatism added another blotch to baseball's tarnished image. Disgusted over falling attendance in Cleveland, Director Robison in 1898 arrogantly chose to punish the local fans by transferring several home games to other cities. Convinced that Cleveland did not "deserve" a contender, he sought to plant his best men in some more remunerative city. Since Von der Ahe at this time was bankrupt and his Browns were under the auctioneer's gavel, Robison's front man, Edward Becker, purchased the franchise in July, 1898. Now the proud owner of two league franchises, plus his Indianapolis "farm team" in the Western League, Robison launched his power play. Under his 1899 war plan all of the best men went to St. Louis, the rest going to Cleveland or to Indianapolis. Of course, there was the problem of securing league approval, but this was carried after bitter debate, punctuated by fist fights and drawn pistols. But with the help of votes from the "little seven," Robison won his point and announced the formation of the "American Base Ball and Athletic Exhibition Company" and the renaming of the Browns. They were now called the "Perfectos."

But with the 1899 stage cleared for a massive struggle between the titanic Superbas and Perfectos, the latter failed to live up to their billing and flopped both financially and artistically. If this was not disastrous enough, Cleveland fans deepened Robison's woe by a thorough job of snubbing the syndicate outpost in town. Attendance was so poor over the last half of the season that Robison sent the team on the road. To the tune of mocking jeers from sportswriters, this inept team became known as the "Exiles" and the "Wanderers."[29]

Yet such threats to the league balance of power prompted Freedman and Soden to enter into a community of interest. While falling short of an outright pool, Freedman "sold" ace pitcher Jouette Meekin to Boston for a trifling $5,000, a sum paid in "stage

[28] *The Sporting News*, October 8, 1898, February 18, August 12, 1899; *New York Clipper*, August 22, 1891, April 8, October 14, 1893; Celler Committee, *op. cit.*, 38.
[29] *The Sporting News*, April 1, June 17, 1899; *Sporting Life*, September 10, 1898.

money" according to a cynical reporter. While Freedman's motive was doubtlessly to make it rough on Brooklyn, he did his best sabotage as a city realtor, arranging it so there would be no subway stop within many blocks of Brooklyn's Washington Park.[30]

Such baronial arrogance in treating the game as a mere matter of dollars and cents affronted many who already were alarmed at attempts by magnates to control the minor leagues. Of course, the purchase of minor-league clubs as "farms" was of older and independent origin. Also, the National Agreement long since had regulated the drafting of minor-league stars. However, what frightened minor-league fans was the new trend toward outright ownership of minor-league teams as pioneered by Magnate Brush. Called "Brushism" (along with that magnate's puritanic proposals), the tactic was bitterly fought by Byron B. Johnson, president of the Western League. In 1899, Johnson convinced the league of the need for a deadline on all player drafts, and he emerged from this bitter battle with a fine reputation for competence and boldness, qualities which came in handy when he founded the rival American League in 1901.[31]

At the height of these controversies many predicted that major-league baseball would be killed by these two threats. Yet after a brief existence, syndicatism failed, because it not only proved unprofitable, but it seemingly worsened attendance by killing interest in the "expendable" cities. The death blow to this tactic came in 1900 when the league lopped off its four weak clubs and returned to eight teams. This was a virtual admission of imbalance, the problem that had plagued the league for more than a decade. But in paring down to eight teams, the remaining magnates were saddled with the costs of the departing franchises. Faced with a $110,000 war debt, a sum nearly equal to that which was paid in 1892 to buy out the association, some barons must have thought back to 1892 and wondered if any progress had been made. Born in debt, the monopolistic league died in debt.[32]

[30] Mrs. John McGraw, *The Real McGraw* (ed. by Arthur Mann), 176–77.

[31] *The Sporting News*, October 31, 1896; *Sporting Life*, November 24, 1900. *Tribune* (Chicago), February 4, 1898.

[32] *The Sporting News*, October 13, 1900.

"Napoleon" Lajoie of the Philadelphia National League and American League, as well as of the Cleveland American League, was one of the game's most formidable batsmen. He had a career batting average of .339. Here he poses at his second base position.

"Ee-yah" Hugh Jennings was player-manager of the Detroit Americans, 1907–18. He had a career batting average of .314.

*John McGraw played third base for the Baltimore Orioles, 1891–
99, and was player-manager of the New York Giants, 1902–32.*

"Three Finger" Mordecai Brown, the pitching phenomenon of the Chicago Cubs, 1904–12.

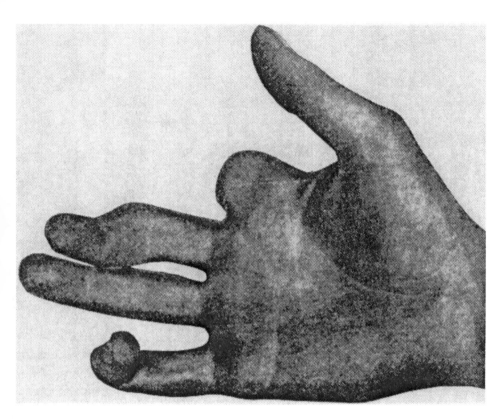

The gnarled and twisted right hand to which Mordecai Brown owed much of the success of his mystifying curve ball.

Baseball Magazine

Frank Chance of the Chicago Cubs tries to tag out Bill Isbell of the White Sox during the 1906 World Series.

MacGreevy Collection, Boston Public Library

"Cy" Young won 511 games and pitched 3 no-hitters during his twenty-two years in the major leagues. Here he holds a trophy awarded him in the early 1900's for his pitching prowess.

This cartoon, depicting the tribulations of a baseball fan of the 1890's, appeared in Sporting Life, *August 24, 1895.*

Quite possibly, Freedman's counterproposal calling for a genuine national baseball trust might have worked, but such a cause already was lost. Fearful that the fans already were repelled by the very words "magnates," "Syndicates," and "trusts," and well aware that the players were strike-minded, baseball men looked back to the 1880's as if it were indeed a golden age.[33]

Such collective nostalgia offered a rare opportunity for a well-organized interloper to move in with a rival major-league team and complete the restoration of the old order. Hence, when portly Byron "Ban" Johnson made his move with his Western League in 1900, he found the road surprisingly clear. To be sure, the league men would go through the motions of a war, but accommodation would come with surprising speed, for Johnson was the key the magnates sought, the chance to return to the womb of the 1880's. Although some yearned to be thought of as gentlemanly sportsmen once again, most wanted to hear the hum of turnstiles and to count big profits once more. By accommodating Johnson's newly named American League as a rival major league, such dreams would come true. Side by side after 1902, the two majors entered a half century of profitable rivalry, based on the imitation of the golden age of the 1880's. Thus, the new "silver age," as a stylized imitation of that bygone era, was an age of returning prosperity and public interest.

As for the fading feudal age, baseball men who survived it would recall with a shudder the arrogance of the barons. Writing in 1911, Spalding denounced the robber barons as one of three all-time evils faced by major-league baseball (along with gambling and drunkenness). Recalling their lack of grace and their inordinate greed, he marveled that the spectacle could have been strong enough to survive the idiocies of its leaders.[34]

[33] *Sporting Life*, August 24, 1901; Celler Committee, *op. cit.*, 38.
[34] Spalding, *op. cit.*, 10.

13

The Big League

I F BY CHANCE some pedantic teacher would someday test his class on baseball high lights of the 1890's, a student would have no difficulty memorizing the key points, because all pennants in the "big league" (as fans called the National League twelve-club monopoly) were won by cities with names beginning with "B"— Boston, Baltimore, and Brooklyn. Also, all champions were managed either by Frank Selee of Boston or by Ned Hanlon of the Baltimore-Brooklyn entries. Of course, such a summary offers only a sketchy outline, and to get the full flavor of this spirited era, some discussion is needed in order to develop the outline.

In 1892 the big league was launched on its maiden voyage, the first peacetime baseball season after two years of bitter interleague fighting. Since the barons desperately wanted a return to profitable days, not to mention the retiring of the league war debt of $130,000,

242

they hoped to entice maximum public support by dividing the championship season. Thus, the first half of the season would end on July 15, after which competition would begin anew with all clubs having a clean slate. If different clubs won each half, there was to be a climactic play-off series following the October 15 closing date. It was a bold plan, calling for tight scheduling and good weather, and it meant jamming each half's slate into only eighty playing dates.[1]

Perhaps in voting the above schedule, club owners had realistically assessed the strength of the Boston Beaneaters. Certainly this team held the inside track in the race for cash and glory, because it had an advantage due to the fortunes of the two previous wars. For one, it was a strong Boston club that won the Players League race of 1890, and when this circuit surrendered, most of its good men went to the Boston league team. With such a boost Boston won not only the league pennant, but also the local popularity contest over its association rivals, which enabled them to pick up another player windfall after their rivals collapsed in 1891. Hence, for the second straight year the Beaneaters were able to pick prize players from the roster of a defeated rival.

Under the circumstances Manager Frank Selee was able to field a team of superstars in 1892. The lineup included: three prize catchers, Mike Kelly, Charles Bennett, and Charles Ganzel; a pitching staff of John Clarkson, Charles "Kid" Nichols, Jack Stivetts, and Harry Staley; an infield of Tom Tucker, Joe Quinn, Bill Nash, and Herman Long; and an outfield of Hugh Duffy, Harry Stovey, Tom McCarthy, and Bob Lowe. As an added bonus, this fighting machine included natural leaders like Captain Nash and Duffy.

Commanding the array was taciturn Frank Selee, in his fourth year as Boston manager. Little was known of this serious, publicity-shy strategist, except that he had been a good minor-league pilot. Belittled by many as a figurehead, Selee had almost no playing background.[2] No doubt his reticence stemmed from such criti-

---

[1] *New York Clipper*, January 9, 1892.

[2] *Sporting Life*, October 7, 1893; *Reach's Official Base Ball Guide*, 1899, p. 104; *ibid.*, November 2, 1899.

cism, yet it also made it difficult for writers to assess his worth. *Sporting Life* called him the "best judge of a player" in America, adding, "He has never failed, in minor or major league, to get together a team of winners."[3] It was this record of success, coupled with a dearth of available hands during the brotherhood war, that led to his Boston appointment. But it was his arrival that triggered the success of the Beaneaters and helped them to capture five league flags during the 1890's. And through it all Selee continued to manifest his dead-pan manner. When once asked for the secret of his success, he enigmatically answered, "My success in base ball has been due in part to the consistent people I have . . . associated with."[4]

The first of Boston's five pennants came under suspicious circumstances. During the 1891 association war, the Beaneaters gained a great psychological advantage by snaring the prodigal Kelly from their association rivals. Prior to that coup, Anson's Colts looked like a sure bet. But with Kelly in fold, Boston won eighteen straight games to snatch the prize from Anson. It was this skein that bothered some, and the end of the season found an investigating committee looking into the charge that the Giants tossed some of their games to Boston. The Giants, it was alleged, played four games without using three of their superstars. However, the committee finally accepted such explanations as one had needed a rest, another had suffered a sprained ankle, and the third had needed to return home for "personal reasons." Although the committee verdict of innocent gave Boston its first flag in nearly a decade, the inquiry soured the victory.[5]

Desperately anxious for an untainted 1892 victory, Selee trained his men in the South, and, before breaking camp, he warned his men that their jobs depended on good performances. He not only warned the men that many hungry rookies were eager to replace them, but he also tightened discipline by insisting on early morning reveille, two hard practices a day, and a curfew of 11:30 P.M. In

---

[3] *Sporting Life*, September 23, 1893.

[4] *Reach's Official Base Ball Guide*, 1899, p. 104.

[5] *New York Clipper*, October 24, 1891; *Daily Globe* (Boston), October 1, 1891; Anson, *op. cit.*, 297.

banning drinking and restricting smoking, Selee concluded his ukase by urging the men to "Do all you can to advance the profession you represent."[6]

Badgered by such advice, but heartened by promising crowds, the team broke fast, winning eleven of their first thirteen games. Although Selee continued to worry about his smokers, urging them "to let up a little on the weed," he did so needlessly, because his Beaneaters stormed through the first half, playing at a .700 clip and clinching the flag by the end of June.

Unhappily, this brilliant effort was marred by universally bad attendance. So alarming was the decline in popular interest that all magnates began cutting playing rosters, dismissing high-priced stars, and peremptorily renegotiating contracts. In Boston this panic button was pushed in June and led to salary slashes and to the dismissal of fading heroes like Kelly and Stovey. Following the practices of other clubs, Boston demanded that all players take pay cuts, and when Bennett and Clarkson balked, Clarkson found himself cut from the squad.[7]

Perhaps it was this shabby treatment, following their heroic effort, that demoralized the team. Subsequently, it played sluggishly during the second half, which led to the recall of Kelly, who was named captain in hopes of "gingering" up the squad. Meanwhile, a fighting Cleveland team, under the fiery leadership of playing-manager Oliver "Pat" Tebeau, drove to the fore. An advocate of rowdy baseball, Tebeau frequently harassed opponents and umpires. He said, "My instructions to the players are to win games and I want . . . aggressive hustlers. . . . A milk and water, goody-goody player can't wear a Cleveland uniform."[8]

On the positive side Tebeau had a brilliant pitching staff, including Cy Young, George Cuppy, and George Davis, and it was he who took on Clarkson after that embittered genius left Boston. Backing this staff was: catcher Charles "Chief" Zimmer; an infield of Jake Virtue, Charles "Cupid" Childs, Ed McKean, and

---

[6] *Daily Globe* (Boston), April 14, 1892.

[7] *Ibid.*, May 1, July 14, 1892; *New York Clipper*, July 16, 1892.

[8] *Ibid.*, January 13, 1894.

Tebeau himself; and an outfield of Jess Burkett, Jim McAleer, and Ed O'Connor.[9]

Thus, while Boston foundered, Tebeau's Spiders built a commanding lead. Bolstered by having a number of home games, they built an imposing lead, which a late Boston drive managed to cut to three games by the end of the campaign.[10]

With two pretenders to the 1892 league championship, confused fans deluged local papers with queries as to the true champion. Although a play-off was the logical answer, Boston found itself accused of "hippodroming," of dragging its feet during the second half. It was such charges that prompted worried magnates to scrap the double championship, and to seriously consider junking the play-off by awarding the flag to Boston on the basis of its better overall record.[11]

But, since Cleveland's honor demanded satisfaction, the play-off was held as scheduled. The results did little to allay the charges; indeed, the ease with which the Beaneaters defeated the Spiders only added more credence to them. Commenting on Boston's five straight victories, one writer said that Cleveland "was highly successful in the manufacture of nothingness, surrounded by an elliptical fence." Responding to this gibe, Cleveland papers accused Boston of bullying and "shrieking like madmen . . . coaching hoodlum style . . . kicking at every decision." Magnified several times over, such acrimony speeded the decision to scuttle the split-season idea.[12]

At the same time sagging attendance figures led magnates to adopt other conservative measures. That year second-half attendance was 300,000 less than the first half, and only Cleveland and Pittsburgh showed profits, with the Giants as heavy losers. Hence, all clubs adopted niggardly practices, and Boston, which broke even, rewarded its heroes by giving them $1,000 to be divided fifteen ways. Moreover, the Beaneaters were ordered to use horse-

[9] *Sporting Life*, July 16, 1892.

[10] *Daily Globe* (Boston), September 11, October 16, 1892.

[11] *Ibid.*, October 16, 1892; *The Sporting News*, October 8, 1892.

[12] *Spalding's Official Base Ball Guide*, 1893, pp. 54–60; *Sporting Life*, October 29, 1892.

car transportation to save the expense of rented hacks. Of course, the biggest blow came in the form of new salary slashes. In urging players to accept them, Chadwick suggested that major-league baseball was entering a famine epoch. Such times called for magnates to take profits and players to content themselves with the leavings.[13]

Faced with the grim reality of being cut loose, players acquiesced in their degradation, for the records warned of the futility of resistance. In 1893 only 54 of the 128 men who joined the brotherhood in 1890 remained active in the league. And of 121 active National League men of 1890, only 52 remained. This evidence pointed to the rise of a new and hungry generation of players. Although veteran Dan Brouthers took the batting title, he was pressed hard by Childs of Cleveland, Bill Hamilton of Philadelphia, and Duffy of Boston. Among the new pitching heroes, men like Nat Hutchinson, Nichols, Stivetts, and Young eclipsed old heroes like Clarkson and Galvin. Not only were many newcomers anxious to make the grade in the big time, but they were also content to play for less pay. To them, the salaries of the golden age seemed hardly credible.[14]

Faced with a burgeoning talent surplus, the barons made the most of the opportunity. From every office contracts were sent out calling for reduced salaries, and in some cases players took 40 per cent cuts in order to bring their pay in line with the new $2,400 maximum. During midwinter huddles, magnates reportedly were seeking to hold total payrolls to a figure below $30,000. To legalize such cuts in the eyes of players, magnates also decided to shorten the contract period to six months.[15]

With the salary burden lightened, magnates attempted to entice more fans. Some owners thought that the public wanted to see more slugging, and this faction blamed the new crop of "cyclone" pitchers for deadening the game. As "cures" some ventured zany suggestions like allowing pitchers to throw only fast balls, or introducing

[13] *Spalding's Official Base Ball Guide*, 1893, pp. 8–11; *Daily Globe* (Boston), May 10, 1892; *Reach's Official Base Ball Guide*, 1893, pp. 2–12.

[14] *The Sporting News*, May 27, 1893.

[15] *Reach's Official Base Ball Guide*, 1893, pp. 2–12; *Daily Globe* (Boston), October 5, 1892, April 23, 1893.

a lively ball, or ordering outfielders to remain in specially marked zones. But in the end the rules committee rejected these in favor of the time-honored plan of increasing the pitching distance. Hence, a rule was adopted extending the distance to the present day mark of sixty feet, six inches. A further boost to batting averages came in the form of a rule ordering scorers not to charge a sacrifice hit as a turn at bat.[16]

At this time some club owners urged a return to the old dual major-league system, but the final decision called for retaining the twelve-club league and making the 1893 season a single race.[17]

But legislators could do nothing to insure a tight race. Despite the usual preseason optimism, Boston looked like the sure winner. To be sure others were improving, for the Giants were under strong leadership with John Ward as captain, and the Baltimore Orioles were gaining ground. One Oriole in particular was outstanding— "Mickey McGraw, the little tough citizen . . . pretty young to die."[18] Two others looked promising, Wright's Phils with Ed Dele-hanty in the line-up, and the Pittsburghs, with Connie Mack breaking in as catcher. But the smart money was on Boston, and Richter stated that only overconfidence or managerial stupidity could bar their way. Since the Beaneaters "are by far the best team in the race," they must avoid "hippodroming" charges by playing seriously all the way.[19]

It was a shrewd forecast, and although Boston was again charged with hippodroming because of its sluggish start, Wright's Phillies broke fast and for a time gave local fans a taste of pennant fever. During the first three months the Phillies drew so well that the Senators transferred some of their home encounters to Philadelphia, hoping to cut a big slice of the visitor's share of gate receipts.[20] Yet the honeymoon was brief, because late in July the Beaneaters came to town and systematically dashed all of Wright's hopes. After that the Bostons tore the league apart, leading by twelve

16 *Spalding's Official Base Ball Guide*, 1893, pp. 150–54.
17 *Sporting Life*, November 5, 1892, April 1, 1893.
18 *Daily Globe* (Boston), April 10, 1893.
19 *Ibid.*, May 8, June 14, 1893.
20 *Sporting Life*, July 8, July 29, 1893.

games in September and cooling public interest in baseball even earlier.

The easy victory set critics to arguing how much Selee had to do with it. To some reporters he was a "clear-headed, bright, diplomatic man," a good handler of men and a sound strategist, who invented the hit-and-run play. To others he was a mere ornament, since it seemed that anyone could have won with such a team. Pitching was the strong suit, and the Boston staff had little trouble with the increased distance. Kid Nichols, winning thirty-two games and losing fourteen, led all, and Stivetts and Staley each won nineteen. At the same time Boston batters benefited from the changes with Duffy batting .382. That year the number of .300 batters multiplied, and Delehanty slugged nineteen home runs, portending the revolutionary batting style of the modern era.[21]

Of course Boston now bore the brunt of the blame for falling attendance, and the cry "Break up the Boston team" was heard. This charge was attacked by the Boston *Daily Globe*, which pointed out that the club's record road attendance figures hardly indicated that the public wanted the team destroyed. Anyway, internal erosion was taking effect, and pride, which often attends too much success, was already revealing itself in symptoms of arrogance and greed. With the pennant in the bag, several late season incidents revealed bitter feelings between Selee and some stars.[22] Because some players left early, causing the team to fritter away much of its lead, and because others tried to cash in on their godlike status by playing winter ball as the "All American team," the team's image was tarnished.[23]

Public reaction to these escapades suggested that many would welcome a Boston collapse. Indeed, baiting the Bostons had become a popular pastime by the end of the 1893 season. In Pittsburgh the returning Bostons were stoned in their hack en route to the hotel, and cries for help were ignored by the police. Only fast driving saved the team from serious injury. Meanwhile, sports-

---

[21] *Daily Globe* (Boston), August 1, 26, October 1, 1893.

[22] *Ibid.*, September 22, 1893; *Sporting Life*, September 30, 1893.

[23] *Daily Globe* (Boston), October 1, 1893; *The Sporting News*, October 7, 1893.

writers launched verbal missiles, with some Darwinian writers mocking the team for playing a sissified bunting game in an age when fans wanted manly slugging. Even Chadwick, while defending the Boston offense as "scientific," scolded them for their noisy, aggressive style of play.[24] Thus, even though a third straight pennant enabled them to retire the coveted Dauvray Cup, the Beaneaters were learning that the price of excessive excellence is envy.

Commenting on the financial result of 1893, a year of severe financial depression all over America, President Young rejoiced in the fact that the league had paid its association war debt. As of 1894, clubs would no longer have to tithe on gate receipts, and since 1893 had bettered the record of 1892, except for cellar-dwelling Washington, prospects were bright enough to convince the barons not to tamper with the playing rules. Indeed, 1893 had been the best hitters' year since 1887, and the public seemingly liked the new style that enabled Jake Stenzel to win the batting title with a .400 plus average, and his Pittsburgh team to post a .319 batting average.[25]

Although outslugged and outfielded by other clubs in 1893, most realists expected the scrappy Beaneaters to win again in 1894. Unhappily, however, a pair of tragic incidents early in 1894 demoralized the team, and one put an end to the brilliant career of catcher Bennett. Embarking on a hunting trip in January, he slipped while trying to board a moving train and fell under the wheel of a car; the tragedy led to the loss of his leg. The other misfortune came early in the campaign, when a carelessly tossed cigarette started a fire, which destroyed the park and $70,000 worth of equipment. Forced to take refuge in the old Congress Street grounds, the club suffered financially and psychologically.[26]

Meanwhile, the fire of determination now sparked the hitherto hapless Orioles. Some inkling of their upsurge appeared in a cautious appraisal of their new power by *Reach's Official Base Ball*

24 *New York Clipper*, September 30, 1893; *Sporting Life*, August 26, September 30, 1893.

25 *Spalding's Official Base Ball Guide*, 1894, pp. 8–57, 61–65; *Reach's Official Base Ball Guide*, 1894, pp. 60–61, 87–98.

26 *New York Clipper*, January 20, 1894; *Daily Globe* (Boston), May 16, 1894.

Guide. Yet, while admiring Baltimore's pitching and the spirit of McGraw and Joe Kelley, the editor stated that the veteran Brouthers and rookies Jennings and Keeler were hopelessly washed up. Convinced at last of the team's imbalance, the guide accepted Selee's opinion and consigned the team to eighth place.[27]

This evaluation seemed sound because Baltimore had never posed a pennant threat since its entry into the majors in 1883. Seemingly the owner, Harry Von der Horst, worried more about beer sales, which until 1893 were sufficient to balance the losses at the gate. Hence, he seldom sank money into playing talent before 1891, and his recent change in heart owed much to Ned Hanlon, who became manager of the team in 1892. One of baseball's superstars, the thirty-five-year-old Hanlon had saved much of the $25,000 that he had earned as a player. Eying an investment opportunity, he jumped at Von der Horst's offer, and, in 1893, having invested in the club, he took over as president with full authority. Obviously pleased with the new arrangement, Von der Horst stuck to his brewery and to his task as club treasurer, while gaily sporting a lapel button which read, "ASK HANLON."

In reaching for fame and fortune, Hanlon now banked on his vast experience as player and captain. Well schooled in coaching players, he was respected by his men, and his keen knowledge of the player talent market served him well in 1894.[28]

Determined to improve his eighth place finish in 1893, Hanlon swapped Young Tim O'Rourke and cash for first baseman Harry Taylor and infielder Hugh Jennings of Louisville. In selecting Jennings, a popular Colonel, who had been sidelined by illness, Hanlon gambled on the player's fiery determination. However, Hanlon's master stroke fell late in 1893, when, after some haggling, he swapped two outfielders for Brooklyn's aging Dan Brouthers and a rookie named Willie Keeler. Meanwhile, Hanlon snatched up castoffs like pitcher Bill Gleason, outfielder Walt Brodie, who was called a troublemaker by the Browns, and Joe Kelley. Recog-

[27] *Reach's Official Base Ball Guide*, 1894, pp. 58–59; *Sporting Life*, April 24, 1894; Mrs. John McGraw, *op. cit.*, 60.

[28] *Sun* (Baltimore), June 21, 1894; *New York Clipper*, May 21, 1892; Mrs. John McGraw, *op. cit.*, 70; Fred Lieb, *The Baltimore Orioles*, 34–35, 40–42.

nizing that pitching was the chief weak spot, Hanlon grasped at other castoffs, picking up Tony Mullane, Duke Esper, and George Hemming in 1894. Such acquisitions were fitted to a nucleus of tested players, including catchers Wilbert Robinson and Bill Clarke, pitchers Bill Hawke and John McMahon, infielders Mc-Graw and Henry Reitz, and utility man Frank Bonner.[29]

As team captain, the burly twenty-seven-year-old Robinson had shouldered most of the catching since 1890. Although never a heavy hitter, he was a good fielder and handler of pitchers. Over the years he gained a legendary reputation for playing despite illness and injury. Indeed, legend later pictured this team as utterly reckless in daring and stoically heedless of personal injury. Helping to cement the myth was a 1911 feature article in the Baltimore *Sun*, which compared Robinson's left hand with that of a noted pianist. Robby's unprotected "meat hand" had every finger broken at least once, and the tip of the little finger had been amputated to arrest the spread of blood poison. The article then quoted Robby's "aw shucks" prescription for such injuries, which was "go to bed with a lemon wrapped around a swollen joint." Since he was no longer active as a player, Robby freely inveighed against the softness of the present generation of players.[30]

Like most baseball myths, this one conflicted with reality. In truth, records of games played in the 1890's show that Robinson was often replaced when hurt by a foul tip, and once the fierce McGraw had to be reassured by a physician that what he thought to be a hip dislocation was only a bruise. Also, the mainstay of the Oriole pitching staff, "Sadie" McMahon, was a veritable hypochondriac, whose fits of depression frequently kept him from pitching.[31] Such accounts suggest that the Orioles were no more rugged than their contemporaries and considerably less Spartan than some men of the gloveless 1870's and 1880's.

[29] *Sporting Life*, June 10, 1893, October 6, 1894; *The Sporting News*, July 15, 1899; *Reach's Official Base Ball Guide*, 1895, pp. 10–15, 35; *New York Clipper*, May 27, 1893.

[30] *Sun* (Baltimore), December 31, 1911.

[31] *Ibid.*, July 11, 1894, June 11, 1948; *Reach's Official Base Ball Guide*, 1895, pp. 10–15, 35.

Still another legend brands the Orioles as a rowdy team, which resorted often to villification and trickery to gain advantages. While this myth has more truth to it than the previous tale, one must keep in mind that earlier clubs like the Browns, Beaneaters, and Spiders all had similar claims to this dubious honor. Thus, McGraw as the bad boy of Baltimore was a carbon copy of Latham, the onetime bad boy of the Browns. One of six children of an Irish immigrant father, he was twelve years old in 1885 when diphtheria carried off his mother and four siblings. Left with a distraught father who despised his son's baseball interest, McGraw ran away a year later after suffering a terrible beating. While supporting himself, he devoted his spare time to baseball, and by 1890, he was good enough to land a minor-league berth. Over the next season he played in two minor leagues and developed rapidly, which persuaded Baltimore to take him on late in the 1891 season. Once a big leaguer, this ambitious player refused to be sent back to the minor leagues, and in 1892, he induced Hanlon to reconsider such a move by displaying fantastic willingness and spirit.

Such competitive spirit obscured his deep knowledge of the game. All along he had studied hard, and he believed that one must know the rules in order to circumvent them. In this way he far surpassed Latham in legal trickery, and he brought the skill of the shyster lawyer to bear on the rules of the game. Among his gimmicks was the trick of slapping a ball out of an infielder's hands, the terrorist tactic of sporting well-sharpened cleats, the verbal tactic of berating umpires and opponents, the confusing tactic of switching balls, and the propagandist tactic of inciting beered-up home-town crowds to threaten the opposition.[32]

In a short time McGraw's deviousness was damned in the sporting press. Early in 1894, he was dubbed "Muggsy," because he behaved like a "mug." Reporter Joe Vila hung the label on him because of his rowdy, hot-tempered attitude, saying, "These tough mugs who want to fight on all occasions, and who use foul language . . . should be chased out of the business." His reputation horrified

[32] Mrs. John McGraw, *op. cit.*, 24–55; McGraw, *op. cit.*, 43; Sun (Baltimore), June 30, July 11, 1894; *The Sporting News*, September 2, 1899.

Chadwick, who blasted the team in general, and singled out Mc-Graw as the worst offender.

However, in an age whose ideology valued the Spencerian "survival of the fittest" ethic and the Rooseveltian "doctrine of the strenuous life," McGraw was not without defenders. Reporter Albert Mott hotly defended him, arguing that crowds like winners and will go along with peppery tactics, "short of physical violence." Mott added that since fans like winners, "a thousand more will come to see the young scrapper at Baltimore. Not a display of good morals? Well, perhaps not, but you must not expect too much of it at a ball game."[33]

What mattered most, of course, was Hanlon's appreciation of McGraw's style. In fact, Hanlon taught his men similar tricks, like diving into the first baseman after he had caught the ball, throwing masks in front of runners at home plate, catching a base runner by his clothes, interfering with base runners, and blocking the view of the opposing catcher. Asked to comment on these charges, Hanlon usually denied them or refused comment, but, in 1898, he admitted that he condoned "hoodlumism" to some degree. He said that he "winked at the evil," because his headstrong men argued that all other clubs did the same. Anxious to justify himself, he insisted that he and Von der Horst repeatedly scolded the offenders and made them pay their own fines.[34]

With natural leaders like McGraw and Jennings pressuring others to adopt this rowdy style, it became a *modus vivendi*. In 1899 moody Jack Doyle, a onetime Oriole, told how the Orioles took each other to task for the slightest shortcomings. Personally, Doyle found Jennings' sarcasm more cutting than McGraw's profanity. But Oriole pitchers suffered most, and Doyle recalled how Joe Corbett, after enduring bitter heckling from his mates, threw the ball over the grandstand, allowing three runs to score.[35]

Although only one of many agitators, McGraw came to per-

[33] *Sun* (Baltimore), July 23, 1894; *Sporting Life*, April 22, 1893, April 28, July 7, 1894; *Spalding's Official Base Ball Guide*, 1895, pp. 12–40.

[34] *The Sporting News*, June 30, 1894; *New York Clipper*, March 5, 1898.

[35] *Sporting Life*, June 3, 1899.

sonify a brutal style of play. As early as 1894, President Young branded him a menace and warned him to "calm down somewhat" or face discipline. But as umpires well knew, Young's threats carried little weight during the feudal age. Long afterwards two umpires of this era recalled McGraw's tactics with shudders. According to Tom Lynch, it was a tossup between Cleveland and Baltimore as to which was the rowdiest team of this era, and McGraw was rivaled by Tebeau of Cleveland. However, John Heydler unhesitatingly pronounced Baltimore and McGraw as hellhole and devil. The Orioles, said he, "were mean, vicious, ready . . . to maim a rival player or umpire," and their insults "were unbelievably vile." Heydler saw umpires "bathe their feet by the hour after McGraw and others spiked them through their shoes." What was worse, they not only got away with this, but inspired other clubs to emulate them.[36]

Yet even Heydler admitted that the Orioles were a well-trained club, excelling in orthodox tactics like base-stealing and the hit-and-run. Since most Orioles aspired to future managerial careers, they studied the game, and in time McGraw, Robinson, Jennings, Gleason, and Kelley became noted managers. And "Dad" Clarke became an institution as baseball coach at Princeton. But as the latter-day "Napoleonic genius" of baseball, McGraw topped them all. According to his second wife, such a goal was his obsession, and his zeal stamped him as the baseball equivalent of those inner-directed types who were then imposing their personalities on the business world of the 1890's. But if in that era such tactics were applauded, McGraw lived long enough to see them become anachronistic. However, he never abandoned the philosophy that he so clearly expressed in 1898: "I have been trying to play ball for all there was in me to help my club win games. This I will continue to do. . . . Should my temper get the better of me the only thing left will be to abandon the profession entirely."[37] Such a philosophy of professionalism broke completely with the sportsmanlike philos-

---

[36] *Sun* (Baltimore), June 23, July 17, 1894; Chadwick, Scrapbooks, II, 34; *Reach's Official Base Ball Guide*, 1897, p. 94.

[37] *New York Clipper*, March 19, 1898.

ophy of the gentleman's era, and it left little room for alternatives, but, when finally the Giants cut him loose in the 1930's, death was his alternative.

In 1894 this spirited aggregation of castoffs was touted as a "dark horse" by shrewd John Ward. Already he regretted sending Keeler to Baltimore for he admired the youth's "scientific hitting." Before the season was over, Ward's fears were reified, for Keeler helped the Orioles make the hit-and-run style a fearful weapon, so much so that it became basic offensive strategy until the home-run era of the 1920's. In 1894, Keeler not only tutored his new mates in the hit-and-run, but also gave Jennings useful batting tips. Keeler's own success at the plate soon had reporters quizzing him; to one Keeler replied, "I have already written a treatise and it reads like this: 'Keep your eye clear and hit 'em where they ain't; that's all!'" Of course, there was more to it, and Keeler depended heavily on his bunting ability and his ability to fake an infielder in by threatening to bunt.[38]

Another offensive weapon was the Orioles' speed on the bases. Again McGraw was the leader, a dervish who repeatedly unnerved opposing pitchers with his provocations. In time speed became the hallmark of the Orioles, and, in 1901, statistics showed that the season before sixteen Orioles stole 338 bases, one fifth of the league output.

The team's blind spot, however, was pitching. Deperate for help, Hanlon sought to use boxer Jim Corbett, but league officials vetoed it, because they believed that hiring Corbett was a cheap publicity stunt. In time Hanlon proved that one Corbett, Joe, was big-league material, but in 1894 only McMahon and Mullane were the team's best pitchers. When others pitched, their pitched balls were belted regularly, and pitching became a nightmare.[39]

During the spring of 1894, while "General" Jacob Coxey turned his unemployed "army of the commonweal" toward Washington to protest the wretched conditions of the poor, Hanlon loosed his

[38] *Ibid.*, February 24, 1894; *Sporting Life*, November 17, 1894.

[39] *Ibid.*, October 7, 1893, October 6, 1894, May 4, 1895; *Reach's Official Base Ball Guide*, 1901, p. 54.

hungry ball players. While others chose economy measures and trained at home, Hanlon took his men to Georgia for warm weather training. There his Spartan regimen took root and enabled the team to go undefeated through sixteen exhibition games. Although some laughed at the pretentious Orioles, Ward predicted that the sun-tanned crew would steal the pennant. Worse yet, he knew his Giants must face the Orioles in the 1894 opener in Baltimore, where the park was newly linked with an electric trolley car system.

Beginning on April 19, Ward saw his fears realized. In the opener 15,235 fans saw "Hanlon's bronzed campaigners of the South" swamp the Giants with the help of some enthusiastic fans, who crowded Ward's fielders. Starting with this victory, the Orioles swept the series, and each man received a new hat from Von der Horst as a reward.[40]

With enemies alerted, Hanlon's team had to overcome a determined resistance, and he saw his team move in and out of first place as his pitching faltered. After July the purchase of "Kid" Gleason and Al Esper helped, but the collapse of the Bostons did more. At last in late August the team moved into first place as Hanlon made one more move to bolster pitching by buying Inks from Louisville.[41]

Burning with pennant fever, Baltimoreans jammed the park, and the combination of local expectations and Ward's pursuing Giants created great strain for Hanlon's bachelors. Although frayed tempers led to bitter strife among players, the team stayed ahead, and fired by the war cry "Get at 'em," his Orioles clinched the pennant in Cleveland in late September. Back home, eighteen hundred loyal fans caught a primitive version of play-by-play transmission of the contest at Ford's Theater, and when the victory was secured, the yell from Ford's touched off a riot of joy: "Scores rushed into the nearest saloon to take a drink on it; prohibition men . . . plunged recklessly into buttermilk. . . . Men were laughing, girls . . . giggling, boys . . . yelling, horses braying, dogs barking . . in one cloudburst of happiness that ought to have cured all

[40] *Sun* (Baltimore), March 24, April 20, April 23, 1894.
[41] *Ibid.*, July 31, September 1, 1894; *Sporting Life*, July 21, 1894.

the gout, rheumatism, dyspepsia and putrified livers in . . . the best State in the Union."[42] Upon returning home, the heroes were feted with a parade, banquet, and reception.

Unhappily, not all returns were in, for as the Orioles drank deeply of adulation and potables, Ward's second-place Giants grimly awaited the 1894 postseason showdown, which was the first of the Temple Cup Series, an idea hatched by a Pittsburgh sportsman who offered a $500 cup to the winner. Temple's plan called for the first-place team to defend its honor in a series against the second-place team, thereby hoping to sustain public interest in the twelve-team league. By the end of September this initial match had been arranged, and it required the winner to take four games of the seven-game series. The profits (after expenses) were to be divided among the players on the basis of 65 per cent to the winners and 35 per cent to the losers.

Recognizing that Ward's men were in better shape, McGraw demanded that his team be given the bigger share since they had won the league flag. However, when Temple refused this and McGraw's next suggestion for a fifty-fifty split, McGraw threatened a one-man strike after the Orioles dropped the opener. Too late, his mates saw his point, but the threat of no-play, no-cup now forced them to play the games as scheduled.[43]

The upshot was that Ward's well-conditioned athletes drubbed the Orioles four games straight in a series marked by fights in Baltimore and mass jeering of the Orioles in New York. Adding to the bad blood were reports that some Orioles and Giants had entered into informal agreements to split their shares, thus insuring each party a half-share. However, the Giants reportedly repudiated these agreements, leaving each Oriole with $450, while each Giant took $800. In addition to this, reporters had a field day berating the Orioles, with Caylor gibing about the Orioles' having to eat at lunch counters in Baltimore. Indeed, reporters so celebrated the

[42] *New York Clipper*, May 5, 1894; *Sun* (Baltimore), September 25, 1894.
[43] *Reach's Official Base Ball Guide*, 1894, p. 110; 1895, pp. 29–30; *New York Clipper*, October 13, 1894.

Giant victory that Young reminded a *Clipper* man that the Orioles were, after all, the true champions of 1894.[44]

Believing this to be a supreme moment of glory, Ward decided to retire, but time would reveal that the Temple Cup Series would never again be so popular. Indeed, today the Orioles are remembered as three-time champions of this era, and few recall the Temple Cup defeats.

Financially, Hanlon and Von der Horst made $40,000 in profits, a figure matched by the Giants, who drew well only when the Orioles came to town. Overall, two clubs lost, one broke even, and the others returned modest profits.

Since a great gap had been left in the Giant line-up after Ward's departure, prospects looked good for a repeat victory. However, a new league ruling threatened to cramp Baltimore's psychological warfare tactics with possible $100 fines for "vulgar, indecent, or improper language." But by now the team was practicing more subtle arts, like conniving with their groundkeeper on landscaping the base lines to prevent their bunts from going foul, loosening the dirt in front of the pitcher's mound to harass rivals, hiding spare balls in the tall outfield grass, and improving the base-path turf in order to give speedy Orioles further advantages. Later McGraw, who admitted engineering most of these devices, defended all of them, rationalizing that others did it and that baseball was not for the mentally weak.[45]

But early in the 1895 season the club faced the expense of building a new park to replace the old one that fire had destroyed. Since the Oriole fire was the league's fourth in a year, many feared that a baseball pyromaniac was on the loose, thereby prompting insurance companies to raise their rates. Since some companies no longer insured wooden stand, Baltimore constructed a concrete and steel structure that would seat sixty-five hundred fans. A new feature was a bike barn and track, which were necessary concessions to a

[44] *Times* (New York), October 9, 1894; *New York Clipper*, October 20, 1894; *The Sporting News*, October 12, 1894.
[45] *Spalding's Official Base Ball Guide*, 1895, pp. 9–10; Mrs. John McGraw, *op. cit.*, 94–95.

leisure fad that was sweeping the country and threatening baseball attendance.[46]

These expenses were used to justify holding salaries down, and this was done despite loud protests. The resultant ill feelings were concealed, however, behind new uniforms, which the team sported on opening day. With a new park and fifteen thousand fans on hand, the management rented a condor from a local zoo to symbolize its own high-flying birds. A Negro lad had been hired to shinny up a two-hundred-foot pole with a rope, after which he was to pull the condor up. However, the condor refused to co-operate, as did the Phils who thrashed the Orioles. To the superstitious this was a bad omen, and the Orioles lent credence to it by lagging seven games behind first place in May.

Of course, there were more natural explanations, which included the pitching problem and a rash of injuries that incapacitated many players, but which failed to debunk the myth of Oriole stoicism. The Orioles pitching was weak with ace pitcher McMahon refusing to work until "arm trouble" left him. Not until August did the temperamental ace return, but when he did, he was superb. Reeling off ten straight victories, he led the patchwork staff in a great stretch drive, which not only overtook Cleveland, but landed the flag. The decisive game was held at home, where the team enjoyed a fantastic fifty-four and fourteen record. Because of this and the fact that the team barely broke even on the road, reporters continued to score the Orioles' disgraceful badgering tactics which they used at home. One writer wrote, "I don't see how any team can win in Baltimore with the treatment that is accorded visiting teams." Some proof of this was provided during the Temple Cup Series, which Cleveland won, four games to one. Taking advantage of their home park, Cleveland won the first three games, but when the series moved to Baltimore, the Orioles won with the help of a bombardment of eggs and rocks from their partisans. When Cleveland won the next day, an angry crowd threatened their safety.[47]

This latest blow to the Orioles' pride fell more lightly, especially

[46] *Sporting Life*, January 26, 1895; *Sun* (Baltimore), March 28, April 6, 1895.
[47] *Sporting Life*, May 25, September 28, October 5, 1895.

since the series paid the winners more poorly than in 1894. Each winning player's share fell from $800 to $600. To many the series was degenerating into a weak anticlimax. For the most part, fans regarded the league race as the big show, and the Cup matches as a hippodroming scheme to enrich players. Agreeing with this evaluation, Oriole fans had plenty to brag about. Their team mounted a strong attack, leading all clubs in sacrifices and stolen bases; and in batting, there were six Orioles above .365. Once again the club topped all others in fielding, but lagged behind most others in pitching.

Facing financial losses in 1895, some owners put star players on the auction block, and the Orioles snared Jack Doyle, first baseman of the Giants. At this time, too, Hanlon finally solved his pitching problem by signing rookies Joe Corbett and Arlie Pond. But now new troubles loomed, the most serious being McGraw's siege of typhoid fever. Then, too, there was ominous evidence that the local fans were becoming satiated by success. Perhaps the national depression helped, but enthusiasts attended games in large numbers only when contenders came to town.[48]

With the Orioles lagging behind Cincinnati during much of the campaign, it began surging ahead in August when the vibrant McGraw returned, sporting an arrogant mustache. His return coincided with a number of home games, which also sparked the team to take the initiative. By the end of the month the team was firmly in first place, and, in September, they routed the Reds, beating them three times. The Birds went on to finish the season nine games ahead of the Spiders.

Although the Orioles at last took a Temple Cup Series, this time beating the Spiders four games straight, the series (like the season) was "a frost, financially speaking." A winning player's share was only $200, a sum swelled by $75 thanks to local benefits. Perhaps the Orioles had a right to complain, but even after considering hard times, their open expressions of disappointment tarnished their image. Reportedly, they had tried to get the last

[48] *Ibid.*, October 12, November 23, 1895; *New York Clipper*, October 19, 1895; *Reach's Official Base Ball Guide*, 1896, pp. 107–108, 1897, pp. 9–13.

cup game transferred to New York, and they looked even worse by telling De Wolfe Hopper that they would not attend his benefit show unless they shared in the receipts. Cleveland too, angered its fans with the same "gimme spirit," and Tebeau was censured for calling Cleveland and Baltimore "dead rabbit towns."[49]

Aware of the fact that continuous glory was spoiling Baltimoreans, Hanlon still refused to listen to voices urging him to break up his team. Ambitious competitors zeroed in on Baltimore by rebuilding with touted rookies and by replacing unsuccessful managers. Two of the most acclaimed rookies were Nap Lajoie of the Phillies and Lou Sockalexis of Cleveland, the latter acclaimed the direct descendant of Sitting Bull (which was untrue, for he was a Penobscot Indian).[50]

But the most solid rebuilding job took place in Boston. Early in 1896 the Beaneaters rocked the baseball world by trading Captain Nash to the Phils for speedy Bill Hamilton. With another outfielder, Chick Stahl, and Jimmy Collins, a flashy third baseman capable of stopping the Orioles' bunting attack, the Bostons had a solid club. Even its already strong pitching staff was strengthened by the acquisition of newcomers like Fred Klobedanz, Jim Sullivan, and Ed Lewis. Backing up this staff was moody Marty Bergen, the most promising catcher since Bennett.

Yet few expected this untried team to end the Oriole tyranny. Indeed, the Orioles thrashed them three straight games at the beginning of the season, while jumping off to a commanding lead. But in June Selee's team jelled, and by July its seventeen-game winning streak was the talk of the league. At home a low left field fence offered easy home runs, which gave many sleepless nights to Mr. F. Norton, the cigar manufacturer who had rashly promised a box of "Sleeper's Perfectos" for each such run.

On the road the team was more vulnerable, yet only Baltimore could match them. August found the two locked in fierce struggle,

---

[49] *The Sporting News*, October 17, 1896; *Spalding's Official Base Ball Guide*, 1897, p. 167.

[50] *The Sporting News*, November 21, 1896; *Sporting Life*, April 17, 1897.

and when they met, fists and cleats threatened players and umpires.[51] To sportswriters the struggle was one of *good* vs. *evil*, and
late in September a western fan, anxious for good to win, offered
$500 to any pitcher who beat the Birds and helped Boston. Yet the
race came down to a win-or-else proposition for Boston, and they
needed to take two of three games in the Orioles' private roost to
triumph. Backed by the redoubtable pitching of Nichols and supported by a trainload of "Boston Rooters," the team accomplished
this feat and then remained in Baltimore for one more week of play.
The pennant clinching touched off a wave of messianic rejoicing
around the league, with Chadwick crowing, "Clean Ball Wins,"
and Richter dropping palms to the effect that "old-fashioned, clean
and legitimate style" had triumphed over "modern, noisy, rowdy"
style.[52]

Unhappily for the rejoicing meek, the devil was back in business a few days later, since Baltimore won the Temple Cup, or
"pimple Gup" as a writer irreverently called it. Although the
Orioles trounced Boston four games to one, few cared because the
series was well on the road to extinction. Attendance, though better,
still kept the winning share to $310, and a cloak of popular indiffer-
ence spared Boston from humiliation. After the deciding game, the
two clubs held a joint banquet, at which the cup was used as a
collective champagne goblet. Unknown to them, they were attending the last supper of the Temple Cup Series, because Temple himself now denounced the shabby conduct of his classic. Yet if he
hoped to frighten the barons into boosting the ritual, he was mistaken, for the magnates seized the opportunity to scuttle the affair.
As Jim Hart put it, the cup games no more resembled the World
Series than "a crabapple does a pippin." Such an act spared a defense of the Bostons. Instead, their fans could boast of the mighty
pitching staff, led by Nichols' record of thirty-one victories and
twelve defeats. In other departments their pets had been out-

---

[51] *Sporting Life*, April 24, 1897; *Daily Globe* (Boston), April 5, September 4, 1897.

[52] *Ibid.*, October 2, 1897; *Sporting Life*, October 9, 1897; *New York Clipper*,
February 18, 1899.

gunned by the Orioles, but the team had a splendid .700 winning effort, and it won plaudits for "pluck, perseverance and good management."[53]

Yet the Boston victory did nothing to correct the league's imbalance, which was made painfully apparent by the horrible 29 wins and 102 losses posted by Von der Ahe's last-place Browns. In the countinghouses the same imbalance persisted, prompting Chadwick to urge the destruction of the Boston-Baltimore monopoly in the name of "sound business." Financially, the gap showed almost all clubs to be poorer, with the Boston directors $100,000 wealthier.[54]

That winter, while clubs wearily turned to the task of coping with the Selee-Hanlon monopoly, the sound of genuine war alarms jolted public interest away from baseball and toward the prospect of war with Spain. Amidst the martial background one major baseball story stood out—the firing of Anson by the pennant-starved Chicago club. Thus ended the long career of the big captain, who still batted over .300 in 1897. As long as he played, the league retained a link with the past, and although voices screamed in protest, in the end these were only the niceties which the situation demanded. As ever, there were new heroes to fawn over, and the war with Spain quickly drove Anson from the news columns.

In April, war came, and, with the call for volunteers, the baseball world was shunted aside. But in an odd way, America's "splendid little war" paralleled a typical league baseball campaign. The usual preseason breast-beating by various club spokesmen had its counterpart in the press assault upon Spain. The war declaration came about the time the baseball war began, and on May Day, the time of high hopes for all teams, Dewey won his victory at Manila. Over the next six weeks, a time when writers maintained their ritual of watchful waiting in the critical weeks of a typical baseball race, people in the East anxiously sweated out the whereabouts of a second Spanish fleet under Admiral Pascual Cervera y

[53] *Reach's Official Base Ball Guide*, 1898, pp. 36–37; *Spalding's Official Base Ball Guide*, 1898, pp. 21, 65–90, 104–107.

[54] *Ibid.*, 1898, pp. 24–25, 43–64; *The Sporting News*, October 23, 1897.

Topete. Then in early June, often the time when a strong team scores its big break-through, the American admirals, Sampson and Schley, bottled up Cervera and crushed the Spanish fleet in Santiago harbor. In Cuba, July ended with the surrender of Spanish arms, and August and September found Americans occupying strong points, exploiting their victory. In a baseball campaign these months would have found a front-running club mopping up its opposition. Afterwards came October, a time of celebration and benefits for baseball champs, and in 1898 a time for greeting returning soldiers, who were flushed with easy victory.

Although short and decisive, the war diverted many fans from baseball. Boston again won a fairly close race, but not until the last games did the Beaneaters get front-page notice at home. Elsewhere the slack in the usual free publicity prompted Cincinnati magnate John T. Brush to post war news at the parks, hoping to satiate the curiosity of fans for such fare. But most magnates learned to resign themselves to empty stands and large losses, especially the eastern magnates. Although western clubs did better, Cleveland attendance fell off so sharply that Director Robison stupidly sought to "punish" local fans by ordering the Spiders to play its late-season games on the road. Incredibly, Robison defended his move by telling fans that baseball was a money-making proposition, not a public service. In the face of such arrogance it was a tribute to the American character that Cleveland fans of 1899 staged a genuine boycott, which ultimately killed Cleveland as a National League franchise. Meanwhile, in 1898, Robison's "Wanderers" were but one of many losers. Despite the Oriole heroics, Hanlon complained of losses amounting to $400 a day, and Chadwick marveled at the league's ability to survive the financial nightmares of 1898.[55]

In retrospect the 1898 season was a time for navel-gazing as the barons desperately sought to explain the decline of the leisure pastime. Still unwilling to admit that they might be at fault, most magnates blamed the war and with the arrival of peace dropped any

[55] *Spalding's Official Base Ball Guide*, 1899, 3–12; *The Sporting News*, September 10, 1898.

further consideration of baseball's wartime role. Now the talk turned to lesser causes, and some blamed the wet weather, while others, like Brush, blamed hoodlumism and urged a tough, repressive policy to combat the threat. Still others thought that the public was offended by the 154-game schedule which was adopted in 1898. This may have been true, for in the 1890's charges of "mercenary tactics" and "Hippodroming" could affect attendance, as Robison well knew.

Meanwhile, a *Clipper* man called attention to the expanding leisure market place, with its new outlets for fun-seekers, such as bicycling and motion pictures. The writer found the public flocking to the "flickers," and noted the great popularity of war pictures. For those who wanted a home variety of this medium, magic lanterns filled the demand.[56]

Since so many "causes" were beyond their control, magnates did little in the way of new legislation. Indeed, they brushed aside an alarming threat of a player revolt by holding to the hard salary line, although sweetening it a bit by tolerating incentives for good play. Powerless to buck the barons, players resented the continuing low pay. In Baltimore, two of Hanlon's ace pitchers, Corbett and Pond, quit baseball for more remunerative careers. Boston, too, faced a major holdout problem in the case of pitcher Nichols, who wanted more than the $2,400 limit. Although he finally yielded, neither he nor his mates were happy with the paltry $235 that each received as the management's thanks for winning the 1898 flag.[57]

At this time most magnates felt that the heart of their financial problem was the Boston-Baltimore monopoly of the championships. To break this stranglehold in 1899, the Robison brothers of Cleveland launched their syndicate plan. Having purchased Von der Ahe's franchise in 1898 at a sheriff's auction, Robison had two teams with which to work, and he decided to plant his best men in St. Louis. In favoring St. Louis, he let it be known that he did

[56] *Sporting Life*, April 16, 1898; *Spalding's Official Base Ball Guide*, 1898, pp. 195–98.

[57] *The Sporting News*, April 26, 1898; *Reach's Official Base Ball Guide*, 1899, pp. 46–47; *Daily Globe* (Boston), March 26, October 16, 21, 1898.

not appreciate the attitude of the Cleveland fans, and he contemptuously announced that brother Stanley would manage the Cleveland team as a "side show."

Perhaps, if Hanlon had not worked out a similar strategy, Robison might have won in 1899, but since attendance had dropped alarmingly in Baltimore, and since the death of President Byrne of Brooklyn had offered a chance to buy into that club, Hanlon grasped the opportunity. Moving into the troubled Brooklyn situation, Hanlon persuaded Frank Abell, a major stockholder, to go along with his idea. When the combine was completed early in 1899, Hanlon and Von der Horst held 50 per cent of the stock, Abell 41 per cent, and Charles Ebbets the remainder.

From the start Hanlon regarded Brooklyn as the money-making arm of the syndicate, and there he stationed his best players. On paper it was a good strategy, for Brooklyn had a big new park, and the borough itself was now a part of Greater New York, having been linked by trolley lines to the other boroughs.[58]

With the Brooklyn *Eagle* supporting his "progressive policy," Hanlon faced the problem of selecting the team which would bring victory to Brooklyn. This was no easy task for there were many talented players. Also, having installed McGraw as head of the Baltimore arm of the syndicate, Hanlon could expect stiff competition. Indeed, McGraw had actually outwitted Hanlon in the selection of players by concealing a fine rookie pitcher, Joe McGinnity. McGraw had also protected his coup by extracting from Hanlon a promise not to pre-empt any Oriole players after April 15.

Nevertheless, Hanlon managed to pack his "Superbas" with superstars. As captain he chose outfielder Joe Kelley and flanked him with Keeler and Fielder Jones. The infield consisted of Dan McGann, Tom Daly, Jennings, and Bill Dahlen. Brooklyn's pitching was quite good with men like Jim McJames, Jim Hughes, Jack Dunn, "Roaring Bill" Kennedy, Al Maul, Joe Yeager, Joe Quinn, and Welcome Gaston. Because McGraw insisted on retaining Robinson as his assistant, catching remained mediocre. Altogether,

[58] *New York Clipper*, July 23, 1898, April 8, 1899; *The Sporting News*, February 11, 1899; *Eagle* (Brooklyn), March 9, 1899.

Hanlon screened forty men from the Baltimore-Brooklyn rosters before making his selections.[59]

With hopes high, Hanlon took this dream team south for training, where it proceeded to slaughter service teams in exhibition games. Back home Ebbets took charge of the opening-day plans, and his open-house plan attracted many fans to the new grounds and convinced him of the need for more trolley cars on the line. Finally, when opening day came, Ebbets saw his dream for a "$10,000 house" come true, with twenty thousand fans watching the Superbas bow to Boston.

Meanwhile, in victory-starved St. Louis, a promising throng turned out to watch Tebeau's "Perfectos" begin their season, and as expected the team broke fast and set a stiff pace.[60]

By mid-May, however, the damaging effects of the syndicate plan were obvious, and, if the top-half of the league was well matched, the bottom-half was never so inept. Indeed, May 20 found Washington with a record of five wins and twenty-one losses, and brother Stanley's Cleveland team with three wins and twenty losses. Even without brother Fred's patronizing remarks about Cleveland fans, such a gait was bound to have had adverse effects at the turnstiles. In truth the club never had a chance; opening day found only five hundred on hand for a double-header, and regularly thereafter Manager Lave Cross's men played to virtually empty houses. In time the team's predicament became so ludicrous that writers gave inordinate attention to the situation. Elmer Bates, for one, did several features on "Brother Stanley's" team, to which he variously referred as the "Misfits" and "Leftovers." He noted that the players were so shell-shocked by regular drubbings that they practiced "for dear life." Only once did they win two games in a row, a feat that enriched several betters, who cashed in on four-to-one odds against this ever happening. By June the team attracted a total of 3,179 home-town fans, an average of less than 200 per game. Since home receipts came to less than $25 a game, visiting clubs raised such a storm that Robison fired the manager

[59] Mrs. John McGraw, *op. cit.*, 114–21; *New York Clipper*, March 18, 1899.
[60] *Eagle* (Brooklyn), March 21, April 16, 1899; *The Sporting News*, April 22, 1899.

and ordered the team to play its remaining games on the road. At least this would save rivals the expense of coming to Cleveland. At the end of the season the "Exiles" posted a record of 20 wins and 134 losses, for a percentage of .129, a record of futility unsurpassed by a league team.[61]

Nevertheless, the Robison syndicate took comfort for a time in the record of its St. Louis entry. But in June the team foundered, and, when the Superbas brushed by, attendance in St. Louis fell off. At this point an *Eagle* reporter made this unkind remark, "Patsy Tebeau's Perfectos haven't the quality of a five cent Reina." He went on to predict that nothing would stop the victory parade of the "Trolley Dodgers."[62]

When a July slump brought relief to the battered opposition, many "Dodger" rooters wrote to the *Eagle* asking whether hippodroming was afoot. But faith in Superba superiority reckoned without the shrewd mind of McGraw, who had put together a fighting team in Baltimore. Paced by the tireless pitching of McGinnity, a onetime ironworker, and the sparkling infield play of Gene DeMontreville, whom McGraw boldly purchased on his own from Chicago, the team was snapping at Hanlon's heels and outdrawing the Superbas on the road. When the angry Hanlon tried to cramp McGraw's style by attempting to draft "Demont" and pitcher Dick Nops to the Superbas, McGraw slyly informed the press, which soon had the baseball world down on Hanlon and the syndicate system.[63] The system was already taking a beating, and Boston's purchase of Giant pitcher Meekin for a paltry fee merely added to its discredit.

In August injuries to key men like Jennings forced Hanlon to turn once again to the market place. At one point he was on the verge of swapping Jennings to Louisville for Honus Wagner, a deal that might have been the steal of the century. Jennings, however, queered it by writing the Louisville president, "Don't consent to deal. Am in no condition. Will play no more this season. Bad arm."

[61] *Sporting Life*, May 20, July 1, 1899.

[62] *Ibid.*, June 3, 1899; *Eagle* (Brooklyn), June 14, 1899.

[63] Mrs. John McGraw, *op. cit.*, 122–29; *Sporting Life*, August 12, 1899.

Unquestionably, McGraw's rivalry and Jennings' "honesty" bothered Hanlon. But he should have known how vulnerable he was, for with him it was a case of win or else. Although he did win, McGraw emerged as the managerial genius, and many said that the only thing that saved Hanlon was the death of McGraw's wife, which took the genius away from the Oriole helm in September. Although the Orioles collapsed, McGraw lost none of the glory.[64]

But much harder to bear was the financial failure of Hanlon's Brooklyn club, which did well enough at home, but drew poorly on the road. What really hurt was a week of patriotic pageantry, which ruined the team's final home game. From Hanlon's viewpoint, the villain was Admiral Dewey, who brought his flagship into Brooklyn one week earlier than expected. With a war hero in their midst, Greater New York forgot about the Superbas in their orgy of hero worship. The celebration overshadowed the team's pennant clinching, and probably accounted for the small attendance at the postseason benefits.[65]

However, if Dewey furnished a convenient excuse for the low profits, it was also true that the team was too good. Noting the "unsurpassed record" of holding first place for twenty-one weeks, Chadwick said the Superbas bored the fans. As for the Perfectos, they finished a disappointing fifth place behind the Orioles. Nevertheless, some profits were made, and McGraw made an unexpected $6,000 profit with the Orioles, but total figures ran far behind the anticipated $100,000 profits. That year the Phils and Beaneaters made the most money, each earning $50,000. For the rest of the clubs, however, it was another grim year with the Louisville's giving "Brother Stanley's exiles" competition as heaviest loser.[66]

The demoralizing financial losses of the have-nots, plus the scandals of syndicatism, finally forced reforms in the league's structure. Moreover, "the melancholy wreck," as Richter called the twelve-club monopoly, now faced competition from an organized rival. This was the revived American Association, whose backers claimed

[64] *Eagle* (Brooklyn), July 14, August 7, 1899; *Sporting Life*, September 9, 1899.

[65] *New York Clipper*, July 29, 1899; *Eagle* (Brooklyn), September 26, October 22, 1899.

[66] *New York Clipper*, October 28, 1899; *The Sporting News*, May 12, 1900.

to have franchises in the big cities and the support of such celebrated baseballers as Anson, McGraw, and Robinson. But when
the showdown came, the backers faltered, and the association was
stillborn.

Although unsuccessful, the attempt to resurrect the American
Association concealed the activities of more resolute interlopers.
While league men worried about this threat, Ban Johnson quietly
launched an attempt to win major-league status for his Western
League. Boldly blackmailing the league barons, he demanded and
received, as the price for his loyalty, the right to rename his circuit
the American League and to plant franchises in Chicago and Cleveland. As a result *Reach's Official Base Ball Guide* predicted "a
new and probably highly promising career for the American
League."[67]

Yet who could say that the barons were not calling the tune?
At the annual league meeting, the powerful voices of Soden, Brush,
and Freedman now advocated a return to an eight-club league and
the end of syndicatism. In an unusual spirit of compromise, the
league men closed ranks and dropped its four weakest members. In
putting the ax to Baltimore, Cleveland, Louisville, and Washington, the league had to purchase the assets of these profit-poor clubs
for $104,000. The blow not only ended the syndicate system, but
it greatly pacified the dropouts. In the case of Louisville, President
Barney Dreyfuss was paid $10,000 in cash and received the right to
sell his stars on the open market and the opportunity to take over
the presidency of the Pittsburgh club. Delighted with this settlement, Dreyfuss kept Fred Clarke and Honus Wagner and quickly
built the Pirates into a first-rate power. Although mere greenbacks
served to pacify the other dropouts, it left the surviving barons
with a collective debt, one which would have to be paid off by more
tithing at the box office.[68]

There remained, however, the knotty problem of mutinous players, who now threatened to organize a new union. At this point they

[67] *Reach's Official Base Ball Guide*, 1900, pp. 52–57.

[68] *Ibid.*, 1900, pp. 48–51; *Spalding's Official Base Ball Guide*, 1901, pp. 10–19;
Sporting Life, December 23, 1899.

were fearful of new salary cuts, and many were afraid that the contraction of the big league would cause a wholesale loss of jobs. But before long the players realized that Johnson's American League offered plenty of new job opportunities and a chance of breaking the salary log-jam. Although at this point the handwriting on the wall was still illegible, major-league baseball was entering a new era. With the American League moving into the defunct territories and vigorously validating its claim to major-league status, it was becoming clear that baseball was returning to the dual-league structure of the golden age. Although the barons felt the need to go through a face-saving war with their new rival, by 1903 nearly all welcomed the restoration of the old *status quo.* Hence, the new "silver age" seemed like a frank attempt to rebuild along the structural lines of the 1880's with the hope of rekindling public interest in the spectacle. That the formula worked was evidenced in the returning profits of the 1900's, and the clink of silver dollars in the countinghouses was a welcome sound to the ears of disillusioned promoters. In time nothing more clearly underscored the wisdom of the move than the fact that for half a century after 1903 there was not one franchise shift in any of the sixteen cities.

Although a new era was dawning in 1900, the old order remained for another season. Once again Hanlon faced the problem of selecting the best seventeen men from two clubs, but this time the leftovers went to the have-nots or to the American League. Although he won the pennant and dispatched rivals McGraw and Robinson to St. Louis, Hanlon's star of empire was setting.[69]

Hanlon, however, did not have an easy time in 1900. When two of his pitching stars quit the game, he faced the problem of acquiring replacements. Meanwhile, a rising Pittsburgh team almost turned the tide. But the bellwether work of "Ironman McGinnity," who pitched and won six consecutive games in six days in September, saved Hanlon. For this, McGinnity received a $700 bonus in addition to his base pay of $1,800. Brooklyn also won a post-season World Series from the second-place Pirates, but overall the

69 *Eagle* (Brooklyn), January 26, March 12, 1900.

Superbas lost money. Only Pittsburgh, Boston, and Philadelphia made respectable profits, the rest either broke even or lost.[70]

With the 1900 season at an end and since some managers were subletting their parks to professional football tenants,[71] few realized that an era had ended. Many magnates feared a baseball war was coming, but a few shrewd ones looked upon the American League rivals as a blessing. Onrushing events would not only prove them correct, but would also show that the Selee-Hanlon monopoly was at end. With the rise of new dynasties like Pittsburgh, Chicago, and New York and healthful competition from the American League, the austere era of the monopolistic "National League and American Association of Professional Base Ball Clubs" was at end.

[70] *Ibid.*, September 28, October 4, 8, 1900; *New York Clipper*, October 20, 1900.
[71] *Sporting Life*, September 29, 1900.

14

The Big Leaguers

I T WAS THE BEST of times, it was the worst of times," said Charles Dickens, and this description aptly describes the lot of ball players in the feudal age. On the gloomy side, they saw their cherished dreams of controlling the spectacle reduced to ashes. Worse yet was the fact that the victory of the magnates had been complete, for it led to restricted salaries and the continuance of the reserve rule—in short, to the proletarization of players.

Yet serfdom had its compensations, for the very monopoly that made the league the baseball world's unquestioned master also made its players unique. For this reason the fans began calling the league "the big league," and the players "big leaguers." In a short time both phrases became complimentary colloquialisms of the American language, and the glory of being one of a select company of two hundred "big leaguers" partially assuaged feelings

274

of oppression.[1] For many players ultimate glory came when large woodcut likenesses appeared in sporting journals for on picture cards inside packages of cigarettes; in such joy many churls found paradise.

More than ever, newspapers, advertisers, and drummers were using endorsements of player-heroes to help sell their products. Especially did newspapers continue to expand their baseball departments. If news of the spectacle sold papers, it is also true that papers sold players, for it was the newspapers which introduced most fans to players and most players to fans.

Among the star catchers of this decade were Kelly, Ewing, Robinson, Connie Mack, Joe Sugden, Charley Farrell, Chief Zimmer, Marty Bergen, and John Clements, all of whom were well known. Yet pitchers commanded top headlines despite a trend toward larger staffs. Because of the lengthened pitching distance, which increased the strain of pitching nine innings, managers hired more men; in 1897, league reserve lists showed two teams with eight and none with fewer than five. Although such numbers meant greater anonymity, players quickly learned to adapt. In an attempt to prevent batters from hitting home runs, the better pitchers adopted defenses like the "Cyclone" fast ball, the curve, and a bewildering variety of trick deliveries. Pitching mastery enabled men like "Cy" (Cyclone) Young, Amos Rusie, "Kid" Nichols, Clark Griffith, Jess Tannehill, "Sadie" McMahon, and Ted Breitenstein to emerge as heroes and to eclipse older titans like Clarkson and Radbourne.

At other positions changes of personnel came less dramatically. At first base the old guard of Anson, Brouthers, Comiskey, and Connor held the limelight far into the decade, although eventually they were overshadowed by newcomers like Jake Beckley, Jack Doyle, and Tom Tucker. Likewise, at second base Fred Pfeffer and "Bid" McPhee continued their long tenures, but were soon obscured by men like the "most graceful" Nap Lajoie, Henry Reitz, "Cupid" Childs, and Bob Lowe. Generally speaking, a pride of fine athletes excited fans, including Honus (John Peter) Wag-

[1] *Spalding's Official Base Ball Guide*, 1897, p. 106.

ner, Herman Long, Gene DeMontreville, Bill Dahlen, and Hugh Jennings. McGraw and Jim Collins were heroic third basemen, but Bill Joyce and Bill Nash acquired a following of their own.

Seemingly, the outfielders carried the best-known names of this era, for this was the traditional locale of great hitters. As hitters, some like Keeler and Jess Burkett won acclaim for their scientific place-hitting; others, like Bill Hamilton, starred as base-stealers; still others like Ed Delehanty, Sam Thompson, and Buck Freeman dazzled fans with their slugging. As a slugging "Phillie," Thompson achieved a career total of 127 home runs, a record that stood until Babe Ruth's day. And little Bob Lowe, playing in a makeshift Boston park in 1894, once hit four home runs in one game, a record still unsurpassed.

Aside from the stellar deeds of diamond virtuosos, newsmen also singled out the ridiculous, awkward, exotic, and pathetic deeds of players. In spicing accounts with such fare, they tended to make a player's whole life public property. Since "yellow journalism" regularly treated socialites and public figures the same way, the sports page merely aped the current journalistic trend. Like some public figures, some players sought notoriety and deliberately performed zany feats. Thus, in 1893, Louisville outfielder Weaver celebrated the Fourth of July by whipping out a revolver and placing five shots into a fly ball before catching it.[2] And after several attempts over a period of years, Catcher Bill Schriver finally attained immortality by catching a ball dropped from the Washington monument.[3] By catering to the diverse tastes of fans, some players earned reputations as "rowdies" for their aggressive style of play. For a time this "tough" style seemed a quick and sure way of ingratiating oneself with many fans, much to the regret of the purists.[4]

But by whatever means, once a baseballer became a superstar, his reputation was secure. In Kelly's case, his sudden death in

[2] *Baseball Magazine*, "The Baseball Bat Bag: Forty Years of Odd Baseball Records," *passim*; *New York Clipper*, July 5, 1893.

[3] *Ibid.*, July 5, 1893.

[4] *The Sporting News*, July 17, 1897; *Reach's Official Base Ball Guide*, 1893, pp. 69–73.

1894, coming in the twilight of his career, was followed by his virtual transfiguration. No doubt he would have enjoyed knowing that five thousand Bostonians viewed his corpse as it lay in state at the Elks Hall.[5] In sharp contrast was the furor over Marty Bergen's suicide, which followed his murder of his wife and children. His funeral attracted the curious, and newsmen spared none of the grisly details.[6]

Sometimes in a manner that went far beyond the limits of good taste, a player was forced into notoriety. Such was the case of Cleveland outfielder Lou Sockalexis. Well-educated and a brilliant player, this six-footer in 1897 set a fast pace which attracted fans and reporters. Such raucous publicity would have taxed the emotions of any rookie, and in this case it ruined Sockalexis' career, for he was a Penobscot Indian, a fact that fans and writers never let him forget. Whenever he appeared, he was greeted with derisive war whoops, and Cleveland writers began calling the team the "Indians." Thus, whenever Tebeau's rowdy crew stirred up emotions, the most menacing threats were directed at Sockalexis. Although some writers urged fans to lay off the "Ki Yi's" and war whoops, it is likely that such pleas merely provoked more of the same. As for Sockalexis, two months after he began playing, he was suspended and fined for drunkenness, although he was batting .413 at the time. Although the end of the 1897 season found him too far gone to save, he now proved useful to reporters as an example of the evils of drink.[7]

A similar fate might have befallen Outfielder William Hoy, for this intelligent, well-educated player was deaf and dumb as a result of the ravages of childhood "brain fever." Called "Dummy" by fans, players, and writers, he had to learn to accept the nickname for the rest of his life. However, his silent world protected him from barbed catcalls, and he enjoyed a brilliant career. In time his mates in the outfield accepted his cleverly contrived system of signals, which enabled him to make the adjustments demanded by

[5] *Sporting Life*, November 12, 1894.

[6] *New York Clipper*, January 27, 1900.

[7] *Sporting Life*, May 8, August 7, 1897; *Daily Globe* (Boston), June 13, 1897.

his affliction. That he was a successful athlete was evidenced by his long career in both the National League and the American League.[8]

As studies in inhumanity, the aforementioned cases were overshadowed by the collective intolerance afforded Negroes, who hoped to use the game as a means of acquiring status. In the 1880's the Walker brothers, Fleet and Weldy, played briefly in the association until the lowering of the color barrier forced them out. According to the studious Weldy Walker, it was Anson's influence that barred Negroes from the majors. In 1887, Ward tried to sign Pitcher George Stovey to a Giant contract, but Anson, "with all the venom . . . of a Tillman or a Vardaman," made his admission unacceptable. Moreover, in his memoirs Anson admitted this act of prejudice, but declined to give any reason other than his personal dislike of all Negroes. Yet this reason and Anson's popularity were enough to dissuade others from bringing "the black man" into "the white leagues." At best, fans regarded Negro players as curiosities; at worst, they harassed them with venomous catcalls. Players suspected of being Negroes, because of some phenotypical characteristics, were hounded from the league. Such was the case of Lou Nava in the 1880's and George Treadway, a fine Oriole outfielder, in the 1890's. In 1901, McGraw signed Charles Grant to an Oriole contract by passing him off as an "Indian," but when some of Grant's Negro friends publicly congratulated him, American League officials demanded his peremptory dismissal.

Indeed, as the 1890's wore on, hostile racism, reflecting the social Darwinian ideologies of the era, steadily worsened. As Jim Crowism was applied to the social institutions in American life, it affected both big-league and minor-league baseball. In this decade there were instances of white players conspiring against Negroes.[9] Harried from white teams, these aspiring baseballers formed strong Negro teams, like the Cuban Giants, and during this era there was even a Negro National League. But such acquiescence merely

[8] *Ibid.*, September 22, 1892; *The Sporting News*, October 8, 1898.

[9] *Sol White's Official Base Ball Guide*, 1907, pp. 60–128; Anson, *op. cit.*, 148–50; *Sporting Life*, June 4, July 23, 1884; *New York Clipper*, June 11, 1887, June 14, 1890.

hastened *de facto* segregation. According to Sol White's guide, the official organ of Negro baseball, by 1900 the best Negro stars earned salaries of $466, which were considerably less than the $571 average paid to a white minor leaguer, and far below the $2,000 average of white big leaguers.

But far worse than the denial of cash and glory was the deprivation of human dignity. In Walker's bitter account one reads of Negro players being barred from hotels and forced to walk the streets at night seeking a bench to rest upon. Desperately needing exhibition games with white clubs to make ends meet, Negro teams scheduled encounters with white opponents, but in doing so, they ran the risk of being humiliated by players who might object to competing with Negroes.[10]

As segregation became a reality, Negro players were not only refused the same accommodations as white players but were also ridiculed by whites, as evidenced by Tim Murnane's comment: "There is an array of colored players around the large cities. Their playing is more picturesque to look at than their pale-faced brothers." Some white managers, Ted Sullivan for example, deliberately belittled Negro teams by humiliating them with such gags as holding the score eleven to seven (a "craps" score) and by breaking watermelons in front of the Negro player bench.[11]

Today, apologists excuse such conduct on the grounds that men of the era were "prisoners of their times," for many Americans of the 1890's believed in the validity of racial inferiority theories and cast the Negro in roles depicted in the popular "coon songs" and "nigger jokes." This rationalization, however, persuades the more objective individual to view major-league baseball as a reflector of the emotions and the values of a culture and to question the claim that the game builds character by its "intrinsic" values of "Americanism" or "gentlemanly sportsmanship."

Half a century had to pass before external changes in values persuaded major-league moguls to remedy the bigotry of this era.

[10] *The Sporting News*, April 1, 1899; *Sporting Life*, February 26, 1898; *Reach's Official Base Ball Guide*, 1896, pp. 138–39.

[11] *Sporting Life*, August 9, 1890; *Daily Globe* (Boston), April 1, 1897; Sullivan, *op. cit.*, 176–79.

Meanwhile, the white man's road to cash and glory remained a tortuous challenge to the hard-nosed young men who sought to become major leaguers, for never was competition for playing berths as keen as after 1891, the year of the association's collapse. As one survey showed, veterans of the 1880's faded fast in the competition of the 1890's. In 1897, only 35 National League players had played in 1889, and of 123 association veterans of 1889, only 28 continued to play. In the interim the annual recruiting of rookies from the minors or from "farm clubs" regularly dislodged veterans. The odds, however, were against these hopefuls, for according to an 1895 estimate, only one in five men who were *drafted* by big-league teams made the grade.[12] But still they came, and for the most part from eastern and midwestern states. Only three big leaguers of 1897 came from as far south as Virginia, and the seven from California and Oregon were the only far westerners. Of the 168 big leaguers of 1897, 34 were Pennsylvanians, 31 Massachusettans, 20 Ohioans, 19 New Yorkers, 11 Missourians, and the rest were from other eastern or midwestern states.[13] Most of these were average performers, who rarely tasted the sweetness of adulation, and for them the stay at the top was quite brief, with no sentiments wasted on their departure. A *Clipper* man, tallying the number of players released by the league in 1898, dismissed them cavalierly: "It is 'off with the old and on with the new.' . . . There is little sympathy with them. As long as a player is a star he is received with open arms, but as soon as he begins to derogate in his work . . . a cry is set up for someone to take his place. Such is the ball player's life."[14]

One rare exception to the above rule was "Bid" McPhee, the Cincinnati second baseman. A twenty-year veteran, he played eighteen years with Cincinnati, a record for sustained service matched only by Anson. Although Anson's tenure was supported by his credentials as a manager and stockholder in his club, McPhee's only asset was his playing skill. In an open letter to Cincin-

12 *Reach's Official Base Ball Guide*, 1897, pp. 103–104; *New York Clipper*, April 14, 1900; *The Sporting News*, November 30, 1895.
13 *Reach's Official Base Ball Guide*, 1896, pp. 138–39; *ibid.*, 1897, 104–105.
14 *New York Clipper*, February 12, 1898.

nati fans in 1900, McPhee announced his voluntary retirement because "... my presence on the team would only handicap its chances." The club, he said, gave him permission to stay as long as he liked, which was a warm tribute to a man who was most proud of the fact that the had not once been fined or ejected for misconduct.[15]

Yet, for most, the prospect of being cast adrift was a constant fear, and, even when expected, was seldom taken lightly. Although some castoffs joined minor-league teams, most found themselves on the same economic level as a blue-collar workingman. Periodically, the guides published stories of how retired players busied themselves. Saloon-keeping lured an estimated 80 per cent, according to Chadwick. On the other hand, deaths and dissipation took a large toll.[16]

But for those who replaced them, conditions seemed somewhat improved over those of previous decades. By 1895 some clubs employed "professional trainers" to care for the routine injuries. Also, doctors assisted by new "Roentgen rays," could give better care to the classic baseball ailments like broken fingers, "glass arms," and "crooked arms." The latest scientific and shamanistic fads found their ways into spring training camps, where players, having fattened all winter, would sweat themselves back into shape. Under the guidance of trainers, "Heavy sweaters, long walks, quick runs, hard rubbing baths, and often great doses of cleansing medicine are used to get rid of the fat winter coat." And even without the benefit of massive research by the surgeon general's office, some shrewd trainers discouraged smoking, linking it with batting slumps and other failings. One manager, imploring his men to smoke cigars if they had to smoke anything, told them to avoid cigarettes because they ruined King Kelly's batting eye.[17]

Although cheaper, this advice provided less immediate comfort

15 *Sporting Life*, May 31, 1900.

16 *The Sporting News*, January 23, 1897; *Spalding's Official Base Ball Guide*, 1894, p. 104.

17 *Sporting Life*, May 13, 1893, October 26, 1895, May 1, 1897; *Reach's Official Base Ball Guide*, 1893, pp. 62–63; *Courier-Journal* (Louisville), March 10, 1890; *Spalding's Official Base Ball Guide*, 1897, p. 88.

than did the improved playing equipment. In the 1890's comfortable flannel uniforms and separate sliding pads replaced the quilted knickers of the 1880's, although the cost of a complete uniform soared to fifty-six dollars. Travel, too, was more enjoyable as a result of speedier rail transport and better eating and sleeping facilities.[18] Anson believed that the current generation of players lived much better than did those of the 1880's. Noting that most clubs were beginning to select better hotel accommodations, he hoped that the trend would attract college graduates, who would make a career of baseball. Fifty years later, thanks to a spate of high bonus offers and a proliferation of college "gut" courses, Anson's wishes were fulfilled.[19]

Moreover, the baseball profession seemed to gain prestige during the 1890's. Such progress was supported by the growing number of social elites who frequented games. Washington's opener in 1894 attracted diplomatic dignitaries like Richard Olney and Sir Julian Pauncefote; on other occasions cabinet members, congressmen, Supreme Court judges, and lesser diplomats attended games. Theodore Roosevelt praised major-league baseball in 1890 for "popularizing a most admirable and characteristic American game," which avoided most of the pitfalls of other commercial leisure pastimes.[20]

Encouraged by the growing support of baseball, league spokesmen pledged further improvements in the game. Under the league monopoly, said one, players not only are more sober and thrifty, but need less discipline than their brethren of the past. These men are also more intelligent and quick-witted, because the new scientific style of baseball requires its participants to develop mental and physical dexterity rather than brute strength.[21]

Yet there were dissenters, and few more adamant than the pompous lawyer Robert Todd Lincoln, the only surviving son of the martyred President. Incensed over his daughter's marriage to a Chicago pitcher, Lincoln denounced his unwanted son-in-law as

18 *Times* (New York), February 1, 1959; *Sun* (Baltimore), June 25, 1894.
19 Palmer, *op. cit.*, 9–19.
20 *Reach's Official Base Ball Guide*, 1894, p. 109; *Eagle* (Brooklyn), August 8, 1890.
21 *Ibid.*, May 1, 1899.

"a base ball buffoon."[22] The denunciation prompted Warren Beckwith to enlist for service in the Spanish-American War, hoping to raise his father-in-law's opinion of him, but the marriage later ended in divorce. Meanwhile, some hotels refused to accommodate ballplayers, and a Michigan YMCA refused to allow teams to train in its gym, because they feared that they might be asked to extend similar privileges to prize fighters.[23]

Because of the collapse of their brotherhood, players escaped being identified with the militant labor struggles of the decade. The price of their respectability, however, was serfdom, and base-ballers were forced to accept lower salaries "for their own good and the salvation of the game." This tendentious logic of President Young was echoed by Chadwick, who compared players with dollar-a-day laborers. In the midst of the panic of 1893, Chadwick urged players to be "patriotic" in the face of "the general ... loss."[24] If high income was an index of high professional status, players suffered serious status deprivation when the magnates slashed their salaries. Some rose to protest, but their voices were unorganized, and when some tried to hold out for higher pay, they were peremptorily fired, although here and there a few indispensables won concessions. But usually, players' attempts to better their lot were a lost cause, for as Giant infielder Danny Richardson explained, "Baseball is a big monopoly. Players can't kick with only one major league. They must accept the reductions or retire." This was a fair evaluation, for it was the plentitude of available talent, as much as the baron's united front, that enabled the magnates, with minor concessions like bonuses for heroic play, to maintain the $2,400 maximum throughout the decade.[25]

If low salaries were the sharpest goads, restrictions rubbed players raw. Especially aggravating were the puritanical behavior codes imposed by the league owners. In 1899, clean-living, hard-working

[22] *Sporting Life*, May 14, 1892.
[23] *Ibid.*, April 2, 1892.
[24] *Daily Globe* (Boston), October 3, 1892; *Spalding's Official Base Ball Guide*, 1893, p. 68; *ibid.*, 1894, p. 104.
[25] *Reach's Official Base Ball Guide*, 1893, pp. 57–59; *New York Clipper*, March 11, November 18, 1893; *Sun* (Baltimore), May 4, 1894.

Jess Tannehill criticized these ordinances, pointing out that the codes regarded players as children. Among other impositions, players were required to sign temperance pledges, which actually prompted resentful baseballers to sneak "snorts" of whisky to prove their manliness.[26]

Eventually such repressions drove players to reorganize. In 1897, Clark Griffith openly urged players to unionize, and sportswriter Joe Campbell called him, "the free silver politico-pitcher of the Colts, supporter of Bryan, Debs and Tillman."[27] Elsewhere, others lit the brush fires of revolt; in 1898 the Orioles threatened to strike for higher wages. The logic of their cause was quite simple: since the league's schedule was to be increased twenty-two games, they wanted the equivalent in extra pay.[28] Two months later the same team faced another crisis. Playing the Giants in New York, Oriole outfielder "Ducky" Holmes was taunted by his former Giant teammates, until he shouted, "Well I'm glad I'm not working for a sheeny any more." Enraged by this thoughtless slur against his Jewish ancestry, Freedman ordered the umpire to expel Holmes, and, when this demand was refused, Freedman carried his case to the arbitration committee and got Holmes laid off. This affair almost triggered an all-out revolt on Holmes's behalf. Boston's *Daily Globe* published a petition signed by the Boston team, denouncing Freedman for his "spirit of impatience, intolerance, arrogance and prejudice toward players, a spirit inimical to the best interests of the game and the public."[29] After emotions had been quieted, a compromise cleared the air, but the battle lines had been drawn.

By 1900 a backlog of hostile incidents stirred the players to unionize. The latest outrages included a proposal by magnate Jim Hart to put all players into a pool for annual redistribution. Although intended to break the Selee and Hanlon monopoly, the suggestion alarmed the players, and when the Brush Resolution

26 *Sporting Life*, February 25, 1899.
27 *Post* (Washington), July 5, 1897.
28 *Tribune* (Chicago), March 11, 1898; *Daily Globe* (Boston), April 9, 1898.
29 *Ibid.*, July 26, August 20, 1898.

was passed, their fears were merely deepened.[30] Early in 1900 a story broke telling of labor-leader Samuel Gompers' organizing the players. In an interview Gompers said that he was a baseball fan and was glad to furnish assistance to the men. In his opinion the magnates were oppressors, and he likened players to merchant seamen, who had been in a state of slavery before the union came to their aid. Since baseball careers were brief, Gompers defended the demand for higher wages, and he branded the contract, the reserve clause, and the unfair punishments as major evils. "The great mass of the people who find recreation in baseball today," said he, "are the working classes and the club owners fully recognize this fact."[31]

Scarred veterans of the brotherhood agreed. In Philadelphia, Richter launched new editorial attacks on "the feudal barons of the National League," and in New York, Ward, now a successful lawyer, won a $700 judgment against Freedman for his "illegal suspension" for Fred Pfeffer. In June, players held a union organizational meeting in Brooklyn. Despite a militant atmosphere, cool heads took charge. One of these, Harry Taylor, another player-turned-lawyer, furnished legal counsel and drew up the form of The Protective Association of Professional Ball Players. The members agreed not to affiliate with Gompers' AF of L, unless magnates withheld recognition. Likewise, strikes would be a last resort, to be used only if negotiations failed.[32]

At this point the occurrence of a major revolt seemed so likely that sportswriter Murnane urged young "Turks" among the journalists to lessen their "muckraking." Meanwhile, a delegation of players stood ready with demands, which insisted that contracts be revised, the reserve clause rewritten, salaries raised, and farming and trading abuses curtailed. In return the association promised to curb "disorder and rowdyism" among players.

Although a showdown was scheduled for the league's December meeting, magnates were reluctant to treat with the association.

---

[30] *Sporting Life*, August 27, 1898; *New York Clipper*, June 24, 1899.

[31] *Sporting Life*, April 7, 1900.

[32] *Ibid.*, April 21, June 23, August 18, 1900.

For three days the delegation of players was ignored, while their tempers smoldered. Years later, Clark Griffith, a member of the delegation, recalled that most men wanted the salary limit raised to $3,000 and the owners to pay the cost of uniforms. With these as their minimum aspirations, they waited several days for a response from the barons. Finally, Griffith encountered the irate President Young, who had been temporarily stripped of his power and sent from the room—an all-too-common experience for this figurehead. Angered by this exclusion, Young blurted to Griffith, "They aren't going to give you a thing."[33]

Forewarned, the players were able to discern the barons' stalling tactics, and from then on they gave their adversaries no rest. Once Griffith followed Soden into a saloon, where in the presence of reporters he demanded to know whether Soden had received a copy of the player petition. When Soden replied that he had not, Griffith proved him a liar by grabbing the document from Soden's coat pocket.[34] Apparently, this incident and Young's disclosure turned the tide of public sympathy in favor of the players, and since the new American League had also sided with the players, Taylor felt that he could make more demands. The new ultimatum charged that a player may not be reserved for less than he had earned the previous year, owners must pay a doctor to care for injured players, players must be represented when league officials meet, and player suspensions must not exceed two weeks.[35]

Because the upstart American League had agreed to some of these requirements and submitted its contract forms to the players association for their approval, Taylor's strategy was vindicated. Now isolated, the league barons not only capitulated and recognized the association, but they conceded the same points that their American rivals had accepted. Although the players made no revolutionary gains, the total effect was to free them from abject serfdom and to elevate the status of the profession.[36] Of course, players

---

[33] *Ibid.*, December 22, 1900; *New York Clipper*, December 22, 1900.

[34] *Sporting Life*, December 29, 1900, March 2, 1901; *The Sporting News*, February 9, 1901.

[35] *Reach's Official Base Ball Guide*, 1901, pp. 13–15, 75, 183.

[36] *Sporting Life*, January 30, June 11, November 26, 1892, April 22, 1893.

continued to act like individualists, which was evidenced in the rapid decline of association memberships after 1902. All that they had really wanted was a reasonable chance to sell their services in an open market, and although this market place was nonexistent in 1902, at least the way was cleared for players to bargain on the basis of individual achievement and to have the opportunity to secure a better return for their efforts.

2. THE BIG-LEAGUE STYLE

Baseball's feudal age witnessed the last significant changes in the rules of major-league baseball and the hardening of their basic structural aspect. In applying the finishing touches to the rules, the rules committee put the quietus on the long debate over the pitching distance. Arguments over "how far back" reached a new boiling point in 1892 and forced baseball leaders into two embattled camps. One, led by Harry Wright, insisted that the distance be kept at 55½ feet in order to retain the essence of the scientific game, but the other, championed by many younger strategists, favored extending the distance to allow "manly slugging."

With a showdown slated for March, 1893, propaganda warfare raged in the newspapers. The most extreme solution was suggested by Clifford Spencer, who wanted to replace the diamond-shaped infield with a pentagon-shaped one, which would have a fourth base for better balance. If adopted, Spencer promised that the plan would yield better balance, better fielding, fewer fouls, more stealing, and higher status for the second baseman.[37]

Although the Spencer plan intrigued many, most advocates of the slugging game simply wanted to extend the pitching distance to sixty-three feet. The rules committee, however, compromised and voted to advance the distance to the present day sixty feet, six inches. Except for minor additions such as ruling on the pitcher's footwork, introducing the rubber slab, and defining a balk, the rules have remained unchanged since 1900.

In announcing their decision, the committeemen made further concessions to the "manly" proponents. By outlawing the flat bat,

[37] *Spalding's Official Base Ball Guide*, 1892, pp. 160–61; *ibid.*, 1893, pp. 150–54.

a handy tool for push-bunting, the committee sought to make more batters swing away. The following year witnessed another assault on bunting: a batter was out if he bunted foul with two strikes on him.[38] Although two 1894 rules might be construed as victories for the manly-slugging school, the adoption of the infield-fly rule, which prohibits an infielder trapping such flies for double plays, and a rule restricting the size of fielders gloves offered advantages to the scientific school as well. Nevertheless, the changes won praise from the manly proponents, who predicted that they would "ginger up the game."[39]

In 1900 the last major change, one which substituted the modern pentagon-shaped home plate for the old diamond-shaped one, completed the playing rules. However, a host of technological innovations kept influencing the style of play. After the rash of 1894 ball-park fires had leveled three wooden grandstands, new building codes and the availability of structural steel and concrete made possible new and impressive structures, like Cincinnati's "steel amphitheatre," the first steel and concrete grandstand. Another useful innovation which helped baseball promoters was the introduction of electric trolley cars.[40]

Other technological innovations, like the mechanical pitching machine invented by Professor Hinton of Princeton were beyond criticism. Actually, the machine was a smoothbored, breech-loading cannon mounted on two wheels, and was fitted with curved prongs attached to both sides of the muzzle for the purpose of curving a ball. By shifting these prongs to the left, or right, or top, or bottom, Hinton claimed that his machine could "pitch" curve, drop, and "raise" balls. The speed of the pitches depended on the amount of the powder charge, although even a little boom terrified most players.[41] Never more than a curiosity, Hinton's machine anticipated latter-day mechanic marvels whereby modern players practice hitting.

[38] *Sporting Life*, April 28, 1894, March 9, 1895.
[39] *New York Clipper*, November 26, 1898; *The Sporting News*, February 27, 1897.
[40] *Reach's Official Base Ball Guide*, 1894, p. 74; *Sporting Life*, June 30, 1894; *Daily Globe* (Boston), August 30, 1894; *Sun* (Baltimore), April 20, 1894.
[41] *Reach's Official Base Ball Guide*, 1897, p. 106; *Post* (Washington), June 11, 1897

Meanwhile, further evidence of a slugging trend was the increased consumption of baseballs. In the 1880's a ball a game was the norm, and if batted out of the park, the game's continuance awaited the pleasure of some anonymous "urchin." If he chose to return it, he was given free admission, if not, the house reluctantly put a new one in play. With the manly-style increasing the number of long hits, a new rule of 1896 required a club to keep a dozen balls on hand, and ordered an umpire to introduce a new ball whenever an old one was soiled, blackened, or scratched. Since pitchers had purposely defaced balls to gain an advantage over batters, such a rule further cramped a hurler's style.

The tug of war over playing rules suggests that the modern synthesis really was a blending of ideologies from two embattled schools of baseball philosophers. Indeed, both groups had labels in this era: one was the proponent of "scientific baseball," and the other advocate of the "manly game." Yet the two schools were similar in many ways, for example, each derived mental attitudes from the current American faith of scientism. Defined as a passion to apply science to nearly every realm of human experience, this credo was a major guide of action in the 1890's. Not to be scientific in this age was to be hopelessly old-fashioned; hence, baseball had to align itself with science.

Even before 1890 some baseball men had sought to apply science to baseball, and this school of scientific baseball dates back at least to the 1870's. Resembling a martinet conception, it stressed drilling a team until the nine functioned like an efficient machine. In Chadwick's words it meant "playing for the side," and, as an offensive weapon, it stressed scoring a few runs by place-hitting, bunting, and stealing bases. Once having scored, the well-drilled defense banked on overpowering pitching to maintain their lead. Although favored by many managers, including Wright, its detractors criticized it as being "effeminate entertainment" and said that it bored fans.

Men like sportswriter Albert Mott preferred the manly game, which they likened to Herbert Spencer's "survival of the fittest ideology." In supporting this philosophy, its followers believed that victory should belong to the heaviest sluggers and the most aggressive players. They defended their belief by arguing that the fans preferred this style of play.

Although the Spencerian school won concessions from the rules committees of the 1890's, they failed to win total victory. Indeed, the safest position for the committee appeared to be a middle course between the two extremes. At least this was the posture of Fred Pfeffer's popular book, *Scientific Ball*, a manual on how to play the game. According to Pfeffer, baseball "evolved" from a stone age game of the 1870's, which he depicted as the primitive, "first-cause" style. Following the style of the muscular era was a "doubly scientific" style, which linked muscular science with the subtle science of superior brains. To bend science to their will, Pfeffer told managers to use deceptive signs, to concentrate on defensive positions which take account of "percentages," and to place fielders where they can always "back up" one another on plays. With the fielders so deployed, "every player is in the right place at the right time." The double play was also a scientific ploy, and to insure getting a fair share of these, the manager was advised to station his most scientific-minded man at shortstop, while posting the dull-witted behemoths at first. Furthermore, all infielders must know how to anticipate where the batter will hit the ball. In addition to tips on scientific fielding, the book included tips on scientific batting and scientific base-running, which required the use of applied social science to bluff and unnerve opponent fielders.[42] Similar advice was to be found in Arthur Irwin's 1895 volume, *Practical Ball Playing*.[43]

Authors like these won plaudits, if not royalties, for their works. Supporting both was Chadwick, who preferred the older scientific style. The elder statesman argued that this style was less taxing physically than the debilitating slugging game. Hence, he praised the bunters and the place-hitters. However, to an impartial English observer, pitching was more than a science in baseball. "This may be science," he quipped, "but it savors of magic."[44]

[42] Fred Pfeffer, *Scientific Ball*, 15–71.
[43] Arthur Irwin, *Practical Ball Playing*, 6–14, 16–18, 20–26.

Because of high-level support, and because of the brilliant play of heroic place-hitters, like Keeler, the scientific school dominated baseball strategy during this decade, and would continue to do so until the home-run era of the 1920's. Indeed, Manager "Pat" Tebeau's outspoken criticism of this time-honored style may have cost him his managerial post with the "Perfectos" in 1900. At the time, Baltimore's brilliant success with the old scientific play of the hit-and-run was popular, and it included specialized tactics like walking a batter deliberately to set up a double-play opportunity. Also, fans greatly admired the speedy base stealers, and when Bill Hamilton stole seven bases in one game, he was acting in the best scientific tradition. Such feats would overwhelm the modern fans, if they did not know that the rules of this era credited a batter for stealing a base when he "stretched" a hit by taking an extra base.[45]

Nevertheless, there were some indications that the manly school was growing in popularity. With the increased pitching distance, batting averages increased, creating new heroes out of sluggers like Delehanty, Sam Thompson, and Buck Freeman, whose twenty-nine home runs of 1899 stood until Babe Ruth set a new record. Also, there was another side to the manly game, namely the tough-guy approach of brawling with rivals, arguing with umpires, stealing signs, and using sharpened cleats to terrorize infielders. Such devices, often in the hands of a scientific team, introduced elements of intrigue, conflict, and bloodshed into the spectacle, and these tactics were defended as a manly example to tough-minded Americans. Thus, to break a rival's code of scientific signals was regarded as a feat of mental toughness, although such accomplishments excited purists to ask, "Has [baseball] really fallen into the hands of a lot of card sharks and bunco men?" This question was prompted by the disclosure that the Phillies were guilty of the twin crimes of sign-stealing and of dampening their infield to slow down the speed of batted balls.[46]

44 *Eagle* (Brooklyn), September 24, 1890; *Sporting Life*, September 17, 1892.

45 *The Sporting News*, August 11, 1900; *Eagle* (Brooklyn), September 1, 1899; *Reach's Official Base Ball Guide*, 1893, pp. 76–77; *Inquirer* (Philadelphia) September 1, 1894.

46 *The Sporting News*, October 6, 1900; *Eagle* (Brooklyn), October 15, 1900.

Of course, the writers who scolded teams for using such tactics were likely to criticize the use of gloves. One writer charged that gloves took both the beauty and the skill out of baseball. To these unyielding purists, nothing was more offensive than the "cushion mitt" used by catchers. Yet if few were sadistic enough to deny fielders protection from batted balls or catchers the security of inflated "breast plates," many were concerned about the dangers of cleated shoes. By 1895 the aggressive style had led to incidents and accusations of deliberate "spiking" of infielders by base-runners. Such incidents triggered brawls and prompted many to plead for a ban. A Chicago pitcher testified, ". . . those spikes cut like knives. . . . You might as well arm a man with a pitchfork." Having been victimized himself on several occasions, this player advocated the use of rubberized cleats, "like those used in football."[47]

Another aspect of the rowdy style of play was the loud cursing by players, who often trained their "fourcabularies" on umpires. Called the "kicking evil" by Chadwick, this style took such forms as cursing, punching, and inciting mobs against umpires. To curb the evil, the league repeatedly increased the amount of fines, and finally resorted to the use of suspensions. Indeed, the Brush Resolution was the high-water mark in countermeasures. As evidenced by the amount of money collected, umpires had a rough life in the 1890's. In 1895, a total of $2,000 was collected from twenty-one guilty players, including five Orioles; in 1897, $1,355 was paid, with the Giants replacing the Orioles as the bad boys. But the amount of money collected is deceiving, for some umpires believed that fining should only be used as a last resort. Also, magnates encouraged aggressive "kicking" by paying the fines of some offenders, and many argued that fans of the 1890's paid to see "scrappiness" in the games.[48]

Of course, a genuinely scientific magnate might have sought available statistics as an aid to discovering what his fans were

[47] *New York Clipper*, July 6, 1895.

[48] *Sporting Life*, November 6, 1897; *Reach's Official Base Ball Guide*, 1896, pp. 108–109; *Spalding's Official Base Ball Guide*, 1898, pp. 195–98.

really like. Above all else, the data would have revealed the rapid growth of the industrial-urban way of life.

Statistics tell the tale of onrushing urbanism when they show that during the period of 1870–90 the number of American cities with populations of 100,000 or more had doubled. By 1890 there were twenty-eight such centers, and in 1900 there were thirty-eight. The trend clearly indicated that in time most Americans would probably live under urban-life conditions. Indeed, 1900 would find a population of 31,000,000 urbanites and 46,000,000 ruralites.

Of great significance was the change taking place in the work habits of urbanites. While the average work day in nonagricultural industries was 10.5 hours in 1870, by 1890 this figure would drop to 10 hours; indeed, workers in selected industries like construction worked 9.4 hours a day. Accompanying this trend was a slow rise in wages, although the depression of the mid-1890's reversed this trend, bringing widespread unemployment. At the close of this decade came the Spanish-American War, which further diverted attention from baseball. Nevertheless, the over-all trend toward fewer work hours and larger pay checks justified a "bullish" outlook for the future of the spectacle.[49]

These changes affected the values and attitudes of Americans. The popularity of science, especially the work of the evolutionists, certainly colored American ideas and thoughts. Veteran manager Gus Schmelz observed that the fans of the 1890's wanted "quick and vigorous action in their sports," although he believed that most fair-minded fans wanted only a minimum of "scraps."[50]

More objective insights into the changing character of American baseball fans came from foreign observers, whose detachment from American culture sharpened their perceptions. Some British sportsmen claimed that baseball crowds indeed reflected basic American values. Writing in the London *Saturday Review*, one noted the "hurried" aspect of baseball crowds. Since Americans

---

[49] U.S. Department of Commerce, *Historical Statistics of the United States, 1789–1945*, 25, 29, 66.

[50] *Sporting Life*, September 17, 1892.

operated on strict time budgets, they wanted baseball games to be finished in a short length of time, and for these people, cricket would never do, because "The American has plenty of tomorrows, but in the meantime holds tightly to his todays and even in his recreation has no intention of wasting all too valuable time."[51]

Recounting his experience as a member of a baseball crowd, the Britisher Henry Furness was impressed by the feverish, purposeful movement of the crowd as it surged into the Washington park. The discipline of this crowd contrasted sharply with sporting crowds of his native England. English crowds were surging masses "of excited, struggling people," but those in America moved like "trained soldiers or obedient schoolboys" as they lined up by twos, forming "one great winding snake, with its head at the gates . . . and its tail a mile away." Furness approved of the way that American crowds observed the rule of first come, first served, and wished "Would it were so at home." But on the other hand, American crowds also mirrored American materialism and its "search of the almighty dollar." He had seen hucksters mingle with the lovers of sport, and watched them sell their places in line to late-comers; "Coin changes hands, and the early bird picks up the greenback worm and departs." Yet there were few thieves; indeed, Furness had prepared himself for pickpockets by putting "watch and . . . purse in an obscure pocket," but this precaution had been unnecessary. If the American crowd had brought out Furness' observational powers, the game itself left him cold. "Verily," said he, "is base ball a game which passeth all British understanding!"[52]

Certainly, when seated at the park, fans expressed themselves as individuals. For *aficionados* who wanted a studious approach to the game there were up-to-date score cards supplied by concessionaire Harry Stevens, "the Score-Card Man." By 1900, this entrepreneur had obtained the score-card concession at most league parks, and his sales prompted barons to rise to public demand and put numbers on the backs of player uniforms so that fans could

[51] *Ibid.*, April 13, 1901.

[52] Frederick S. Tyler, *Fifty-Five Years of Local Baseball, 1893–1947, passim*; *Daily Globe* (Boston), July 17, 1891.

make better use of their score cards. Since there was no electronic amplifying service, and since the announcers using megaphones were inefficient, a fan could not identify players at this time without a Stevens card. Besides meeting the needs of studious fans, "Hustling Harry" also catered to the hungry ones, selling them the immortalized ball-fan's supper of hot dogs and soft drinks.[53] By providing this service, he laid the groundwork for a future million-dollar enterprise.

Although most crowds were orderly, individual members differed in their definitions of order and disorder. This was also true of sportswriters, some of whom excused swearing and brawling as mere "scrappiness," while to others loud shouting by players or merely arguing with umpires was an affront. As for fans, some thought nothing of venting their emotions by throwing rented cushions at the heads of players or at the occupants of reserved seats. Although such behavior offended many fans, more seemed to resent profanity and cursing. One man whose wife had been upset by purple language wrote to the newspaper demanding to know why a "foul-mouthed cur" was not "lifted bodily out of the seats" and ejected. Some spectators claimed that they could no longer take their wives to games. Still others were affronted by the use of words like "thief," "robber," or the phrase "How much are they paying you?" which were directed quite regularly at umpires.[54]

Foul language was only one of baseball's problems. Another, the possibility of riot, would remain a constant threat as long as owners permitted fans to occupy part of the playing field. Although the newer parks had eliminated this problem, most owners still allowed spectators to position themselves on the field, and many fans subsequently interfered with games. Once, Clark Griffith, standing on the side lines, tried to help his Chicago mates retrieve a ball that was batted into a standing crowd. Although he managed to kick the ball in the direction of a Chicago fielder, a Giant fan grabbed it

---

[53] *Ibid.*, August 23, 1891; *Sporting Life*, September 16, 1899; *The Sporting News*, August 6, 1898.

[54] *New York Clipper*, August 29, 1896.

and ran off with it. Under the rules, the Chicago fielders had to get it from the fan, and when they did, the batter already had his home run.[55]

A less violent form of crowd misbehavior confronted President Ebbets of Brooklyn and persuaded him to curtail ladies'-days in 1899. According to Ebbets, many serious-minded fans had complained about ladies who were using ladies'-days for outdoor "conversation bees." Some brought children, "who made the stand a playground," while mothers talked.[56]

Now and then one read nice things about crowds. The Britisher Furness was highly impressed by the Washington fans in their treatment of Bill Hoy. When outfielder Hoy made a brilliant catch, the crowd arose "en masse" and wildly waved hats and arms. "It was the only way in which they could testify their appreciation to the athlete, for he was both deaf and dumb!"[57]

But charges of rowdyism persisted and marred baseball's public image. To counter this, a Boston writer claimed that the "better classes" made up most of the baseball fans in America. Needless to say, the validity of his conclusion is questionable since it was drawn from a poll in which only 100 pollees were involved. His paper announced that anyone sending name, address, and the price of return postage would receive a printed baseball schedule. Of the 100 responses 46 were written on "professional" letterhead stationery. Thus, the "sample" convinced the reporter that most patrons "were necessarily of the better classes."

While charges of indecorous behavior raged, league baseball in Pittsburgh lost 450 of its most regular and best behaved fans, when the Roman Catholic chancery forbade priests to attend baseball, football, or theater performances. Although the edict stated that attendance was not a sin, it expressed fear that younger priests were running off and leaving their elders with too much work.[58]

Since baseball crowds are heterogeneous in structure, it is un-

---

[55] *Ibid.*, April 15, 1899; *The Sporting News*, April 22, 1899.
[56] *Sporting Life*, April 13, 1901.
[57] *Ibid.*, May 7, 1892, January 12, 1895.
[58] *The Sporting News*, January 1, 1898; McGraw, *op. cit.*, 82–86; *The Sporting News*, September 8, 1900.

just to stereotype them on the basis of a few members. Yet some crowds and cities were stereotyped by some of the noted characters who regularly attended the games. Boston had its "Hi Hi" Dixwell, New York its "Well Well," Baltimore its Major Fulton, and Philadelphia its "Smitty." While some of these characters immortalized themselves by their omnipresence and their peculiar yells, others became noteworthy for what they said on a single occasion. At a close game in Washington a Negro fan once screamed that if the Senators' pitcher got the team out, he could lynch the fan. When the pitcher did so, the fan convulsed all by shouting, "jist name the spot." Another example was the memorable case of the Milwaukee Dutchman who, as he entered that city's American League park in 1900, was told that he needed a rain check. Said he, "I wants no rain check, what for do I? I have mine umbrella mit me."[59]

Meanwhile Americans with no interest in baseball worried about the spectacle's encroachment on the sacred domain of the Sabbath. During this decade harassment mounted as Sabbatarians secured the arrest of league players on several occasions. By 1896, Sunday baseball divided league magnates, with the "big five" opposing Sunday games and the "little seven" favoring them. Because the "big five" refused to play Sunday games, President Young's task of scheduling games became so formidable that he turned it over to Jim Hart. In 1899, Hart's task was lightened when four of the "big five" joined the pro-Sunday ball forces, leaving Boston as the last stronghold of such Puritanism. However, this breach in the ranks of the opposition did not mean that the four would play ball at home; it only meant that they would consent to playing Sunday games when on the road. Nevertheless, it became apparent that the dollar would triumph, for what magnate would argue with such records as the crowd of 27,489 which turned out to see a Chicago home game played on a Sunday in 1899? Since making money was the chief goal of the owners of baseball clubs, it was just a matter of time before magnates would shuck off their social inhibitions in favor of turnstile figures. By 1900, 19 out of 26

[59] *Post* (Washington), May 17, 1897; *The Sporting News*, April 10, 1897. *Spalding's Official Base Ball Guide*, 1900, pp. 44–45; *Sporting Life*, April 7, May 5, 1900.

Sundays on the league schedule had at least one game carded,[60] which suggested that the Sabbatarians were fighting a war that they had already lost.

If baseball moved with the secular tide in the matter of Sunday ball, in other matters of change the tide ran against the spectacle. For example, those barons who believed that baseball was America's national game or favorite sport found themselves at a loss to explain the public interest in new leisure pastimes. Undoubtedly the first cycling craze of the 1890's cut into baseball attendance. At first the "dude contrivances," as blustery Dan Brouthers called them, were expensive, but, by 1890, they sold for as little as $40 and could be bought on installment terms. With popular interest in "scorching" reaching mania proportions, shrewd magnates accommodated the cyclists by providing bicycle parking facilities and bike tracks at the parks. Yet all but Spalding worried, for he was busily forming a bicycle trust.[61]

Another challenge came from the "armored knights" of the football gridiron, and this new field sport showed every indication of matching baseball's popularity. Alarmed by football's successes, Chadwick stated that baseball "was temporarily at a discount," and blamed this phenomenon on public interest, claiming that America was in an era of brutal sports enthusiasm. Although brash football promoters predicted that their game would displace baseball as the national game, baseball barons regarded the new spectacular as a second-rate rival. Since ball parks could be adapted for football, and since the baseball season ended when football began, some big-league magnates sought to organize the "American League of Professional Foot Ball Players," with franchises in the eastern cities of the National League. In their egotism they believed themselves to be the farsighted founders of the "Out-Door Sport Trust," but public apathy and collegiate competition resulted in infant professional football being stillborn. Yet the lost $2,000 investment was cheap enough,[62] and time would eventually

---

[60] *Ibid.*, October 15, 1892, May 30, 1896.

[61] *Ibid.*, May 30, 1896.

[62] *Ibid.*, December 3, 1892, November 11, 1893, October 27, 1894.

show the soundness of big-league professional football. The decade also witnessed the birth of an infant indoor spectacle, basketball. Eventually, baseball promoters realized that they would have to accept America's preference for a *smörgasbord* of leisure pastimes, with baseball merely being one of several spectacle sports. Yet the future would reveal that there would be plenty of cash and glory for all, but in the meantime chauvinistic baseball magnates continued to acclaim baseball as "America's National Game."

 IV. *The Return of the Old Order*

15

The Silver Age

1. WAR AND PEACE, 1900–1903

DEPENDING ON WHETHER THEY BELIEVED that the new century began on New Year's Day, 1900 or 1901, some literal-minded American Christians watched apprehensively for signs of a coming millennium. But for most baseball magnates there was no such hope; instead of watching the horizon for signs of millenial prosperity, they covered their heads to avoid new blows which might come from any direction. From outside the league, telling salvos were directed by the invading American League. Having made good their threat to compete with the National League, Ban Johnson's henchmen busily prepared for further forays in 1901, while proudly proclaiming their circuit's major-league status.

If made a decade earlier, such a threat would have driven league magnates into each other's arms, but in recent years they had seen too much bitterness poured into too many fraternal feuds. Although the situation cried out for a war chieftain to arise and sound the tocsin, no one came to the fore. Tired Nick Young, too long a sycophant, hoped only to avoid dethronement at the hands of a western cabal headed by Jim Hart. In 1901, he was caught between two embattled camps of club owners, who were locked in the last internecine battle of the feudal era. Forced to act as a mere care-taker and denied the right even to name umpires, Young sym-bolized the spirit of *Weltschmerz* that gripped the league. Know-ing that he no longer had a future in league baseball, he frankly told a reporter that he favored the American League cause, because the restoration of the old dual-league pattern offered the last hope for returning prosperity.[1]

Such candor only inflamed his enemies and hastened his ouster. The showdown between the two camps came late in 1901 at the time of the annual re-election of the president. Heading one camp was the mighty Andrew Freedman of New York, who was backed by Soden and his old enemies, Frank de Haas Robison and John Brush. This combination of strange bedfellows had recently been fashioned at a meeting held at Freedman's mansion in Red Bank, New Jersey. There Freedman spun his plan for converting the league into a true baseball trust, one which would pool players, franchises, and profits under a single organization. By shifting players and franchises wherever and whenever profit opportunities were promising, the plan would have stripped the spectacle of any claim to being a sport. Yet it was a sound scheme, and it held forth hopes of restoring profits and coping with the upstart invaders. To assure its adoption, the quartet chose to support pliable Nick Young for another term.

Unfortunately for these plotters, their grand design was no secret, and reporters had a field day detailing its mercenary aspects. Thus, at the time of the election the opposition was thoroughly united behind Hart, Ebbets, Rogers, and Dreyfuss. Posing as true sportsmen, this faction fitted its halos and named Spalding as their candidate. The ensuing struggle deadlocked the league's December meeting and resulted in no election. Renewing the fight at the

[1] *Sporting Life*, October 6, 1900, January 26, March 9, 1901.

March meeting, this faction waited until the Freedman forces retired and then announced, by a dubious quorum ruling, that Spalding had been elected. When Spalding seized the books, it looked as if the coup had been successful, but then Freedman secured an injunction prohibiting the take over. With both sides hopelessly pinned down, Spalding resigned and Young gratefully grabbed a chance to retire with a pension. With the 1902 season under way, both camps agreed to allow Hart, Soden, and Brush to operate as the league's Control Commission, which was to manage the league affairs until a president could be elected.

Although undefeated, Freedman realized the futility of his plan; also, he wanted to be free to pursue his lucrative Gotham real-estate and subway-building ventures, which always took priority over his baseball interest. Thus, in July, 1902, he completed a complicated settlement whereby the league paid $125,000 for his interest in the Giants. At his insistence Brush became president of the Giants, with one of Freedman's men remaining on the board. Moreover, Freedman managed to plant his friend Julius Fleischmann, the yeast king, as owner of the Cincinnati franchise. As a final ploy, showing to what lengths he would go to save face, Freedman named one of his New York political friends, Frank Farrell, as one of the directors of the American League's New York franchise. That the American League agreed testifies not only to Freedman's powerful influence in major-league baseball, but also to the fact that the league was willing to accommodate the interlopers in the interests of order and prosperity.[2]

Freedman's passing still left the league facing an uncertain future. The unwieldy Control Commission was powerless to do more than handle necessary administrative chores, and the question of the presidency remained an open sore until Harry Clay Pulliam was elected as a compromise candidate late in 1902. Meanwhile, magnates fought magnates, players fought magnates and umpires, and the American League fought to validate its claim to

[2] J. N. Lewis and J. Durant, "Law of Baseball," *New York Law Journal*, May 14, 1945. *Reach's Official Base Ball Guide*, 1916, pp. 44–45; Mrs. John J. McGraw, *op. cit.*, 174–80; *The Sporting News*, November 17, 1900; *ibid.*, October 27, 1900, February 2, August 24, 1901.

big-league status. Since the ten-year National Agreement had expired in 1901, the American League felt free to launch all-out raids on National League playing rosters. Having exhausted the surplus talent supply made available by the league's recent contraction to eight clubs, the Americans were after bigger game, which delighted league players who saw opportunities for higher salaries. Hence, in 1901, the Players Protective Association encouraged members to take advantage of the situation, and this enabled the Americans to snare one hundred league men, including top-flight stars like McGraw, Cy Young, and Lajoie.

It was the flashy Frenchman Lajoie who became the prize catch. Lured from the Phillies for a nominal salary increase, this batting champion joined the American's Athletic franchise. His signing touched off a hot legal controversy, which led to a Pennsylvania Supreme Court decision in favor of the Phillies; the court ruled that Lajoie was so skilled that the loss of his services did irreparable damage to the plaintiff. An injunction was issued restraining the Athletics from playing Lajoie, but the American League circumvented this by transferring him to Cleveland, which in turn prudently refrained from playing him in Philadelphia. In Cleveland, Lajoie became such an attraction that the team was nicknamed the "Naps"; more importantly he restored the local baseball interest that Robison's syndicate had quashed.

Other state courts disagreed with the Pennsylvania decision, thus rendering the league's weapon most uncertain. In Missouri, when Lajoie's case came up, the Americans won, and other suits followed the ruling of a New York State court decision. In scoring these victories, the Americans merely secured verification of older court decisions which had ruled against the league's reserve clause. Once again the clause was held to be lacking in equity and mutuality, and the action of the league in conspiring to control salaries by such means was branded as unjust.[3]

3 John Stayton, "Baseball Jurisprudence," *American Law Review* (May-June, 1910), 388–91; L. A. Wilder, "Baseball and the Law," *Case and Comment*, Vol. XII, No. 3 (August, 1912), 151–62; Lewis and Durant, "Law of Baseball," *New York Law Journal*, May 14, 1945; *Sporting Life*, April 13, 1901; *The Sporting News*, March 2, 9, 1901.

But if the courts again served notice that the league was operating on unsound ground, again the players failed to take advantage of the breakthrough. Instead, they exercised their usual individualism in deciding to jump to the Americans. Although players had a protective association working for them, by 1901 this association was torn by petty bickering. Its president, Chief Zimmer, complaining of ingratitude, was accused of pursuing his own interests, and Lawyer Harry Taylor was charged with collecting too fat a fee. Subsequently, dues fell off, and although Johnson wooed the association with promises of better contractual relationships, he was prudent enough to retain the reserve clause, and Machiavellian enough to undercut Zimmer as "one of the worst characters in baseball."[4]

This velvet-glove policy revealed the basic conservatism of the American League leaders. Obviously, they were most interested in winning acceptance as a competing major league. This attitude impressed the league leaders, many of whom wanted a return to the old dual major-league system. Yet "face" had to be saved, and for a time the league gave the invaders grape and canister by hitting them with snubs, court battles, ticket price-wars, counter salary offers to defectors, and even the tactic of encouraging other major-league pretenders to move in on the Americans. Indeed, Brush tried to lure Johnson away by offering him the league presidency, while others sought to wreck the Americans by offering its strongest clubs franchises in a revived twelve-club league.

Yet for the most part league magnates seemed to be testing the mettle of the invaders, who had fought their way from an 1899 status of "elite minor" league to nominal major-league recognition in 1901; the Americans had now advanced to the point where they seriously sought to outdraw their rivals at the ticket offices.[5] Not only did the Americans meet each test, but they managed to hold their financial backers firmly in line and even to shift their backers to cities of greater opportunity. Thus, in 1901, the Americans

---

[4] *Sporting Life*, March 30, May 18, 1901.

[5] *Ibid.*, December 22, 1900, March 30, 1901; Paul Gregory, *The Baseball Player*, 155–56; *The Sporting News*, May 6, July 17, October 27, 1900.

dropped Indianapolis, Kansas City, Minneapolis, and Buffalo and picked up Philadelphia, Boston, Baltimore, and Washington. The following year St. Louis replaced Milwaukee, and when Baltimore proved a "dead town," Johnson announced his determination to replace it with New York City.[6] With Freedman's help, Johnson made good this threat and in 1903 the New York Highlanders were ready to do battle. The eight-club circuit which the Americans had fashioned by this year was to prove durable enough to last for half a century without a single franchise shift.

Late in 1902, the meaning of these developments seemed clear to league magnates. That fall they met and elected Pulliam their president. A former Louisville newsman, the thirty-three-year-old Pulliam was a friend of Barney Dreyfuss, the magnate of the powerful Pittsburgh club. A unanimous choice, Pulliam's election signaled the failure of the three-man Control Commission. Although Pulliam lacked the autocratic charisma of his rival Johnson, his businesslike image helped restore order to the league. Upon receiving his commission, with the blessing of the magnates, he immediately sued for peace with Johnson.[7]

Anxious for peace, Johnson along with Comiskey met with Pulliam and August Herrmann at a 1903 baseball conference. Meeting in a mood of *rapprochement*, the delegates eventually concluded a remarkable settlement. In only two days of negotiating, it was agreed that the two rivals would function as separate and equal major leagues, joined together by common playing rules, harmonious playing schedules, and common contracts. The last point was most important since it restored the primacy of the reserve clause and put an immediate end to the player raids by recognizing the present status and territory of each of the sixteen franchises. The delegates also validated the American's claim to a New York franchise. Adopting Manhattan as its home town, this club would win legendary fame in twenty years as the New York Yankees. But at the time, this forlorn newcomer merely gave the Americans the prestige of being represented in America's largest city.

[6] *Sporting Life*, February 2, May 25, December 4, 1901, March 15, 1902.
[7] *Reach's Official Base Ball Guide*, 1910, p. 190; Richter, *op. cit.*, 16–18.

Time would show that this Cincinnati peace gave major-league baseball fifty years of rock-ribbed stability, with not one franchise shift taking place in either league. Certainly such an outcome went far beyond the dreams of the realists who devised the peace. In drawing up this National Agreement in 1903, the emissaries modestly put a ten-year limit on their handiwork, after which another conference was to be held to review the situation. Meanwhile, the agreement set a new rank order for all professional leagues in America, stabilizing playing rules, player drafts, and the classifications of minor leagues. By creating an efficient board of arbitration, which represented the interests of both majors and high minors, it ushered in a new era of baseball history. Certainly this stimulated the growth of minor-league baseball in America, for in less than ten years twenty-five more minor leagues were operating.[8]

As usual though, the losers were the players, who once again found themselves bound by the reserve clause. Indeed, the new arrangement was far more extensive in its benevolent tyranny than was the twelve-club monopoly. If the new agreement included no measure as flagrantly repressive as the salary-limiting laws of the 1890's, its tyranny was hardly the less. From a legal standpoint, the agreement was a deliberate attempt to enforce the reserve clause and to control "by its own decrees . . . enforcing them without the aid of law, and answerable to no power outside its own." Such weighty power over a commercialized sport came not from any legal right, but from the massive public interest in baseball, which condoned a "legal sin" by its enthusiastic patronage.[9]

2. Baseball's Supreme Court

Since it took men to make the new National Agreement work, the heart of the compromise was embodied in the National Commission, a top level executive and judicial group charged with keeping the peace. In 1903, it was decided that the two major-

[8] *The Sporting News*, January 24, March 14, May 19, 1903; J. G. Taylor Spink, *Judge Landis and 25 Years of Baseball*, 41–47; National Association of Professional Base Ball Leagues, *Minutes of New York Meeting*, October 24–26, 1901.

[9] Stayton, "Baseball Jurisprudence," *American Law Review* (May-June, 1910), 374–76.

league presidents would serve on the commission along with "Garry" Herrmann, the Cincinnati magnate who was named chairman. Although this seemed to favor the National League, it really did not, for Herrmann and Johnson had been lifelong friends. Pulliam contributed much to the smooth working of the commission, but he was overshadowed by his convivial colleagues. Nor did Pulliam wield the authority of "Czar" Johnson, because the National League magnates were by no means willing to submit to central authority.

The first decade of the new century found the owners contrite and more willing to work for the good of the order, but, nonetheless, the sensitive Pulliam was constantly harried by enemies like Brush. In 1909, tensions arising from such petulance drove him to a nervous breakdown, and a year later he took his own life. His death was followed by a period of bitter politicking over a successor, and the ensuing brief terms of men like former umpire Tom Lynch or former governor of Pennsylvania, John Tener, failed to provide strong leadership for the National League. When Tener quit in disgust in 1918, he was succeeded by the zealous John Heydler, whose record of service as league secretary began with the Pulliam era. Although admirably qualified by such long experience, his first three-year term coincided with the 1919–20 Black Sox scandal, which culminated in major-league baseball coming under the personal rule of High Commissioner Judge K. M. Landis.

Hampered by insecurities, several league presidents perforce occupied the subordinate position on the National Commission. With the charismatic Johnson wielding dictatorial power in the American League, and with the popular Herrmann enjoying repeated re-election as chairman of the body, real power came into the hands of the Johnson-Herrmann clique. Under their leadership the commission speedily won recognition for having saved baseball from anarchy, and in 1906 the body was christened the "Supreme Court of baseball." Among its official duties was the formidable task of arbitrating a host of disputes between major and minor leagues over the rights to players' services. In 1905 the commission handled seventy-three cases, agreeing unanimously every time. At the same time the commission's recommendations for revising the player draft rules were approved by both major leagues. The commission also adjudicated disputes between umpires and players, which enabled it to impose and collect fines. Other cases found the commission black-listing players for contract or disciplinary breaches, recommending improvements in player contracts, ruling that all National Agreement clubs use either Spalding or Reach balls, striking out at the abuses of the "farming systems," blunting the threat of a new players' union in 1913, and helping the major leagues fend off the invasion of the Federal League. In the last crisis the commission ruthlessly black-listed players to discourage major leaguers from jumping their contracts for lucrative outlaw offers.[10]

Of course, the most celebrated task of the commission was the regulation of the annual World Series. The peace pact between the two leagues was followed by the revival of this classic in 1903, and after a year's suspension, it was institutionalized. Indeed, so great was the public's interest that the series quickly became the capstone of the baseball season. Although dedicated fans could be counted on to maintain constant vigil over the regular major-league campaigns, the spectacle of major-league baseball gripped the nation at series time. Recognizing this trend, the commission took its series obligations seriously, and its feverish work included appointing umpires, designating eligible players, overseeing the public accommodations, and, most important, disbursing the receipts among contenders, players, and the two leagues. Since 10 per cent of the receipts passed directly to the commission, this windfall covered most of the commission's annual expenses and helped give it a measure of freedom from prying magnates. Because the orderly conduct of the series was essential to the commission's independent existence, one can well understand how a scandal like the "thrown"

[10] *Spalding Base Ball Record*, 1910, p. 4, 1911, p. 15, 1916, pp. 2–5, 1919, p. 127; *Spalding's Official Base Ball Guide*, 1914, pp. 5–7; *Reach's Official Base Ball Guide*, 1906, pp. 69, 175, 1909, pp. 13, 423, 1915, pp. 366–67; Spalding, *op. cit.*, 333.

World Series of 1919 could discredit the body and lead to its disso-
lution soon afterwards.[11]

3. The Age of Ban Johnson

In spite of occasional blunders and the humiliation of the 1919–
20 Black Sox scandal, the National Commission deserves credit
for restoring prosperity and public interest in major-league baseball. If any one man deserves the most credit for leading the spectacle into its twenty-year-long silver age, that accolade goes to
Byron Bancroft Johnson. The son of an Ohio professor, Johnson
developed a love for baseball and journalism as a student. Returning to his native Cincinnati upon graduation from college, he became a baseball writer for the *Commercial-Gazette*. As a reporter,
Johnson's blunt-spoken, inner-directed character led him to criticize the twelve-club monopoly in general and the policies of Cincinnati mogul John T. Brush in particular. Irked by the fire, Brush
challenged Johnson to "do something about it," and it was Charles
Comiskey who supplied the opportunity. When "Commy" challenged Johnson to accept the presidency of the shaky Western
League, Johnson accepted on condition that he was to be given a
four-year term and free rein. Moving in with a gusto, he set out to
make the circuit an elite minor league, which was an almost in-
surmountable goal in the light of the fact that some western clubs
were "farms" of the big league. Among the most notorious was
Brush's Indianapolis holding, which quickly became Johnson's
prime target.

An obvious "mark," Brush not only drafted Indianapolis men
for his Cincinnati team, but he often did so in order to resell them
to some rival for a profit. Since the practice was illegal under the
terms of the prevailing National Agreement, Johnson patiently
gathered incriminating evidence until he had enough to prosecute
Brush. Thus, in 1897, he made Brush sell his Indianapolis holding
under threat of expulsion from the National Agreement.

In daring to strike against so strong a rival, Johnson alarmed

---

[11] *Reach's Official Base Ball Guide*, 1904–21, *passim*. Each guide provides annual
coverage to the National Commission's World Series work.

some of his promoters, including those who depended on player sales to pay their operating expenses. But majority opinion not only sustained the action, but widened his powers. Convinced that the Western League would forever be at the mercy of big-league exploiters, Johnson began seeking ways to obtain major-league status for it. During the 1897–98 seasons, Johnson personally drew up the playing schedules and persuaded the magnates to let him plan the railroad travel in order to spread costs equally. In the austere year of 1898, Johnson took on the additional tasks of signing players, adjusting salaries, and shifting franchises. Thus, when Omaha failed, Johnson shifted it to St. Joseph and subsidized the transfer from his general fund. This prompt action saved the Western League in 1898 and won dictatorial powers for its president in 1899.[12]

These powers equipped Johnson to face his moment of truth which came with the failure of the league's syndicate ventures in 1899. When the league decided to drop four clubs and return to an eight-club circuit, Johnson persuaded his followers to occupy the abandoned towns. Having crossed the horsehide Rubicon, Johnson waited until his circuit passed the test of the 1900 season before announcing his claim to equal status with the National League. When the nationals agreed to recognize the circuit as a major league, Johnson immediately led his forces into Baltimore and Washington and drew up plans to invade New York. Fully aware that war was inevitable, Johnson shored up defenses by requiring his franchises to sign long-term leases and deposit them with him. Next, he launched an offense by encouraging raids on national rosters, justifying them on the grounds that the National Agreement had expired. While hoping to land at least twenty league stars, he did much better, snaring men like Lajoie, McGraw, Robinson, Young, and Duffy, while taking on solid new financial backing from men like Ben Shibe of Philadelphia.[13]

Anxious to consolidate his gains, Johnson reformed his circuit as a major league in January, 1901, and bound the eight clubs with

[12] *Sporting Life*, March 6, July 16, 1898; *Reach's Official Base Ball Guide*, 1901, p. 41; *The Sporting News*, July 17, 1899, December 15, 1900.
[13] *Sporting Life*, April 6, 1901.

313

a ten-year membership pact. At the same time he received a ten-year term as its president, with an annual salary of $7,500. That the owners now trusted him completely was evidenced by their willingness to submit to his executive control over the entire league, for he now held the posts of president, secretary, and treasurer. Fully determined to avoid the traps that crippled earlier intruders, the doughty generalissimo demanded that each owner not only deposit his lease, but also a majority of its stock and an option to buy both the plant and franchise. Such a policy was conceived to protect magnates from treason within, and it also made Johnson the most powerful league president in baseball history.

As baseball's autocrat, Johnson wielded power with genius. In exploiting the gulf between league players and magnates, Johnson placated the players association by granting a "graded system of contracts," which bound men to long terms with the same club. The pacts offered annual salary increases, while effectively protecting the American League from contract jumpers. Players were also pleased by the announcement that they would not be sold, traded, or farmed out without their consent. Such conservative concessions convinced Johnson's owners that they would not face a costly salary war for player talent, and Johnson's decision to withhold release of his 1901 schedule until after the National League had released theirs, cleverly avoided the ruinous competition of a box-office showdown. Meanwhile the owners got added assurance in the continuation of Johnson's policies of equalizing travel costs, sharing gate receipts, and retaining the attractive 25 cent base-admission rate to all American parks.[14]

The years 1901–1902 marked the crisis of the American League. With his rivals divided among themselves, Johnson chose to hang on and strive hard for popular support. Bending his back to this task, he traveled the American circuit, working tirelessly and despotically to curry public favor. Convinced that the public disapproved of the National League's condoning rowdy ball, Johnson tyrannically snuffed out incidents in the American League that might suggest collusion with the nationals. Thus he ordered a

[14] *Ibid.*, February 2, July 20, 1901; *The Sporting News*, October 27, 1900.

manager to cut his squad to avoid any hint of a "farming plot," and later he suspended McGraw for umpire-baiting.[15] In taking on McGraw, however, Johnson caught a tartar who fought back viciously. At one point, Johnson charged McGraw with treason, but McGraw snarled back, "So the 'Julius Caesar' of the American League calls me a 'Benedict Arnold' does He?" The bitterness between the two and Johnson's decision to replace Baltimore with a New York franchise, prompted McGraw to jump to the National League, where he became manager of the Giants. Coming in mid-1902, McGraw's defection was interpreted as a serious blow to the Americans. For his part, McGraw was hotly criticized in the press, but McGraw later insisted that his departure was part of the complicated agreement between the two major leagues. Not only did McGraw's defection clear the way for Johnson's invasion of New York, but with Freedman's assistance, the plot ended the major-league war.[16]

With the dawn of peace in 1902, Johnson saw baseball returned to the dual-league system. As the strong man on the new National Commission, he was called the "Czar of Baseball." Yet even in peace he continued to play the role of the autocratic Puritan. Knowing that some league men were bitter over the peace settlement, Johnson feared reprisals, and he and his lieutenants favored the continuation of his iron rule. To retain their leader, they voted in 1906 to increase his annual salary to $15,000, and, in 1910, he easily won another ten-year term.

At this point a godlike leader might have laid his sword aside and adopted a posture more attuned to the relaxed prosperity of the new age. But most men are not godlike, and the burly Johnson was no exception—he was not blessed with a flexible personality. Thus, he continued to rule from Olympus and hurl his thunderbolts at players, umpires, and owners who dared to step beyond the bounds of his definition of propriety. Bolstered by his great prestige, he had his way up to 1910, but not without opposition. During

[15] *Sporting Life*, July 20, August 31, 1901.

[16] *Ibid.*, May 25, June 8, July 21, August 3, 1901; Mrs. John J. McGraw, *op. cit.*, 155–58.

this time he offended his old friend Comiskey by publicly chiding him for umpire-baiting and by suspending one of his players. For a time relations between the two friends were frosty, but the feud was resolved; and in 1910, Commy proposed that Johnson be given a $25,000 annual salary to accompany his ten-year term of office. As it was, Johnson got the salary and a twenty-year term of office. Yet three years later, the two again clashed over Johnson's suspension policies, and Commy tried unsuccessfully to have Johnson dismissed.[17]

During the following year, 1914, the rival Federal League made its bid for major-league recognition, and the haughty Johnson refused to treat with the invaders. But the well-organized federals appealed to the courts and obtained injunctions against Johnson's black lists. At this time, too, a new players union questioned the legality of the reserve clause and Johnson's highhanded suspensions. This was a fine opportunity for fence-mending statesmanship, but Johnson contemptuously rebuffed the player fraternity's bill of charges, thus incurring more desertions along with the ill will of more realistic magnates.[18]

But in Johnson's defense, it must be said that he believed World War I, with its adverse effects on baseball attendance, would deliver a *coup de grâce* to the federals, but the invaders showed great staying power. In 1915 the federal suit against the major's reserve clause reached Judge Kenesaw Mountain Landis' district court. By reserving decision on the matter, while at the same time publicly announcing his unwillingness to strike a blow at America's "national institution," Landis became the new hero of the major-league moguls. By 1915, Landis' dilatory tactics gave the majors time to negotiate a costly settlement, which eliminated the federal threat. This spared Landis from making his decision, and preserved the major-league *status quo*. From this point onward, the National

---

[17] Axelson, *op.cit.*, 187–88; *Reach's Official Base Ball Guide*, 1906, p. 23, 1907, p. 56; *Baseball Magazine* (March, 1913), 57–68.

[18] *Baseball Magazine* (November, 1912), 29–34, 124–26, (September, 1913), 80, (November, 1913), 82–83, (January, 1914), 81–85.

League strove to replace the National Commission with Landis as high commissioner.[19]

Although Johnson had insisted that the courts would rule in favor of baseball's unique position under the antitrust laws, few magnates wanted to test the matter. Thus, instead of siding with Johnson who called Landis a "showboat," most magnates considered the judge their champion and Johnson a blundering fool.[20]

Yet even this blemish did little to diminish the prestige of the testy Johnson. Furthermore, he retained the support of American owners who resented national assaults on their president. For the time being, at least, he remained their "Czar," and his edicts were obeyed unquestioningly. But in the profitable postwar era, Johnson would see his control ruthlessly shattered by newcomers who knew that he was only mortal. The explosion came with telling effect in 1919 after Johnson sought to impose another of his final decisions on a matter of which American club had the right to a player. Hitherto, club owners automatically accepted his decision, but in this instance the owners of the New York Yankees took their protest to the courts and obtained an injunction against the president. When Johnson protested loudly and publicly, several American owners joined with their national counterparts and supported Landis for baseball's high commissioner. At the 1919 fall meeting, this cabal narrowly missed carrying their point, and it was evident that the supreme court era was tottering.[21] The final onslaught was prompted by the shocking revelation that the Chicago White Sox had thrown the 1919 World Series. Clearly this was the end of the old commission, but even in that black hour baseball men trusted Johnson to carry out the investigation. This he did, courageously and tirelessly, knowing that the evidence he uncovered would be used by the new high commissioner who must overshadow him.

The following year the old commission was abolished and was replaced by Judge Landis, the first high commissioner of baseball.

[19] Spink, *op. cit.*, 29–40.

[20] *Ibid.*, 40–50; *Baseball Magazine* (April, 1916), 62–66.

[21] Spink, *op. cit.*, 48–56; *Reach's Official Base Ball Guide*, 1920, pp. 358–74, 1921, pp. 44–48.

Although Johnson remained American League president, he was no longer omnipotent. His passing ended baseball's silver era, but his rule would be remembered as the time in which the spectacle regained the heights lost in the 1890's.

Bibliography

PRIMARY SOURCES

Unpublished Material

Chadwick, Henry. Scrapbooks. Spalding Collection, New York Public Library.

Cincinnati Base Ball Club Bills, Receipts, Cash Books, Correspondence, 1882–88. Hauck Collection, University of Cincinnati.

Craig, Peter S. "Organized Baseball: An Industry Study of a $100 Million Spectator Sport." Unpublished bachelor's dissertation, department of economics, Oberlin College.

The Orr-Edwards Code for Reporting Base Ball. Orr-Edwards, Copyright 1890. Spalding Collection, New York Public Library.

Wright, Harry. Correspondence of Harry Wright, Baseball Manager. MSS, 7 vols. Spalding Collection, New York Public Library.

———. Note and Account Books. MSS, 18 vols. Spalding Collection, New York Public Library.

Public Documents

Brech, E. Y., ed. "In Equity: *Allegheny B.B.C.* v. *Charles W. Bennett*," *Pittsburgh Legal Journal*, XIII (August, 1882–August, 1883), 152–54.

National Reporter System. *The New York Supplement*. Vol. IX, St. Paul, West Pub. Co., 1890.

State of New York. *Laws of the State of New York*. 100 sess.,

Chap. 178, "An Act in relation to bets, wagers, and pools." Passed April 25, 1877.

U.S. House of Representatives. *Organized Baseball*. Report No. 2002 to accompany H.R. 95, 82 Cong., 2 sess., 1952.

Books

Anson, Adrian C. *A Ball Player's Career*. Chicago, Era Pub. Co., 1900.

Axelson, Gustav. *"COMMY": The Life Story of Charles A. Comiskey*. Chicago, Reilly & Lee, 1919.

Chadwick, Henry. *The Art of Base Ball Batting*. New York, A. G. Spalding Co., 1885.

———. *The Art of Fielding: With A Chapter on Base Running*. New York, A. G. Spalding Co., 1885.

Detroit Tribune Pub. Co. *The Detroit Tribune's Epitome of Base Ball*. Detroit, Tribune Pub. Co., 1887.

Ellard, Harry. *Baseball in Cincinnati: A History*. Cincinnati, Johnson & Hardin, 1907.

Griffith, William R. *The Early History of Amateur Base Ball in the State of Maryland, 1858–1871*. Baltimore, John Cox, 1897.

Irwin, Arthur. *Practical Ball Playing*. New York, American Sports Pub. Co., 1895.

Kelly, Mike. *"Play Ball": Stories of the Ball Field*. Boston, Emery & Hughes, 1888.

Lawson, Thomas W. *The Krank: His Language and What It Means*. Boston, Rand Avery Co., 1888.

McGraw, John J. *My Thirty Years in Baseball*. New York, Boni & Liveright, 1923.

Mack, Connie. *My 66 Years in the Big Leagues*. Philadelphia, John C. Winston Co., 1950.

Morse, Jacob C. *Sphere and Ash: History of Baseball*. Boston, J. E. Spofford & Co., 1888.

Palmer, Harry. *Stories of the Base Ball Field*. Chicago, Rand McNally & Co., 1890.

Pfeffer, N. Fred, ed. *Scientific Ball*. Chicago, N. Fred Pfeffer Pub. Co. 1889.

Rankin, June. *The New York and Brooklyn Baseball Clubs*. New York, Richard Fox Printer, 1888.

Richter, Francis C. *A Brief History of Baseball*. Philadelphia, Sporting Life Pub. Co., 1909.

———. *Richter's History and Records of Baseball: The American Nation's Chief Sport*. Philadelphia, Richter Pub. Co., 1914.

Spalding, Albert G. *America's National Game*. New York, American Sports Pub. Co., 1911.

Spink, Alfred H. *The National Game: A History of Baseball*. St. Louis, Sporting News, 1910.

Sullivan, T. P. *Humorous Stories of the Ball Field*. Chicago, M. Donohue Co., 1903.

Ward, John Montgomery. *Base Ball: How to Become a Player*. Philadelphia, Athletic Pub. Co., 1888.

Wright, George. *Record of the Boston Base Ball Club Since Its Organization*. Boston, Rockwell and Churchill, 1874.

PERIODICALS

1. Newspapers

Commercial. Cincinnati, 1868–70, 1881–82.

Courier-Journal. Louisville, 1877, 1884, 1890.

Daily Globe. Boston, 1877–78, 1883, 1890–98.

Daily Mirror. New York, 1950.

Daily Journal and General Advertiser. Providence, R.I., 1879, 1884.

Eagle. Brooklyn, 1889–1901.

Enquirer. Cincinnati, 1880–82, 1940.

Free Press. Detroit, 1882, 1885–88.

Globe-Democrat. St. Louis, 1882, 1884–89.

Harper's Weekly. 1857–71.

Herald. Boston, 1872–73, 1883.

Inquirer. Philadelphia, 1883–84, 1900–1901.

Leslie's Illustrated Weekly. 1870–71.

North American and United States Gazette. Philadelphia, 1864, 1871.

Public Ledger. Philadelphia, 1889.
Register. Rockford, Ill., 1867, 1870–71, 1915.
Sun. Baltimore, 1894–99, 1911, 1948.
The Evening Star. Washington, D.C., 1867–69, 1914, 1927, 1933, 1944, 1954.
The Illustrated Graphic News: The Great Western Pictorial Weekly. Cincinnati, 1886.
The Times. Philadephia, 1878.
Times. New York, 1872–83, 1888–89, 1957.
Tribune. Chicago, 1870–71, 1876, 1880–86, 1898.
Washington Post. 1897.
World. New York, 1876.

2. Sporting Journals

Baseball Magazine. 1908–21.
New York Clipper. 1868–1903.
Sporting Life. 1883–1910.
Sporting Times and Theatrical News. 1870.
The Sporting News. 1886–1921.

3. Baseball Guides

Beadle's Dime Base Ball Player. 1871–81.
Chadwick's Base Ball Manual. 1870–71.
DeWitt's Base Ball Guide. 1872–83.
Manual. Ed. by Henry Chadwick. 1874.
Reach's Official Base Ball Guide. 1883–1921.
Spalding's Base Ball Record. 1908–21.
Spalding's Official Base Ball Guide. 1876–1921.
The Base Ball Ready Reference. 1880.
The Player's National League Official Guide. 1890.
The Sporting Life's Official Base Ball Guide and Hand Book of the National Game. 1891.
The Universal Base Ball Guide. 1890.
Sol White's Official Base Ball Guide. 1907.
Wright & Ditson's Base Ball Guide. 1884–86.

4. Articles in Periodicals

Ward, John Montgomery. "Is the Base Ball Player a Chattel?" *Lippincott's Magazine*, Vol. XL (August, 1887), 310–19.

REPORTS

Constitution and Playing Rules of the National League of Professional Base Ball Clubs. Official 1. 1876. Philadelphia, Reach and Johnston, 1876.

National Association of Professional Base Ball Leagues. *Minutes of New York Meeting*, October 24–26, 1901.

Proceedings of the National Association of Professional Base Ball Players Held in New York City, March 17, 1871. Washington, Beresford Printers, 1871.

Wright, George. "Sketch of the National Game of Baseball." *Records of the Columbia Historical Society.* Vol. XXVII. Ed. by John Larner. Washington, Columbia Historical Society, 1920.

OTHER SOURCES

Voigt, David Q. Interview with Clark Griffith, president of Washington American League Baseball Club, August 11, 1955. On magnetic tape.

Voigt, David Q. Interview with S. O. Grauley, sports editor emeritus of the *Philadelphia Inquirer*, December, 1956.

SECONDARY SOURCES

Books

Adams, Samuel Hopkins. *Grandfather Stories.* New York, New American Library of World Literature, Inc., 1959.

Allen, Lee. *The Cincinnati Reds.* New York, G. P. Putnam's Sons, 1948.

Bartlett, Arthur. *Baseball and Mr. Spalding: The History and Romance of Baseball.* New York, Farrar, Straus & Co., Inc., 1951.

Brosnan, Jim. *The Long Season.* New York, Dell Pub. Co., Inc., 1961.

Cady, Edwin Harison. *The Gentlemen in America: A Literary Study in American Culture.* Syracuse, Syracuse University Press, 1949.

Davidson, Marshall B. *Life in America.* 2 vols. Boston, Houghton Mifflin Co., 1951.

Davis, Mac S. *Lore and Legends of Baseball.* New York, Lantern Press, Inc., 1953.

Dulles, Foster Rhea. *America Learns to Play: A History of Popular Recreation, 1607–1940.* New York, D. Appleton-Century Co., 1940.

Federal Writers Project. *Baseball In Old Chicago.* Chicago, A. C. McClung & Co., 1939.

Finch, Robert L., ed. *The Story of Minor League Baseball.* New York, National Association of Professional Baseball Leagues, 1953.

Gregory, Paul Michael. *The Baseball Player: An Economic Study.* Washington, Public Affairs Press, 1956.

Henderson, Robert W. *Baseball: Notes and Materials on its Origin.* New York, New York Public Library, 1940.

Holliman, Jennie. *American Sports, 1785–1835.* Durham, N.C., Seeman Press, 1931.

Huizinga, Johan. *Homo Ludens: A Study of the Play Element in Culture.* New York, Roy Publishers, Inc., 1948.

Kaplan, Max. *Leisure in America: A Social Inquiry.* New York, John Wiley & Sons, Inc., 1960.

Kier, Malcom. *The Epic of Industry.* Vol. V of the *Pageant of America.* Ed. by Ralph Gabriel and D. R. Fox. New Haven, Yale University Press, 1926.

Kiernan, John. "Henry Wright." *A Dictionary of American Biography.* Vol. XX. Ed. by Dumas Malone. New York, Charles Scribner's Sons, 1936.

Klapp, Orrin E. *Heroes, Villains, and Fools: The Changing American Character.* New York, Spectrum Books, 1962.

Kouvenhoven, John A. *Adventures in America, 1857–1900: A Pictorial Record of Harper's Weekly.* New York, Harper, 1938.

Krotz, Ernest. *Collector's Guide to Baseball Publications*. Cleveland, Baseball Bureau, 1943.

Krout, John Allen. *Annals of American Sport*, Vol. XV of the *Pageant of America*. Ed. by Ralph Gabriel and D. R. Fox. New Haven, Yale University Press, 1929.

Larrabee, Eric and Rolf Meyersohn, eds. *Mass Leisure*. Glencoe, Ill., Free Press, 1958.

Lerner, Max. *America As A Civilization: Life and Thought in the United States Today*. New York, Simon & Schuster, 1957.

Lieb, Frederick G. *The Baltimore Orioles*. New York, Rees Press, 1953.

Lindsay, Vachel. *Collected Poems*. New York, Macmillan Co., 1931.

McGraw, Mrs. John J. *The Real McGraw*. Ed. by Arthur Mann. New York, David McKay, Inc., 1953.

Mott, Frank Luther. *American Journalism: A History of Newspapers In the United States Through 250 Years, 1690–1940*. New York, Macmillan Co., 1941.

Nevins, Allan. *The Emergence of Modern America, 1865–1878*. New York, Macmillan Co., 1928.

Peek, Hedley and F. G. Aflalo, eds. *The Encyclopedia of Sport*. New York, G. P. Putnam's Sons, 1897.

Schlesinger, Arthur M. *Paths to the Present*. New York, Macmillan Co., 1949.

———. *The Rise of the City, 1878–1898*. New York, Macmillan Co., 1933.

Seymour, Harold. *Baseball, The Early Years*. New York, Oxford Press, 1960.

Smigel, Erwin, ed. *Work and Leisure: A Contemporary Social Problem*. New Haven, College and University Press, 1963.

Spink, J. G. Taylor. *Judge Landis and 25 Years of Baseball*. New York, Thomas Y. Crowell Company, 1947.

Turkin, Hy and S. C. Thompson, eds. *The Official Encyclopedia of Baseball*. New York, A. S. Barnes & Co., Inc., 1951.

Tyler, Frederick S. *Fifty-five Years of Local Baseball, 1893–1947*. *Records of the Columbia Historical Society of Washington, 1946–1947*.

Wecter, Dixon. *The Saga of American Society: A Record of Social Aspiration, 1607–1937.* New York, Charles Scribner's Sons, 1937.

Weir, L. H. *Europe at Play: A Study of Recreation and Leisure Time Activities.* New York, A. S. Barnes & Co., Inc., 1937.

Articles and Periodicals

Baker, Russell. "Poor Richard's Almanac," New York *Times,* March 7, 1965.

Catton, Bruce. "The Great American Game," *American Heritage,* Vol. X, (April, 1959), 17–25, 86.

Daley, Robert. "Sports Explain the Nations," New York *Times Magazine,* Vol. CVIII (August 23, 1959).

Gross, Edward. "A Functional Approach to Leisure Analysis," *Social Problems,* Vol. IX (Summer, 1961), 2–8.

Henderson, Robert W. "How Baseball Began," New York Public Library Bulletin, 1937.

Keating, James W. "Sportsmanship As A Moral Category," *Ethics,* Vol. LXXV (October, 1964), 25–35.

Lewis, J. N. and J. Durant. "Law of Baseball," *New York Law Journal,* May 14, 1945.

Pimlott, J. A. R. "Christmas Under the Puritans," *History Today,* Vol. X (December, 1960), 832–39.

Stayton, John W. "Baseball Jurisprudence," *American Law Review,* Vol. XLIV (May–June, 1910), 380–81.

Tarvin, A. H. *75 Years on Louisville's Diamonds.* Louisville, Public Library Report, 1940.

Wilder, L. W. "Baseball and the Law," *Case and Comment: The Lawyer's Magazine,* Vol. XIX (August, 1912), 153.

Wittke, Carl. "Baseball In Its Adolescence," *The Ohio State Archaeological and Historical Quarterly,* Vol. LX (April, 1952), 118–21.

Woody, Thomas. "Leisure in the Light of History," *The Annals of the American Academy of Political and Social Sciences,* Vol. CCCXIII, (September, 1957), 4–10.

Index

Doubleday, Abner: 5; "Doubleday legend," 5, 7
Dow, Clarence: 203
Doyle, John Joseph: 254, 261, 275
Dreyfuss, Barney: 226f., 271, 304, 308
Drinking and drunkenness: 31, 41, 53, 75, 79, 84f., 91, 103, 108f., 111, 123, 135, 158, 172f., 177f., 190, 241, 245, 277
Duffy, Hugh: 104, 243, 247, 249, 313
Dunn, John Joseph: 267
Dunnigan, Joseph: 189

Eastern League: 134
Ebbets, Charles Hercules: 145, 267f., 296, 304
Eliot, Pres. Charles William: 196, 205f.
Ellard, George: 25
Ellick, Joseph J.: 186
Elysian Fields, Hoboken, N.J.: 12
Emslie, Robert Daniel: 191–92
Engel, Nick: 115, 168
Equipment, protective: 206, 282; masks, 85f., 210, 215, 217; chest protectors, 85f., 210, 215, 217; gloves, 86, 210, 215f., 288, 292; mitts, 215, 217, 292
Esper, Charles H. (Duke): 252, 257
Ewing, William (Buck): 116, 163, 175, 275
Expenses, travel: 10, 15, 43, 58, 70, 131, 148, 174, 226, 313f.
Exposition Grounds, Pittsburgh, Pa.: 125

Farrell, Charles A.: 275
Farrell, Frank: 305
Federal League: 311, 316
Ferguson, James: 48n.
Ferguson, Robert V.: 42, 70n., 175, 191, 200
Fielders and fielding: 19, 51, 88, 94ff., 103, 105, 140, 180, 202, 210, 215f., 248, 253, 256f., 261, 276, 288, 290ff.
Fleischmann, Julius: 305
Force, David W.: 50, 62
Forest City Club, Rockford, Ill.: 17, 100
Fort Wayne, Ind.: 18, 211
Fort Wayne Kekiongas: 39
Foster, John B.: 226
Foutz, David Luther: 141, 145
Fowle, Charles A.: 63f.
Fowler, Mr. (substitute with 1869 Cincinnati Red Stockings): 29

Franchises: 36, 59ff., 62, 64, 67, 73, 91, 117, 121, 128, 133, 148, 164, 167, 201, 228, 230f., 235, 240, 272, 298, 304f., 307ff., 315; Syracuse, N.Y., 77; Detroit, Mich., 105, 112ff., 115; Providence, R.I., 110; Washington, D.C., 110, 131; New York, N.Y., 122f.; Philadelphia, Pa., 123, 166; Worcester, Mass., 126; Troy, N.Y., 126; Toledo, Ohio, 131; Indianapolis, Ind., 131; Brooklyn, N.Y., 131, 145, 161, 227; Cleveland, Ohio, 135f., 233, 271; St. Louis, Mo., 139, 153, 239; Kansas City Mo., 110, 145; Boston, Mass., 150; Cincinnati, Ohio, 150f., 161, 212, 238; Milwaukee, Wis., 151; Baltimore, Md., 227; Omaha, Neb., 313; St. Joseph, Mo., 313; Minneapolis, Minn., 141; Bay City, Mich., 141; Pittsburgh, Pa., 144; Chicago, Ill., 271
Freedman, Andrew: 104, 227–29, 237, 239ff., 271, 284f., 304f., 308, 315
Freeman, Mr. (sponsor of the "Female Base Ball Club"): 211
Freeman, John F. (Buck): 276, 291
Fulton, Major: 297
Fulton, Chandos: 93
Furness, Harry: 294, 296

Gaffney, John H.: 186, 189–91
Galvin, James F.: 174–75, 177, 247
Gamblers and gambling: 16f., 19f., 29f., 32, 38, 50, 53, 61, 68, 71, 73, 81ff., 84, 91, 158–59, 174, 241
Ganzel, Charles W.: 243
Garfield, Pres. James Abram: 106
Gassette, Norman: 54n.
Gaston, Welcome Thornburg: 267
Gillam, H. M.: 194
Gleason, William J. (Kid): 251, 255, 257
Goldsmith, Frederick E.: 102, 176
Gompers, Samuel: 285
Gore, George F.: 103, 111, 163
Gosham, Alfred: 25
Gould, Charles Harvey: 27, 33, 51n.
Graffen, S. Mason: 55n.
Grant, Charles: 278
Grant, Pres. Ulysses Simpson: 28
Graves, Abner: 5
Griffith, Clark Calvin: 104, 275, 284, 286, 295
Griffith, William: 10